From Mesopotamia to t

Tannaitic Inheritance Law in its Legal and Social Contexts

From Mesopotamia to the Mishnah

Tannaitic Inheritance Law in its Legal and Social Contexts

Jonathan S. Milgram

Boston
2019

Library of Congress Cataloging-in-Publication Data

Names: Milgram, Jonathan S., 1971- author.
Title: From Mesopotamia to the Mishnah : Tannaitic inheritance law in its legal and social contexts / Jonathan S. Milgram.
Description: Paperback edition. | Brighton, MA : Academic Studies Press, 2019. | First published: Tubingen : Mohr Siebeck, 2016. | Includes bibliographical references and index.
Identifiers: LCCN 2019004488 | ISBN 9781644690277 (pbk.)
Subjects: LCSH: Inheritance and succession (Jewish law) | Inheritance and succession (Assyro-Babylonian law) | Mishnah. | Jewish law—Assyro-Babylonian influences.
Classification: LCC KBM632 .M55 2019 | DDC 346.05/2—dc23
LC record available at https://lccn.loc.gov/2019004488

ISBN 9781644690277 (paperback)

Cover design by Ivan Grave

Paperback edition published by Academic Studies Press in 2019

28 Montfern Avenue
Brighton, MA 02135, USA
press@academicstudiespress.com
www.academicstudiespress.com

Este libro es dedicado a la
Memoria de mi mamá, Noemi Milgram (1942–1999),
Cuya herencia a sus hijos, aunque no material,
Fue espiritual y aún más importante: el ejemplo del amor incondicional

אוי, ווער עס האָט פארלוירען, דער ווייס שוין וואָס איך מיין...
(From the song: א יידישע מאמע)

Table of Contents

Preface to the Paperback Edition

From Mesopotamia to the Mishnah: Tannaitic Inheritance Law in its Legal and Social Contexts was first published just two and a half years ago.[1] And now, such a short time later, the demand for another appearance of its contents and methodology justifies a second printing. There is, perhaps, no greater gratification that the author of a scholarly work can have.

I extend my heartfelt appreciation to all those who made the publication of the paperback edition possible. My thanks to Gregg Stern, former Acquisitions Editor at Academic Studies Press, for his initial interest in the republication of my book and for all of the time that he invested in bringing the project to fruition. To Kira Nemirovsky (Production Editor) and Alessandra Anzani (Senior Editor) at Academic Studies Press, I also express my gratitude. Finally, I would like to thank the former Provost of the Jewish Theological Seminary, Alan Cooper, who enthusiastically endorsed the allocation of a generous subvention grant for the republication of this work.

Since its original publication, my book has benefitted from serious attention by a wide-ranging group of scholars. Both in oral communications at conferences and in written book reviews,[2] colleagues have shared their enthusiasm for some of the ideas and analyses presented as well as their disagreement with others. The republication of the book provides me with the opportunity to respond thoughtfully to some of the observations made by scholars. The responses are embedded in the footnotes of this edition's Postscript, the primary goal of the Postscript being to present to the reader, in more explicit fashion, the methodological underpinnings specific to my argument that both the legal and social contexts of tannaitic Palestine—and especially Roman law—likely impacted the inheritance laws of the tannaim in meaningful ways.

The body and footnotes of this paperback republication are identical to the body and footnotes of the original work. The only differences between this edition and the earlier printing are: (a) the pagination of the original Preface and (b) the addition of a new Preface and Postscript. It is my hope that the paperback edition will enable many more scholars and laypeople alike to gain some insights into the inheritance laws of the tannaim and, just as significantly, to observe the benefits of employing philology and source criticism for the study of comparative ancient law in its legal and social contexts.

---

[1] Jonathan S. Milgram, *From Mesopotamia to the Mishnah: Tannaitic Inheritance Law in its Legal and Social Contexts* (Tübingen: Mohr Siebeck, 2016).

[2] For a listing, see the Bibliography to the Postscript.

I would like to note the timeliness of the publication of this paperback edition. The year 2018, during which I prepared this manuscript, is the fiftieth anniversary of the death of Boaz Cohen, a pioneer in the study of Jewish and Roman law, whose work has informed my own study in meaningful ways. 2018 is also the seventieth anniversary of the publication of J.N. Epstein's, *Mavo le-nusaḥ hamishna*, a veritable watershed in mishnaic studies that has powerfully impacted the entire field, and the influence of which is apparent on almost every page of this book. Most importantly for me personally, my family and I were recently blessed to welcome a sixth child, Stav Hoshana. The republication of *From Mesopotamia to the Mishnah* is lovingly dedicated to her.

Jonathan S. Milgram
February 2019

Preface

This book is a study of the key areas of tannaitic inheritance law and has three major goals. The first is to clarify the ways in which the tannaim perceived the operation of the procedures for inheritance that they promoted. Using source-critical tools, I consider the numerous and conflicting traditions recorded in tannaitic literature, and I explain the conceptualization behind them. The second goal is to show the degree to which tannaitic inheritance laws are the product of their ancient legal context. In the absence of significant rabbinic interpretation of Scripture on which to base the tannaitic innovations, I argue that the laws are often the product of the adoption and adaption of inheritance customs known from other ancient legal collections in the region. Accordingly, I examine the laws, customs, terms, conceptions, and technical formulae of multiple legal traditions in the ancient world—biblical, ancient Near Eastern, Greek, Roman, Elephantine, and Judean desert—and consider the possible relationships between inheritance traditions that are external to the rabbinic canon and the inheritance laws of the tannaim.

The third goal of this study is to suggest the possible impact, if any, of the social and economic contexts of tannaitic Palestine—specifically, the nuclear household structure and privatized landholdings in an urbanized setting—on the development of tannaitic inheritance law. In the final analysis, this book argues that tannaitic inheritance law—as a conglomerate of often previously attested concepts, terms, and formulae—cannot be identified as a complex of laws that was born in isolation and developed independently or as a collection of rules anchored in biblical laws or their interpretation. Rather, tannaitic inheritance law lies at the pinnacle of a great historical and geographic continuum of ancient inheritance laws, in many ways metaphorically related more closely to customs we know from the civilization of Sumer and the city of Sepphoris than to those of biblical Bet El and Beer Sheva. Therefore, an overarching question of this book is: If grounding in the Hebrew Bible or its interpretation is indicative of Jewishness, then how Jewish is Jewish inheritance law? I contemplate an answer to this question in the final chapter ("Conclusions").

Previous studies of tannaitic inheritance law, for the most part, emphasize the overall conceptual and terminological overlap between Greek sources and tannaitic traditions (see below). To a lesser extent, scholars address the potential parallels of specific tannaitic laws and terms with those of other legal traditions.[1] No work prior to the present one, however, combines a broad comparison to laws from multiple legal traditions in the ancient Near East and Mediterranean while also integrating a meaningful discussion of the

[1] I address these works in each chapter in their appropriate location.

social and economic contexts and their possible effects on the development of tannaitic inheritance law.[2]

Below, I identify the main contributions of three major scholars who preceded me in the study of tannaitic inheritance law: Yitzhak Baer, Ephraim Elimelech Urbach, and Reuven Yaron.[3] Following my digest, I summarize my general approach in light of the works of these scholars. For a full exposition of my conclusions, I refer the reader to the section in the "Introduction" entitled "The Present Study" and to the chapter called "Conclusions." At the end of this preface, I indicate the main methodological assumptions that operate throughout the book and list the editions of the Bible and rabbinic literature I consulted.

In his 1962 article, "The Historical Foundations of the Halakhah,"[4] Baer correctly notes that aspects of inheritance procedure in the Bible and the Mishnah are significantly different. According to the mishnaic order of succession, sons *and their descendants* precede other male heirs. Baer also points to the rabbinic innovation of brothers supporting their unmarried sisters after the former inherit from the father that the brother(s) and sister(s) have in common. These principles are not stated explicitly in biblical literature, and Baer argues that the innovations in tannaitic law are a direct result of the Hellenistic context in which the rabbis lived. In that setting, contends Baer, the rabbis are exposed to a new concept of extended family ties, and they adopt ancient Greek legal principles found primarily in the writings of the Attic orators Isaeus and Demosthenes.[5]

Urbach, in his lecture at the Fourth World Congress of Jewish Studies in 1965, entitled "Inheritance Laws and After-Life," correctly critiques Baer, pointing out that the concept of descendants of sons inheriting before (or together with) other male heirs is already evidenced in legal collections from ancient Mesopotamia, as is the concept of brothers supporting their unmarried sisters from the inheritance bequeathed by their father.[6] Urbach further notes that it is fairly common to locate parallels to tannaitic inheritance laws in multiple collections of ancient law external to the rabbinic canon, a fact that presents a significant methodological hurdle to those scholars wishing to find the origins

---

[2] Schremer, *Male and Female*, is an excellent example of a study that incorporates both comparative ancient law and socio-economic history for the analysis of another area of rabbinic legal development, that of marriage laws.

[3] In his important study of the history of inheritance law, *Inheritance and Wills*, Joseph Rivlin impressively collects ancient (and medieval—esp. from the Cairo Genizah) sources, pointing to abundant parallels to biblical and rabbinic traditions. I address Rivlin's approach, ideas, and methodology in the appropriate sections of this book (see, esp., the Appendix). Similarly, I deal with the significant contributions on the development of rabbinic inheritance law by Aryeh Edrei in the notes where appropriate.

[4] Baer, "Historical Foundations."

[5] Baer, "Historical Foundations," 133.

[6] Urbach, "Inheritance Laws and After-Life," 133–134. See also Driver and Miles, *The Babylonian Laws*, 331, (cited by Urbach, 134 n. 12).

of, and influences on, rabbinic inheritance laws. Only broad comparative studies, argues Urbach, would result in accurate conclusions about the impact of ancient legal traditions on tannaitic laws. Therefore, in his lecture, Urbach does not focus on ancient legal parallels to rabbinic laws. Rather, he addresses another matter entirely: the complex question of the relationship of inheritance customs, mourning, and burial rituals to conceptions of afterlife in the ancient world (an affiliation actually absent from tannaitic discourse and that I address in Chapter 3). For Urbach, because of the effects of war, the destruction of the Second Temple, and the general shifting of landholding patterns (due to economic and social change in the centuries leading up to the rabbinic movement), the theological ideal of transferring one's landholdings to progeny as essential to immortality could not endure. Namely, the role of the son, and then the grandson, as replacing and, in essence, continuing the identity of the father (after his death) on ancestral property could not be maintained. New ideas about reward and punishment in the afterlife began to be integrated into tannaitic discourse and,[7] in tandem, ways for distributing wealth among family members, as well as non-relatives, began to be absorbed into rabbinic law.

Although Urbach disagrees with Baer's bold statement about Greek influence on tannaitic inheritance law, he does agree that there are clear indications of the entry of Greek inheritance terminology into tannaitic legal discourse, most notably the presence of *diathēkē*,[8] the Greek word for a written disposition in case of death. It is Yaron who, earlier in his magnum opus *Gifts in Contemplation of Death* published in 1960, demonstrates that not only the word *diathēkē* entered tannaitic legal discourse. Actually, the entire formula of the *diathēkē* was copied from the original Greek.[9] Furthermore, Yaron argues throughout his book for the general influence of Hellenism on rabbinic inheritance traditions while denying any affinity with, or impact of, Roman legal conceptions on the inheritance laws of the tannaim.

In my study, I affirm the contention of Baer, Urbach, and Yaron that the Greek language and formulae and Hellenism in general had a significant impact on the production of tannaitic inheritance laws. At the same time, I embrace Urbach's challenge to investigate multiple ancient legal traditions before arguing for the origins of tannaitic rules. Accordingly, as already

---

[7] Urbach, "Inheritance Laws and After-Life," 138–141. However, I agree with Edrei's critique of Urbach in which he argues that, more than the changing views on afterlife, in all likelihood new landholding patterns and the ability to freely sell land contributed to legal innovation; see Edrei, "To Fulfill," 137.

[8] Urbach, "Inheritance Laws and After-Life," 134. Following Gulak, *Das Urkundenwesen*, 126, Urbach also maintains that elements of the *diathēkē*'s original accompanying formula (but not the entire formula) are preserved in tannaitic texts; see the next note. See also the discussion in the translation of Gulak's work into Hebrew; Gulak, *Legal Documents*, 155 n. 5.

[9] Yaron, *Gifts*, 24–26. Earlier, Gulak pointed to an affinity between part of the formula of the rabbinic and Hellenistic *diathēkē*; see previous note. For Urbach's argument with Yaron regarding the formula of the *diathēkē*, see "Inheritance and After-life," 134 n. 21; and my comments in the section entitled "Yaron on the Tannaitic *Diathēkē*," in the Appendix.

noted, my analysis includes a review of a broad range of legal traditions. I examine parallels carefully before arguing for the possible relationships between them. Indeed, at times, tannaitic inheritance laws are paralleled in multiple collections of ancient law and, therefore, cannot be traced back to specific influences or processes. These tannaitic laws are simply the product of a general outlook on the division of property prevalent throughout the ancient Near East and Mediterranean. Other times, however, I argue for a more direct line of contact and even the influence of specific laws and formulae on tannaitic conceptualization and formulation. One of the most important arguments that I make in this book—departing from Yaron's view—is that Roman inheritance terminology and conceptualization did, indeed, affect the choice of terms and legal approach of the nascent tannaitic movement (for more information see, especially, Chapters 1 and 3).[10] Lastly, throughout this work, I entertain the possibility that the social and economic conditions experienced by the rabbis may be related to the integration of practices and traditions into the rabbinic web of inheritance laws despite the fact that I do not argue for direct cause and effect.

Throughout this book, the mention of inherited or gifted property refers specifically to real property, that is, land, unless otherwise stated. Hebrew citations and translations of the Hebrew Bible are drawn from *The JPS Torah Commentary* (Philadelphia: The Jewish Publication Society, 1989–1996). Hebrew quotations from the Mishnah are taken from the Kaufmann manuscript, Georg Beer, ed., *Faksimile-Ausgabe des Mischnacodex Kaufmann* (Haag: Nijhoff: 1929) with the addition of full spellings. English translations of the Mishnah are based on Herbert Danby, ed. and trans., *The Mishnah* (Oxford: Oxford University Press, 1933), and reworked as needed. Hebrew citations of the Tosefta are taken from Saul Lieberman, *Tosefta* and *Tosefta Ki-fshuṭah* (New York and Jerusalem: Jewish Theological Seminary, 1955–1988) with the addition of full spellings. English translations of Tosefta texts are adapted from Jacob Neusner, ed., *Tosefta* (New York and Hoboken, NJ: Ktav, 1977–1990). Original citations from the Palestinian Talmud are taken from *Talmud Yerushalmi: According to Ms. Or. 4720 (Scal. 3) of the Leiden University Library with Restorations and Corrections*

---

[10] My study is a further affirmation of an emerging trend in the study of tannaitic law that increasingly points to Roman and tannaitic parallels, indicating the possible influence of Roman legal conceptualization and terminology on the development of tannaitic laws. For an impressive discussion of the parallels between the rabbinic *takkanah* and the Roman edict, see Hayes, "Abrogation." More recently, see Novick, "Borer," 1–8; and Furstenberg, "Eating in a State of Purity," 163–164. Shaye Cohen, however, questions the impact of Roman and Hellenistic traditions on the legal innovation of the rabbis; see S. Cohen, "Judaean Legal Tradition," 127. One scholar even writes, "I have not yet seen a single convincing argument for any particular instance of reception of Roman law into Jewish law" (Katzoff, "Children of Intermarriage," 286). See also Moscovitz, "Legal Fictions," 132; and Jackson, "Roman Influence," 184. Certainly, the possible channels of transmission that may have led to the rabbis' awareness of Roman legal terminology and conceptualization were present in tannaitic Palestine because it was, for the most part, a typical Roman province in its political and organizational structure (see Schwartz, "Political Geography," 77–78).

(Jerusalem: Academy of the Hebrew Language, 2001) with the addition of full spellings, and I include the pagination of this edition in parentheses when citing. English translations of the Palestinian Talmud are adapted from Jacob Neusner, ed., *The Talmud of the Land of Israel* (Atlanta: Scholars, 1999). The manuscripts from which original quotations of the Babylonian Talmud derive are cited in the footnotes, where relevant. The translations of Babylonian Talmud texts are adapted from Isidore Epstein, ed., *The Babylonian Talmud* (London: Soncino, 1935–1952).

Acknowledgements

Although the writing of a book is the sole responsibility of the author, a book is never really the product of one person's efforts in isolation. So many people and institutions contribute to the final product. Certainly, the scholarship of others, who preceded the author, contributes significantly to the backdrop against which a scholar presents ideas. Without prior scholarship to engage and dispute, an academic can barely get started. From the outset, therefore, I acknowledge the important contributions of the scholars who wrote on inheritance in the ancient world and related topics before me. Their accomplishments enriched this work in meaningful ways.

I also acknowledge the contributions of fellow colleagues who shared their work, agreed to read chapters, and who, at conferences or over coffee, offered critiques and advice. The idea for this book was born out of a series of conversations in 2008 with Menahem Kahana, my teacher years earlier at The Hebrew University in Jerusalem, while he was on sabbatical in New York. I thank Professor Kahana for encouraging me to take up tannaitic inheritance law in comparative context as the topic of my first book and for giving me invaluable advice on methodology from the earliest beginnings of the project. Two other former teachers, whose roles in the actual conceptualization of this work may have been less active but whose methods and contributions to scholarship continue to inform me at every stage of my work are Shamma Friedman and Haym Soloveitchik. Both taught me the importance of the implementation of proper methodologies in scholarship. Shamma Friedman was my *Doktorvater* at Bar Ilan University and, in all the years I have known him, has given me undeserved attention both on a professional and personal level. For that, and so much more, I am forever indebted to him. It was Haym Soloveitchik, with whom I studied at Yeshiva University, who recommended that I study with Shamma Friedman. His sound advice proved to be life-changing.

During my years as a student of Talmud criticism, I have enjoyed the friendship and professional guidance of Yaakov Elman, also among my former teachers at Yeshiva University. He has steadfastly supported my initiatives to expand my methodological approaches from primarily philological to comparative. In this endeavor, Christine Hayes also has proven to be a wonderful sounding board, colleague, and friend. Her willingness to engage my ideas seriously and encourage me as I employ interdisciplinary methodologies has helped propel my intellectual activities as a comparatist. I thank her, especially, for introducing me to the scholarship of the legal scholar John Fabian Witt.

Several scholars read earlier drafts of chapters or the entire manuscript of this book. These include: Stephen Geller, Bernard Jackson, Richard Kalmin, Aaron Koller, Tzvi Novick, Michael Satlow, and Sacha Stern. I thank all of them for their insights and for challenging me to produce the best work possible. Among these readers, I am especially grateful to Aaron Koller for his meticulous engagement with the material in this book and meaningful suggestions for improvement. I also thank Aaron for introducing me to the scholarship of the American historian Gordon S. Wood, with whose work I open the introduction and whose ideas impacted my synthesis of the data. Bernard Jackson's detailed observations on the legal content of this book, for which I am grateful, proved to be extremely helpful. Always the proper English gentleman, Bernard has a genteel way of suggesting improvements and has been supportive of this project from its inception. Finally, Richard Kalmin, my first Talmud teacher—during my undergraduate studies at The Jewish Theological Seminary—has transitioned over the years from teacher to colleague and friend. He has read several drafts of the chapters in this book. Always supportive and professional, Richard is the best kind of colleague one could have.

Colleagues from around the globe, several of whom I have never met in person, were willing to share their work, at times even unpublished, and deserve my deepest expressions of gratitude. I begin by mentioning the late Raymond Westbrook, whom I never met, but who through email correspondence shared his enthusiasm and encouragement for this project as it began. Professor Westbrook generously sent me many offprints of his articles and an impressive bibliography when I first contacted him. I thank Shalom Holtz and Yobu Jindu who initially suggested I get in touch with Westbrook. Westbrook's students and collaborators Bruce Wells, F. Rachel Magdalene, and Cornelia Wunsch were of great assistance as the details of this study unfolded. All three scholars happily shared their unpublished work with me. Meir Malul, Phyllis Bird, and Zvi Szubin also graciously shared unpublished scholarship with me. The Serbian legal historian Sima Avramović generously shared his articles and conducted a meaningful email exchange with me on the development of inheritance practices in the ancient world. The following scholars also directed me to studies in their respective fields: Alejandro Botta, Hannah Cotton, Judith Evans Grubbs, Michael Gagarin, Norbert Lohfink, David Marcus, Paul du Plessis, Joseph Rivlin, and Seth Schwartz. I thank Steven Fine, who invited me to lecture at a conference he chaired and later published (along with Aaron Koller) my remarks at a critical time in the development of my thesis.

Special thanks are due to Joel Roth and Jack Wertheimer, former department chair in Talmud and provost at the Jewish Theological Seminary, respectively, whose joint efforts brought me (back) to the Seminary to be a member of its faculty. I also wish to thank Ismar Schorsch, under whose chancellorship I was hired. I am fortunate to be a member of a distinguished faculty, especially in my field, and I thank all of my colleagues for their constant encouragement and support. Alan Cooper, the current provost, has always been more than supportive and, in fact, due to his policies, was instrumental in enabling the completion of this project, for which I thank him. I enjoyed two sabbatical leaves, the first during the academic year 2010–2011 and, the second, during the fall semester of 2013. Under the leadership of the current chancellor Arnold Eisen, the Jewish Theological Seminary continues to be a pleasant and productive place to engage in serious scholarship.

My research was enhanced by access to the libraries of Columbia University and their staff members. I also thank the staff of the library of The Jewish Theological Seminary for its outstanding service to me during the writing of this book. The Teaneck Public Library and the library of the Kaplen JCC on the Palisades served as great "hiding places" while writing during summers and sabbaticals. I also thank the Memorial Foundation for Jewish Culture and Targum Shlishi, a Raquel and Aryeh Rubin Foundation, for their financial support toward the preparation of this book for publication. To my copy editor Leslie Rubin, my deep gratitude for the wonderful job she has done on the manuscript.

Four personal friends deserve mention here as well. Barry Wimpfheimer, among my closest friends for two decades, has always been a voice of unwavering support for my work. Zvi Kaplan, through his parodies and caricatures of the academic, has never ceased to make me laugh at myself (and at him and our colleagues) in only the healthiest ways. Neil Danzig and Jason Rogoff are steadfast in their encouragement and genuine interest in my progress and have listened patiently as I complained about the endless details involved in the production of this book. To the editors at Mohr Siebeck, and especially Azzan Yadin-Israel, I extend my sincere thanks for their interest in my scholarship and desire to publish this volume.

I acknowledge with profound gratitude my supportive family—who, not only through prodding and encouragement but also by understanding the demands of the life of the scholar, seemingly on a neverending trajectory to add just one more detail, insert another footnote, or edit a chapter yet again—contributed immensely to my ability to dedicate seemingly endless hours, days, weeks, and years to thoughtful and immeasurably meaningful research and writing. So, above all, I thank my wife, Adina, and my children Maayan Noemi, Aron Benjamin, Tiferet Tzahala, Reut Hadas, and Yarden Gilad. I have been blessed by all a scholar needs to accomplish successful work, but above all I have been blessed by the presence in my life of the six aforementioned individuals. This book is dedicated to the memory of my mother, Noemi Milgram, who, as stated on the dedication page, bequeathed to her children no material fortune but did leave the most important legacy—her example of giving unconditional love. *Yehi zikhrah barukh.*

Jonathan S. Milgram
May 2016

Abbreviations, Terminology, and Transliteration

Abbreviations

In general abbreviations of biblical and other ancient sources follow the *Chicago Manual of Style* (16th ed.) or the *SBL Handbook of Style* (1st ed.).

Primary Sources

Citations to rabbinic sources use the following system of abbreviation: Lowercase single letter (in italics) to indicate Tosefta, Mishnah, or one of the Talmuds:

b	Babylonian Talmud (Bavli)
m	Mishnah
p	Palestinian (Jerusalem) Talmud (Yerushalmi)
t	Tosefta

Mixed case letters (in italics) to indicate the tractate name:

BB	*Baba Batra*
Bekh	*Bekhorot*
Bik	*Bikkurim*
BM	*Baba Metsi'a*
Dem	*Demai*
Eruv	*Eruvin*
Git	*Gittin*
Ker	*Keritot*
Ket	*Ketubbot*
Meg	*Megillah*
Ned	*Nedarim*
Pes	*Pesaḥim*
San	*Sanhedrin*
Shab	*Shabbat*
Shek	*Shekalim*
Sot	*Sotah*
Suk	*Sukkah*
Yad	*Yadayim*
Yev	*Yevamot*

EXAMPLES*: tKet, mBB, bYev,* and so forth

Additional Primary Sources

NOTE: For publication information about the following sources, see the bibliography.

BIN	Babylonian Inscriptions (in the Collection of J. B.) Nies
BM	Museum Siglum of the British Museum, London (UK)
D	*The Digest of Justinian*
TAD	*Textbook of Aramaic Documents from Ancient Egypt*
VAS	Vorderasiatische Schriftdenkmäler

Terminology

Although I employ terms familiar to lawyers trained in the Western legal tradition, the institutions and procedures in tannaitic law are not always an exact match for those in the Western legal tradition. Therefore, below I provide a list of terms, defined specifically for the presentation of the phenomena I observe in tannaitic law. That is, below I summarize the main institutions discussed in this book, at times the entries also serving as stipulative definitions.

DISTRIBUTION A unilateral mechanism (not requiring an act of acquisition by, or on behalf of, the recipient) effected by the original property owner for the apportionment of inheritance shares to immediate heirs (such as a son or sons) during the owner's lifetime that does not affect the size of the portion(s) each heir would receive in the event of regular intestacy. On distribution, see Chapters 2 and 3.

GIFTING IN CONTEMPLATION OF DEATH A bilateral mechanism (requiring an act of acquisition by, or on behalf of, the recipient) for the transfer of assets from the original owner, known as the donor, during the donor's lifetime to a recipient, known as the donee. The gift takes full effect and becomes finally irrevocable only upon the death of the donor. In Jewish law, the two most common gifts in contemplation of death are called (by the amoraim), *mattenat bari* and *mattenat shakhev mera*. See Chapter 1 and the Appendix.

INHERITING A unilateral mechanism (not requiring an act of acquisition by, or on behalf of, the recipient) for the transfer of property upon death from a person to an immediate heir or heirs (such as a son or sons) in the event of intestacy (i. e., without the express intervention of the original property owner) by force of law or custom. That is, inheriting by the heirs is effected when the original property owner dies intestate. See Chapter 1 and "Intestacy/ Intestate Succession."

INTESTACY/INTESTATE SUCCESSION The absence of the express intervention of the original property owner (i. e., the donor) for the apportionment of property upon the property owner's death, resulting in the automatic division of the property by force of law or custom. That is, dying intestate effects inheriting by the heirs according to the order of succession. See Chapter 1 and "Inheriting."

TESTACY/TESTATE SUCCESSION AMONG SONS The unilateral transfer or devolution of property to a specific son(s) designated heir(s) by the property owner (= father), not in accordance with the established division as per the order of (intestate) succession, taking effect at the time of the original property owner's death. Tannaitic law only recognizes testate succession among sons or among agnates (see "Testacy/Testate Succession among Agnates") and not to strangers. See Chapter 1 n. 2 and Chapter 3.

TESTACY/TESTATE SUCCESSION AMONG AGNATES The unilateral transfer or devolution of property to specific agnate(s) (family members through the male line), designated heir(s) by the property owner and not in accordance with the established order of (intestate) succession, taking effect at the time of the original property owner's death. See also "Testacy/ Testate Succession among Sons" and Chapter 3.

Transliteration

My transliteration system aims for simplicity and clarity.

I do not indicate *alef* or *ayin* at the beginning or the end of a word. When an *alef* or an *ayin* appears in the middle of a word, an apostrophe (') indicates that letter.

For the purposes of transliteration, the legend below indicates the diacritics or English letters that represent Hebrew letters that do not have direct English equivalents.

ʾ	*alef* or *ayin* in the middle of a word
ḥ	*ḥet*
k	*kaf* and *kof*
kh	*khaf*
ts	*tsadi*

NOTE: When citing an author or documenting a source, I retain the transliteration system of that author or source.

Introduction

In his acclaimed book, *The Radicalism of the American Revolution*, the historian Gordon S. Wood examines, among other matters, the effects of the social and economic conditions leading up to and after the American Revolution on inheritance practices in the American colonies. Wood argues that due to social and economic changes – including shifts in family make-up and landholding patterns – the customary procedures for dividing inheritances known from England were transformed. Young men starting their families had more autonomy than they previously experienced in their patriarchal households.[1] Time-honored traditions such as primogeniture (landholdings passing only to the eldest son in the English model) and entail (a strategy enabling an estate to remain intact and in the hands of a specific line of the family) eventually were abandoned.[2] Post-revolution, daughters and widows, in particular, began to benefit from greater equality in the division of estates.[3]

In this book I suggest that a radical transformation of inheritance law may emerge against the background of the dynamic differences between the social and economic contexts – namely, family structure and landholding patterns – presumed in biblical law and literature, on the one hand, and those reflected in the tannaitic legal collections, on the other.[4] The biblical model of an extended family in an agrarian economy, residing on its jointly owned ancestral estate and populated by subordinate daughters, invisible wives, and the firstborn at its head, is not manifest in the later, tannaitic law and lore. Rather, tannaitic inheritance law – like other areas of tannaitic law[5] – supposes a situation in which the nuclear family is predominant,[6] land is privatized,[7] and rabbinic society is

[1] Wood, *Radicalism*, 129.

[2] Wood, *Radicalism*, 46–47; for additional economic factors, see 134.

[3] Wood, *Radicalism*, 183.

[4] On the question of the historicity of these models, see the section below entitled "On the Relationship of Ancient Laws to Ancient Societies."

[5] For a general overview on the supposition of the predominance in tannaitic literature of the nuclear family and its possible effects on tannaitic law, see Z. Safrai, "Family Structure." See also n. 17.

[6] The nuclear family was most likely made up of parents with unmarried children and perhaps elderly grandparents living in the same household (see below "On the Textual and Archeological Evidence for the Presumed Family Structure and Landholding Patterns in the Bible and Tannaitic Literature").

urbanized.[8] In tannaitic texts, generally the firstborn son enjoys no honored position within the family,[9] the division of estates is assumed, and laws addressing the welfare of widows and the economic independence of daughters dominate. Indeed, although the relationship of biblical law to the social and economic realities external to the texts remains uncertain,[10] tannaitic inheritance law – in all of its variety – seemingly reflects the social and economic conditions the rabbis observe and experience in tannaitic Palestine. It contains principles, terminology, and formulae drawn from the legal landscape of the greater regions of the ancient Near East and Mediterranean. That is, the rabbinic construction of inheritance law – although in all likelihood only theoretical in nature[11] – is crafted out of the legal traditions of the ancient world that had spread to the rabbinic centers from far and wide and represents principles for property division apparently appropriate to the social and economic conditions known to us from tannaitic Palestine.[12] (On the question of cause and effect, see the section entitled "Tannaitic Society and Tannaitic Inheritance Law: Cause and Effect?" below).

Unquestionably, the colonial condition is not comparable to the tannaitic situation. The state of affairs in the American colonies was the product of rapid and intentional change. Considerable documentation demonstrates that over the course of just a few decades, the laws were refashioned by jurists desiring to address the needs of a quickly growing and increasingly modern and mobile population. The players sought actively to break free from earlier archaic models to create a new and singular system relevant to current social and economic con-

[7] Z. Safrai, *Baalut al hakarka*, 9. Here, and throughout this book, I use the terms "privatization," "privatized," and "private," synonymously for land owned by individuals and not held jointly as an extended family estate. Others use these terms to distinguish between land owned by the king or government (non-private) and land owned by others (private), even when jointly owned by members of an extended family (see, e. g., B. Levine, "Farewell to the Ancient Near East," 228). For some preliminary thoughts on the parameters of the terminology, see Hudson's Acknowledgments in *Privatization*.

[8] See L. Levine, *Rabbinic Class*, 23–33; Schwartz, *Imperialism*, 129–176; Sperber, *City*, and, more recently, comments specifically regarding the tannaim in Lapin, *Rabbis as Romans*, 78–79 and 88. Throughout, when I mention urbanized society, urban centers, and the like, I refer specifically to the building of cities in antiquity and the cosmology of social life that the construction of cities creates and fosters (cf. Hudson, "New Economic Archaeology of Urbanization," 9–10). That is, residence in urban centers has the potential to affect family size because of space constraints, as well as to alter the roles of family members due to the intensity of interaction and duties that are less well defined than in a rural context. For example, paternal influence may be diminished due to sons living apart from their father. I focus here on the building of cities and the possible effects on landholding patterns and family structure and, consequently, inheritance laws. See also n. 138.

[9] See Chapter 2 for possible exceptions.

[10] See the section entitled "On the Relationship of Ancient Laws to Ancient Societies."

[11] On the lack of evidence that tannaitic laws were actually practiced by Judeans during the tannaitic period, see below in the body of this section.

[12] Edrei, "To Fulfill," 137–138, argues that without the appropriate social and economic contexts, legal adaptation would not have occurred. See also Edrei, "To Fulfill," 134.

ditions.[13] The tannaitic scene, however, is a sparsely documented circumstance. It is the culmination of a centuries-long, protracted process of, in all likelihood, unconscious legal development by historically unidentifiable characters on behalf of an equally unverifiable populace.

The transformation, the outcome of adopting and adapting existing local customs and traditions, culminates in a cacophony of conflicting conceptions, opinions, and abstractions embedded in disputes between sages and traditions from different tannaitic schools,[14] which correspond to the social and economic conditions the tannaim likely experience. As different as they are, though, the two models – the American and the tannaitic – do share something: each, in its own way, may be representative of the interplay between the formulation of law and the social and economic contexts in which it is created.

Significant scholarship of the last century casts doubt on the actual role of the rabbis and their laws in Roman Palestine.[15] Indeed, the idea that tannaitic law represents rabbinic legislation for the masses, or, for that matter, is at all related to the actual practice of Jews in antiquity, is largely rejected.[16] But, as recent scholarship on the laws of the tannaim affirms,[17] even the acceptance of this thesis does not lead to the conclusion that elements of the social and economic contexts in which tannaitic laws are created are not somehow reflected in its legislation. Law is seldom created in a vacuum, and in this book, I contend that in the absence of the hermeneutic underpinnings for tannaitic innovations on inheritance,[18] the laws cannot be attributed to the rabbinic imagination's penchant for inventive interpretation of Scripture.[19] As the evidence adduced later

---

[13] See Wood, *Radicalism*, 46–47; 124–145; 181–185.

[14] On conflicting traditions in the tannaitic legal corpus, see below "Tannaitic *Laws* and not Tannaitic *Law*: The Philological-Historical Approach and the Legal Legacy of the Tannaim."

[15] The details of this thesis need not be repeated here. For a summary of the issues and the relevant scholarship, see Lapin, *Early Rabbinic Civil Law*, 13–34. Specifically on Jacob Neusner's important contributions regarding the relationship of, primarily, the Mishnah to the social and economic contexts in which the tannaim live, see Lapin, *Early Rabbinic Civil Law*, 22–29.

[16] See the previous note. However, see also the discussions in Chapters 4 and 5 regarding how the tannaim may build their laws on actual practices documented in contemporary Judean desert documents.

[17] For recent scholarly views on the interplay between rabbinic texts and the social and economic contexts in which they are created, see e.g., Lapin, *Early Rabbinic Civil Law*, 19–34; Schremer, *Male and Female*, 23–31; Satlow, *Jewish* Marriage, xxiii–xxvi; Tropper, "Economics of Jewish Childhood," 189–233; Tropper, "Children and Childhood," 299–343; Weissberg, *Levirate Marriage*. On inheritance specifically, see Edrei, "To Fulfill," 105. See also n. 5.

[18] Cf. Edrei, "To Fulfill," 129–130; Edrei also notes the significance of the lack of scriptural interpretation on matters pertaining to inheritance.

[19] In her important study on the Talmudic prohibitions relating to idol worship (*avodah zarah*), comparing the Palestinian and Babylonian Talmuds, Christine Hayes works with data representing, in a way, the inverse phenomenon. That is, Hayes demonstrates that the differences in approach between the Talmuds is not due to distinctions in the social make up of amoraic Palestine and Babylonia, but rather hermeneutic approaches unique to each center; see Hayes, *Between the Babylonian and Palestinian Talmuds*, 3–30 (esp., 17–30).

in this book supports, tannaitic inheritance law is primarily the product of the adoption and adaption of principles and formulae evidenced in sources outside of the tannaitic canon, which typically conform to the social and economic contexts of Roman Palestine. Indeed, tannaitic inheritance law is seemingly the outcome of the irrecoverable interplay between the legal legacy of the ancient Near East and Mediterranean and the social and economic conditions the rabbis likely experience in Roman Palestine despite the fact that causation is seldom, if ever, definitively determinable (see "Tannaitic Society and Tannaitic Inheritance Law: Cause and Effect?").

In summary, tannaitic inheritance law overlaps significantly with rules and regulations, as well as terms and formulations, known from the rich repositories of inheritance law in the ancient world. These include ancient Near Eastern, Second Temple, Greek, Elephantine, Judean desert, and Roman.[20] The principles and parallels integrated into the tannaitic corpus are often appropriate to the social and economic contexts in which the rabbis function historically: a state in which the nuclear family structure with private landholdings in urbanized centers predominates. Applying the tools of philological-historical analysis to tannaitic traditions, as described in the next section, throughout this book I examine the inheritance laws of the tannaim within their legal and social contexts.

Tannaitic Laws and not Tannaitic Law: The Philological-Historical Approach and the Legal Legacy of the Tannaim

Among the most important observations of the philological-historical school during the course of the twentieth century is the degree to which tannaitic legal collections in general, and the Mishnah in particular,[21] are not representative of a fundamental unity of legal conceptions.[22] Rather, the compilations are comprised of conflicting earlier tannaitic sources, at times harmonized within the tannaitic corpus and at other times, not. These disparate traditions appear in

[20] See also the suggestions for comparison to mishnaic law in S. Cohen, "Judaean Legal Tradition," 121–143.

[21] On the origins of the philological-historical school, see most recently Gafni, "Emergence of Critical Scholarship." English-language essays on, and (at times, unnecessarily harsh) critiques of, the scholars who employ the methods of the philological-historical school appear in Neusner, *Modern Study*. See also the citation relating to Epstein in n. 26.

[22] Some scholars of Jewish law, usually not trained in the philological-historical method, tend to assume a (relatively seamless) conceptual unity between conflicting sources from the same period (such as Mishnah and *baraitot*) and accept the harmonization of the contradictory sources in later works of the rabbinic canon (esp. the Babylonian Talmud and even medieval legal works) as the historical meaning of the earlier sources. For a critique of the school of thought engaged in this exercise, the *Mishpat Ivri* school (with specific reference to capital punishment), see Berkowitz, *Execution and Invention*, 41–47.

three different forms: disputes between sages (*maḥlokot tanna'im*), discrete units of tannaitic tradition that conceptually conflict (*trei tanna'ei*), and newly discovered tannaitic traditions uncovered by the application of critical methods.[23] The third category entails the use of form and source criticism to determine the relationship between the (harmonized) component parts of a tannaitic text or multiple tannaitic texts to each other,[24] and this, only after a rigorous comparison of medieval manuscripts and linguistic forms to establish the best versions of the texts analyzed.[25] A corollary to the notion that disparate sources make up tannaitic literature, significantly developed by J. N. Epstein,[26] is that each tannaitic tradition, whether presented in one collection or another, whether attributed or anonymous, offers an equal glimpse of the richness of conceptualization, beauty of expression, and – above all – variety of approaches that embodies tannaitic literature: competing laws and collections.[27] For the study of tannaitic inheritance law, in particular, the presentation of competing and conflicting legal conceptions contributes – immeasurably – to the reconstruction of what the tannaitic law of inheritance or, perhaps more accurately, the tannaitic *laws* of inheritance are. By examining the various anthologies of tannaitic literature and not limiting ourselves, for example, only to an appreciation of the mishnaic laws of inheritance, a more accurate account of the variegated legal situation of the tannaim emerges.[28]

---

[23] See the presentation of methods for identifying the disparate and discrete sources of the Mishnah in Epstein's lecture at the opening ceremony of the Hebrew University in 1925; Epstein, "Hamada hatalmudi utserakhav."

[24] Among the most famous scholarly disputes in Mishnah studies is the debate between J. N. Epstein and Hanokh Albeck regarding how actively the editor of the Mishnah harmonizes and changes earlier sources, which I mention here only in passing for the benefit of the reader. Epstein argues, generally, for a heavy-handed redaction, and Albeck argues, generally, that the editor does not rework earlier sources often. Epstein's approach is evident on almost every page of his magnum opus *Mavo* and throughout his other works, including, of course, *Tannaim*. See, by way of an example related to inheritance, *Mavo*, 659–660, which I deal with in detail in Chapter 4. For an impressive list of cases where Epstein contends the editor's active hand results in deciding the law in accordance with the view of Rabbi Judah the Prince (the presumed editor of the Mishnah), see *Tannaim*, 225–226. In addition, for examples where Epstein presumes the editor leaves clusters of sources untouched or leaves evidence of earlier sources he adapts, see *Tannaim*, 212–224. Perhaps the most remarkable example of the editor's active reworking of sources is exhibited in an outstanding, yet rarely cited, article by E. S. Rosenthal, "Leferushah shel mishnat Taanit 1:1–2." Albeck's view is clearly explained in H. Albeck, *Mavo lamishnah*, 99–115. For a similar approach promoted by Avraham Weiss, see Weiss, "Laḥeker hasifruti."

[25] See Rosenthal, "HaMoreh," 15, who explains that the philological-historical approach rests on the exploration of the following elements in the exact order listed before reaching conclusions: the textual version, the linguistic formulation, and the literary-historical context.

[26] The greatest systematic summary of Epstein's weighty oeuvre remains that of E. Z. Melamed, *Pirkei Mavo*. Baruch Bokser wrote two English-language summaries of Epstein's views on the Mishnah and its redaction. See Bokser, "Epstein's Introduction," 13–36; and Bokser, "Jacob N. Epstein," 37–55.

[27] See, e. g., Epstein's opening remarks in Epstein, *Tannaim*, 13.

[28] Neil (Nachman) Danzig argues that the use of the term *baraita* (a term pointing to a tannaitic teaching external to the Mishnah) only among fourth-generation Babylonian amoraim

In this book I embrace the methods of the philological-historical school and probe the different strands of inheritance procedure included in tannaitic sources, drawing from the Mishnah, the Tosefta, halakhic midrashim, and the collections of *baraitot* found in the Palestinian and Babylonian Talmuds.[29] After identifying the numerous notions of inheritance practice, I trace parallels and antecedents from various traditions of ancient law (see above). I argue that these parallels attest to the place of tannaitic law as a collection of legal traditions in the ancient world and, in each instance, suggest the relationship, if any, of the tannaitic views to those extant in other ancient legal traditions. Are we dealing with common origins, the same effects of comparable societal conditions on unrelated legal systems, entirely independent – yet similar – legal development in separate legal traditions, or the influence of the law in one ancient legal compilation on the law in another?

Tannaitic Law(s) and Comparative Ancient Law: Context, Influence, and Internal Development

In a recent study, legal scholar John Fabian Witt discusses the pitfalls and profits of three competing theories of legal development: immanence, contingency, and inevitability.[30] Immanence, explains Witt, is the idea that there exists a fundamental logic behind the evolution of law and that individual legal systems develop independently but similarly, often leading to a greater openness, rationality, and freedom in the law. According to the theory of contingency, the development of law is free from any connection to a deep, inner logic or systematic move toward a greater good. On the contrary, the evolution of law is the random working out of legal principles over time. Advocates of the theory of inevitability argue that the development of law is primarily guided by social and economic changes in the course of history.

I contend that the three approaches examined in Witt's inquiry are biased toward the study of the evolution of single, individual legal traditions. However, after one compares legal traditions directly and discusses the conceptual and ter-

---

and later, indicates the lateness of the advent of the Mishnah's authority. For, only once the Mishnah is considered authoritative would other tannaitic sources be referred to as external to it. If Danzig is correct, then, to be sure, scholars should not, anachronistically, give priority to the Mishnah as *the* representation of law in the tannaitic period. All of the various tannaitic collections would have been considered equal before the advent of the use of the term *baraita*. Despite this, scholars continue to prioritize the Mishnah as representative of tannaitic law and lore. See Danzig, "Hitpatḥut" and Danzig, "Lehitpatḥut." See also Epstein, *Mavo*, 166–352. For a critique of Danzig, see Wald, "Baraita," 127.

[29] For a summary of scholarly issues pertaining to the authenticity (or not) of texts presumed to be tannaitic but only preserved in the Talmuds, see Diamond, "Rabbinics," 178–179.

[30] Witt, "Contingency, Immanence, and Inevitability," 1–41.

minological parallels, the assumptions of each individual theory are challenged. A more nuanced approach, incorporating elements of all three theories, must be employed to explain the possible evolution and relationship of specific laws. Certainly, the scholar of comparative law considers whether parallel developments identified in multiple legal collections are actually the product of a natural evolutionary process (immanence), a coincidental overlap of the working out of legal principles (contingency), or the outcome of comparable socioeconomic conditions, necessarily yielding similar legal conclusions (inevitability). But the comparatist benefits from putting distinct laws into dialogue with one another, and at least when dealing with legal traditions of the ancient Near East and Mediterranean, gains immeasurably from comparing and contrasting the principles and practices in legal collections that, while inarguably independent, reign throughout the same general region for millennia – at times simultaneously – and overlap conceptually, procedurally, and on occasion, even terminologically.

Thus, the comparative approach challenges the three previously mentioned theories. The common development from intestate succession to testate succession in ancient law is an appropriate example to subject to the theory of immanence;[31] for we witness a possible progression from the prohibitive to the permissive, a narrative in which the law moves toward greater freedom. Implicit in the discussion in Deuteronomy[32] of property allocations to sons is that, in accordance with the laws of intestacy, each son receives a single share of the inheritance while the firstborn inherits two portions. It is unclear what rights of allocation, if any, exist according to Deuteronomy (see Chapters 1 and 2) even if there may be narrative evidence from Genesis that at least the firstborn's inheritance may be subject to reallocation under certain circumstances (see below). By the tannaitic period, however, multiple methods for transferring property among family members and even strangers become available, including forms of testate succession (see Chapters 1 and 3), a fact that attests to the individual's right of allocation in tannaitic law.[33]

Similar evolutionary processes take place in multiple ancient legal contexts. Regarding the ancient Near East, sources from early dynastic and Sargonic Mesopotamia provide evidence of only intestate succession but in material from the Old Babylonian period onward, testate succession is available.[34] In Athenian

[31] For the definitions of these terms, see "Abbreviations, Terminology, and Transliteration."

[32] 21:15–17.

[33] On the methodological challenge of a legal history approach beginning with the Bible and ending with the tannaim, see below "The Legal Legacy of the Tannaim: Ancient Parallels and Antecedents," and n. 53. Nevertheless, I cite this example here because in many areas of law, the tannaim see historical continuity between their laws and the earlier laws of the Bible.

[34] Here, too, an argument can be made against viewing different ancient Near Eastern legal traditions as outgrowths of one another (see, e.g., the discussion in Greengus, "Issues"). However, on the overarching and unifying spirit of legal conceptualization in ancient Near Eastern law, see Westbrook, "Introduction," and n. 36.

law, according to pre-sixth-century BCE accounts, only intestate succession exists, after which a shift takes place, with the innovations attributed to Solon, enabling testate succession as well. And, for Roman law, although it is assumed that in its earliest stages only intestate succession is practiced, according to some, by the advent of The Twelve Tablets in the fifth century BCE, traces of testate succession are codified.[35]

The fact that similar developments are documented in multiple bodies of ancient legal material might strengthen the assertion of immanence that an independent inner logic to the development of law exists. The comparatist asks, however, whether parallel trajectories point to common traditions. Put differently, does the shift from intestate to testate succession in multiple ancient legal contexts – two of which presumably do so in the fifth and sixth centuries BCE – suggest a possible dependence of legal traditions on each other?[36] That is, can points of contact be discovered that thereby undermine the central assumption of the immanence school?[37] Even if in the final analysis the answer is a resounding no, the comparatist's questions must be entertained for the fruit they may yield.

The study of comparative ancient law poses a challenge to the theory of contingency as well, especially when the convergence of coincidences is an untenable argument. The parallels between ancient gifts in contemplation of death from different legal traditions,[38] in fact, contest the basic assumption of contingency, the specific case of deathbed bequests being particularly instructive. In the narrative about a (seeming) deathbed bequest found in Gen. 27:2, Isaac, addressing his son Esau, declares, "Behold now, I have become old and I know not the day of my death." The gifting here simply seems like an act generated by the circumstances of the storyline: Isaac contemplates his approaching demise and wishes to gift his possessions. For the advocate of contingency, here gifting is, in fact, nothing more than a function of the coincidental situation in which the literary characters Isaac and his son Esau find themselves.

The later tannaitic deathbed bequest, the *mattenat shakhev mera*, is a formal legal instrument employed by the seriously ill and (at least according to amoraic law) revocable upon the donor's recovery (see Chapter 1 and the Appendix). For the proponents of contingency, here, too, we witness just haphazard happenings. The desire of the ill to gift in anticipation of death, combined with the possibility

[35] See further on this matter in Chapters 1 and 3.

[36] The greatest advocate for the idea of a "shared tradition" among ancient legal traditions is Raymond Westbrook. For a summary of his views and methodology, see the introduction in *Tigris to Tiber*, the volumes published in his memory by Wells and Magdalene. See also the approach espoused in Burkert, *Babylon, Memphis, Persepolis*. For a critique of Westbrook, see Greengus, "Issues."

[37] On the legend of a Roman delegation sent to Athens to examine Solon's laws and the legend's import for the historical study of parallels in Greek and Roman sources, see Watson, *Legal Transplants*, 25–27.

[38] See "Abbreviations, Terminology, and Transliteration," Chapter 1, and the Appendix.

of a change of mind after recovery, spawns the creation of a flexible institution. For the legal comparatist, however, the accidents of history actually weaken the stance of contingency. For, it is the coincidence that the Bible is the product of the ancient Near East and the circumstance that the rabbis formulate their laws within a Greco-Roman context that make the argument for contingency here unreasonable. The formula employed by Isaac is, in fact, attested as technical terminology for deathbed gifting in ancient Mesopotamia,[39] and the tannaitic *mattenat shakhev mera* is parallel to the Roman *donatio mortis causa*. Other tannaitic forms of gifting in contemplation of death also find their parallels in Greek and Roman sources. The *mattenat bari*, which transfers ownership immediately to the donee while use and management are retained by the donor until death, is parallel to the Greco-Egyptian *meta tēn teleutēn* and the Roman *donatio deducto usufructu*.[40] The *diathēkē*, Greek for a written disposition in case of death, retains its original Greek name and formula in rabbinic sources![41] Engaging in the comparative approach, therefore, points to the weaknesses of contingency; for, what are the chances that the same function or formula would be applied independently in contexts with such potentially close contact, such as the biblical and the ancient Near Eastern or the Greek and the tannaitic?[42]

The theory of inevitability, too, is challenged by the comparative approach, and here an examination of the previously mentioned, possible flexibility regarding the firstborn's receipt of his double portion of inheritance is in order. According to the Deuteronomic laws of intestacy,[43] the firstborn has a special status and receives a double portion of inheritance while the other sons receive one portion each. It is unclear if any flexibility exists with regard to allocating the portions in Deuteronomy. However, flexibility regarding the designation of firstborn status and the allocation of the double portion seemingly exists in biblical narratives and in tannaitic law.[44] Indeed, the patriarchal narratives in Genesis present flexibility regarding the appointment of the firstborn. In two narratives it is the second son who replaces the first – Isaac takes the place of Ishmael, and Jacob supersedes Esau. In another, Joseph supplants Reuben, the double portion possibly granted to Joseph by their father Jacob through Joseph's sons Ephraim and Manasseh (on the firstborn and these narratives, see Chapter 2).[45]

---

[39] This is a point of serious debate among scholars. See most recently the defense in Malul, "Deathbed Dispositions," 35–63.

[40] See the Appendix for my extended discussion of the matter.

[41] Yaron, *Gifts*, 124–126; for my treatment, see the Appendix.

[42] However, see, below, "On the Relationship of Ancient Laws to Ancient Societies" regarding to what extent the Bible is representative of ancient Near Eastern law and culture.

[43] Deut. 21:15–17.

[44] See, below, "On the Relationship of Ancient Laws to Ancient Societies," regarding the fact that not all of the narratives and law collections preserved in the biblical canon are representative of the same legal and cultural traditions.

[45] This may be overstated here. See the fuller discussion in Chapter 2.

Tannaitic law is less ambiguous regarding flexibility. A father has considerable liberty when allocating assets. A tannaitic tradition preserved in the Mishnah (*BB* 8:5) grants a man the right to give the firstborn a single portion and another son the double portion (see Chapters 1 and 2). To be sure, the presumed household structure in biblical literature and tannaitic texts – although different from each other – might account for the existence of possible flexibility in both spheres. The biblical model is an extended family household that requires a family leader or administrator at its head. The firstborn leader is designated either through lineage or appointment. If we can learn from the ancient Near Eastern record, in all likelihood a firstborn has financial obligations to the widow and other members of the extended household; hence, he receives an extra portion.

The family unit known to the tannaim, however, is a nuclear one, without a family leader with obligations to an extended clan determined by lineage or otherwise. The theory of inevitability could explain the possible flexibility present in both biblical and tannaitic sources as a product of the social institution of the family that is the presumed background in each context. In the biblical model, following the lead from parts of the ancient Near East, at times a son or other relative, favored or more capable than the biological firstborn, is appointed to lead the family, preserve the estate upon the father's death, and receive an additional inheritance. In the nuclear family of the tannaitic period, however, a role for the firstborn family leader generally is not acknowledged.[46] Tannaitic family organization enables a flexible approach to the allocation of a double portion to the firstborn to emerge in tannaitic law as well but for a different reason: since the firstborn has no official role, he can be granted a single share, or a son other than the firstborn can be given extra inheritance at the discretion of the father.[47] However, the scholar of comparative law investigates further. Is it not reasonable to entertain the possibility that the two models of flexibility, similar in concept and (as part of the ancient Near Eastern tradition) employed in the same general geographic region over centuries, share a common origin? Or, at least, is it plausible that the "local practice"[48] of biblical/ancient Near Eastern flexibility plays a role in the eventual emergence of the flexible approach among some tannaim? And what of the impact of the Greco-Roman context in which tannaitic law is formulated where a firstborn enjoys no privilege?

In light of the challenges that comparing ancient legal traditions poses to dogmatic theoretical views on the evolution of law, I endeavor to provide a more nuanced understanding when comparing the legal complex of tannaitic inheritance laws to other ancient laws. But, as the examples above illustrate and the

[46] For possible exceptions, see Chapter 2.

[47] For this line of argument, see Milgram, "Transformation," 19–28. However, my comments in Chapter 2 come to supersede my initial thinking in that article.

[48] On my use of the term "local practice," see, below, "The Legal Legacy of the Tannaim: Ancient Parallels and Antecedents."

case of firstborn flexibility stresses, even the most successful study of these historical relationships depends on more than just the examination of overlapping traditions and terminology. A serious consideration of the social and economic contexts is also in order and follows in the section called, "On the Relationship of Ancient Laws to Ancient Societies." Before addressing that matter, however, in the next section I explore the appropriateness of certain ancient legal traditions for comparison with tannaitic laws.

The Legal Legacy of the Tannaim: Ancient Parallels and Antecedents

Following Alan Watson's observations on the enterprise of comparative law,[49] the subject of this book is, above all, a study of the similarities and differences between the rules of inheritance in several ancient compilations of law in the context of the historical relationship of the rules to one another. I discuss laws that have potential points of contact (whether direct or indirect) or historical overlap with tannaitic laws. These include biblical laws; representations of pre-rabbinic local custom in ancient Near Eastern legal codes and records of legal transactions (primarily from Mesopotamia but also from Anatolia and the Levant);[50] pre-rabbinic Jewish legal interpretation in Second Temple sources relevant to our study (e.g., in Philo, Judith, and Tobit); antecedent and parallel documentary evidence in the papyri from Elephantine and the Judean desert; and Greek and Roman legal sources.

I compare the laws of inheritance preserved in all of the above collections to those found in tannaitic literature with the goal of accomplishing methodological thoroughness. This broad and ambitious comparative study enables a fuller appreciation of the possible origins of and parallels to tannaitic inheritance laws and facilitates the achievement of more nuanced conclusions about the relationship of specific tannaitic approaches to those present in the greater ancient Near East and Mediterranean before and during the tannaitic period. The reader can find a summary of my conclusions below in the section entitled, "The Present Study." In the paragraphs that immediately follow, I mention the general contributions of several comparatists whose work guides the enterprise of examining tannaitic

---

[49] Watson, *Legal Transplants*, 9.

[50] On the distinction between the two kinds of evidence, see "On the Relationship of Ancient Laws to Ancient Societies."

laws in various ancient legal contexts,[51] and I illustrate the relevance of each of the legal traditions I choose for comparison with tannaitic inheritance laws.[52]

Certainly, any study of tannaitic law should begin with an analysis of the possible biblical antecedents to rabbinic legislation despite the fact that verifiable historical continuity from biblical law to tannaitic law is lacking for most, if not all, areas of law.[53] This fact makes any legal history approach (such as mine) beginning with the Bible and ending with the tannaim methodologically challenging. The endeavor remains useful, and perhaps even imperative, because the rabbis see themselves as a legacy, a link in a long and unbroken legal continuum beginning with the Bible and as the arbiters of biblical literature's most authentic interpretation. It is not only because of the rabbis' religious inspiration, however, that the comparison of tannaitic law to biblical law is so essential. Because the rabbis rely so heavily on biblical law and literature to buttress their authority and innovation – and, perhaps needless to say, preserve such a vast and magisterial tradition of interpretation of biblical literature – research in tannaitic law must begin with discussions of biblical antecedents, first and foremost, to understand the degree to which the rabbis do or do not simply replicate biblical laws and how the rabbis employ biblical interpretation to uphold their innovation. The present study demonstrates that, in general, the inheritance laws formulated by the tannaim bear little resemblance, if any, to their biblical counterparts and that tannaitic legal innovation in the area of inheritance law is not generally linked to biblical commentary.

The case for the study of rabbinic law in light of ancient Near Eastern traditions is made by many scholars.[54] Most recently Samuel Greengus,[55] building

[51] J. J. Rabinowitz, in articles and in his book *Jewish Law*, argues for the historical influence of Jewish legal institutions and formulae on multiple legal systems from antiquity onward. I address the relevant discussions from Rabinowitz's studies primarily in the Appendix.

[52] For a discussion of prior scholarship on tannaitic inheritance laws in a comparative context, see the Preface.

[53] To be sure, areas of continuity exist between Israelite religion and rabbinic Judaism, such as the circumcision of males, the relative lack of consumption of pork, the centrality of Jerusalem, and the worship of Yahweh as mentioned by Schwartz, *Imperialism*, 19–20. Stephen Geller reminds me that the use of the Hebrew language also is an area of continuity.

[54] For a general impression on the influence of ancient Near Eastern law and culture on tannaitic Judaism, see Geller, "Influence," who correctly argues the probability that "[t]hrough Aramaic much of the technical vocabulary of the Near East found its way into Jewish texts" of the Hellenistic period and beyond (43). To be sure, the strongest argument for common origins can be made when there is terminological overlap. See, e. g., on the Akkadian parallels to the rabbinic *nikhsei melug*, B. Levine, "Mulugu/Melug," 271–285, and my comments in Chapter 4; on *din napishtim* and *dinei nefashot*, see S. Friedman, "Plotting Witness," 827 n. 88. See also on divorce terminology, most recently in Holtz, "To Go and Marry," 241–258. See also works cited throughout my book. A comprehensive list of works on the overlap between ancient Near Eastern law and rabbinic law first appeared in Muffs, *Love and Joy*, 139–141. Some additional studies include Yaakov Elman's early work: see Elman, "Authoritative Oral Tradition," 19–32 and "Babylonian Echoes," 12–19. A partial listing of significant studies on the subject by Sham-

on his previous work,[56] collects parallels between rabbinic law and ancient Near Eastern law for multiple areas of legislation. Whereas most scholars shy away from directly addressing the question of which "channels of transmission"[57] lead to the parallels between ancient Near Eastern law and rabbinic law, based on specific examples of ancient Near Eastern laws from the second millennium BCE that "reemerge" in rabbinic collections (2nd and 3rd centuries CE), Greengus suggests that "[t]his long trail of continuity supports the postbiblical Jewish claim concerning the existence of ancient 'oral laws' that had been 'handed down' alongside of the written laws of the Pentateuch."[58] Although the question of whether Greengus's examples attest to oral traditions that necessarily accompanied the written text of the Pentateuch requires further consideration, his attention to the circulation of oral traditions in the ancient world as a possible mechanism to account for the legal overlap is valuable. In this study, when applicable based on the evidence,[59] I take a different approach. I claim that various ancient Near Eastern traditions, by virtue of being present in one form or another in the general region of the ancient Near East as the local practice or local tradition for millennia, possibly have an impact on the production of law by the tannaim. I mention this possibility even though it cannot be demonstrated that the rabbis actually knew of, or read, ancient Near Eastern codes or transactional records.[60]

A close examination of Second Temple literature to gain an adequate appreciation of legal antecedents to rabbinic laws is, to be sure, a methodological desideratum.[61] Studies of Qumran and its religious practices as antecedents to tannaitic traditions abound.[62] Other Second Temple works, under the assumption of some cultural, legal, or historical continuity with the tannaim, also provide compelling points of comparison and even evidence for stages of development between biblical religion and rabbinic Judaism.[63] Although the treasure trove of Qumran does not provide source material relevant to this study, other important works from the period of the Second Temple do, including the writings of Philo and the books of Judith and Tobit, all three of which provide meaningful data for comparison (see primarily Chapters 3 and 4). For a general overview, the classic work

ma Friedman includes Friedman, "Woman with Two Husbands," 530–558; "Plotting Witness," 801–829; and "Ben-Drosai," 77–91.

55 *Laws*.

56 See Greengus, "Filling Gaps," 149–172.

57 I thank Bernard Jackson for suggesting the use of this phrase.

58 Greengus, *Laws*, 282. For another possible channel of transmission, see n. 54.

59 See, e.g., Chapter 1 on gifting vs. inheritance, and see Chapter 2 on firstborn inheritance.

60 On the distinction between ancient Near Eastern codes and transactional records as sources of law, see, below, "On the Relationship of Ancient Laws to Ancient Societies."

61 For a general description, see Piatelli and Jackson, "Jewish Law during the Second Temple Period," 19–56.

62 See, e.g., the works by Vered Noam and Lawrence Schiffman cited in my bibliography.

63 See, e.g., Flusser, *Judaism of the Second Temple Period*.

by Samuel Belkin, *Philo and the Oral Law*,[64] remains the most comprehensive survey of the legal material in Philo's writings and its potential relationship(s) to rabbinic law. The possible preservation of pre-rabbinic (Jewish) laws in the books of Judith and Tobit is addressed by Yehoshua Grintz in his critical edition with commentary to the book of Judith[65] and in his study, *Chapters in the History of Second Temple Times*.[66]

An invaluable collection of legal practices to consult when searching for legal antecedents to tannaitic laws is preserved in the documentary papyri from Elephantine, a fifth century BCE Jewish military colony. As the dean of Elephantine studies, Bezalel Porten, succinctly stated almost a half century ago, the documents from Elephantine "provide the earliest documentation for the political, economic, social, religious, and corporate life of a Jewish community."[67] They are, therefore, essential for understanding identifiably Jewish antecedents to tannaitic law. The only systematic presentation of the law of the Elephantine papyri compared to Jewish sources remains Reuven Yaron's useful, if dated, *Introduction to the Law of the Aramaic Papyri*,[68] which includes an entire chapter on succession. The availability of editions of the Elephantine papyri, both in the original and in translation,[69] enabled more studies on specific topics to be authored.[70] Inheritance law is no exception, as represented by the thoughtful scholarship on testamentary practices at Elephantine with reference to Talmudic parallels authored jointly by Porten and Zvi Szubin,[71] from which I draw when relevant.

A recent volume entitled *Law in the Documents of the Judaean Desert* reminds us of the importance of a different set of much later documentary papyri.[72] This written testimony deals with the activities of private individuals from the late-first and early-second centuries CE. For the study of Judaism in Roman Palestine, in general, and law as practiced during the tannaitic period, in particular, this collection is of great importance. Beginning with the research of scholars such as Yigal Yadin in the 1960s,[73] the documentary evidence for traditions among these presumed non-rabbinic Jews became useful for a clearer understanding of

[64] Belkin, *Philo*. For additional bibliography, see Chapter 4.

[65] Grintz, *Judith*.

[66] Grintz, *Chapters*.

[67] Porten, *Archives from Elephantine*, vii.

[68] Yaron, *Aramaic Papyri*. See also, of course, the relevant sections – scattered and embedded throughout – in Muffs, *Studies,* and the appropriate chapters in Porten, *Archives from Elephantine*.

[69] See, e.g., Porten, *Elephantine Papyri in English;* and Porten and Yardeni, *Textbook*.

[70] For the studies relevant to inheritance, see the literature cited in Chapters 1 and 3 and the Appendix. See also Botta, *Aramaic and Egyptian Legal Traditions*.

[71] See the listings in the bibliography for Szubin and Porten. For my discussion, see primarily Chapter 3.

[72] Katzoff and Schaps, *Documents of the Judaean Desert*.

[73] See, e.g., "Expedition D," 227–257.

the relationship, if any, between the laws preserved in tannaitic legal collections and the actual practices evidenced in Palestine of the tannaitic period. More recently, the important work of Hannah Cotton on the content of the actual laws represented in the papyri and their comparison with tannaitic laws further enhances our ability to paint a partially reconstructed picture of this pre-rabbinic (and postbiblical) Judaism as actually practiced.[74] If the rabbis are aware of the inheritance customs of their early contemporaries, then we must postulate why, at times, there is conceptual and formulaic overlap between the laws preserved in the tannaitic collections and the practices preserved in the Judean desert documents and why, at times, the traditions in the two collections exhibit divergent paths (see in particular Chapter 5).

As demonstrated by two eminent scholars of the previous generation, Saul Lieberman[75] and David Daube,[76] the Greek language as well as significant elements of Hellenistic thought and culture are embraced by the tannaim on multiple levels. In the realm of the strictly legal, Asher Gulak's early comparative studies, primarily based on papyrological evidence – even if authored three-quarters of a century ago – remain valuable for the analysis of potential intersections between tannaitic law and the law of the Greek papyri.[77] More recently, the contents of an entire volume dedicated to exploring the degrees of contact, accommodation, and response among the tannaim to all things Greek, *Hellenism in the Land of Israel*[78] affirms, once again, the deep level of interaction that exists between the rabbis and their Hellenized non-rabbinic and non-Jewish contemporaries. Regarding tannaitic inheritance law specifically, it is Yaron in his magnum opus *Gifts in Contemplation of Death*, who fleshes out the most significant parallels and points of potential influence of Greek dispositions in case of death on the nascent inheritance laws of the tannaim, a matter I address in detail throughout this work (see the Preface and below "The Present Study").

The final body of ancient law that I consult when discussing tannaitic inheritance principles is classical Roman law. The comparative study of rabbinic and Roman law was championed by Boaz Cohen in his many erudite articles

[74] The following is only a partial listing of Cotton's work: "Babatha's Property," 211–24; "Deeds of Gift," 179–86; "Law of Succession Again," 115–23; "Archive," 171–208; "Marriage Contracts," 2–6; "Rabbis and Documents," 167–179; "Women and Law," 123–147.

[75] Indeed, two of the most important works in the English language remain Lieberman's, *Hellenism* and *Greek*. Important for the subject of this book is Yaron's *Gifts*, in which the author emphasizes the influence of Hellenistic inheritance law on rabbinic inheritance law. See also Baer, "Historical Foundations," and the critique in Urbach, "Inheritance Laws and After-life," 133–134. These three works are discussed in the Preface.

[76] The first volume of *Collected Works of David Daube* is dedicated to Daube's studies on Talmudic law and Greek, as well as, Roman law.

[77] For examples of the contribution of Asher Gulak to the study of Greek and rabbinic law, see the two titles cited in n. 84.

[78] *Hellenism in the Land of Israel.*

on specific legal topics.[79] In his studies Cohen preserves a conservative balance between determining when there is "mutual indebtedness" for specific laws[80] among the tannaim and the Romans[81] and when comparative study serves only "to illumine dark corners in sundry branches of the law by opening up new vistas and perspectives afforded by the aggregate of analogies and contrast."[82] Here, too, David Daube in his numerous studies on the potential interconnections between Roman law and tannaitic law, with an attention to detail and a clarity of expression perhaps unparalleled among scholars engaged in similar work, explores the historical, cultural, and legal implications of contact between rabbis and Romans.[83] To a certain extent, Gulak, here as in his studies of Hellenistic Judaism, precedes both Cohen and Daube in parts of this endeavor.[84] Regarding inheritance law specifically, Yaron, in *Gifts in Contemplation of Death*, mentioned above, denies any influence on Jewish law by Roman law,[85] a matter with which I disagree and address directly in the Preface and Chapters 1 and 3 and summarize below in the section entitled, "The Present Study."

In summary, the parallels from the distinct collections supply essential data for determining to what degree the inheritance laws formulated by the tannaim are representative of concepts, customs, and laws generally known in the ancient Mediterranean. At times, we can determine that a particular approach, formula, term, or concept is in fact appropriated from a specific and identifiable compilation external to the tannaitic corpus.[86] Therefore, the legal, literary, and archival

[79] Most of these are collected in Cohen's two-volume work *Jewish and Roman Law*. Important methodological issues are covered on pp. vii–xxvii, 1–30 (see, e. g., the exploration of parallels between The Twelve Tablets and rabbinic law on 17–22). The author also discusses the views of other scholars of the previous generation (such as Zechariah Frankel and Louis Ginzberg) on the general question of the impact of Roman law, if any, on rabbinic law.

[80] See, however, the critique in Morton Smith's review of B. Cohen, "[c]onsequently the relationships noted between Jewish and Roman law are occasional and superficial. It is justifiably observed that the general development of Roman law and the direct pressure of the Roman administration probably influenced the tannaitic lawmakers… . But there is no systematic examination of either influence, only a scattering of instances" (Smith, Review of Cohen, 240).

[81] E. g., Cohen argues that, in general, the concept of usufruct in Jewish law is *likely* borrowed from Roman law; see B. Cohen, *Jewish and Roman Law*, 557–577. However, see my comments in the Appendix.

[82] B. Cohen, *Jewish and Roman Law*, 13–14. An important survey of the methodological issues is in Jackson, "Roman Influence," 157–203; see also Jackson, "Evolution," 372–390 and "History, Dogmatics and Halakhah," 1–26.

[83] See n. 76.

[84] See, e. g., Gulak, *Legal Documents*; see also, Gulak, *Yesodei Hamishpat Haivri*.

[85] Yaron, *Gifts*, 38 and 125.

[86] In his recent essay, "Beyond Influence," Michael Satlow urges scholars to reconsider the historiographical models of analysis employed for writing the history of the Jews in antiquity. Up until recently, argues Satlow, works on rabbinic historiography reduced "culture into static binary encounters characterized by … 'influence,' 'assimilation,' 'acculturation,' and 'appropriation' (38). In this study, I embrace Satlow's challenge not to reduce and oversimplify the relationship of the tannaim and their laws to those external to their group and to view the rabbis

evidence is treated throughout as possibly parallel and antecedent to tannaitic inheritance law.

The comparison of tannaitic inheritance laws to the customs and practices found in the literary, legal, and documentary collections described above makes up only part of the work undertaken in this book. The construction of law is usually in some way related to the presumed cultural complex – whether just the literary or also the social and economic ones – from which the works in which the laws are embedded originate. One of the observations of this book is the degree to which in constructing inheritance laws based on the legal contexts of the ancient Near East and Mediterranean, the rabbis fashion laws that generally correspond to the social and economic contexts prevalent in Roman Palestine. In a later section entitled, "Tannaitic Society and Tannaitic Inheritance Law: Cause and Effect?," I deal with the complex question of causation, that is, did the social and economic contexts in Roman Palestine actually cause the tannaim to formulate their inheritance laws as they did? Before tackling that matter, however, for each of the law collections that I compare to tannaitic laws, in the section immediately following, I address the more general question of the relationship of ancient laws to the ancient societies in which they are created.

On the Relationship of Ancient Laws to Ancient Societies

As mentioned previously, scholars dismiss the notion that the rabbis function in any real capacity as legislators for the masses of Judeans in Roman Palestine.

---

as part of the general population of Roman Palestine, "assuming the similarities." A study like mine, however, which is much more about tannaitic legal history than historiography, must work under different assumptions than a purely historical monograph (the subject addressed by Satlow). The bulk of the evidence examined by Satlow (archeological and papyrological and often, due to its nature, unverifiable in its connection to the rabbis), is studied in order to understand what may have been actual practice among the general populace in Roman Judea. My pursuit here, however, is to unravel the legal makeup of the rabbinic movement as it is represented in tannaitic literature. And, in carefully employing the comparative approach to deepen my understanding of rabbinic conceptualization and formulation, I often turn to discrete bodies of law, themselves verifiable as external to the rabbinic canon and the product of specific groups in identifiable locations throughout the ancient Near East and Mediterranean, to compare and contrast them to the tannaitic evidence. While Satlow's commendable search for the historical-cultural truth requires a focus on scattered and unrelated material evidence, often not verifiable as linked to the rabbis, my hunt for the textual-legal truth is founded on evidence that, in its preserved state, is identifiably tannaitic and is compared to data that, in its preserved state, is verifiably external, enabling some degree of confidence when arguing that the practices and principles of the latter are appropriated by the former. Nevertheless, some procedures for inheritance in tannaitic literature existed in much of the ancient world. Accordingly, it is not possible to trace if, when, or how tannaitic law embraced them. In several of these instances I suggest that the phenomena observed in tannaitic law are representative of the local and regional customs for transferring property that reigned for millennia (see "The Legal Legacy of the Tannaim, Ancient Parallels and Antecedents").

Moreover, academics remain agnostic to this day regarding what, in fact, tannaitic law is in its time.[87] Still, that there is a relationship in some areas of law between the laws of the tannaim and those recorded in sources external to the rabbinic canon,[88] as well as a possible connection between tannaitic laws and the social and economic contexts in which the authors of the laws lived, is compelling based on the research conducted in several studies.[89]

Inheritance law is no exception. Parallels discussed throughout this book attest to the terminological, formulaic, and conceptual origins of tannaitic inheritance law. Furthermore, also as previously noted, the rabbinic construction of the inheritance procedures that are adopted and adapted is appropriate to what we believe to be the social and economic contexts experienced by the tannaim in Roman Palestine.[90] The absence of tannaitic scriptural interpretation – and, indeed, the paucity of biblical verses – to buttress rabbinic inheritance procedures attest to the fact that the complex of tannaitic inheritance laws cannot be attributed to rabbinic exegesis. Rather, the laws are the result of an unclear, and likely unrecoverable, interplay between the formation of laws – even theoretical ones – and the legal, social, and economic contexts in which they are constructed. What remains apparent is that in the realm of inheritance, unlike the claims in other recent studies of tannaitic law, an argument attributing tannaitic innovation primarily to rabbinic invention and imagination cannot be maintained.[91] In this

[87] Note the issue of *Association for Jewish Studies Review* (32:2, 2008) dedicated to the question, "What is (the) Mishnah?"

[88] See the section called, "The Legal Legacy of the Tannaim: Ancient Parallels and Antecedents."

[89] See n. 5 and n. 17.

[90] See, below, "The Social and Economic Dimension: The Nuclear Family, Private Landholdings and Urbanization in Tannaitic Palestine."

[91] In her recent study *Execution and Invention*, Beth Berkowitz argues that the rabbis invent a complex death penalty ritual under their control to strengthen their claims for authority in the context of Roman political sovereignty. As Berkowitz correctly points out, the rabbis, in part, are in dialogue with biblical sources on execution. Accordingly, their innovations are anchored in scriptural interpretation, and their construction of the legal complex, therefore, cannot be solely attributed to the adoption and adaption of existing legal principles external to the rabbinic canon or the social and economic contexts of Roman Palestine (see Berkowitz's critique of the latter possibility, specifically, scattered among other discussions on 34–52; on the literary use of Roman capital punishment practices by the rabbis, see 153–179). Similarly, Ishay Rosen-Zvi, in his book *Mishnaic Sotah Ritual*, demonstrates the degree to which the rabbis, in part, reshape the biblical ritual of *soṭah* (=suspected adulterous wife) through reactions to and interpretations of biblical texts; for a sampling, see 1, 22, 50–51, 67–69, and 183–218 (on the possible overlap with imagery from the Roman arena as well, see 219–223). Naftali Cohn recently published *Memory of the Temple*, where he claims that the prominence of the Temple and its ritual in the Mishnah is intended to bolster rabbinic authority under Roman dominance. Without relating the specifics of Cohn's argument, I note that here, too, the nature of the data is different than that for inheritance. Based on Cohn's examination of the topic, seemingly no external evidence exists regarding other ancient temples from which the rabbis may draw for their Temple imagery.

section, I review aspects of the historicity of the laws in the legal collections discussed in this book, and in the next section I consider the possible relationship of the presumed social and economic contexts of biblical Israel and tannaitic Palestine to the inheritance laws present in the Bible and tannaitic literature.

The establishment of the relationship of ancient laws to everyday life in the societies in which they are formulated is a complex methodological problem by no means limited to the study of tannaitic law. Almost every body of law and literature consulted in this book is plagued by similar and, even additional, methodological limitations. For example, although generally in agreement that biblical law is an essential part of a greater biblical culture, separate from the specifically legal discourse of the Bible, scholars of biblical law disagree to what extent the laws represent daily life in ancient Israel or even reflect historically verifiable social or economic situations.[92] Furthermore, distinctions are made, for example, between the customs possibly reflected in the patriarchal narratives, the traditions in the Pentateuchal law collections, and later biblical books (such as Ruth and Job, treated here).[93]

Regarding inheritance practices in particular, it is evident that the presumed procedures put into place upon the death of the head of household – such as the joint ownership of the estate until its eventual division, (upon division) the granting of extra inheritance to the firstborn son, and the exclusion of daughters from the order of succession – are all intrinsically related to the Bible's larger construction of ancient Israel's presumed social framework. The extended clan resides on the jointly owned ancestral estate with a family leader at its head and in an agrarian (and male dominated) society. Whether historically such family arrangements and landholding patterns actually existed in ancient Israel, however, is debated by scholars.[94] For our purposes, the historicity of the biblical sources is less important than the fact that the rabbis – knowing all too well the models of the family and landholding patterns presented in biblical texts – construct a complex of laws not only divorced from the Bible's conceptions but also, uncharacteristically, independent of creative interpretation of Scripture to uphold their innovations. And, all the while, the procedures that are promoted remain apparently appropriate to the social and economic conditions in which the tannaim themselves live.

Returning to the problem of the relationship of biblical law to historical Israelite society, the attempt to define what biblical law actually is – since it is embedded within a work that is largely narrative in scope and whose ideological goal is the telling of the Hebrews' election, exodus, and occupation of the promised land – remains for many a riddle requiring resolution by the examination

---

[92] See Chavel, "Biblical Law"; Westbrook and Wells, *Everyday Law.*

[93] See, in particular, Chapter 3.

[94] See Maeir, "Rephaim," 289–297. My thanks to Aaron Koller for this reference.

of external sources. The outside evidence is drawn from the ancient Near East (primarily Mesopotamia).[95] Yet, the body of source material from the ancient Near East is, in its own right, methodologically challenging to engage.

Assyriologists distinguish between transactional records, such as marriage, divorce, adoption, and testamentary documents and the supposed codes of ancient Mesopotamian law, most famous among them the Code of Hammurabi (ca. 1750 BCE) and the earlier Code of Lipit Ishtar (ca. 1930 BCE). The former genre of source material is documentary evidence for practices in ancient Near Eastern communities; from it, we glean significant insight about the activities among the people (even if not the formal laws), as well as details about the social and economic make up of specific ancient societies. The latter are codes, called into question as charters of actual law because they never are clearly binding on communities (or even cited in court cases and transactional records!).[96] In all likelihood they are theoretical laws that are the product of scribal schools.[97] Still, some scholars point to the important observation that the laws in the codes are often representative of a common legal culture with the transactional records,[98] at least at the level of conceptualization, if not always in exact content.[99] The question of to what extent biblical law is generally part of the cultural and legal continuum of the complicated legacy of ancient Near Eastern law – whether relying on it and/or responding to it – occupied scholars over the last century and continues to occupy them.[100] As Gershon Brin and Raymond Westbrook,[101] among others, observe, and as affirmed by the investigation carried out in this book, with respect to biblical inheritance practices some continuity between biblical inheritance law and ancient Near Eastern tradition is, at times, discernible.

Questions of cohesion concern scholars in other fields of ancient law as well. For example, the lack of continuity among the various *poleis* (=city-states) in ancient Greece that contributes to what might be contentiously called Greek law is the topic of a recent and engaging essay by Michael Gagarin entitled, "The Unity of Greek Law."[102] Pointing specifically to matters of inheritance (and marriage), Gagarin argues that the intrinsic differences among the laws of separate city-states

[95] There has been significant debate among biblicists about whether the Bible represents continuity or discontinuity with the greater legal traditions of the ancient Near East. On this see Malul, *Comparative Method,* and, further, see Barmash, *Homicide*, 1–7. See also the classic, Finkelstein, *Ox that Gored.*

[96] For a review of the scholarship on the codes and the question of their normativity, see the essays in Lévy, *La codification des lois dans l'antiquité.*

[97] Roth, *Law Collections*, 4.

[98] Westbrook, "Introduction," 4–21.

[99] These two bodies of evidence – together with a third type, royal decrees, which are often cited in records – constitute the bulk of the ancient Near Eastern data from which I draw in this study.

[100] See n. 95.

[101] See, in particular, Chapter 2.

[102] Gagarin, "Unity of Greek Law," 29–40.

are enough to call into question the presence of an underlying conceptual unity implied by the term "Greek law."[103] The inheritance laws in the three Greek city-states treated here – Athens, Sparta, and Gortyn – do, indeed, show significant variation. Certainly, of the three judicial traditions, the one best documented and, therefore, most easily described by a general characterization is the Athenian tradition.[104] We, nevertheless, draw from the laws of Sparta and Gortyn as well, due to the significant – even if, at times, limited or unclear – evidence for inheritance customs there and the richness of the comparisons resulting from their inclusion.

The inheritance laws of each city-state represent but one facet of the larger social and economic framework of each *polis* and, as elsewhere in the ancient world, the make up of inheritance laws is intimately related to the presumed structure of family life and landholding patterns. Significantly, unlike the skepticism justifiably maintained by students of biblical law and ancient Near Eastern codes, scholars of Athenian law in particular generally rely on the historicity of their main body of evidence – about one hundred court speeches.[105] That is, these speeches likely were recited in court settings and represent various aspects of the actual law known and practiced in classical Athens (ca. 435–322 BCE). Their study is, nonetheless, marred by methodological problems, including – but not limited to – the exact historical verification of the attributed orators.[106] Perhaps more significant for a legal study such as ours, the speeches only present one side of the case adjudicated. They are perforce, therefore, an incomplete representation of the laws.[107] A significant debate around the Law Code of Gortyn ensued in recent years with Gagarin arguing that the code, indeed, represents true historical legislation,[108] while others disagree.[109] The field of Spartan law is plagued primarily by the fact that reports of Spartan law are transmitted in ancient Greece exclusively by non-Spartans, some of whom live hundreds of years after the supposed legislation comes into being in Sparta itself. Accordingly, the relationship of the accounts to historical practices is debatable.[110]

---

[103] Gagarin, "Unity of Greek Law," 29–40. Gagarin builds on the previous work of Sir Moses Finley (see Gagarin, *Writing Greek Law*, 7) and suggests focusing on elements of the Greek way of thinking about how law is practiced and how it functions within the *polis* in place of a conceptual unity. See also D. Cohen, "Problems," 92 and n. 28 there.

[104] Indeed, such descriptions appear in several volumes, two of which include Harrison, *Law of Athens*, and Macdowell, *Law in Classical Athens*.

[105] MacDowell, *Law in Classical Athens*, 8; Todd, "Law and Oratory at Athens," 97–99; Lanni, "Relevance in Athenian Courts," 112–115.

[106] See MacDowell, *Law in Classical Athens*, 9.

[107] MacDowell, *Law in Classical Athens*, 8.

[108] Gagarin, "Early Greek Law," 82–83; Gagarin, "Inscribing Laws," 9–20; Gagarin, *Writing Greek Law*.

[109] For the summary of other views, see scattered references in Gagarin, *Writing Greek Law*; Whitley, "Cretan Law and Cretan Literacy," 635–661.

[110] On some of the methodological problems, see MacDowell, *Spartan Law*, 2–3; and, more to the point, D. Cohen, "Problems," 97. See also, Hodkinson, *Property and Wealth*, 1–7.

Despite the methodological challenges unique to the study of the law of the Greek city-states, the comparisons to tannaitic law that their inclusion enables are significant. All three bodies of law, from Athens, Gortyn, and Sparta, include rich expositions on inheritance practices that contribute meaningfully to our discussion. The legal distinction between (what I consider) the Athenian form of testate succession,[111] that is, the *diathēkē* with *eispoiēsis* (=adoption),[112] and gifting in contemplation of death, that is, the *diathēkē* without *eispoiēsis* (=without adoption)[113] – the latter attested in different forms both at Sparta and Gortyn – is a case in point. The word *diathēkē* and its Greek formula are both absorbed into tannaitic legal discourse.[114] Yet, neither of the two institutions – as they originally functioned in classical Greece – makes its way into tannaitic law. For a discussion of how the original forms of the Greek *diathēkē* are transformed among the tannaim, see Chapters 1, 3, and the Appendix (for a summary, see "The Present Study").

Significant Roman legal parallels to tannaitic inheritance law exist as well.[115] These, when absorbed into the tannaitic complex of laws, are transformed in their new tannaitic environment in ways different from their Greek counterparts. However, before noting the most significant parallels, in line with the theme of our section, I first mention methodological matters concerning the historicity of classical Roman sources.

According to legend, the origin of the earliest code of Roman law, The Twelve Tablets, is attributed to the defeat of the patricians by the plebeians regarding the question of the publication of law.[116] The mythical account firmly places the work as a response to social upheaval during the period of the earliest legal development in Rome. Although some historians of Roman law accept the fundamentals of the legend – that the compilation represents the victory of the plebes around 450 BCE – as historical,[117] others propose that the laws are just as likely the product of the elite's desire for self-regulation.[118] As for Gaius's *Institutes* (ca. 160 CE) – a textbook considered to be an exemplary exposition of the laws centuries later by Justinian's compilers (ca. 533 CE)[119] – much more is known about its relevance for Roman legislation hundreds of years after its

[111] On all this, see Chapters 1 and 3.

[112] It transfers both rights and liabilities; see Chapter 1.

[113] It only transfers a right or good; see Chapter 1.

[114] On all this, see Chapters 1, 3, and the Appendix.

[115] See, esp., Chapters 1 and 3.

[116] See the account by the great Roman historian Livy in *Ab Urbe Condita Libri* 3.31–59 (*History of Rome*, 196–232).

[117] Jolowicz and Nicholas, *Historical Introduction*, 14.

[118] Crawford and Cloud, *Roman Statutes*, 560. See also Watson, *Rome of XII Tables*, 3–4.

[119] Jolowicz and Nicholas, *Historical Introduction*, 387.

publication than during the author's lifetime.[120] Although Gaius writes that "an act is law which the people decide and enact," (1:3),[121] the relationship of such a statement to what possibly spawns actual legislation in Gaius's time cannot be verified.[122] Regardless of the questions arising as to the historicity of these bodies of Roman law, the parallels to tannaitic law remain significant. And here, unlike their Greek counterparts, the Roman terms and principles are integrated differently. I argue that tannaitic terminology for the legal distinction between gifting in contemplation of death and inheriting is rooted in Roman terminology. The tannaitic gift, called a *mattanah*, and inheritance, known as *yerushah*,[123] are seemingly translations of the Roman legal terms *donatio* and *hereditas*, respectively.[124] Furthermore, the concept of testate succession among agnates in tannaitic law, an innovation attributed to the tanna Rabbi Yoḥanan ben Beroka, may find its origins in Roman legal conceptualization as well (on all this, see "The Present Study").[125]

The other bodies of law that I discuss in this work include documentary materials whose relationship to actual practice in their specific locales cannot be denied. The records from the military colony at Elephantine and the Judean desert provide substantive data for the function and role of custom and law in daily life.[126] The former archive supplies meaningful formulaic and conceptual antecedents among presumed Jews. The latter repository provides a glimpse at the law practiced by Jews in the Roman province of Judea, living at the same time as some tannaim and in cities geographically not far from the rabbis' own centers. Accordingly, the Judean desert texts afford the researcher an opportunity to discuss why the rabbis may or may not promote living laws that they, themselves, may be aware of.[127]

---

[120] Gordon and Robinson, *Institutes*, 7–10. For a broader view of the work's afterlife and relevance to Western jurisprudence and social thought, see Kelley, "Gaius Noster," 619–648.

[121] Gordon and Robinson, *Institutes*, 21. The Latin reads: "Lex est, quod populus iubet atque constituit" (Gordon and Robinson, *Institutes*, 2).

[122] On the different approaches to this question and related matters, see Honoré, *Gaius*, xi–xiii.

[123] That is not to say that there is a historical etymological connection between the Latin and Hebrew terms. To be sure, both the word *mattanah* and the word *yerushah* existed in the classical Hebrew lexicon prior to contact with their Latin counterparts. That is, the words did not come into existence as a result of rabbinic contact with Roman legal terminology. Still, the choice of the tannaim, in the context of disposition of assets, to label opposing mechanisms in accordance with their Roman legal counterparts is significant. On this and related matters, see Chapter 1.

[124] For additional parallels between the concepts, see Chapter 1.

[125] See Chapter 3.

[126] Also pertinent is my mention of the evidence from the Greco-Roman papyri from Egypt when relevant. I address this in the notes with reference mostly to Taubenschlag, *Law*. See also n. 196 and n. 200. In general on the topic, see Modrzejewski, "Jewish Law and Hellenistic Legal Practice."

[127] See, in particular, Chapter 5.

Less encouraging is the final category of evidence investigated – what seem to be laws and customs preserved in Second Temple writings. Here I address primarily the work of Philo[128] and the books of Judith and Tobit.[129] Methodological limitations abound because it is not always clear whether inheritance procedures presented in the texts are representative of some living law, entirely fictitious narratives without any kernel of historical accuracy,[130] or the creative interpretation of Scripture.[131]

As noted, the methodological problems relating to the historicity of each body of law used in this study abound. However, our main concern is not the historicity of the laws or their application in their own time. Whether as theoretical or as living law, minimally these collections provide useful points of comparison for legal conceptualization in the ancient world and maximally, the possible origins of some tannaitic laws. Furthermore, despite the methodological limitations, inheritance laws, even when theoretical, do, at times, relate to and reflect the presumed social and economic structures of the literatures in which they are contained and the societies in which they are produced. In the next section we turn to some aspects of the relationship between inheritance laws and the presumed social and economic structures of biblical Israel and tannaitic Palestine, that is, family structure and landholding patterns.[132]

On the Relationship of Inheritance Laws to Presumed Social and Economic Settings in the Bible and Tannaitic Literature

If we rely on the biblical accounts, the Israelite laws of inheritance reflect a social and economic context in which the extended family resides on jointly owned ancestral land with a family leader,[133] often the firstborn son, at its head. Indeed, according to some, the biblical laws of inheritance seem to be representative of the tightly knit clan structure and tribal origins[134] of historical Israelite soci-

[128] See Chapter 4.

[129] See Chapter 3.

[130] On Judith, see Nickelsburg, "Stories," 48. On Tobit, see Nickelsburg, "Stories," 40.

[131] On Philo, see my comments in Chapter 4.

[132] In this book I make reference to the social and economic settings not only of biblical Israel and tannaitic Palestine, but also of ancient Mesopotamia, the Greek city-states, and Rome. Although my book addresses comparisons between the social and economic contexts reflected in biblical vs. tannaitic literature, it is beyond the scope of this work to compare and contrast the degrees of urbanization or nucleation of families in all of the centers mentioned.

[133] On family ownership of land, see B. Levine, "Farewell to the Ancient Near East," 228.

[134] The Israelites "[a] seminomadic people at the time of their first settlement, they remained, through the period of the Judges, a tribal society" (Barkay, "The Iron Age II–III," 305–306). See also van der Toorn, *Family Religion*, 24; and Milgrom, *Numbers*, 482. See Roaf, *Cultural Atlas*, 68, where the author discusses the fact that the Uruk period in Palestine and Anatolia was largely unaffected by the urban developments in Mesopotamia.

ety.[135] Specific examples in the law of this representation include the passing of property only to a son (see Chapters 1 and 4) and the biblical law of endogamy for inheritance purposes, whereby a daughter (without brothers) preserves her father's estate by marrying within the family or tribe. There is no clear biblical evidence that women can own land (see Chapters 4 and 5). By marrying among her own, a daughter seemingly serves as a conduit for the passing of a father's assets to sons (and grandsons) (see Chapter 4). More examples of the reflection in biblical law of the presumed social and economic make up of biblical society include: the institution of land redemption whereby a kinsman redeems the land sold by a family member forced into poverty,[136] the aforementioned role of the firstborn as administrator of the ancestral estate (see Chapter 2), and levirate marriage.[137]

However, family structure and landholding patterns are not uniform throughout the ancient Near East, a matter illustrated when we turn to even one example (and the earliest), Sumer. Parts of the ancient Near East experience what the famed archeologist V. Gordon Childe calls the "urban revolution"[138] as early as the fourth millennium BCE,[139] and documentation from third-millennium BCE Mesopotamia[140] affirms the predominance of nuclear families.[141] Based on the archeological and literary evidence combined, Claus Wilcke comments that regarding the order of succession in Sumerian law, "[t]he witnessing members of an extended family attested in sales contracts are possible claimants of inheritance rights in the same way as inheritance may in our days be claimed by

---

135 See Milgrom, *Numbers*, 482.

136 See Lev. 25.

137 Levirate marriage is not treated in this book. The topic benefited recently from a monograph dedicated exclusively to it; see Weissberg, *Levirate Marriage.* On levirate marriage within the social context of ancient Israel specifically, see Weissberg, *Levirate Marriage*, 200.

138 See Childe's now classic "The Urban Revolution," 3–17. To be sure, Childe's use of the term he coined, "urban revolution," is far broader than the sense in which I am employing urbanization in this book. Childe includes a series of interconnected societal transformations such as the emergence of the powers of kings and government along with social stratification, the expansion of economic activities, and the building of cities characterized by writing and literacy. On Childe's concept and its continued influence on current scholarship, see Smith, "V. Gordon Childe and the Urban Revolution." I focus here on the building of cities and its effects on landholdings, family size, opportunities for the society's female members, its property ownership patterns, and inheritance practices. See also n. 8.

139 Roaf, *Cultural Atlas*, 58. For a geographic survey of the development of cities in different parts of Mesopotamia, see Stone, "Development of Cities," 235–248. For a broader geographic survey, see Roaf, *Cultural Atlas*, 58–73.

140 Wilcke, *Early Ancient Near Eastern Law*, 14.

141 Wilcke, *Early Ancient Near Eastern Law*, 67. Compare this to the biblical presentation where clans and larger family groups exercise the property rights described above. This may reflect the late arrival of urbanization in historical biblical Israel. Although the tenth century BCE marks the beginning of the drive toward the urbanization that continues throughout the Iron Age, biblical Israel is markedly urban only by the eighth century BCE (Barkay, "The Iron Age II–III," 305–306, 329).

relatives of different degrees of relationship."[142] That is, the order of succession at Sumer may not reflect the structure of the household at all. It may merely echo remnants of practices and perceptions from prehistoric times, before urbanization and the nucleation of families take hold (or may be representative of assumptions about earlier family ties that never existed historically).[143] Returning to the specific subject of inheritance by daughters, the condition expected in an urbanized context in which women could own property is actually present at Sumer.[144] Legislation declares that daughters can inherit (see Chapter 4). The possible reflection in biblical and Sumerian law of the presumed social and economic contexts in which the respective laws are formulated, therefore is, at times, perceivable (even if at other times not).

Tannaitic inheritance law also may reflect elements of the presumed framework of the society in which it is formulated, enabling not the discovery of a genetic link between ancient laws but rather a possible morphological analysis of inheritance practices promoted by the tannaim and those known from other urbanized societies in the ancient world with nuclear families and privatized landholdings[145] (such as Sumer, as in the paragraph above, and, of course, the great ancient cities of Athens[146] and Rome).[147] That is, perhaps the realization of specific inheritance laws should be expected in certain social and economic contexts.[148] Certainly the biblical inheritance practices that typify the specific social and economic structure of biblical society (as per biblical texts) are transformed or abandoned by the time of the tannaitic period. Endogamy for

---

[142] Wilcke, *Early Ancient Near Eastern Law*, 14.

[143] Cf. Milgrom, *Numbers*, 482.

[144] Wilcke, *Early Ancient Near Eastern Law*, 14.

[145] On the evolution of privatization in Sumer, in particular, see Hudson, "Dynamics of Privatization," 33–72.

[146] On the (almost) scholarly consensus regarding the *oikos* as representative of the nuclear family, see the discussion and bibliography in Cox, *Household Interests*, 131–134. While Cox argues that the real make up of *oikoi* is more complex (see her lengthy discussion on the diverse make up of *oikoi* and the use of their wealth; Cox, *Household Interests*, 134–208), she acknowledges that the classical literature represents the basic unit of the *oikos* and its elements as serving the needs of the nuclear family (Cox, *Household Interests*, 134). On the urbanization of ancient Greece, see the now standard work of Martin, *L'Urbanisme*.

[147] Roman jurists depict the household as made up of a nuclear family (Saller, *Patriarchy, Property and Death*, 82); see also Dixon, *Roman Family*, 11. That is not to say, however, that there is not significant diversity among households within Roman society. On aspects of the multifaceted nature of Roman households, see Dixon, *Roman Family*, 8–11; cf. Saller and Kertzer, "Historical and Anthropological Perspectives," 2; and Saller, *Patriarchy, Property and Death*, 82. On the pool of evidence as derived from the testimony of the urban elite, see Saller, *Patriarchy, Property and Death*, 4.

[148] On the possible correlation between the decline of the extended family and the diminished sociological link between families and their ancestral land, see Z. Safrai, "Family Structure," 133.

inheritance,[149] for instance, is not evidenced in tannaitic law at all,[150] and family land redemption along with the firstborn's family leadership role (see Chapter 2) and levirate marriage disappear as well.[151] What does emerge among the tannaim, therefore, are laws which – even in all of their variety – still reflect their time and place. The new laws not only drop archaic biblical institutions but also embrace new methods that the rabbis observe. Among those in the ancient Near East, Greece, and Rome, these arrangements grant citizens the freedom to design individual approaches to inheritance that meet personal patterns of fluctuating family bonds.[152] In tannaitic law the adoption and adaptation include options attested to throughout the ancient world for a daughter to share in her father's estate (see Chapter 4) and for a wife to partake of her husband's fortune (Chapter 5), multiple forms of gifting in contemplation of death (see Chapter 1 and the Appendix), the demotion of the firstborn son, and distinctions between ways of transferring wealth – even to strangers.[153] In the following section, I discuss the textual and archeological evidence, as well as the scholarly consensus, regarding the assumptions I enumerate above about the contrasting family structure and landholding patterns presumed in biblical and tannaitic literature.

On the Textual and Archeological Evidence for the Presumed Family Structure and Landholding Patterns in the Bible and Tannaitic Literature

A study of the tannaitic textual evidence points to a background in which the nuclear household is predominant as opposed to the extended family scholars presume in biblical literature.[154] If, in fact, the biblical literary accounts are representative of historical family situations, then the structure of the household changes dramatically from the biblical to the tannaitic period through a process likely protracted over the course of centuries.[155] The presumption in biblical

[149] See my discussion in Chapter 4.

[150] It exists, however, in Athens and elsewhere in ancient Greece. For a full discussion, see Chapter 4.

[151] Z. Safrai, "Family Structure," 132–133, 139.

[152] On Rome, see Saller, *Patriarchy, Property and Death*.

[153] See Z. Safrai, "Family Structure," 141–142, who, building on Büchler's *Studies*, 15–44, suggests that changes in the structure of the family must have contributed to the emergence in the first century of a practice whereby fathers transfer inheritance rights to someone other than their sons (see, in particular, Büchler, *Studies*, 19 and 34).

[154] For parts of the discussion below on matters pertaining to the nuclear family in the postbiblical period, I benefited from the summaries and bibliography in Fiensy, *Social History*, 120–121 and 126–130.

[155] Scholars debate if and when such a shift takes place. For a discussion about the shift taking place during the rise of the First Temple monarchy, see Bendor, *Social Structure*, 210–215; the Second Temple period, see Urbach, "Inheritance Laws and After-Life," 133–141; the Hellenis-

texts of an extended family, jointly owning property and with a firstborn, or his appointed substitute, as administrator at its head, is replaced by the representation in tannaitic literature of the nuclear family with private landholdings in an urban setting, without an appointed or inherited head of household with obligations to the extended family.[156]

In its literary representation, the biblical *bet av* (literally, house of the father), the extended family unit, includes parents, children, spouses of sons and their offspring, and possibly unmarried relatives and servants all living in close physical proximity (even if not in the same house)[157] as part of a jointly owned estate.[158] The firstborn (or his replacement; see below) functions as the family leader.[159] The structure of the household presumed in tannaitic texts is different.[160] The nuclear household – parents with unmarried children – owning private property[161] is predominant,[162] and the firstborn son seemingly has no official role within it.[163] Indeed, tannaitic traditions about housing arrangements imply nuclear families and private ownership of property. Mishnah *Eruvin* 6:7, for example, mentions brothers[164] who "ate at their father's table but slept in their own houses," referring to a father and sons who reside in adjoining houses with a common courtyard, "the most characteristic type of domestic architecture in Palestine."[165] Although according to the text the father and the sons live in the

tic and Roman periods, see Rubin, "For Whom Does One Mourn?" 111–122; Rubin, *End of Life*, 87–102; Fiensy, *Social History*, 121, 146, and 178. See also Halpern, "Jerusalem and the Lineages."

[156] On aspects of the transformation of the firstborn's role specifically, see Chapter 2.

[157] Van der Toorn, *Family Religion*, 190–205. See also the seminal study on the structure of the household in ancient Israel, Stager, "Archaeology of the Family," 18–23; and the discussion of Stager's findings in Schloen, *House of the Father*, 167–171. On the *bet av* as a biblical notion of kinship relations, see Bendor, *Social Structure*, 45–67.

[158] Westbrook, *Property and Family*, 118–141.

[159] Westbrook, *Property and Family*, 140.

[160] Some texts do speak of "brothers who are jointholders," *ha'aḥin hashutafin*. See, e.g., *mEruv* 6:7. Even in this text, however, there is no joint ownership of property per se. See the discussion of this *mishnah* below.

[161] Z. Safrai, *Baalut al hakarka*, 9.

[162] See Chapter 2. Some scholars, however, maintain that the extended family is predominant into the Hellenistic and Roman periods. See S. Safrai, "Home and Family," 732; Dar, "Agriculture and Agricultural Produce," 144; Dar, *Landscape and Pattern*, 84. See the critique of this view in Tropper, "Economics of Jewish Childhood," 200–203; and Tropper, "Children and Childhood," 336–339. See also Stager's carefully formulated observation about the possible persistence of the *bet av* type of housing compounds in the Roman period in Capernaum and references to such compounds in the writings of Philo and in the New Testament in "Archaeology of the Family," 22.

[163] See, Milgram, "Transformation," 20 n. 19. For a fuller discussion and possible exceptions, see Chapter 2.

[164] On the concept *ha'aḥin hashutafin*, "brothers who are jointholders," see n. 160.

[165] Guijarro, "The Family in First-Century Galilee," 52. On additional types of housing in ancient Palestine, see the summary in Guijarro, "The Family in First-Century Galilee," 49–55; and the extensive study in Hirschfeld, *Palestinian Dwelling*.

same courtyard complex, according to *mEruv* 6:7,[166] the residents perform an act that creates a shared domain, an *eruv ḥatserot*. The *eruv ḥatserot* is created by the residents jointly depositing foodstuffs. The *eruv* enables them to carry items on the Sabbath between the homes adjoined by the courtyard (otherwise prohibited on the Sabbath).[167] The author(s) of this *mishnah* view(s) each son's nuclear family unit as an individual household, independent of the father's, at least under certain circumstances.[168] Other tannaitic texts refer to partners and neighbors, not family members,[169] sharing a courtyard, demonstrating the degree to which – at least according to the textual evidence – courtyard housing is not representative of extended family housing or joint family ownership per se.[170] According to the textual testimony, even independent nuclear families reside together in such complexes.

Although the literary evidence implies changes in the situation from the extended family of the Bible to the nuclear family of tannaitic literature,[171] determining family relationships based on archeological remains[172] – and, therefore, anything more about the historical structure of the household and ownership of property relying on archeology – is, at best, challenging. Even so, scholars point to developments in the structure of the family and landholding patterns based on archeological evidence. For instance, archeological data relating to funerary practices provides, for some, evidence for the changing structure of the family.

---

[166] However, see *tEruv* 5:10.

[167] See *mEruv* chapters 6 and 7.

[168] On this source, see Lapin, "The Construction of Households," 58 and 65. See also the comments in H. Albeck, *Mishnah*: Mo'ed, 2:109; Goldberg, *Eruvin*, 181; Z. Safrai, "Family Structure," 150; Fiensy, *Social History*, 128.

[169] See the discussion in Fiensy, *Social History*, 129–130; see also the comments in Z. Safrai, "Family Structure," 133 n. 13.

[170] Contra Guijarro, "The Family in First-Century Galilee," 52 and 59; and Dar, *Landscape and Pattern*, 84. Guijarro does contend, however, that the "majority of the inhabitants of Galilee were members of nucleated families" (Guijarro, "The Family in First-Century Galilee," 60). For an objection to some of Guijarro's estimates on family size, see Meyers, "Roman-Period Houses," 497.

[171] Nisan Rubin even sees a shift within tannaitic literature itself. He argues that a move away from the extended family toward the nuclear is reflected in the tannaitic laws of mourning. The earliest layers of tannaitic literature state that mourning rites are observed for members of the extended family; the later layers of tannaitic literature shift mourning to only members of the immediate family ("For Whom Does One Mourn?" 111–122; *The End of Life*, 90–92). Following Rubin's model, Zeev Safrai contends that the shift to the nuclear household structure results in the generally enhanced role of the nuclear family in several areas of tannaitic law ("Family Structure," 129–130). See also the acceptance of Rubin's findings in Dar, *Landscape and Pattern*, 85; and Fiensy, *Social History*, 129. However, note the fundamental critique of Rubin's textual analysis in Schremer, *Male and Female*, 333–336 and, now, a response to Schremer in Sabato, "Elu hen hakerovin," 106–108.

[172] See, e. g., the statements by Meyers regarding the challenges faced by archeologists trying to determine the relationships among residents of courtyard housing based on archeological evidence; Meyers, "Roman-Period Houses," 492.

Archeologists note, for example, that First Temple rock-cut tombs likely serve large numbers of people – probably extended families. Tombs from the Second Temple period, however, seemingly house only the immediate family.[173]

For others, archeological evidence for changes in landholding and settlement patterns in rural parts of Israel also reflects a shift in the make up of household structure. Shimon Dar's study of settlement and landholding patterns in Samaria over the course of fourteen centuries,[174] together with Shimon Applebaum's interpretations of these findings, contribute significantly to the understanding of this development. Dar suggests that farmsteads dating to the Early Iron Age II–III (1000–586 BCE), similar to farmsteads found in both the Negev and Judea,[175] represent "a characteristic model of settlement by kinships (extended families)."[176] He observes that the farmhouses located on the grounds are large structures that likely house twenty to thirty people.[177] Furthermore, due to the lack of clearly marked boundaries for (what would have been) individual properties, Dar concludes that the data is representative of landholdings of members of the same *bet av*. Namely, according to Dar, at least in this period,[178] multiple farmsteads are viewed as related to one another by those who work and manage them.[179]

Dar also identifies field towers from the Hellenistic period that provide more defined divisions for the cultivated areas. According to Applebaum, the towers point to a shift in the structure of the household by the Hellenistic period. Applebaum writes that the social-agrarian importance of the evidence is that each tower represents a family unit and defines the precise area cultivated around a tower.[180] The multiple towers, argues Applebaum, can "only be interpreted as representing units of nuclear families rather than the single unit of the extended *beth av* (kinship group)."[181] Applebaum sees in the archeological evidence, therefore, a clear development from the extended family of early Iron Age II–III Israel to the nuclear family of the Hellenistic period in Palestine. If Applebaum's

---

[173] See the statements in Hachlili and Killebrew, "Jewish Funerary Customs," 126; Hachlili and Killebrew, *Jericho*, 172. For a similar statement, see Barkay, "Burial Caves," 106. See also the discussion and bibliography in Faust and Bunimovitz, "Judahite Rock-Cut Tomb," 150–170.

[174] Dar, *Landscape and Pattern*.

[175] See the discussion and bibliography for similar types of farms in the Negev and Judea in Dar, *Landscape and Pattern*, 8, 270–271, nn. 12–15; and the discussion in Fiensy, *Social History*, 120–121.

[176] Dar, *Landscape and Pattern*, 2.

[177] Dar, *Landscape and Pattern*, 7.

[178] For earlier Israelite settlement patterns, see the summary and bibliography in van der Toorn, *Family Religion*, 187–190. For a summary and discussion of earlier scholarship on the archeological evidence for extended family housing arrangements, see Faust, *Archaeology of Israelite Society*, 159–163; and Chapter 1.

[179] Dar, *Landscape and Pattern*, 7–8.

[180] Applebaum, "Historical Commentary," 258.

[181] Applebaum, "Historical Commentary," 258. Applebaum's view regarding the Hellenistic period towers is contrary to Dar's opinion that the more clearly demarcated areas were still inhabited by extended families; see Applebaum, "Historical Commentary," 262.

observations are correct, then the data also suggest a move toward the privatization of landholdings. For, as the evidence from the rural context intimates, by the Hellenistic period, land is likely no longer jointly owned by extended families but is, rather, in private hands.

These findings, representing the evolution of the family on its landholdings and related to the rural landscape, if accurate, are significant. The observation that tannaitic law reflects the nuclear family on private landholdings in urban centers does not depend, however, on the tannaitic historical situation replacing a different biblical circumstance that historically precedes it. That is, regardless of whether the structure of the family and its landholdings change over the course of time, the tannaim and their nuclear families live and function in cities. Indeed, by the advent of the tannaitic period – after the establishment of Tiberias and Sepphoris as Roman cities[182] and the characterization of settlement mainly in villages and the evidence of relatively few estates[183] – urban life and the nuclear family with private landholdings are part and parcel of the society the rabbis[184] know and experience.[185] The make up of society in which the highly urbanized tannaim[186] live is much closer, therefore, to that known from some ancient Mesopotamian urban centers, Athens, and Rome than to the society presumed in biblical literature. The inheritance laws formulated by the rabbis – crafted out of laws prevalent throughout the ancient world – seem to reflect these realities.

Tannaitic Society and Tannaitic Inheritance Law: Cause and Effect?

Laws are seldom formulated in a vacuum,[187] and the inheritance laws of the tannaim are no different. Tannaitic inheritance laws are created in specific social and economic contexts and, as argued above and throughout this work, these circumstances are generally reflected in the laws themselves. That is, the

[182] Leibner, *Settlement*, 332.

[183] Leibner, *Settlement*, 348 and 373. On some aspects of the ownership of several disconnected plots of land, see Satlow, *Marriage*, 199–209; Satlow, "Marriage Payments," 51–65.

[184] I emphasize here the rabbinic class, the creators and fashioners of tannaitic law, since it is their experience and its possible impact on the law they produce that is most important for my argument for legal development. The social and economic conditions outside of the cities and, therefore, the experience of non-rabbis, are of less importance to me. However, see the next note.

[185] Other factors, such as the decline of Palestine's agrarian economy under Roman rule, certainly would have contributed to changes in landholding patterns as well; see, Gil, "Decline of the Agrarian Economy," 285–328. See also on the proliferation of the peasant landowner in Roman Palestine of the first three centuries CE, Rosenfeld and Perlmutter, "Landowners," 327–352. On the status of Israel after the Bar-Kokhva revolt, see Gafni, "Ma'amadah," 224–232. See also Schwartz, "Political, Social and Economic Life," 38–43.

[186] See L. Levine, *Rabbinic Class*, 23–33; Schwartz, *Imperialism*, 129–176 and, more recently, the comments specifically regarding the tannaim in Lapin, *Rabbis as Romans*, 78–79 and 88.

[187] However, for Watson's problematization of the presumed relationship of law to society, see "Legal Transplants to Legal Formants," 469–476; and *Society and Legal Change*, 98–114.

inheritance laws of the tannaim are often appropriate to a context in which the nuclear family is predominant, landholdings are privatized, and (rabbinic) society urbanized; in short, the conditions that historians assume obtain in Roman Palestine in rabbinic circles.

The appropriateness of laws to the social and economic contexts in which they are formulated leads to the obvious question of causation. Do, in fact, the social and economic conditions in Roman Palestine cause the rabbis to adopt, adapt, and formulate laws in accordance with what they observe and experience? One could posit the existence of a rabbinic class that creates a complex of laws – even theoretical laws – that still corresponds to the social and economic experience of their formulators.[188] Indeed, due to the general lack of evidence for the interpretive origins of many tannaitic[189] traditions on inheritance and the significant terminological, formulaic, and conceptual parallels with other bodies of ancient law, as already mentioned, it cannot be argued successfully that the laws are the result of rabbinic hermeneutics and its tendency toward creative scriptural exegesis. Rather, one could argue that the rabbis are motivated by their social and economic contexts to adopt and adapt existing inheritance practices, terminology, and formulae known throughout the region in order to construct laws appropriate to those contexts.[190] The result is the creation of inheritance

[188] As Adiel Schremer, among others, correctly points out, the question of whether the rabbis frame and formulate their laws in accordance with their lived reality does not necessarily relate to the question of whether the rabbis rule for masses of followers (see *Male and Female*, 24 and the earlier literature cited there in nn. 39–40).

[189] The amoraim, however, differ and attempt to attribute inheritance institutions to biblical sources. See, e.g., *bBB* 147a where two amoraim endeavor to find the source of the death-bed bequest in 2 Sam. 17:23, the story of Aḥitophel setting his house in order; on this, see the comments in Yaron, *Gifts*, 8. See also the comments by Urbach, "Inheritance Laws and After-Life," 137 n. 46.

[190] Here I suggest an adaptation of the method of Haym Soloveitchik who repeatedly demonstrates the degree to which social and economic factors affect the course of medieval halakhic rulings. For Soloveitchik, the assumption is that if not for social and economic influences, certain rulings of medieval rabbinic decisors (=*rishonim*) would represent compelling readings of the Talmudic sources and reflect normative principles for deciding between the rulings of previous generations (cf. the description in Woolf, "Methodological Reflections"). Therefore, Soloveitchik seeks "the crucial angle of deflection that is necessary for any demonstration that extraneous factors were impinging on the course of immanent developments" ("Can Halakhic Texts Talk History?," 176; compare his more recent statement in "Halakhah, Hermeneutics and Martyrdom," 77–80). While the medieval example is starkly different from the ancient – in the former, the rabbis legislate for confirmable communities – the method is, nonetheless, valuable for my purposes. It provides a model that may account for the origins of innovation when the verifiably expected tendency (in the tannaitic case dependence on scriptural interpretation) is seemingly absent. Accordingly, in this study, I mention that, due to the lack of laws based on rabbinic readings of Scripture – and, for that matter, biblical verses to draw from – rabbinic innovation might be seen as the outcome of the adoption and adaption of legal principles and formulae present in other ancient legal traditions in order to make the laws appropriate to the social and economic conditions in tannaitic Palestine (however, see my comments above in the body of the chapter). As mentioned earlier, for this study I draw from tannaitic midrash, Mish-

laws that are quite independent from the biblical complex of laws – or even the biblical text – and often much more related to the laws of the neighbors of the tannaim or biblical Israel's predecessors and contemporaries than to the laws of the biblical forefathers. By ensuring that their inheritance laws correspond to the social and economic contexts of Roman Palestine, perhaps the rabbis prepare laws that would be appropriate in the event they are to legislate. Or, put differently, it may be that the construction of these inheritance laws is an expression of the rabbis' desire to legislate a livable law for their time or for a time when their laws would be accepted.

The question of cause and effect, however, is infinitely more complex than we can determine based on our current knowledge of the rabbinic movement and its goals, the social and economic contexts of tannaitic Palestine, as well as the relationship of the rabbinic texts in our possession – all medieval or later copies – to the actual oral texts redacted in the early centuries of the Common Era.[191] Throughout this book, therefore, I prefer to point to the correspondence, when applicable, of rabbinic laws to the presumed social and economic contexts of Roman Palestine (in accordance with the current state of the field), suggesting at times the possibility of causation while at the same time attempting to avoid concluding definitively that the social and economic contexts result in specific laws.

The Present Study

With the aim of tracing the origins of tannaitic inheritance laws, I engage in a multidisciplinary exercise of combining the results of philological-historical analysis of tannaitic texts, social and economic history of tannaitic Palestine, and comparative ancient law. I argue that only the engagement of all three disciplines ultimately yields the most accurate results about the development of tannaitic law as an ancient legal collection within the social and economic contexts of Roman Palestine. Indeed, in this study I contend that, as previously mentioned, in the absence of rabbinic interpretation locating the origins of inheritance laws in Scripture, the contributions of the tannaim cannot be considered the product

---

nah, Tosefta, and *baraitot* preserved in the Palestinian and Babylonian Talmuds; and whereas it is correct not to expect the Mishnah and the Tosefta to cite significant amounts of scriptural interpretation, it is abundantly clear that these works usually depend heavily on Scripture. As Neusner points out regarding the Mishnah (and, as is also applicable to the Tosefta): "The superficial relationship of the Mishnah to Scripture is ambiguous only because the Mishnah never links its legal statements to Scripture or claims that it rules in accord with Scripture... . So, on first glance the Mishnah, whatever it claims to be or to do, in no way links itself to Scripture. But, of course, hardly a second glance is needed to reveal the opposite, which is that the Mishnah depends in a deep way, for both thematic agendum and the facts of its topics and rules, upon Scripture" (*Judaism: The Evidence of the Mishnah*, 171–172).

[191] Compare Sussmann, "Torah shebe'al peh," 212.

of the creative and imaginative enterprise of rabbinic scriptural exegesis. Rather the innovations are the result of the appropriation and adaptation of inheritance practices known throughout the ancient world. Moreover, the traditions traced in this work – in all of their variety – reflect the social and economic contexts of Roman Palestine, a locale where the nuclear family was predominant and private landholdings in an urbanized setting were the norm the rabbis experienced.

Based on the evidence, in the following pages I show that some of the developments in tannaitic inheritance law simply represent the expected result of laws formulated in the legal landscape in which the rabbis function. That is, some tannaitic traditions are widely paralleled in the ancient world and cannot be attributed to traceable rabbinic adoption from any specific body of legal material. Their origins are to be found, as Saul Lieberman was wont to comment in other contexts, in "hoary antiquity,"[192] attesting to some tannaitic laws as the product of their ancient legal context. In Chapter 1, for example, I point to the conceptual-legal distinction between gifting and inheriting in tannaitic sources and present in multiple legal traditions in the ancient world although seemingly absent from the Bible.[193] It is clear that the legal-conceptual distinction is prevalent in a significant cross section of independent, ancient legal traditions such as from Nuzi, Athens, and Rome. Therefore, its presence in tannaitic law cannot be attributed to direct borrowing from one tradition. I do argue, though, that the tannaim likely take from Roman law its terminology for this distinction and perhaps even the idea for a bilateral procedure for gifting. The Hebrew terms for gifting and inheriting, *mattanah* and *yerushah*, respectively, appear to be literal translations of the parallel Roman legal terms *donatio* and *hereditas*. That is not to say, however, that there is a historical etymological link between the Latin and Hebrew terms. The words *mattanah* and *yerushah* each existed in the classical Hebrew lexicon prior to the rabbis coming into contact with Roman inheritance terminology. Therefore, the Hebrew terms do not come into existence due to said contact. I do suggest, however, that the choice to apply the terms *mattanah* and *yerushah* to inheritance procedures comes about due to the presence of the parallel Latin terms in Roman legal discourse. Furthermore, procedurally, gifting is bilateral – requiring an act of acquisition on the part of, or on behalf of, the donee – only in tannaitic and Roman law (among the ancient legal traditions explored here), suggesting that an element of the implementation of gifting may originate in Roman practice, even if actual Roman acts of acquisition are not adopted by the tannaim.[194] Furthermore, in Chapter 1 I note that the distinctions between gifting and inheriting adopted by the tannaim are appropriate to the

[192] See, e.g., "The methods applied in the understanding of dreams were invented neither by the Jews nor by the Greeks. They go back to hoary antiquity" (Lieberman, *Hellenism*, 75).

[193] For short definitions and the differences, see "Abbreviations, Terminology, and Transliteration" and Chapter 1.

[194] See Chapter 1.

social and economic contexts in which the rabbis find themselves, namely, where approaches to enable the partibility of the estate are fitting.

In Chapter 2, I consider the matter of the firstborn son's double inheritance portion and the flexibility of its allocation found in *mBB* 8:5. Certainly the flexibility is the outcome of the adoption of gifting as a method for transferring property. In light of the complex legal as well as social and economic contexts in which this tannaitic source is likely produced, I suggest the possibility that the flexibility also may come about due to the convergence of three additional factors: the presence of the local practice of flexibility known from biblical and ancient Near Eastern sources, the lack of a role for the firstborn within the nuclear household experienced by the tannaim, and the absence of extra inheritance for the firstborn in Greek and Roman sources.

In Chapter 3, I discuss the form of testate succession that is championed in tannaitic law and attributed to the tanna Rabbi Yoḥanan ben Beroka, that is, testate succession among agnates (anyone in the male line of descendants). Rabbi Yoḥanan ben Beroka's model of testate succession – universal, unilateral, and automatic – is closest in form and function to the Roman testament to the *sui heredes* (those legally considered members of a Roman *familia*). I argue that although in the absence of terminological overlap the degree of dependence of one tradition on the other cannot be shown, Rabbi Yoḥanan ben Beroka's proposal is certainly appropriately formulated and conceptualized for the context of Roman Palestine in which it is conceived.

Chapter 4 deals with inheritance by a daughter. There I emphasize the possible relationship between the social and economic contexts and inheritance by a daughter in tannaitic law and elsewhere in the ancient world. Although the existence in the region for millennia of practices enabling daughters to partake of the patrimony, in all likelihood, duly contribute to the adoption of laws by the tannaim, there seems to be a correlation between the presence of nuclear families in urbanized settings and the proliferation of opportunities for a daughter to acquire a piece of the paternal estate. This is most notable in parts of the ancient Near East and in Rome. This correspondence may exist in tannaitic law as well. Indeed, the presence of dowry, maintenance, and a newly uncovered tradition promoting direct inheritance by daughters (even in the presence of sons!) in tannaitic law is appropriate for the social and economic contexts in which the rabbis live. The adoption and adaption of these practices, therefore, may be the result of some unrecoverable interplay between the production of tannaitic law and its relationship to the social and economic contexts of tannaitic Palestine.

In Chapter 5, I address inheritance by a wife. Although wives are not included in the biblical or rabbinic orders of (intestate) succession, tannaitic law contains several provisions for a widow, including the option for support from the deceased husband's estate. Here significant parallels with evidence from Judean desert documents exist, attesting to the degree to which the rabbis may draw from the living law they observe. The tannaim actually expand the law of the Judean desert documents by granting a wife the automatic right to reside in her late husband's residence, a convention paralleled only in some ancient Near Eastern laws.[195] The tannaitic approach is certainly indicative of the rabbis' wish to adequately provide for their wives – even after death – a priority appropriate to the social and economic contexts the rabbis likely experience, in which, according to some scholars, wives seemingly gain prominence within the family unit. This situation may provide the proper conditions for the adoption and expansion of existing traditions. In the Appendix, I explore the different forms of gifting available in tannaitic law and discuss their characteristics and formulae in light of ancient parallels, demonstrating the overlap and antiquity of some gifting strategies and technical formulae. In light of all of my findings, in the "Conclusions" I entertain the question, 'How Jewish is Jewish inheritance law?'

Each chapter is organized in the same way. I begin with an introduction to the topic of the chapter followed by a detailed examination of the tannaitic sources (often accompanied by a philological-historical analysis). Then, I address the biblical legal heritage and lead into discussions of the possible ancient Near Eastern, Second Temple, Elephantine, Judean desert, Greek, and Roman parallels and antecedents,[196] all in light of the social and economic conditions prevalent in tannaitic Palestine.

For the biblical evidence I gather data from both biblical law and narrative. The bulk of the evidence from ancient Near Eastern sources is drawn from legal codes, transactional records (including but not limited to marriage and testamentary documents), contracts, and reports of adoption. In comparing ancient Near Eastern materials to tannaitic law, I do not distinguish between those sources that may be the codification or representation of actual practice and the law that may be solely the product of scribal schools and their manifestations of intellectual processes.[197] I treat all of these laws equally as traditions in the region for millennia, which may be part of the legal landscape from which tannaitic inheritance law draws. I mine the ancient Near Eastern collections and archives and begin with the evidence from the earliest known civilizations in the third millennium BCE

---

[195] To be sure, arguments in favor of real rabbinic influence and against it dominate the discourse in the legal studies of much of the evidence found in the papyri from the Judean desert. For a summary and bibliography, see, most recently, Katzoff, "Rabbinic Law on Widows," 545–547. Significantly, in his erudite and informative analysis of two other documents from Babatha's archive, P. Yadin 21 and P. Yadin 22, Katzoff convincingly argues that the nuanced conditions in Babatha's sale documents of parts of her husband's estate are better understood once they are considered in light of rabbinic texts (see 547–568). This, in its own right, however, does not prove that what later becomes codified as rabbinic legislation, in any global sense, independently impacts on the law practiced in the Judean desert. For more on this, see Chapter 5.

[196] When applicable, I also cite in the notes the law in the Greco-Roman papyri of Egypt (=Taubenschlag, *Law*). See also n. 126 and n. 200.

[197] See above in the body of the text; and Roth, *Law Collections*, 4.

in ancient Mesopotamia such as Sumer and, where appropriate, include source materials from Anatolia and the Levant such as Nuzi, Ugarit, and Emar.

Previous studies of inheritance law already emphasize the Greek, Greco-Egyptian, and Hellenistic conceptual and terminological overlap with tannaitic law and procedure, a matter I consider in the Preface. In keeping with the current trend in the study of ancient Greek law not to prioritize Athenian law as the primary representative of legal traditions from ancient Greece,[198] in this study I include data from both Sparta (5th–4th centuries BCE) and Gortyn (450 BCE), in addition to Athens (5th–3rd centuries BCE). I do not argue that the rabbis know of Spartan and Gortynian legal traditions per se. However, their inclusion in my study provides a more thorough presentation of Greek inheritance traditions and in certain instances, as in Chapter 1 regarding gifting in contemplation of death, the inclusion of these traditions enriches the discussion.

So, too, I build on the significant comparative studies on tannaitic inheritance law and the law of the Elephantine and Judean desert papyri. I also review the evidence for inheritance traditions in Second Temple Jewish sources. I pay added attention to the work of Philo and the books of Tobit and Judith.

As for Roman law, I draw only from Roman legal conceptualization and terminology that could precede or be contemporaneous to the tannaitic movement.[199] I focus on sources representative of the laws of the Republic (5th century BCE) through approximately the second third of the Principate (early 3rd century CE).[200] That is, I cite laws preserved primarily in The Twelve Tablets (ca. 450 BCE),[201] the famed Roman law textbook *The Institutes of Gaius* (ca. 160 CE),[202] and at times I cite the opinions of the classical jurists, for example, Ulpian (died ca. 223 CE), preserved in the (much later) works of Justinian, such as in his *Digest* (ca. 533 CE).[203] The significance of citing The Twelve Tablets, the earliest code of Roman law and the foundation of the *ius civile* (civil law),[204] is abundantly clear: much of the later legislation finds its beginnings here. The rules and regulations summarized by Gaius are of great significance because as one scholar writes, this work is "the only evidence for the classical law which we can with reasonable certainty believe to be free from alteration by postclassical

198 See D. Cohen, "Introduction," 4. See also D. Cohen, "Problems."

199 Of course, I do address the relevant sources for the contemporary practice in the Roman province of Judea when I deal with the Judean desert documents (see above).

200 See n. 126 and n. 196.

201 Citations in the book are from M.H. Crawford and J. Cloud, eds., *Roman Statutes*.

202 Texts throughout are taken from W.M. Gordon and O.F. Robinson, *Institutes of Gaius*.

203 Texts throughout are cited from Alan Watson, ed., *Digest of Justinian*.

204 The *ius civile* is based on *lex*, that is, laws and/or statutes based on traditional common law and *interpretatio*, the authoritative interpretation of the *ius civile* by the classical jurists. *Ius civile* should be contrasted with *ius honorarium*, magisterial law, which is a supplement and, at times, a qualification of the civil law instituted by the magistrates in their efforts to apply the law. On all this, see Nicholas, *Introduction to Roman Law*, 14, 19, 26 n. 1, 59; du Plessis, *Borkowski's Textbook*, 33, 35–38.

editors or by Justinian's compilers."[205] This work is verifiably representative of Roman law that overlaps historically with the tannaitic period. And, finally, the opinions of select jurists are included since it is likely that jurists assisted judges and magistrates in the preparation and issuance of edicts,[206] as well as Roman citizens in the preparation of legal documents such as wills.[207]

In short, in this book I set out to demonstrate the degree to which tannaitic inheritance laws are likely the product of their ancient legal, social, and economic contexts.

---

205 Nicholas, *Introduction to Roman Law*, 35. This is because of the presumed authentic transmission history of the work; see Nicholas, *Introduction to Roman Law*, 35.

206 On magisterial law, see n. 204.

207 See du Plessis, *Borkowski's Textbook*, 37.

Chapter 1

Gifting and Inheriting in Tannaitic Law and in the Ancient World

Introduction

The fundamental features of tannaitic inheritance law include its partibility (the division of an estate after the demise of the head of household), its multiple methods for disposing of assets, and its capacity for transferring property, even to non-family members. In this chapter I argue that these three components do not find their source in biblical inheritance law (which prefers an undivided and jointly held family estate led by the firstborn) or in rabbinic interpretation of Scripture. Rather, we find their origin in the adoption, and adaptation, of well-known ancient legal traditions, with a particular affinity for Roman legal vocabulary and conceptualization. Indeed, I suggest that the tannaim likely borrow from Roman law its terminological distinction between gifting and inheriting and, perhaps, the requirement that gifting be accompanied by an act of acquisition by, or on behalf of, the donee. Furthermore, the assumptions of tannaitic law also seemingly reflect the social and economic conditions known and experienced by the tannaim: a situation in which the nuclear family, in an urbanized setting with privatized landholding patterns, is predominant.

Tannaitic inheritance law assumes a fundamental distinction between two mechanisms for the transfer of property: gifting in contemplation of death (hereafter, gifting)[1] and inheriting in accordance with the order of intestate succession (hereafter, inheriting).[2] The differences between inheriting and gifting are, in fact, significant.[3] Gifting transfers a *mattanah*, or gift, from donor to donee; inheriting

[1] Throughout I subscribe to the definition of gifts in contemplation of death as those gifts that are finally irrevocable only upon the donor's death (cf. the definition in Yaron, *Gifts*, 1). These include the *diathēkē* and two additional forms of gifting, which came to be known in amoraic literature as the *mattenat bari* and the *mattenat shakhev mera*. For short descriptions, see below in the body of the chapter; for a full discussion of each gift, see the Appendix.

[2] Below I also address a corollary of inheriting (in accordance with the laws of intestate succession): the application of some of the properties of inheriting even to cases where there is a discretionary act on the part of the property owner on behalf of a son or sons. I call this testate succession among sons. On testate succession among agnates, see Chapter 3. See also "Abbreviations, Terminology, and Transliteration."

[3] Compare the following list to those in Gulak, *Yesodei Hamishpat Haivri*, 3:75–79; and Rivlin, *Inheritance and Wills*, 18–21.

devolves a *yerushah*, or inheritance, from decedent to heir. Gifting is voluntary and its allocations unbounded;[4] inheriting is automatic and its portions predetermined. Gifting is subject to consent; inheriting is not subject to refusal. Gifting is bilateral, requiring a *ma'ase kinyan*, act of acquisition, by or on behalf of the donee; inheriting is unilateral and requires no act. Gifting takes effect, at least in part, during the lifetime of the decedent;[5] inheriting does not. Gifting can result in bestowing possessions on non-family members; inheriting only entails family members. Gifting, in theory, forestalls future claims by heirs since the property is excluded from the eventual division of the estate; inheriting, if not strictly adhered to, allows for disputes, since the entire property is considered in the division. Finally, gifting transfers only a specific right or good currently in the possession of the donor (*muḥzakim*). Inheriting is accompanied by the adoption of the legal personality of the decedent by the heir, that is, the heir "stands in the place"[6] of the decedent and accordingly inherits even the contingent assets

---

[4] Gifting allocations pose, in theory, a potential problem for heirs who, due to gifting to non-heirs, do not receive inheritance. One tannaitic source, while not forbidding such an approach, still presents it negatively; see *mBB* 8:5 (par. VII; cited below in the body of the chapter). Another source seems to forbid gifting all of one's property and leaving the sons without any inheritance (see my discussion of *mPe'ah* 3:7 and *mBB* 9:6 in the Appendix). In Roman law the concern about leaving heirs with nothing led to important legislation. The *lex Falcidia* (40 BCE) restricts gifts from an inheritance to three-quarters of the net estate (since heirs receive only what remains after the debts are paid and gifts distributed); see D.35.2.1; Stein, "Lex Falcidia," 454–457.

[5] This refers to the *mattenat bari* (see below in the body of the chapter and in the Appendix).

[6] Evidence for heirs standing in the place of the deceased is found in (what seems to be) an early collection of anonymous *halakhot* in the ninth chapter of Tosefta *Baba Batra* (the collection opens with "R. Natan says Naḥum Hamadi was among the *dayyanei gezerot*"). Tosefta *BB* 9:8 states that if creditors come to collect from both donees and heirs, collection from the heirs precedes collection from donees. Based on the interpretation of medieval commentators, Lieberman (*Tosefta: Neziqin*, 161 n. 28) comments that legally "the heir stands in the place of the testator." Cf. the comments in Bird, "YRŠ," 416, regarding the fact that the basic idea of the root *y-r-sh* in biblical Hebrew and its cognate languages is "to take the place of another." The idea that sons take the place of fathers also appears in tannaitic sources relating to the transfer of authority, such as kingship and the priesthood, from generation to generation. On kingship, see *Sifre to Deuteronomy*, par. 162 (212–213, Finkelstein ed.): *she'im met, beno omed taḥtav*, "that if he dies, his son stands in his place," i. e., reigns in his stead (on the idea and its expression with the root *y-r-sh* in biblical Hebrew, see Bird, "YRŠ," 239). On the priesthood, see *Sifra, Aḥarei Mot, Perek 8* (83a, Weiss ed.). Tosefta *Shek* 2:15 actually establishes a link between the transfer of leadership and the order of succession: "whoever takes precedence in inheritance takes precedence in positions of authority." See my comments on this source in Chapter 2 n. 11. Gulak, *Yesodei Hamishpat Haivri*, 3:80, however, argues that in Jewish law there is no merger of the legal personalities (since it is forbidden to appoint an heir). Based on my analysis above, I respectfully disagree with Gulak; see also Chapter 3. On Gulak's view, see also Edrei, "Halakhic Responsibility," 822. In his investigation of tannaitic texts on the obligation of heirs to fulfill the religious duties of their deceased father, Edrei concludes, "[t]he fact that it is the inheritors who are bound to the obligations of the deceased in this world, moves the Halakhic concept of inheritance as it emerges from the cases discussed, towards Roman law" ("Halakhic Responsibility," 854). These remarks concur with my basic impression regarding inheritance

(*re'uyim*), those assets not yet in the possession of the decedent at the time of death but to which the deceased had a right.[7]

Even just a glance at the differences makes it abundantly clear, regarding a related ancient legal context, why one scholar labels gifting in Roman law a "strategy of succession."[8] Gifting in Roman law reflects both the need for mechanisms that enable people to make decisions about the future of their estates and the desire for institutions that deal with the complexities of social relationships, which prove the rigid pre-allocation of intestate inheritance portions impractical. As I demonstrate, the distinction between gifting and inheriting is fundamental to several ancient legal traditions in addition to the Roman and the tannaitic. The distinction is not biblical,[9] however, and, significantly for the study of early rabbinic law, it is not the outcome of tannaitic interpretation of Scripture either. That is to say, while the tannaim locate general parameters for inheriting in what they see as biblical precedent, they make no similar attempt to find the source for gifting in the biblical past. The origins of gifting, and therefore the distinctions between gifting and inheriting, are extra-biblical; the source for the legal-conceptual and terminological opposition between the two mechanisms originates, therefore, not in hermeneutics but rather in history; not in commentary but rather in context.

In the analysis below I survey the evidence for the conceptual-legal and terminological distinction between gifting and inheriting in multiple ancient legal traditions. Certainly, elements of the distinction between the two mechanisms found in tannaitic law also exist in ancient societies as far flung as Nuzi, Athens, and Rome. Despite the parallels, however, the legal-conceptual distinction between gifting and inheriting likely has its own meaning and implications in each legal tradition due to the differences in presumed family structure and landholding patterns unique to each body of laws. Where the extended family would have jointly owned and resided on the rural ancestral plot, gifting is limited only to family members (or those adopted) and attests to the value placed on family posterity through the preservation of ancestral property in family hands.[10] Where

---

(not a religious obligation) as well (explained above). However, regarding Edrei's approach to heirs inheriting the financial liabilities of the decedent, see n. 44; and also n. 115.

[7] See *Sifre to Deuteronomy*, par. 216 (249, Finkelstein ed.); these include interest, outstanding debts, and improvement of the property between the time of death and the division. The first-born, however, only receives two portions of the *muḥzakim*; see *Sifre to Deuteronomy*, par. 217 (250, Finkelstein ed.), *mBekh* 8:9, and *tBB* 7:4. See also Gulak, *Yesodei Hamishpat Haivri*, 3:84.

[8] Saller, *Patriarchy, Property and Death*, 179.

[9] See below, "Gifting and Inheriting in the Bible."

[10] Although the Bible does not explicitly preserve the legal distinction between gifting and inheriting, it does deal in detail, for example, with the redemption of land by family members for a relative who has sold his ancestral plot; see Lev. 25:25–55 (see also the relevant verses in Ezek. 46:16–17). The rights of family to ancestral land were protected according to biblical law so that even land that is sold or gifted is not permanently alienated from the family. See below n. 87 and n. 90. For a discussion of the issues, see Westbrook, *Property and Family*, 58–68.

the nuclear family resides on privately owned land in an urbanized setting and a link to the family plot no longer exists, and gifting even to strangers (without adoption)[11] is possible, gifting – whether due to specific family or other personal circumstances – is likely primarily about benefiting another.

According to both models, the rigidity of intestate succession is avoided by gifting; but within each model, the potential empowerment gifting offers is different and determined by the assumptions about the social and economic contexts. Below I suggest that in tannaitic Palestine, where the nuclear family prevails and lives in an urbanized setting in which private landholdings are the norm, the rabbis may fashion their inheritance laws – whether operative or not[12] – into a framework that reflects the reality they live and experience. Theirs is a condition in which mechanisms for the division of estates was known for centuries; and the socioeconomic circumstances are much closer to those their Greek and Roman contemporaries experience than do their biblical forebears. So it is that, in Athens, holding joint property after the death of the *kyrios* (head of household) is the exception;[13] and when he dies, the original *oikos* (household) is divided and each son holds his own *oikos*, becoming its *kyrios*.[14] J. A. Crook succinctly states, regarding the situation in ancient Rome, "partibility itself does not square well with the 'patriarchal joint family.'"[15] Furthermore, as mentioned, although elements of the distinction between gifting and inheriting are evidenced far beyond the borders of tannaitic Palestine in the great societies of the ancient Near East and Mediterranean, a special affinity seems to exist between the structure and terminology of tannaitic and Roman inheritance law. For example, *mattanah* and *yerushah* appear to be literal translations of the parallel Roman legal terms *donatio* and *hereditas*, respectively, indicating the influence of Roman legal terminology. Although this does not mean that the Hebrew terms *mattanah* and *yerushah* etymologically originate from the Latin – certainly both *mattanah* and *yerushah* exist in the classical Hebrew lexicon before the tannaim come into contact with Roman inheritance terminology – the choice to employ the terms *mattanah* and *yerushah* for inheritance procedures in all likelihood comes about due to the presence of the Roman legal terms *donatio* and *hereditas*. Moreover, both in Roman and tannaitic law gifting is bilateral – requiring an act of acquisition – whereas inheriting is unilateral. It may be, therefore, that the impact of both the terminology of Roman law and its implementation is discernible in tannaitic law. However, as I demonstrate below,

---

[11] On adoption, see Chapter 3.

[12] See the Introduction.

[13] MacDowell, *Law in Classical Athens*, 92. On the Law Code of Gortyn's specific provision for division of the estate, however, see Westbrook, *Property and Family*, 139.

[14] MacDowell, "*Oikos*," 11. On this model as the ideal in legal literature on Athens, see Cox, *Household Interests*, 142.

[15] Crook, "Women in Roman Succession," 60. See also Dixon, *Roman Family*, 4.

due to the evidence for the existence of the conceptual distinction between gifting and inheriting in many parts of the ancient world, it cannot be maintained that the rabbis only know and adopt the distinction between the mechanisms from the Romans. The tannaim likely borrow and apply Roman legal terms to the well-known categories and perhaps also to gifting its bilateralness. Even if the rabbis do the latter, however, they do not also adopt Roman methods of acquisition. Tannaitic law already knows of methods of acquisition for the sale of property such as *shetar* (deed) and *ḥazakah* (acquisition by use)[16] and, accordingly, the rabbis draw from these when seeking methods of acquisition befitting gifting. The evidence follows.

Gifting and Inheriting in Tannaitic Law

As previously mentioned, central to tannaitic inheritance law is its assumption of partibility, the distinction between gifting and inheriting, and the possibility of including non-family members in the disposition of property (even to the point of disinheriting immediate heirs).[17] Mishnah *BB* 8:5 addresses all of these issues and serves as the springboard for further discussions in this chapter. The analysis that follows highlights the degree to which tannaitic law embraces the principles that distinguish its inheritance laws from biblical inheritance laws.

In assuming the partibility of the estate, *mBB* 8:5 frames the question of the freedom to allocate assets among sons around the legal-conceptual and terminological opposition between gifting and inheriting. According to the first tannaitic understanding below, the division of inheritance pursuant to the laws of intestacy is explicitly addressed in the Bible – presumably Deuteronomy[18] – the injunction there forbidding the alteration of the inheritance portions to sons: the firstborn receives two portions, and the other sons acquire one portion each. Attempts to adjust the inheritance allocations, at least when employing terminology connoting inheriting (phraseology seemingly reserved for divinely mandated intestate succession), are forbidden. Indeed, *mBB* 8:5 invokes biblical legislation as its source:

---

[16] Cf. Herzog, *Main Institutions*, 2:6. To my mind the best summary on acts of acquisition in Jewish law remains Abramson, "Acquisition," 216–221.

[17] On the possibility of disinheritance by an *inter vivos* gift of dismission, see, regarding Yaron's position, *Gifts*, 29; Bernard Jackson sees evidence for this practice in the New Testament; see Jackson, "Prodigal Son," 111–150; and Milgram, "Review of Jackson," 432–433. See n. 29.

[18] The exact citation goes unstated.

I.	האומר 'איש פלוני בני בכור לא יטול פי שנים', 'איש פלוני בני לא יירש עם אחיו', לא אמר כלום שהיתנה על הכתוב שבתורה.[19]	A man who says (*ha'omer*), "Such-a-one, my firstborn son, shall not receive a double portion" or "Such-a-one, my son, shall not inherit with his brethren," has said nothing, for he has laid down a condition contrary to what is written in the Torah.

The *mishnah* states that the firstborn son (apparently as per Deuteronomic law)[20] receives a double portion of inheritance and implies that each other son receives a single share.

According to this tannaitic opinion, attempts to change the presumed preset biblical division among sons – giving the firstborn a single inheritance portion, increasing or decreasing the inheritance shares of other sons, or expressly disinheriting a son – employing the terminology of inheriting are forbidden. They contradict the tannaitic understanding of Torah law. Inheriting is a mechanism presumed only applicable to intestate succession. That is, the attempt to engage in a discretionary act to give property to a son or sons employing terminology for inheriting – testate succession among sons[21] – is forbidden. Indeed, while assuming the partibility of the estate, this section of *mBB* 8:5 only provides for the division of the estate in accordance with a specific understanding of the biblical laws of intestate succession.

As the continuation of the *mishnah* teaches, however, the limitation listed could be circumvented through gifting, a more flexible framework for the allocation of assets. In fact, three different forms of gifting in contemplation of death are known to tannaitic law, perhaps themselves proof that the tannaim promote partibility. In the following paragraph I provide short descriptions of each form. For details of the three forms and their ancient legal parallels, see the Appendix.

The first form, the *diathēkē*, is a tannaitic adaptation of the Greek disposition in case of death. Two additional forms of gifting exist in tannaitic law and here,

[19] The seemingly unusual phrase *hakatuv shebatorah*, perhaps better translated as "the written (=verse) in the Torah," here is as per MS Kaufmann (so, too, MS Lowe); this formulation also occurs in MS Kaufmann in *mBik* 1:3. In MS Parma and MS Leiden, as in the Mishnah in the manuscripts of the Bavli (MS Paris [Bibliothèque nationale Suppl. Heb. 1337], MS Vatican 115, MS Hamburg 165, and MS Munich 95) and printed editions, our *mishnah* reads, *mah shekatuv batorah*.

[20] Deuteronomy 21:15–17 states: "If a man has two wives, one loved and the other unloved, and both the loved and the unloved have borne him sons, but the firstborn is the son of the unloved one – on the day he distributes his property to his sons, he may not treat as firstborn the son of the loved one in disregard of the son of the unloved one who is older. Instead, he must accept the firstborn, the son of the unloved one, and allot to him a double portion of all he possesses; since he is the first fruit of his vigor, the birthright is his due." On firstborn inheritance, see Chapter 2.

[21] For more on testate succession among sons, see "Abbreviations, Terminology, and Transliteration."

as throughout this book, I refer to them by their amoraic names. The *mattenat bari* (literally, the gift of one in good health) is an arrangement whereby the donor gifts the land now, immediately passing ownership to the donee,[22] while retaining use of the land and its produce until death. The *mattenat shakhev mera* (literally, the gift of one lying ill) is a deathbed bequest. Mishnah *Baba Batra* 8:5, like so many other sources on gifting, does not indicate the form of gifting referred to.[23] Therefore, in the following interpretations of the *mishnah,* I deal with gifting in general terms, without exploring which gift is referenced. Even so, it should be noted that it is unlikely that *mBB* 8:5 refers to the *mattenat shakhev mera* as it mentions a written instrument (pars. IV and VII; see below),[24] and the *mattenat shakhev mera* in tannaitic literature, unlike the other two forms named, is implemented orally (for more on this matter, see below) and, at least according to amoraic law, does not require an act of acquisition as do the other forms.[25]

Certainly, gifting achieves significant goals for the apportioning of property including those forbidden through testate succession among sons. Indeed, rearranging the allocation of assets under the guise of gifting remains permissible even if the same allotment under the intention of inheritance is not.[26] For example, gifting enables granting the firstborn a single share, increasing or decreasing the portions of other sons,[27] and gifting to non-family members (even to the point of disinheriting sons; see par. VII below). As long as a term for gifting and not for inheriting – not the root *y-r-sh* – is used, the property transfer is valid.[28] It seems the rabbis are of the opinion that because gifting, as opposed to inheriting, is not explicitly attested to in biblical law, it could not be considered a violation of it (or at least not a violation of the letter of the law). The tannaim were correct that gifting, in the sense of a legal category, is absent from the Bible,[29] and they seem to have made no attempt to justify the practice through the interpretation of Scripture.[30] In fact, in biblical texts the two roots *n-t-n* and *y-r-sh* are used interchangeably, affirming that the distinction is not biblical in origin, a matter

[22] Presumably the gift is finally irrevocable only after the donor's death; see n. 1 and the discussion in the Appendix.

[23] On the methodological problem of interpreting sources on *mattanah,* as often they do not specify which form of gift is being referenced, see Yaron, *Gifts*, 21–28.

[24] See n. 46.

[25] Hence, in the Talmud we see references to the rabbis treating the words of the *shakhev mera* "*as if* written and delivered" (=*kikhetuvim umesurin*); see *bBB* 151a, 175a, *bGit* 13a, 15a.

[26] Cf. Yaron, *Gifts*, 37; Brin, "Two Problems," 245; Rivlin, *Inheritance and Wills*, 28.

[27] Cf. Yaron, *Gifts*, 33.

[28] Although *y-r-sh* cannot be employed, *n-t-n* and other phrases connoting gifting are acceptable. See below in the body of the text and, for another example, *tBB* 9:13.

[29] The only possible exception may be what Yaron identifies as gifts of dismission, an arrangement where a son receives property from the father while still alive and loses future claims to the inheritance (as when Abraham gifts to the sons of his concubines; Gen. 25:6); see Yaron, *Gifts*, 2 and 4. In any event, these do not clearly exhibit the criteria of tannaitic gifting. See n. 17.

[30] Not so the amoraim, who, in their midrashim such as *Bereshit Rabbah*, see gifts (like the *diathēkē*) in biblical narrative. For a list, see Rivlin, *Inheritance and Wills*, 138 n. 35.

I address, at length, in the next section.[31] The text of *mBB* 8:5 (in MS Kaufmann 8:5–8:7) continues:

II.	המחלק נכסיו על פיו, ריבה לאחד ומיעט לאחד, הישווה להן את הבכור דבריו קיימין.	One who apportions [*hameḥalek*=gifts][32] his property by word of mouth, increased for one and decreased for one or made the firstborn equal to them his words remain valid.
III.	ואם אמר משם[33] ירושה לא אמר כלום.	But if he had said [*amar*] so that it should be "as an inheritance," he has said nothing.
IV.	כתב בין בתחילה ובין באמצע ובין בסוף משם מתנה דבריו קיימין ...[34]	If he had written down [*katav*], whether at the beginning or in the middle or at the end, that thus it should be "as a gift," his words remain valid ...[35]
VII.	הכותב נכסיו לאחרים והניח את בניו מה שעשה עשוי אבל אין רוח חכמים נוחה ממנו.	If a man assigns his goods in writing [=gifts] to others and passed over his sons, what he has done is done but the sages have no pleasure in him.

These sections of *mBB* 8:5 maintain that asset allocation could only be accomplished by gifting and not by employing terminology for inheriting (reserved exclusively for referring to intestate succession).[36] As explicitly stated in the sections of the *mishnah* here, gifting grants the donor considerable freedom: the right to increase or decrease the portions allotted to sons, including adjusting the firstborn's double portion (par. II);[37] the authority to transfer property to outsiders;[38] and the power to disinherit sons (par. VII). None of these can be implemented by using terminology that hints at inheriting, that is, employing testate succession among sons. Indeed, instructions that use inheriting terminology, at least according to this tannaitic position,[39] do not take effect (par. III).

[31] Although certainly the exception, there are tannaitic traditions in which the clear terminological distinction between gifting and inheriting is blurred. See, e.g., *tBB* 7:3 and Kahana, *Sifre Zuta Deuteronomy*, 306, especially n. 5.

[32] This interpretation is based on context. So, too, H. Albeck, *Mishnah: Nezikin*, 145; Brin, "Two Problems," 245; Falk, *Introduction*, 342–344; Rivlin, *Inheritance and Wills*, 28. However, see below where I discuss this paragraph as originally referring to inheriting [!].

[33] In both occurrences, MS Kaufmann states *mishem*. So, too, MS Parma, MS Lowe, and MS Leiden. The Mishnah in Bavli manuscripts (MS Paris [Bibliothèque nationale Suppl. Heb. 1337], MS Hamburg 165, and MS Munich 95) and printed editions, however, have *mishum*.

[34] I deal with Pars. V and VI of the *mishnah* in Chapter 3.

[35] See the previous note.

[36] Additional tannaitic texts reflect this position, e.g., *tBB* 7:16–17; see also 7:11. Other texts that treat the legal distinction between gifting and inheriting include, *mBB* 3:3, *tDem* 1:16, and *tNed* 5:1.

[37] See *pBB* 8:5, 16b (1254).

[38] On gifting to outsiders, see also *tBB* 7:16; 9:1, 9, 10, and, 11.

[39] However, see below "A Philological-Historical Analysis of *mBB* 8:5" and the discussion of the opinion of R. Yoḥanan ben Beroka in Chapter 3.

The distinction between gifting and inheriting (in the usual sense of intestate succession) is not merely terminological or without legal consequence. Each mechanism brings about a different transfer and determines a legal status for the property transferred. Based on a comparison with other tannaitic texts, we can assume that the distinctions elsewhere between gifting and inheriting apply here as well (see the summary above). Among the major differences are the following. Gifting is a bilateral transaction that requires the donor to transfer the property with intention and that requires an act of acquisition be performed by (or on behalf of) the donee.[40] Inheriting, though, devolves automatically – it happens by itself without the future decedent's intervention – and is unilateral, requiring no action on the part of the recipient.[41] Furthermore, as implied by paragraph VII, which describes gifting to outsiders as final ("what he has done is done"), gifted property is not subject to the later claims of heirs.[42] That is, the division of the estate is calculated excluding the gifted property.[43] Inheriting, however, accomplishes a fixed and predetermined distribution among immediate heirs which, if not strictly followed, can be a source of dispute among heirs. Although, as noted, there are legal distinctions between the status of gifted versus inherited property, there is one common denominator: when a debtor transfers immovable property to another party by gifting or inheriting (or selling), any existing lien obligations attached to the property are passed on to the recipient.[44]

Although my formal discussion of the differences and similarities between the two mechanisms for the transfer of property – gifting and inheriting – ends

---

[40] Tannaitic sources that reflect the bilateralness of gifting include *mBB* 8:6 and 9:7. For a discussion of these sources, see Yaron, *Gifts*, 32–36. For my analysis of *mBB* 9:7, see below "A Philological-Historical Analysis of *mBB* 8:5." For a sampling of primary sources (from different areas of rabbinic law) that affirm that an act of acquisition on the part of the recipient completes the process of gifting, see *tPe'ah* 2:2; *tMeg* 2:15; and *tBB* 9:1 and 11, and 10:1. See also R. Yoḥanan's statement in *bNed* 43a.

[41] Moshe Greenberg demonstrates that late biblical and tannaitic Hebrew grammatical constructions made up of the nouns *naḥalah* and *yerushah* (and usually preceded by the verb *n-f-l*, "fall") connote that an inheritance can "'come (by chance, by succession, as duty), devolve' (the estate fell to his brother)," reflecting a unilateral devolution of assets onto heirs ("The Terms *Nafal* and *Hipil*," 253). On inheritance and gifts of land "falling" to women, see Lapin, "Maintenance," 188 and n. 52.

[42] On those sources that express rabbinic disapproval of the practice of gifting assets and excluding sons, see Yaron, *Gifts*, 39.

[43] See also *tBB* 7:12, where the firstborn receives a gift and, in addition, receives his double portion (presumably only of the remaining assets). On this source, see Yaron, *Gifts*, 45.

[44] See S. Albeck, *Principles of Talmudic Private Law*, 277, and the summary in Yaron, *Gifts*, 130–133. Aryeh Edrei submits a statement of this principle: "[t]he primary significance of the law of mortgaged property is that it affords acquisitional rights to creditors so that the property is available to them even if it was no longer in the possession of the debtor but transferred to a third party by sale, donation or inheritance. The rights of the inheritor are identical to that of a buyer, both of which are superseded by the rights of the creditor" ("Halakhic Responsibility," 823). This is not the case, however, in other ancient legal traditions (see below). See also Edrei's comments cited in n. 6 and n. 115.

here, the next section demonstrates that the distinctions between the mechanisms in *mBB* 8:5 involve more than is evident at first glance. Indeed, as I illustrate, a philological-historical analysis of *mBB* 8:5 both supplies a distinction in the ways that gifting and inheriting are implemented and uncovers a suppressed tannaitic position that allows appropriating the language and the mechanism of inheriting[!] to assign property to sons, that is, it recognizes testate succession among sons.

A Philological-Historical Analysis of mBB 8:5

An examination of the form and language of this *mishnah* is instructive. For, as mentioned, a close look uncovers meaningful new data: the revelation of a concealed tannaitic position that permits testate succession among sons and a difference in the realization of gifting versus testate succession among sons. First, I indicate the textual problems that are the foundation of my analysis; then, I offer solutions to the textual difficulties and explain how they point to the conclusions in this section.

The doubling of *devarav kayamin* in both paragraphs II and IV may be textually problematic. Once the *mishnah* implies in paragraph II that the terms for gifting effectively transfer property, that fact need not need be restated in paragraph IV.[45] Perhaps more importantly, whereas it is clear in paragraph II that the division is executed orally, *hameḥalek nekhasav al piv*,[46] paragraph IV treats paragraph II as if dealing with a written instrument, *katav bein bateḥila*.[47] This point is significant to the discussion below. In the *mishnah*'s other paragraphs, there is a clear distinction between the execution of gifting and attempts to employ the mechanism of inheriting, namely, testate succession among sons, along the lines of whether instructions are given orally or in writing. When treating

[45] Similarly, par. III may be superfluous because its prohibition of the use of inheriting terminology perhaps could be inferred from par. I.

[46] As mentioned, *mBB* 8:5 does not say to which form of gifting (*mattenat shakhev mera* or *mattenat bari*) it refers. Due to the ambiguity created by the appearance of the phrases "by word of mouth" and "if he had written down," in pars. II and IV, respectively, medieval authorities are unclear as to which form of gifting is referred to in the *mishnah*. Rashi (*Yev* 36a, *s. v. al piv*) merely states that the division is in accordance with what one states, whereas Rashbam (*BB* 126b, *s. v. hameḥalek nekhasav al piv*), presumably influenced by the *mishnah*'s statement "by word of mouth," states that the *mishnah* refers to a *mattenat shakhev mera*, an orally executed instrument (see the Appendix). See H. Albeck, *Mishnah: Nezikin,* 145 and 438; and Urbach, "Inheritance Laws and After-Life," 134, both who interpret the words *al piv* as "according to the *diathēkē*," presumably since par. IV mentions a written document. Such an interpretation cannot be maintained, however, since *al piv* (in par. II) does not refer back to a previously mentioned *diathēkē* (or anything else written). Rather it must be translated as "orally."

[47] I say "more importantly" because, ultimately, the disagreement between the paragraphs is more significant as a textual problem than the repetition of the phrase, "*devarav kayamin*," which can still be representative of single authorship.

inheriting, as in paragraphs I and III, an *oral* declaration (*ha'omer, amar*) is referenced; and when addressing gifting, as in paragraphs IV and VII, a *written* deed (*katav, hakotev*) is mentioned.[48] These sections of *mBB* 8:5 are richly complex in their presentation and, below, building on the work of J. N. Epstein and Zeev Falk, I offer my analysis.

Epstein notes that paragraph II stands out because, when mentioning the oral declaration, it does not use a form of the root *a-m-r* as do the other paragraphs in the *mishnah*. Paragraph II uses *ḥ-l-k* in the phrase *hameḥalek nekhasav al piv*. Therefore, states Epstein, paragraph II likely originated in another source and was added here later.[49] Falk takes a somewhat different approach, suggesting that paragraphs III and IV provide a gloss to paragraph II. Originally, argues Falk, paragraph II referred to testate succession among sons, not to gifting. It is worth noting that the possibility that the problem of the juxtaposition of one source (par. I) prohibiting testate succession among sons and the other permitting it (par. II) led to the glosses found in paragraphs III and IV. Falk writes that paragraph II referred to testate succession among sons, and "[l]ater on a limiting statement from a source using the term *amar* was added, and finally the third sentence, taken from a source using the term *kathav*,[50] was inserted in order to qualify the second statement."[51] For Falk, the addition of paragraphs III and IV creates a context in which *hameḥalek* in paragraph II, here translated "one who apportions," must mean "one who gifts." If so, originally paragraph II grants full rights of testate succession among sons,[52] even to the extent of adjusting the firstborn's double portion as inheritance[!], an issue I address in detail in Chapter 2. That is, the original directive enables even the language and mechanism of inheriting (and not just gifting) to be appropriated and employed for allocations not in accordance with the intestate order of succession.

I propose additional data to Epstein and Falk's observations about the unusual formulation and placement of paragraphs II–IV. For example, the grammatical differences in paragraphs III and IV, as compared to other paragraphs in 8:5, support the contention that paragraphs III and IV are later additions to the *mishnah*. There is a switch from the verbal noun forms, *ha'omer* (par. I), *hameḥalek* (par. II), and *hakotev* (par. VII) to *amar* and *katav* in paragraphs III

[48] Later in this same *mishnah* (par. VI), R. Yoḥanan ben Beroka also discusses an oral declaration designed to effect inheriting. See the full discussion of his statement in Chapter 3.

[49] Epstein, *Mavo*, 618; Epstein there points to a parallel in *Midrash Yelamdenu* that quotes par. II in the name of R. Elazar. Since *mBB* 9:7 includes R. Eliezer (a possible interchange with Elazar) and overlaps terminologically with our *mishnah* (see below in the body of the chapter), Epstein sees 9:7 as a possible source for par. II in 8:5; see my comments below in the body of the chapter.

[50] That source may be *tBB* 7:17 or a source similar to it.

[51] Falk, "Testate Succession," 76. See also the discussion of this source in Szubin, "Testamentary Succession," 19–20.

[52] Compare Falk, "Testate Succession," 76; and see Chapter 3.

and IV, respectively, verbs that are in the perfect tense. Furthermore, the assertion that paragraph II originally referred to testate succession among sons can be supported by the fact that mention of the division (*ḥ-l-k*) of assets (*n-kh-s*) among sons (*banim*), as in the context of our *mishnah*,[53] may refer to testate succession among sons specifically and not to gifting.[54] So, too, the emphasis on an *oral* declaration, *al piv*, aligns paragraph II with the other paragraphs in our *mishnah* (see above) that specifically link matters of inheriting (and not gifting) with oral declarations.[55]

Significantly, our *mishnah*'s formulation *hameḥalek nekhasav al piv* is also found in *mBB* 9:7,[56] specifically in the context of gifting.[57] The appearance of *hameḥalek nekhasav al piv* in 9:7 assists in explaining the historical process leading to the glosses in paragraphs III and IV. The author(s) of paragraphs III and IV add(s) the glosses to clarify the meaning of paragraph II. Knowing well that the phrase *hameḥalek nekhasav al piv* in paragraph II could refer to testate suc-

---

[53] To be sure, the context of pars. I–IV and VII is the division of the estate among sons. A genizah fragment and MS Lowe actually read *hameḥalek nekhasav levanav* ["to his sons"] *al piv* (JTS ENA 1487.77; cf. the text in H. Albeck's edition). Note that in my article "Prolegomenon," 183, I erroneously attribute the version including *levanav* to the Kaufmann MS.

[54] Noted by Lieberman in *Tosefta ki-fshuṭah: Neziqin*, 419, relying on the comments in *Mitzpeh Shemuel* by R. Shemuel Avigdor bar Avraham Tosfaa (in the back of standard Bavli printings), to *tBB* 7:11 (there 7:4 n. 70). In addition to *mBB* 8:5 under discussion here and *tBB* 7:11, see *tBekh* 6:8 (where it states *zekharim* and not *banim*). The combination of the root *ḥ-l-k* and the noun *nekhes/nekhasim* (without *banim/zekharim*) is also employed in the Mishnah to indicate inheriting (see *mYev* 4:3; *mKet* 8:6; *mBB* 3:3, 8:3, and 8:6 among others). For some occurrences of *ḥ-l-k* (alone) referring to inheriting, see *mKet* 4:3 and 8:6; *mBB* 8:7–8:8. However, *ḥ-l-k* is also used for gifting in tannaitic literature (for a clear example, see *tBB* 9:13 where the root *ḥ-l-k*, among other roots, is used for gifting; and for an example in which the roots, *n-t-n* and *ḥ-l-k* are used together, see *tBB* 7:16). Accordingly, Lieberman notes that whether *ḥ-l-k* (alone) refers to gifting or inheriting depends on context (Lieberman, *Tosefta ki-fshuṭah: Neziqin*, 419). On *ḥelek venaḥalah* and variations of it referring to inheriting in the Bible, see Gen. 31:14; Num. 18:20 and 26:56; Deut. 10:9, 12:12, 14:27, 14:29, and 18:1; Proverbs 17:2. However for a reference where it means gifts, see 2 Sam. 6:19. In general on the use of *ḥ-l-k* in the Bible, see Tsevat, "Chalaq II," 447–451.

[55] The strict distinction between oral declarations for inheriting and written statements for gifting, as in *mBB* 8:5, is not sustained throughout tannaitic literature. Hence, Lieberman's repeated emphasis that context and outcome must be considered when determining if a given transfer of property is the result of inheriting or of gifting (see, e.g., *Tosefta: Neziqin*, 155 n. 45 and the previous note).

[56] *mBB* 9:7 reads, "If a man apportioned his goods by word of mouth, R. Eliezer says: whether he was in health or at the point of death, property for which there is security can be acquired only by money or by deed or by usucaption; that for which there is no security can be acquired only by the act of drawing into possessions. They said to him: it once happened that the mother of Rokhel's sons was sick and said, 'Give my veil to my daughter,' and it was worth twelve hundred *denars*; and she died and they fulfilled her words… . The Sages say: On a Sabbath his words remain valid, since he cannot write, but not on a weekday. R. Joshua says: If they have said [that he can assign property] on a Sabbath, how much more so on a weekday!"

[57] The tradition deals with methods of acquisition, a matter only relevant to gifting (see previous note).

cession among sons, the glossators were motivated to uproot the contradiction between paragraphs I and II. Moreover, the harmonization of the two paragraphs would eliminate the legal position "contrary to what is written in the Torah." They find support for their interpretation of the phrase *hameḥalek nekhasav al piv* in paragraph II as gifting in 9:7, the location of the parallel formulation, and a place in which the phrase must refer to gifting specifically.[58] In this way the independent tradition in paragraph II, perhaps initially juxtaposed with paragraph I precisely because it contradicts it by promoting testate succession among sons, is transformed.[59] In short, originally two conflicting tannaitic approaches to testate succession among sons exist in tannaitic law; in *mBB* 8:5 as we have it, they are harmonized.

In summary, *mBB* 8:5 provides the foundation for the legal, conceptual, and terminological distinction between the two mechanisms for transfer of property in the event of death in tannaitic law: gifting and inheriting. Gifting, in addition to being bilateral and resulting in the transfer of property excluded from the eventual division of the estate, is effected through a written deed in our *mishnah* and transfers property even to outsiders.[60] Intestate inheriting, however, is unilateral and automatically results in a predetermined partition of the estate. For one tannaitic opinion attempts at adjustments using the mechanism of inheriting, that is, testate succession among sons, is forbidden. For another tannaitic approach, here restored, testate succession among sons can be implemented[61] (even

---

[58] I stress that if the context of R. Eliezer's statement in 9:7 is someone distributing possessions on the Sabbath (compare the parallel in *tBB* 10:12 where the Sabbath context is more explicitly stated), a time when writing is prohibited according to Jewish law, then terms for writing would not have been available to the *mishnah*'s author. Only an oral declaration could be mentioned by the tanna. Accordingly, the use in *mBB* 9:7 of *hameḥalek nekhasav al piv* to mean gifting would not indicate that the phrase, under regular circumstances, implies gifting. Rather, its use in *mBB* 9:7 may only be due to the context which, perforce, disallows references to writing. On R. Eliezer's requirement for an act of acquisition, (also) prohibited on the Sabbath, see the discussion in Lieberman, *Tosefta ki-fshuṭah: Neziqin*, 450 n. 35 and the literature cited there.

[59] I identify four stages in the redaction of this *mishnah* as it appears before us. Initially the *mishnah* consists of pars. I, V, VI, and VII (for pars. V and VI, see Chapter 3). Then, par. II, expressing an opposing position to par. I is added. Next, par. III is appended to neutralize the contradiction between pars. I and II, and finally par. IV is added as a further qualification. Or, alternatively, pars. III and IV are added together as qualifying statements to the contradiction between pars. I and II.

[60] Despite the evidence, however, Büchler in *Studies*, 34, sees the verb *k-t-v* in our *mishnah* as referring specifically to inheriting (=testate succession among sons), presumably because of the existence of written dispositions in case of death in the ancient world and tannaitic law.

[61] The existence of a tannaitic approach promoting testate succession among sons implies, along with its corollary testate succession among agnates, that mechanisms for the transfer of property exclusively for after death (i. e., without the accompanying transfer of any property during the lifetime of the donor/testator as well) are, at least according to some tannaim, permissible. Some scholars assume that Jewish law prefers practices whereby the transfer of some of the property or rights to it, to the donee, are accomplished during the lifetime of the donor/testator as well as after the donor/testator's death. Cf. Chapter 3 n. 6 and the Appendix n. 18 and n. 54.

when adjusting the firstborn's double portion).[62] Testate succession among sons is accomplished by an oral declaration. The multiple options for the division of an estate discussed above may be, in and of themselves, proof that partibility is promoted by the tannaim. The presumed biblical model, which prefers impartible inheritance remaining in family hands, in all likelihood is not the foundation of the construction of the tannaitic laws of inheritance. Rather, tannaitic inheritance laws may have been the product of their own social and economic contexts. Furthermore, in the absence of attempts by the rabbis to find justification for their innovations in Scripture, factors external to rabbinic interpretation must be considered as the source. But, before engaging in a discussion of the possibilities, a review of the biblical model follows.

Gifting and Inheriting in the Bible

Biblical inheritance law is based primarily on the opposite assumptions of tannaitic inheritance law. It does not promote partibility but rather prefers an undivided inheritance, that is, heirs to the decedent jointly owning ancestral property (at least until the division of the estate). If and when a division of the estate takes place, the joint ownership ends and the distribution is only among family members,[63] presumably in accordance with the biblical laws of intestate succession. In addition, there exists no legal-conceptual or terminological distinction between gifting and inheriting.

"Undivided inheritance," an economically advantageous arrangement in ancient agrarian societies,[64] is attested to in multiple societies in the ancient Near East and is the presumed preferred condition in biblical texts (see below). In his discussion of the topic, Raymond Westbrook[65] capitalizes on earlier observations by David Daube[66] and illustrates the ancient Near Eastern context of the biblical institution. In particular, Westbrook highlights the fact that in biblical texts the firstborn (or his replacement) functions as administrator of the jointly owned property (until a division takes place),[67] a matter I discuss in Chapter 2. Regarding gifting and inheriting, while the data reflect a consistent meaning for *y-r-sh* in pre-Deuteronomic biblical as well as in mishnaic usage, this is not the

[62] For more on the inheritance of the firstborn, see Chapter 2.

[63] See the examples in Hiers, "Transfer of Property," 121–155. These distributions are usually to immediate heirs or potential heirs (i.e., in the line of succession). The only possible exceptions are transfers to slaves. Slaves, though, may have been considered members of the household. On the negative view of transferring inheritance to slaves reflected in Ezek. 46:16–17, see Greengus, *Laws*, 71.

[64] Brin, *Studies*, 250.

[65] Westbrook, *Property and Family*, 118–141.

[66] Daube, "Consortium," 71–91.

[67] Westbrook, *Property and Family*, 140.

case for *n-t-n*, thereby establishing that the terminological and legal-conceptual distinction between the two methods is not present in the Bible.[68] Curiously, the absence of a conceptual distinction is not consonant with the broader picture in the ancient Near East (see below).

Phyllis Ann Bird, in her unpublished dissertation on the root *y-r-sh*,[69] writes regarding the pre-Deuteronomic usage:

> The basic meaning of the Qal stem is "to inherit," i. e., to succeed another in ownership of something, usually real estate… . The verb is a legal term; it implies that the person who is heir or inherits has legal title to the property or position acquired. Essential to the idea of acquiring possession and title expressed by *yrš* is the condition of the death or removal of the former owner. The verb, *yrš*, involves as a necessary idea, the extinction of former claims in that manner.[70]

The primary definition of *y-r-sh* in pre-Deuteronomic biblical texts, therefore, is "inherit," in the legal sense of the term, a meaning akin to its mishnaic equivalent.[71] The Deuteronomic usage of the root, however, is almost exclusively limited to conquest references.[72] Accordingly, the word connotes taking possession of or seizing something.[73] When it appears together with *n-t-n,* it actually represents the counter action required in a *bilateral* process of acquisition, such as when God gifts (*n-t-n*) the land of Canaan to the Israelites who later seize (*y-r-sh*) it.[74]

---

[68] Indeed, in the Bible *n-t-n* is not a technical term and is also employed synonymously with *y-r-sh*; see below in the body of the chapter.

[69] I thank the author for providing me with a copy of her dissertation.

[70] "YRŠ," 319. Indeed, as Bird points out in her conclusions, this is the primary meaning of the word in the cognate languages as well: "In the cognate languages, however, this legal usage is without exception the dominant one; it is also frequently the only one. In all of the languages in which the root is attested it is used as a technical, legal term for inheriting and inheritance. While the more general idea of possession may also be represented by some uses of the root, in no language is the specific sense, 'inherit,' lacking. This latter meaning constitutes the universal common denominator and cannot, therefore, be regarded as secondary or derived. It must in some way describe the basic, shared meaning in or behind all the uses" ("YRŠ," 415).

[71] Bird mentions in a footnote (without citing evidence) that "[t]he Mishnaic use of *YRŠ* (and *NḤL*) corresponds in large measure to late biblical usage" ("YRŠ," 101 n. 63). Here, I believe, Bird's comment may be linked to Moshe Greenberg's thesis on the usage of *y-r-sh* in both late biblical Hebrew and mishnaic Hebrew, see n. 41. See also my discussion of *y-r-sh* in tannaitic literature above in the body of the chapter.

[72] Bird, "YRŠ," 328. This is not to say, of course, that Deuteronomy does not have in its lexicon the earlier meaning of *y-r-sh* as well.

[73] Lohfink, "Yaraš," 372. Cf. Lipinski, "Naḥal," 320; see also Thompson, *Historicity*, 204; Malul, "'Āqēb "Heel" and 'āqab "To Supplant," 195, 202; and on some aspects of taking possession in the Bible, whether through sale, gift, or inheritance, see B. Cohen, *Jewish and Roman Law*, 457–471.

[74] See, e. g., Deuteronomy 1:8 and the extensive discussion on the coupling of *n-t-n* and *y-r-sh* in Bird, "YRŠ," 338–357. This usage is paralleled in contracts throughout the ancient Near East. As Bird explicitly writes, *n-t-n* "is used in contracts and treaties throughout the ancient Near East as a technical term to describe the transfer of property either by donation or by sale. In most of these cases *some counter action on the part of the recipient is expected*" ("YRŠ," 341; emphasis mine). See also Lohfink, "Yaraš," 385 and B. Cohen, *Jewish and Roman Law*, 460–463.

So the root *y-r-sh*, an expression of *unilateral* transfer in mishnaic Hebrew (like its pre-Deuteronomic definition), actually expresses the opposite in Deuteronomic usage. The zigzagging of the primary meaning of *y-r-sh* – from inherit in pre-Deuteronomic biblical usage, to seize in Deuteronomic jargon and then back to inherit in mishnaic idiom[75] – may be the outcome of the influence of Aramaic on mishnaic Hebrew,[76] where the Aramaic root *y-r-t* seems to refer primarily, if not exclusively, to inheriting.[77] In any event, even in those biblical texts in which *y-r-sh* is parallel to *n-ḥ-l*[78] and connotes inheriting,[79] it does not appear in contradistinction to gifting, *n-t-n*. Rather, the roots, which by the tannaitic period came to signify opposing mechanisms for the transfer of property, are used interchangeably. Accordingly, several roots are used synonymously,[80] including *n-t-n*,[81] *y-r-sh*,[82] and the related *n-ḥ-l*.[83] In Deut. 21: 15–17, for example, the root *n-ḥ-l* appears to be synonymous with the root *n-t-n*, "when he distributes [*beyom hanḥilo*][84] ... he must accept the firstborn[85] ... and give [*latet*] him a double

On *n-t-n* and *n-ḥ-l* appearing together and indicating two parts of one transaction, see Josh. 17:4, 19:49; Ezek. 46:16 and 47:23; Ps. 111:6; Job 42:15. See also Num. 27:8–11.

[75] This is not meant to imply that one language was the outgrowth of the other but, rather, to highlight that differences in usage may be attributed to certain influences. For an English summary of the relationship of biblical to mishnaic Hebrew, see Bar-Asher, "Mishnaic Hebrew," 570–579.

[76] However, Bird suggests that, "[t]he Aramaic usage we have observed has surely been influenced by the Hebrew of the Mishna – even though the latter is itself heavily Aramaicized" (Bird, "YRŠ," 101).

[77] For Aramaic occurrences of the root, see Bird, "YRŠ," 70–121. Regarding *y-r-t* at Elephantine, for example, Bird writes, "*Yrt* pertains to a body of law describing the rights of survivors to a deceased person's property (including in some cases his debts and duties); ... *yrt* in these contracts assumes such a body of customary law and that it refers primarily to property rights of descendants, relatives, or others designated 'heirs'" (Bird, "YRŠ," 79–80). On talmudic Aramaic, Bird states, "It is exclusively legal and very similar to that of the Elephantine papyri" (Bird, "YRŠ," 91) and on Targumic Aramaic, she notes that, "[o]nly a few minor peculiarities distinguish this technical usage from that of the Talmud" (Bird, "YRŠ," 103). So, too, in Syriac, "[i]t would appear then that the basic meaning of the verb in the Pe. [pe'al] is 'to be heir (in respect to someone or something), to inherit, to lay claim to an inheritance or hereditary possession'" (Bird, "YRŠ," 129–130).

[78] Unlike Bird, Lohfink, "Yaraš," 373 (and following him, Lipinski, "Naḥal," 320) contends that only beginning with postexilic biblical texts, under the influence of Aramaic, did the root *y-r-sh* begin to connote inheritance of possessions, becoming parallel to the root *n-ḥ-l.* If he is correct, then the Aramaic influence did not affect only the semantic range of *y-r-sh*; it also changes the legal function of *y-r-sh* from describing one side of a *bilateral* method of acquisition to eventually describing a *unilateral* method of acquisition.

[79] However, on *n-ḥ-l* as referring to a gift, see B. Cohen, *Jewish and Roman Law*, 463.

[80] In addition to the verbs listed here *a-v-r* (transfer) should be considered, on which, see Chapter 4.

[81] For a list of occurrences and discussion, see Farby, "Nātan."

[82] For a list and discussion, see Lohfink, "Yaraš," 370–376.

[83] For a list and discussion, see Lipinski, "Naḥal."

[84] That is, his estate.

[85] For a discussion of the firstborn, see Chapter 2.

portion." So, too, in the story of Zelophehad's daughters in the book of Numbers, "[t]he plea of Zelophehad's daughters is just: you should give [*naton titen*] them a hereditary holding [*aḥuzat naḥalah*] among their father's kinsmen" (27:7); and "[i]f he has no daughter, you shall give [*u-netatem*] his property [*naḥalato*] to his brothers" (27:9).[86] In short, the distinction is not biblical.[87]

In the absence of clear biblical antecedents and a hermeneutic foundation for the tannaitic traditions,[88] the sources for a preference for partibility, the legal distinction between gifting and inheriting, and the inclusion of outsiders must be sought elsewhere. These characteristics may reflect the social and economic contexts of tannaitic Palestine, a situation divorced from the values underlying the biblical concept of an undivided inheritance with extended family landholdings. The tannaitic condition is exemplified by the prevalence of the nuclear family in an urbanized setting with private landholdings. Certainly, the distinctions between gifting and inheriting and the ability to transfer property to strangers represent the flexibility required in a legal as well as social and economic complex that prefers partibility. As I demonstrate below, the tannaitic preference for partibility and the embrace of the transfer of property to outsiders (without adoption) parallels not biblical or ancient Near Eastern precedent but, rather, practices known from Athens and Rome with a particular affinity for Roman terminology and conceptualization. Even so, there are characteristics common to most of the legal traditions of the ancient world, excluding the biblical, primary among them unilateral inheriting and universal succession. In this sense, tannaitic inheritance law is merely a product of the general legal landscape of the ancient Near East and Mediterranean.

The Universality of Unilateral Inheriting and Universal Succession

Although absent in biblical texts, and devoid of rabbinic hermeneutic foundation, some aspects of tannaitic inheritance law – such as unilateral inheriting[89]

[86] See also Num. 27:4, 10, 11; 36:2.

[87] It may be that there is no need for a distinction between mechanisms for transfer of property in biblical law precisely because within the biblical model, ideally, the estate is held jointly by family members. Indeed, if the primary goal of inheriting in biblical law is family posterity on ancestral land, then it would seem unnecessary to have a distinction between property that is included (inherited) versus property that is excluded (gifted) from the valuation of the joint estate. Furthermore, all of the deceased's property, even if eventually divided, is still representative of the family legacy because the division is only among family members. See n. 10 and n. 90.

[88] I discuss the relevant biblical narratives that deal with matters of gifts and inheritance in their appropriate contexts in the following chapters. Accordingly, I examine the patriarchal narratives in Chapters 2 and 3. I treat the story of Zelophehad's daughters and Job's daughters in Chapters 3 and 4.

[89] That is, not requiring an act of acquisition by or on behalf of the recipient.

and universal succession – have historical parallels in the ancient world.[90] Both of these aspects of inheritance practice attest to a view of heirs as extensions of the deceased, standing "in the place" of the dead.[91] Appropriately, unilateral inheriting is the automatic transfer of ownership to the heirs, and universal succession comprises the contents of the transfer. That is, the heir succeeds to the rights as well as the liabilities of the deceased (see below).

Inheriting through the law of intestacy is, in fact, unilateral throughout the ancient Near East, and universal succession is already present in documents from the Early Dynastic and Pre-Sargonic periods.[92] So it is that in the *Grand document juridique,*[93] heirs inherit not only the property of the deceased but also his obligations[94] and according to document Foxvog,[95] a son inherits a claim to payments due his deceased father.[96] The Neo-Sumerian period evidences universal succession as well,[97] including claims the heir can pursue in litigation.[98] The Code of Hammurabi (12) includes provisions for claiming from the estate of the deceased.[99] Documentation from the Old Assyrian period attests to the fact that an inheritance division can be accomplished only after debts are settled and claims of the deceased collected.[100] The Middle Assyrian period also evidences heirs inheriting both assets and debts.[101] At Nuzi, in testamentary dispositions, the heir inherits both rights and obligations.[102] An unpublished adoption document from the Neo-Assyrian period states explicitly that the heir inherits the assets, debts, and claims of the deceased: "He (the heir) will enjoy his inheritance share with them (his brothers); ... he will settle his (the father's) debts and he will

---

[90] It is true that biblical texts about inheritance do not address universal succession directly. Even so, the transfer, or sharing, of debt obligation did exist. For example, according to biblical law, if a kinsman is destitute and must sell part of his land, fellow kinsmen either buy it preemptively or buy it back after it is sold and then keep it until the Jubilee year; see Lev. 25:35–55. Possible evidence that debt is somehow linked to the personality of the deceased is documented in 2 Kings 4:1–7 where a widow cries out to Elisha the prophet because her sons are going to be sold into slavery to pay for the debts of her husband. See n. 10 and n. 87.

[91] See n. 6, n. 44, and n. 115.

[92] See Westbrook's emphasis on "direct" and "automatic" inheritance ("Introduction," 56–57).

[93] On the *Grand document juridique,* see Wilcke, *Early Ancient Near Eastern Law*, 92–93.

[94] See the texts discussed in Wilcke, "Neue Rechtsurkunden," 47–67.

[95] On document Foxvog, see Wilcke, *Early Ancient Near Eastern Law*, 69.

[96] See Wilcke, "Neue Rechtsurkunden," 44–47; Gelb, Steinkeller, and Whiting, *Earliest Land Tenure Systems*, 32a.

[97] See text no. 183, esp., lines 8–20 in Falkenstein, *Die Neusumerischen Gerichtsurkunden*, 291–293.

[98] See text no. 174, lines 6–18 in Falkenstein, *Die Neusumerischen Gerichtsurkunden*, 276–277.

[99] Roth, *Law Collections,* 84.

[100] See text no. 287 in Eisser and Lewy, *Die altassyrischen Rechtsurkunden vom Kültepe*, 330–334.

[101] Freydank, "*Bitqī batāqu* 'Abschneidungen abschneiden'?" 108.

[102] Paradise, "Nuzi Inheritance Practices," 242–248.

claim payment for the debts due to him (his father)."[103] Neo-Babylonian period documents point to universal succession as well.[104] The terms in loan deeds from Elephantine may demonstrate universal intestate succession there. The deeds mention that the children of a debtor must pay his debts if he dies before repaying.[105] In Athens, intestate succession is both unilateral and universal, including liabilities and debts owed to and by the deceased.[106] This seems also to be the case in Sparta and Gortyn.[107]

In Roman law the devolution of the *hereditas*, or inheritance, is also universal.[108] It includes assets, liabilities, and claims.[109] The principle is aptly captured in the following brocard, *hereditas est successio in universum ius*, "inheritance is succession to the whole right,"[110] and the following from the writings of Gaius gives the background to the Roman concept of universal succession. Note the formulation when describing why heirs from within the family are called *sui heredes*, "heirs to themselves":

> These heirs are called immediate, the testator's own heirs, because they come from inside the family and are in a certain sense thought of as owners even while their parent is alive. That is why, in the event of intestacy, these descendants have the first entitlement. They are called compulsory because they have no choice in the matter. Whether under a will or not, they become heirs automatically (*Institutes*, 2:157).[111]

---

[103] Radner, "Neo-Assyrian Period," 900.

[104] See text no. CM20 59 in Wunsch, *Das Egibi-Archiv*, 82–83. There a son does not pay the debts of his deceased father because he has been adopted by an uncle and seemingly renounces his natural father's inheritance and obligations. In addition, these texts exhibit the power of children to refuse their father's inheritance. One document confirms that heirs reject the inheritance of their father because there are too many debts attached to it; see text no. TCL 12 122, discussed in Wunsch, "Und die Richter berieten," 84–85.

[105] Yaron, *Law of the Aramaic Papyri*, 41. Yaron considers the idea that the heirs would incur the debt based on the terms of the loan contract alone unreasonable. He therefore assumes that the children's future obligation must be due to the practices of intestate succession (Yaron, *Law of the Aramaic Papyri*, 66). See also a Ptolemaic text (in Greek) from Elephantine that indicates that if an unmarried son does not pay the debt of his parents, he will not inherit from the estate; text D3 in, Porten, *Elephantine Papyri in English*, 412–413.

[106] MacDowell, *Law in Classical Athens*, 92–93; cf. Harrison, *Law of Athens*, 1:129.

[107] On Sparta, see Hodkinson, *Property and Wealth in Classical Sparta*, 94; on Gortyn, see Kristensen, "Inheritance, Property, and Management," 92.

[108] See Pomponius, *Sabinus*, book 5: "An heir succeeds to the whole legal position of the deceased and not only to the ownership of individual things, because the assets which take the form of debts due also pass to the heir" (D.29.2.37).

[109] Buckland, *Text-Book of Roman Law*, 307–308; 364; 398; Nicholas, *Introduction to Roman Law*, 235 and 238.

[110] Buckland, *Text-Book of Roman Law*, 307–308. The entire text actually reads, *Nihil est aliud hereditas quam successio in universum ius quod defunctus habuit*, "inheritance is nothing else than succession to the whole right the deceased had" (D.50.16.24).

[111] Gordon and Robinson, *Institutes of Gaius*, 92 and 201; cf. Paul, Sabinus, book 2: "In the case of *sui heredes* ... no inheritance is regarded as having taken place, as if they were already owners, being thought of as in some sense owners even in the lifetime of the father" (D.28.2.11).

Gaius conveys the idea that even before death, the legal personality of the immediate heir and the decedent are considered merged; the rights and obligations are considered one and the same.[112] Heirs succeed universally because even during the lifetime of the deceased, they are already viewed "in a certain sense" as owners of the family property.[113] Inheriting, by being both unilateral and universal, transfers complete ownership, therefore, from one generation to the other "automatically" upon the death of the parent.[114] The stress on "automatically" distinguishes between unilateral inheriting and bilateral gifting, the subject of the next section. As for inheriting, in the final analysis, tannaitic law functions in the same way as the laws known in the region for millennia.[115] As we see below, while much the same is true of gifting as well, the concept of gifting in tannaitic law bears a closer resemblance to the Roman concept of bilateral gifting.

Gifting in the Ancient World

Like inheriting, gifting is also paralleled in multiple ancient legal traditions. Gifting serves the same important function as a strategy of succession throughout the ancient world: it enables the allocation of property that would be excluded from the eventual division of the estate. In this way, gifted property is protected from the heirs. Despite the common purpose that gifting has within multiple legal traditions, distinctions among legal traditions remain. These differences often reflect aspects of the presumed family structure and landholding patterns of the societies in which the laws are formulated. For example, in some ancient Near Eastern societies property has to remain within the family because only those linked to the ancestral land are allowed to possess it; therefore, donees also are always heirs (on adoption, see Chapter 3). At times this seems to be the case even in more urbanized ancient Near Eastern contexts,[116] perhaps a remnant of the

---

[112] See also Taubenschlag, *Law*, 163–164.

[113] In the absence of children, The XII Tablets provide for the nearest agnate (male relation on the father's side) to inherit. See the text of The XII Tablets (V:4–5) in Crawford and Cloud, *Roman Statutes*, 641.

[114] Cf. Gaius, *Lex Julia et Papia, book* 13: "In the case of the *sui heredes*, formal acceptance is not a requisite because they immediately fall to be heirs by operation of law" (D.38.16.14).

[115] Edrei notes that in Jewish law, conceptually heirs inherit the debts of their father because they are in possession of the father's (= the debtor's) land upon which there is a lien (the same as a buyer of land owes debts). Accordingly, the obligation of the heirs is limited by the value of the decedent's land. In Roman law, however, the obligation of the heirs is unlimited. Therefore, the heirs have to pay the creditors from their own property if the inheritance is insolvent. Edrei's article addresses, almost exclusively, amoraic (and later) data. Accordingly, it is premature to conclude that the same conceptualization he describes applies to tannaitic law as well. See "Shi'abud nekhasim," 293; "Mitsvah al hayetomim;" and my comments in n. 6 and n. 44.

[116] See the examples of gifts of land and slaves to a son, unsuccessfully disputed by brothers, in Lafont and Westbrook, "Neo-Sumerian Period," 207.

earlier societal origins of specific practices.[117] Accordingly, in the ancient Near East gifted property retains a characteristic of inherited property: liens remain attached to the property even after transfer. That is, this aspect of universal succession applies both to heirs and donees, a reality unknown to the Greeks and Romans.[118] Indeed, the primary distinction between gifting and inheriting in ancient Near Eastern law, as opposed to Athenian and Roman law, is precisely this: only according to the former does gifted property with a lien remain claimable by creditors. Furthermore, neither Athenian nor Roman law requires the adoption of donees. Donees can remain outsiders and are not considered members of the household. Accordingly, gifts remain separate from the estate in every way. Finally, there is no evidence for the bilateralness of gifts in ancient Near Eastern or Athenian law.[119] Roman law, however, like tannaitic law, requires an act of acquisition by or on behalf of the donee (see below, "Terminology and Implementation of Gifting and Inheriting").

General features of ancient Near Eastern gifting can be gleaned from highlighting the principles governing the *kitru* gift at Nuzi. Although the gift is always granted to someone who is already an heir, it is seen as separate from the inheritance portions and, therefore, not subject to dispute among heirs.[120] As Jonathan Paradise writes, "[t]he purpose of this designation ... is to secure the rights of the person to the entire object from the claims of other relatives ... This suggests that the property could have been part of the normal division of the estate had the gift not been kept separate from the rest."[121] Furthermore, recipients of *kitru* gifts, as heirs, could not escape the obligation to pay the debts of the deceased.[122]

---

[117] See the section entitled "On the Relationship of Inheritance Laws to Presumed Social and Economic Settings in the Bible and Tannaitic Literature" in the Introduction.

[118] On Greek and Roman gifts, see below in the body of the chapter. The only exception, e.g., in Roman law, is when paying the debts and the legacies would leave the heirs without inheritance. This is what the *lex Falcidia* remedies; see n. 4.

[119] Although it may be reasonable to assume that in the ancient Near East acts of acquisition are required by donees as well, clear evidence for this has yet to come to the fore. Regarding another legal context, marriage contracts, scholars note that due to the fact that agreements were often concluded orally, whatever acts and rites accompanied these transactions were lost. See Greengus, "Old Babylonian Marriage Contract," 514–515; Roth, *Babylonian Marriage Agreements*; Paradise, "Marriage Contracts," 3–7. See also, Malul, *Legal Symbolism*, 2–3; and Magdalene and Wunsch, *Manumission, Emancipation, and Oblation*, 31–32 (my thanks to F. Rachel Magdalene and Cornelia Wunsch for sending me a prepublication copy of parts of their book). So, too, acts of acquisition that may have been performed during transfers of property by gift may not be traceable for the ancient Near East. On some aspects of ceremonial and symbolic acts in the area of sales, however, we have benefited from an entire study, Malul, *Legal Symbolism*. On the lack of evidence for acts of acquisition in classical Athens, see Harrison, *Law of Athens*, 1:201 and 244–248.

[120] For a full discussion of the *kitru* gift at Nuzi, see Paradise, "Nuzi Inheritance Practices," 249–253.

[121] Paradise, "Nuzi Inheritance Practices," 252.

[122] Paradise, "Nuzi Inheritance Practices," 252.

In the earlier Old Babylonian codes of Lipit-Ishtar (31)[123] and Hammurabi (165),[124] we also see that gifts to heirs are excluded from the later division of the estate.[125] Scholars of Neo-Assyrian[126] and Neo-Babylonian[127] inheritance practices also document some of the features unique to gifting (as opposed to inheriting). For example, one Neo-Assyrian document records a gift from a father to a son; the division of the father's estate among the heirs coming from the remaining assets only.[128]

Terminology and Implementation of Gifting and Inheriting

The discussion above demonstrates the degree to which a conceptual distinction between gifting and inheriting – in significant ways parallel to the tannaitic distinction – exists in different parts of the ancient world. In the areas of terminology and methods of implementation, however, the distinctions present in tannaitic law are not evidenced broadly, even if they are known to Roman law. Accordingly, in the final analysis, I suggest that some aspects of the affinity between tannaitic and Roman inheritance law are not a coincidence.

As pointed out by F.R. Kraus, references to the division of inheritance in ancient Near Eastern texts commonly use forms of the noun *zittum*, "inheritance share," or the related verb *zāzum* in Akkadian.[129] However, although the Akkadian verb *nadānu*, "to gift," and the related noun *nadānu/nidintu*, "gift," are used for land grants, these terms are not employed in the context of gifting in contemplation of death.[130] Significantly, Jonas Greenfield points to a reflex of one usage of *nadānu*, specifically the formula *našû-nadānu*, in one document from Elephantine, appearing as *hnṣl-ntn*,[131] which is in the context of gifting in contemplation of death.[132] Indeed, at Elephantine, use of the Aramaic equivalent of *n-t-n*, the technical term *y-h-b*, "give," transfers ownership from donor

[123] Roth, *Law Collections*, 32.

[124] Roth, *Law Collections*, 112.

[125] On these two sources, however, not in relation to the subject discussed here, see Greengus, *Laws*, 71–72.

[126] Radner, "Neo-Assyrian Period," 900.

[127] On the possibility of a distinction between gifting and inheriting in Neo-Babylonian documents, see the short comments in Wunsch, "Women's Property," 3.

[128] Kohler and Ungnad, *Assyrische Rechtsurkunden*, 41.

[129] Kraus, "Erbrechtliche Terminologie," 54–55. So, too, the Sumerian logogram ḫa.la, "inheritance share" (Kraus, "Erbrechtliche Terminologie," 55); for a Sumerian text, see Podany, Beckman, and Colbow, "Adoption," 48.

[130] On the use of *nadānu*, see the discussion in Speiser, "Akaddian Documents from *Ras Shamra*," 160–165. See Bird, "YRŠ," 341–342 n. 18.

[131] Greenfield, "*našû–nadānu* and its Congeners," 724.

[132] Szubin and Porten, "Testamentary Succession," 38–39.

to donee,[133] among (a broadly defined category of) family members.[134] That is, after transfer, these gifts of property cannot be reclaimed by the alienor or the heirs.[135] However, these gifts, while given in contemplation of death, unlike the other gifts dealt with here, seemingly are transferred fully during the donor's lifetime.[136] The root *y-h-b* is also employed in deeds of gift in contemplation of death from the Judean desert,[137] possibly establishing, together with the evidence from Elephantine, the antiquity of gifting terminology, parallel to that used by the tannaim, among presumed Jews.[138] Furthermore, the presence in the Elephantine papyri of the root *y-r-t*, the Aramaic equivalent of Hebrew *y-r-sh*, is significant because, together with *y-h-b*, it may point to a terminological antecedent to the tannaitic usage of *y-r-sh* and *n-t-n* as opposing mechanisms for transfer in case of death. Note, however, that *y-r-t* only appears in the context of the widower's rights in the Elephantine papyri,[139] a datum that prevents us from concluding that the terminological distinction at Elephantine functions in the same way as in tannaitic law.

While gifting serves as an important strategy of succession within the context of ancient Near Eastern society, for those legal traditions that allow gifting to outsiders (even without adoption) and in which gifts are unaccompanied by liabilities,[140] gifting certainly seems to serve primarily as a personal benefit to an individual.[141] In Athens, for example, where testate succession requires adoption, it transfers both rights and liabilities (as in cases of intestate succession).[142] The establishment of a gift from the inheritance, which does not require adoption and is unaccompanied by obligations, serves an important social role. Through

---

[133] Yaron, *Law of the Aramaic Papyri*, 80 and Szubin and Porten, "Testamentary Succession," 36. *N-t-n* also appears in the papyri; see Botta, "A Reevaluation," 100–101.

[134] See Chapter 3.

[135] Szubin and Porten, "Testamentary Succession," 36.

[136] Szubin and Porten, "Testamentary Succession," 39.

[137] See the text of P. Yadin 7 in Yadin, *Documents*, 82–83; cited in part and discussed in the Appendix.

[138] However, in the absence of a significant sampling for inheriting terminology, a case cannot be made for terminological antecedents to the tannaitic distinction in the Judean desert. For, it may be that in Judean desert documents the verbs for gifting and inheriting are used interchangeably as in the Bible.

[139] Yaron, *Law of the Aramaic Papyri*, 71. See, e.g., text B28 [=Cowley 15] in Porten, *The Elephantine Papyri in English*, 181 and n. 36 there. Note the different terminology, *shalita* (=control, right to), used regarding the rights of the widow. On this, see Yaron, *Law of the Aramaic Papyri*, 69–73, and the literature cited there. For additional texts, more on the different legal implications of *sh-l-t* versus *y-r-t*, as possession versus ownership, respectively, and a comparison to possible Ptolemaic legal equivalents, see Botta, "Legal Function," 199–200. See also my comments in Chapter 5.

[140] On forms of gifting in tannaitic law and the ancient world, see the Appendix.

[141] Because at Nuzi recipients of the *kitru* gift are usually already heirs, Paradise ("Nuzi Inheritance Practices," 250) rejects Koschaker's comparison of the *kitru* gift to Roman legacies (in Koschaker, "Drei Rechtsurkunden," 190).

[142] On the universal *diathēkē* with *eispoiēsis* or testamentary adoption, see Chapter 3.

the *diathēkē* without *eispoiēsis* (=without adoption),[143] or *Legatentestament*, the donor transfers only a specific right or good to the recipient.[144] Similar forms of gifting, available in Sparta and Gortyn, are considered in detail in Chapter 3. Significantly, however, a clear terminological distinction between inheriting and gifting is not always discernible among these documents.[145] In addition, as in the ancient Near East, the gift is not subject to claims by the heirs as part of the estate,[146] and there is no act of acquisition.[147] Two of the major features of the tannaitic distinction between gifting and inheriting, therefore, the terminological distinction and the bilateralness of gifting, are not paralleled in biblical, ancient Near Eastern, or Greek legal material. A comparison with Roman law, however, yields rich parallels. Indeed, both Roman and tannaitic law maintain a terminological distinction between gifting and inheriting, and both require acts of acquisition for the former. Below is a summary of the Roman legal institutions followed by a discussion of the overlap between Roman and tannaitic law.

In Roman law, gifts from the inheritance transfer only a right or a good without obligations and,[148] as in the other traditions reviewed previously, are not subject to the claims of heirs.[149] The transfer of such gifts, whether a *donatio mortis causa* (deathbed bequest),[150] or a *legatum* (legacy),[151] function generally under the rubric of the law of gifts, or *donatio*,[152] requiring both an act of acquisition and the pronouncement of terminology specific to gifting. Accordingly, the *legatum* (*per vindicationem*),[153] for example, is effected by the donor employing specific gifting terminology, as discussed by Gaius (*Institutes*, 2:193):

---

[143] On the dating of gifting practices, see Asheri, "Laws of Inheritance," 9; Ste. Croix, "Athenian Family Law," 390.

[144] Avramović, "Differences of Substance," 9–18. As this article is in Serbian Cyrillic, I thank the author for providing me with the journal's English summaries and for discussing the contents of the article with me. Also on Greek gifts without liabilities, see Asheri, "Laws of Inheritance," 10.

[145] See Yaron, *Gifts*, 34; and Rubinstein, *Adoption*, 86 n. 58.

[146] Asheri, "Laws of Inheritance," 10.

[147] See n. 119.

[148] Buckland, *Text-Book of Roman Law*, 334.

[149] Nicholas, *Introduction to Roman Law*, 260.

[150] For a detailed discussion of *donatio mortis causa* and its parallels, see the Appendix.

[151] The *legatum* and the *donatio mortis causa* achieve similar goals although they are executed in different ways. For example, the execution of a *legatum* requires listing in a testament. The *donatio mortis causa*, however, originally made only in contemplation of death as the result of a specific eventuality, enables gifting out of the inheritance without the requirement of writing a testament, among other things. On all this, see Nicholas, *Introduction to Roman Law*, 266–267.

[152] Accordingly, *donatio inter vivos* and *donatio mortis causa* are ordered one after the other in *The Digest of Justinian* under the titles, *De Donationibus* and *De Mortis Causa Donationibus et Capionibus*, respectively; so, too, see the order in Buckland, *Text-Book of Roman Law*, 253–258.

[153] On the different types of legacies, see Buckland, *Text-Book of Roman Law*, 335–336; Nicholas, *Introduction to Roman Law*, 264–266.

This is how we make a proprietary legacy: "To Titius I give and bequeath," for example, "the slave Stichus"; but even if either word is used, for instance, "I give" or "I bequeath," this is equally a proprietary legacy; again, the majority would consider "let him take" or "let him have for himself" or "let him accept" as being equally a proprietary legacy.[154]

For gifting, Gaius promotes the specific formula, *do* lego,[155] "I *give* and bequeath," the latter word from the verb *legare*, the noun *legatum* being derived from it. Alan Watson argues that in classical Latin, "[t]he verb is not used to denote the institution of an heir, and the noun is not used to designate the deceased's property in general or the part of it which goes to the heir."[156] That is, *legare/legatum* is specifically employed for the leaving of legacies (= gifts) and not for the institution of an heir (=universal inheritance),[157] the terminology for which is discussed in Chapter 3. Gifting terminology is specific to gifting whereas inheriting terminology is specific to inheriting, as in tannaitic law (even when testacy is considered ineffective and illegal).[158] Moreover, the words *mattanah* and *yerushah* seem to be Hebrew renditions of the Latin *donatio* and *hereditas*,[159] respectively. By this I do not mean, of course, that the Hebrew terms, *mattanah* and *yerushah* etymologically originate from the Latin. To be sure, both *mattanah* and *yerushah* exist in the classical Hebrew lexicon before the tannaim come into contact with the terms employed in Roman inheritance law. The choice of the tannaim to employ the terms *mattanah* and *yerushah* for inheritance procedures, however, likely occurs due to the presence of the Roman legal terms *donatio* and *hereditas*. As pointed out, the parallel functions not only linguistically. *Hereditas* falls on the heir intestate unilaterally as *yerushah* does in tannaitic law. The Roman gift, like the tannaitic *mattanah*, is a bilateral arrangement, which transfers to the donee through an act of acquisition. It may be that the rabbis also draw

---

154 Gordon and Robinson, *Institutes of Gaius*, 101 and 219.

155 The phrase is preserved in the Greco-Roman papyri from Egypt as well; see Taubenschlag, *Law*, 147.

156 Watson, *Rome of the XII Tables*, 59. Note that despite its use of *legare*, "uti *legassit* super familia," V:3 (638), is understood by the classical sources as referring to disposing of property through testament and not legacy (see Crawford, *Roman Statutes*, 639). However, based in part on this text, it is argued that perhaps the earliest forms of "testament" only contain legacies and not the appointment of a universal successor. For a discussion, see Jolowicz, *Historical Introduction*, 129–130. See also the discussion in Watson, *Rome of the XII Tables*, 59–61. Compare also the overlap between the formula for gifting (2:193; 101 and 219), *do lego*, "I *give* and bequeath," and the formula for bequeathing inheritance in the *testamentum* (2:104; 78 and 173), *ita do ita lego ita testor*, "I thus *give*, I thus *bequeath*, I thus attest." Rabinowitz in "Neo-Babylonian Legal Documents and Jewish Law," 164 sees in these formulaic ambiguities reason to assume that by the time of Gaius, the terminological differences for gifting versus engaging in testate succession are void. See also the next note.

157 The formula for which is, *Titivs heres esto*,' "Let Titius be heir," (*Gaius*, 2:117; 81 and 179).

158 See above my discussion of the sections of *mBB* 8:5 that prohibit forms of testate succession and Chapter 3.

159 For a summary of the differences between *legatum* and *donatio,* see de Colquhoun, *Summary of Roman Civil Law*, 2:118–119.

from Roman law its requirement for an act of acquisition.[160] If they do, they do not also adopt the methods of acquisition in Roman law because there is no need to.[161] The tannaitic laws of sale of property already contain methods of acquisition from which to draw into the legal context of inheritance.[162]

Conclusions

Although the notions of gifting, inheriting, and universal succession in tannaitic law originate in the shared context of ancient law, it is the Roman law of succession that provides the closest parallels to both the terminological and the legal-conceptual opposition evidenced in tannaitic literature by the terms gifting and inheriting. The choice of the tannaim to employ the opposing categories *mattanah* and *yerushah* apparently was made under the influence of Roman inheritance terminology,[163] namely, *donatio* and *hereditas*. Not only are the Hebrew terms equivalent to the Latin;[164] in both Roman and tannaitic law, gifting is bilateral, requiring an act of acquisition, a circumstance that may suggest the impact of Roman methods of implementation. If the latter suggestion is correct, though, the tannaim did not borrow from Roman law its methods of acquisition, preferring simply to use those already available in the area of property sales. However, the laws of the tannaim do not attest only to the rabbis' inclusion of terms and concepts they observe and absorb from the greater legal context around them. Through the possibilities for partibility that they promote, including gifting and (in one tradition) even testate succession among sons, the

[160] The other possibility is that Roman law affects Jewish legal usage even outside of rabbinic circles and that the rabbis simply adopt what they observe. There is no evidence, however, for the usage outside of rabbinic circles in tannaitic Palestine. In Chapter 5, though, I argue that, based on evidence from the Judean desert showing what non-rabbis did, the rabbis may have adopted and further developed traditions about inheritance by widows that they may have witnessed.

[161] On *traditio*, see Gordon and Robinson, *Institutes of Gaius*, 57–58 and 131–132 (2:18–20); for a summary of the procedure, see Nicholas, *Introduction to Roman Law*, 117–120; on *traditio* and *meshikha*, see B. Cohen, *Jewish and Roman Law*, 465. On *mancipatio*, see Gordon and Robinson, *Institutes of Gaius*, 31–32 and 79–81 (1:119–121); also see the comments on *mancipatio* of a legacy *per vindicationem* of certain kinds of property in Daube, "Mancipatio of *rec nec mancipi*," 35–38; for a general discussion of *mancipatio*, see Nicholas, *Introduction to Roman Law*, 63. On *in iure cessio*, see Gordon and Robinson, *Institutes of Gaius*, 58–59 and 133–135 (2:24–25); for a general description of *in iure cessio*, see Nicholas, *Introduction to Roman law*, 63–64.

[162] See the discussion in the Introduction to this chapter.

[163] See directly above, at the end of the previous section, where I lay out the nature of the influence I mention here.

[164] In fact, Willem Surenhuys in his 17th-century translation of the Mishnah into Latin seems to concur because he translates pars. III–IV of *m.BB* 8:5 (cited in the original above): "Si vero dixerit, propter *hæreditatem*, nihil dixet fi fcripferit, five in principio five in medio five in fine, propter *dona*, verba illius rata funt" (4:192) [italics mine].

tannaim may affirm the impact of the specific social and economic reality around them – the combined conditions of the nuclear family along with privatized and urbanized landholding patterns – on their formulation and categorization of inheritance laws.

CHAPTER 2

Firstborn Inheritance in Tannaitic Law and in the Ancient World

Introduction

In Chapter 1, I argue that one aspect of tannaitic inheritance law that distinguishes it from its biblical precursor is the presence and function of two mechanisms for transferring property in case of death: gifting and inheriting. In the absence of evidence for its hermeneutic underpinnings, I assert that the innovation is not the result of the rabbinic imagination and its penchant for inventive interpretation of Scripture. Rather, it is a consequence of embracing well-attested ancient legal categories and their Roman terms, which are appropriate to the family structure and landholding patterns that the tannaim experience. Undeniably the appropriation of gifting has a major effect, from a legal standpoint, on the (theoretical) transfer of possessions in ways not in accordance with the order of (intestate) succession.[1] One example is the double portion inherited by the firstborn son, the *bekhor*.[2] Although tannaitic law assumes that in cases of intestacy the *bekhor* receives a double portion of inheritance,[3] and, in fact, several tannaitic traditions prohibit deviation from this practice,[4] gifting – in a paraphrase of *mBB* 8:5 par. II – enables one to give much to one and little to another or to make the firstborn equal to his brothers. This *mishnah* explains that a single portion can be gifted to the firstborn and implies that a double portion can be gifted to another son or to no one at all. Also in Chapter 1, using the tools of source criticism and linguistic analysis, I demonstrate that the hitherto concealed original meaning of this paragraph likely refers to testate succession among sons (and not gifting).

However we read it, *mBB* 8:5 features great flexibility regarding the allocation of a firstborn's shares and should be compared to similar ancient legal traditions specifically regarding primogeniture. In this chapter I describe the

[1] See Chapter 1.

[2] On the possibility that in parts of the ancient Near East the distinction of firstborn also may apply to daughters, see Greengus, *Laws* 72 and n. 127.

[3] For example, *mBB* 8:4 states "the [firstborn] son takes a double portion of the father's property" (and not the mother's); see also the sources cited in the next note.

[4] See *mBB* 8:5, par. I, cited in Chapter 1; *Sifre to Deuteronomy*, par. 216 (249, Finkelstein ed.); and Kahana, *Sifre Zuta Deuteronomy*, 305; see also *pBB* 8:5, 16b (1254). Finally, see Hoffmann, *Midrash Tannaim*, 129 (but note the tannaitic provenance of this tradition is in doubt; see my comments in n. 15).

flexibility in this tannaitic tradition as well as flexibility in a number of biblical and ancient Near Eastern sources. Although a clear genetic link between the legal conceptions cannot be established, below I suggest that the presence of a flexible, ancient "local practice," namely, the custom known in the region for millennia from various biblical texts and ancient Near Eastern laws, contributes to the emergence of a flexible approach among some tannaim. However, the development of legal flexibility in each context – the ancient Near Eastern/biblical and the tannaitic – yields two different approaches. In the ancient Near Eastern/biblical model, flexibility necessarily leads to the appointment of another son with firstborn status.[5] In the tannaitic model, flexibility can actually lead to the absence of a "firstborn" at all.

In some parts of the ancient Near East and in some representations in biblical literature, a firstborn has an elevated status within the family and with regard to the family landholdings; in tannaitic literature, generally, a firstborn does not. The flexibility in ancient Near Eastern and biblical law and literature reflects the presumed importance that accompanies the firstborn's position within the extended family on its jointly owned estate.[6] Indeed, the context demands that there be a firstborn; for, being the firstborn is as much about one's status and role within the family as about an additional share of the inheritance. In parts of the ancient Near East, for example, the firstborn's function includes caring for his widowed mother and unmarried siblings in the household, ensuring the proper burial of the parents, and performing cultic rituals after their death,[7] all duties that justify the firstborn's extra inheritance.

Based on the biblical evidence against its ancient Near Eastern background, Raymond Westbrook argues that after the death of a patriarch in ancient Israel, the firstborn becomes the administrator of the *bet av* (the extended family estate).[8] The firstborn holds this position indefinitely and until such time that the heirs deem it necessary to divide the inheritance.[9] Westbrook contends that due to the importance of the task of family administrator, at times a son other than the biological firstborn receives the double portion and is appointed "firstborn" to head the family estate, a situation central to the patriarchal narratives in the biblical book of Genesis. Whether we accept Westbrook's assumptions about the historicity of the biblical evidence or not, his reconstruction and description of the firstborn's role, as presented in biblical literature, certainly seems accurate.

---

[5] I.e., someone eventually receives an extra portion of inheritance and/or the mantle of family leadership.

[6] On different portrayals of the firstborn as privileged in the Bible and the ancient Near East, see Milgrom, "First-Born," 337–338.

[7] According to Bruce Wells, in all likelihood these duties are prevalent in biblical Israel as well ("The Hated Wife," 132).

[8] This is also the case in Egypt; see Westbrook, *Property and Family*, 140; and Pestman, "Law of Succession in Ancient Egypt," 64–65.

[9] Westbrook, *Property and Family*, 140.

Significantly, although obviously the tannaim are aware of the biblical accounts, they do not explicitly build on the storylines in Genesis to buttress their promotion of flexibility in allocating the firstborn's inheritance.[10] That is, the patriarchal narratives in Genesis, replete with raw material for proving the acceptability of reassigning the firstborn's inheritance, are not tapped by the tannaim to innovate on hermeneutic or interpretive grounds. The effect, if any, these narratives have on the rabbis is due to flexibility being representative of local practice, that is, ancient Near Eastern custom for millennia. In addition, the presence of flexibility in *mBB* 8:5 may be related in part to the social and economic conditions experienced by the rabbis; that is, the tannaim may construct laws that make sense for their social and economic contexts.

In general, tannaitic law and literature do not address the *bekhor*'s leadership function within the framework of the family.[11] There is, in fact, no need for a firstborn, and, perhaps, the developments in tannaitic law can be seen, in part, as brought on by social and economic conditions specific to tannaitic Palestine. The predominant situation known to the tannaim is the nuclear family residing on privately owned partible land and in urban centers. Certainly for the tannaim who defend the redistribution of the double portion, the capacity to do so – like the ability to regulate any inheritance share – attests to the centrality of partibility to the tannaitic complex of inheritance laws. More than just that, however, the flexibility to reallocate the firstborn's inheritance may be connected to the fact that the *bekhor* has no unique place as administrator of an extended family estate. In these ways – the family structure and landholding patterns coupled with the lack of leadership for the *bekhor* – the tannaitic household with its corresponding property coincides more closely with contemporaneous Greek and Roman households, in which the firstborn has no right or role, than with its biblical forerunner.[12]

---

[10] There is no extant tannaitic midrash for Genesis. The relevant tannaitic traditions on the Genesis narratives are collected in Mirsky, *Midrash Tannaim Livreshit*, 144, 150, 161, 192, 196, 199, 200.

[11] See *mBB* 8:3 (=*Sifre to Numbers* 134); 8:4 (cf. *Sifre to Deuteronomy*, par. 215 [247–249, Finkelstein ed.]); 8:5; *tBB* 7:7, 7:11–12; *tBekh* 6:16, 6:18; *tSot* 6:6. The only possible exception is in *tShek* 2:15 and similar conceptual parallels (such as *Sifre to Deuteronomy*, 162 [212–213, Finkelstein ed.]), which discuss the transfer of leadership such as kingship and priesthood and related duties, from a man to his next of kin. The Tosefta there states, "whoever takes precedence in inheritance takes precedence in positions of authority." Presumably, the firstborn would inherit a role of leadership before another son. On these sources, see Alon, "Beneihem shel Ḥakhamim," 91. See also my comments in Chapter 1 n. 6. However, for a bibliography on, and critique of, the assumption that the Patriarchate is passed from father to firstborn son, see Appelbaum, "Rabbi's Successors," 3–11. On a cryptic tannaitic tradition that may have echoes of the role of the *bekhor* in his deceased father's household, see the comments of Menahem Kahana in *Sifre Zuta Deuteronomy*, 306–308.

[12] See in the Introduction the section titled, "On the Relationship of Inheritance Laws to Presumed Social and Economic Settings in the Bible and Tannaitic Literature."

In summary, several combined elements may contribute to the development of a flexible approach to the firstborn's inheritance in tannaitic law. These include the adoption of gifting as a method for transferring property in case of death and the lack of priority for primogeniture among the traditions of the Greeks and Romans. Furthermore, the presence of the local practice of flexibility toward the *bekhor*'s inheritance (as represented in some biblical and ancient Near Eastern sources) combined with the absence of a defined role for the firstborn within the tannaitic household and its realty, may together enable the emergence of legal flexibility among the tannaim.

The Tannaitic Sources

In my discussion of *mBB* 8:5 in Chapter 1, I offer two interpretations of its second paragraph. I base the first explanation, namely, that the firstborn's double portion, like the single portion of every other son, can be reallocated through gifting, on a reading of the text of *mBB* 8:5 in its final redacted form.[13] I base the second elucidation on a philological-historical investigation in which I isolate paragraph II of the *mishnah* as an independent tradition. The conclusion is that a concealed tannaitic opinion, revealed through the process of critical analysis, originally proposes the reallocation of the sons' portions – including the firstborn's double portion – through testate succession among sons.[14] The *mishnah* is explicit that one can grant the firstborn a single inheritance share as inheritance, and not as gift ("made the firstborn equal to them"), and implicit that one can gift the double portion to a non-firstborn son ("gave much to one and little to another") as an inheritance as well. My suggestion that the assignment of inheritance portions, including the firstborn's, can be accomplished through testate succession among sons is restricted to this interpretation of *mBB* 8:5.

In light of the absence of recoverable tannaitic scriptural interpretation supporting legal flexibility for the allocation of the firstborn's double portion, [15] the search for antecedents and parallels across the legal traditions of the ancient world provides meaningful evidence to suggest the origins of the tannaitic tendency. Furthermore, an appreciation of the social and economic settings in which tannaitic laws and customs are produced may provide a framework for realizing the complex interplay between the production of this tannaitic tradition and

[13] This is already pointed out in the Palestinian Talmud, *pBB* 8:4, 16b (1254).

[14] See Chapter 1 and "Abbreviations, Terminology, and Transliteration."

[15] The one tradition in Hoffmann, *Midrash Tannaim*, 129, that might be interpreted along similar lines is likely not of tannaitic origin. An exposition on Deut. 21:16, one verse in a cluster (21:15–17) dealing specifically with the firstborn's double portion, is suspect due to its use of the phrase *kegon she'amar*, barely attested in tannaitic midrash, and wording paralleled in *bBB* 130a. I thank Menahem Kahana for his assistance in dealing with the question of the tannaitic provenance of this text.

the society in which it is formulated. We begin with the evidence from biblical literature and then move on to the ancient Near East.

The Firstborn in the Bible

An examination of the literary evidence in the Bible provides important information. The flexibility featured in biblical literature may be the result of the role of the firstborn son within the presumed extended family on its jointly held estate. Biblical inheritance law prefers an undivided inheritance, an economically beneficial arrangement in the premised agrarian society of biblical literature,[16] with an administrator, usually the firstborn, at the head (see below). This concept dictates that heirs to the decedent jointly own and work ancestral property and, if a division of the estate takes place,[17] the joint ownership ends.

The concept of an undivided inheritance is actually evidenced in some societies in the ancient Near East; and Westbrook,[18] in his study of the institution, specifically highlights the firstborn's function (or that of his appointed replacement) in biblical literature and, hence, according to his view, in Israelite society. The firstborn son is the administrator of the jointly owned property.[19] The work of Karel van der Toorn on the biblical term *bet av* affirms the structure of the extended family unit that resides on the family estate according to biblical literary testimony. Van der Toorn goes further, arguing that the textual, archeological, and ethno-archeological evidence combined suggests that the historical Israelite *bet av* is, in fact, an extended family unit consisting of several houses within close physical proximity.[20] Each contains a nuclear family in which everyone resides under the leadership of a father figure or, in his absence, the firstborn son.[21]

Whether or not we accept Westbrook and van der Toorn's assumptions about the relationship of the biblical texts to historical Israelite reality, there are actually two intertwined aspects to the portrayal of the firstborn in the Bible: receipt

---

[16] Brin, *Studies*, 250.

[17] The division is, presumably, in accordance with the biblical laws of intestate succession.

[18] See Westbrook, *Property and Family*, 118–141.

[19] So, too, in Egypt; see n. 8.

[20] Van der Toorn suggests that archeological evidence from ancient Mesopotamia may support the contention that extended families actually lived under one roof. Spacious homes, from Fara and Abu Salabiḫ specifically, were large enough to house an extended family and would have been under the authority of a single male leader who would bequeath the leadership to his eldest son (van der Toorn, *Family Religion*, 24). See also the detailed discussion of the make up of ancient Mesopotamian households in Gelb, "Household and Family," 1–98, and specific mention of the firstborn's role (Gelb, "Household and Family," 58). See also the section entitled "On the Textual and Archeological Evidence for the Presumed Family Structure and Landholding Patterns in the Bible and Tannaitic Literature" in the Introduction.

[21] Van der Toorn, *Family Religion*, 194–199. See also Stager, "Archaeology of the Family," 18–23.

of the mantle of family leadership and, in addition, acquisition of a double inheritance portion. Both biblical law and narrative address these two facets of the *bekhor*'s role. Deuteronomy 21:15–17, for example, treats the receipt of the double portion by the rightful firstborn:

If a man has two wives, one loved and the other unloved, and both the loved and the unloved have borne him sons, but the firstborn is the son of the unloved one – on the day he distributes (*beyom hanḥilo*) his property to his sons,[22] he may not treat as firstborn the son of the loved one in disregard of the son of the unloved one who is older. Instead, he must accept the firstborn, the son of the unloved one, and allot to him a double portion (=*pi shenayim*)[23] of all he possesses; since he is the first fruit of his vigor, the birthright is his due.[24]

Certainly, according to these verses a father must preserve the double portion of the firstborn and the single portions of each other son (in accordance with the implied practices of intestate succession).[25] A father is empowered only regarding the allocation of the specific fields each son receives – what is known in law as the right of distribution[26] – but not concerning the ultimate size of each lot. Alternatively, it may be that even though a father may prefer one wife over another, he cannot circumvent giving the firstborn a double portion; he can reassign it only based on a preference for one son over another.[27]

Here in Deuteronomy nothing more is added regarding the matter. Elsewhere, such as in the patriarchal narratives in Genesis, however, despite the absence of explicit mention of the *bekhor*'s double portion, family feuds about who is the rightful firstborn – over the course of three generations – appear. In each case a non-firstborn (to the father; see below) prevails. Admittedly, the relationship of Deuteronomy's laws to the patriarchal narratives, however we interpret them, is

---

[22] The root *n-ḥ-l* in the causative (*hifil*) in biblical Hebrew refers specifically to the power to allocate inheritance portions (Lipinski, "Naḥal," 322; cf. Hiers, "Transfer of Property," 148). Compare the use in Ezek. 46:18 and Prov. 13:22. See also Chapter 1.

[23] Ancient translations (LXX, Vulgate, Peshitta, Onkelos, and Pseudo-Jonathan) of Deut. 21:17 and rabbinic literature (*bBB* 118b–119a and 122b–123a) fix the meaning of *pi shenayim* as double portion, i. e., two portions of the estate (so, too, Ben Sira, Philo, and Josephus; see Tigay, *Deuteronomy*, 382 n. 43). The phrase is the topic of considerable discussion due to its possible meaning in Zech. 13:8 as "two-thirds." For a full treatment including ancient Mesopotamian parallels, see Davies, "The Meaning of Pi Šenayim," 341–347. See also Brin's discussion and bibliography in Brin, *Studies*, 240–245, where he points to ancient Mesopotamian and Egyptian sources.

[24] Contra Hiers, "Transfer of Property," 146, who writes that the Deuteronomy "text does not use the expression 'birthright'." The final word in Deut. 21:17, *bekhorah*, may be accurately translated "birthright." See, among others, Brin, *Studies*, 238.

[25] Yaron, *Gifts*, 9; Brin, "First-Born," 261; Goldin, "Youngest Son," 31; Brin, *Studies*, 252; Rofé, *Deuteronomy*, 188.

[26] See "Abbreviations, Terminology, and Transliteration."

[27] Thompson, *Patriarchal Narratives*, 291; Tigay, *Deuteronomy*, 195; Westbrook, *Property and Family*, 20 and 136 n. 2; Wells, "Hated Wife," 134–135. Cf. Hiers, "Transfer of Property," 146.

a complex one.[28] Indeed, the narratives may not be representative at all of what later comes to be considered biblical law (in Deuteronomy). Still, it remains significant that in the patriarchal narratives, to which we now turn, the role of the firstborn son, unique to his station as family leader, is central and simultaneously flexibly transferred.

In the first narrative to be considered, Abraham's wife Sarah, in an effort to provide a son for her husband, offers him her maidservant Hagar. By Abraham cohabiting with Hagar, Sarah will bear a child through her and a legitimate son and successor for the patriarch,[29] his son Ishmael.[30] Subsequently, however, Sarah herself bears Abraham a son, Isaac, and urges Abraham to cast out Hagar and Ishmael (Gen. 21:10).[31] Abraham gives all that he has to Isaac (Gen. 24:36 and 25:5) and gives gifts to the sons of his concubines (Gen. 25:6). Furthermore, although Ishmael is legally entitled to share in the inheritance,[32] he is cast out (Gen. 21:12) and seemingly disinherited.[33] By choosing to designate one son as successor, effectively disinheriting the firstborn, and gifting to the sons of concubines, this narrative reflects the patriarch's general right to dispose of his assets freely[34] and replace his biological firstborn.[35]

The story of the next generation, about Isaac and Rebecca's children Esau and Jacob, shows how two sons from the same wife compete for the rights of the firstborn. Two episodes describe how Jacob, the younger of the twins, comes to be considered the firstborn. In the first account, Esau, the older of the twins, sells his birthright (more precisely defined below) to his younger brother in exchange for lentil stew:

---

[28] See, e.g., the comments in Levenson, *Death and Resurrection*, 55–56. On the canonical treatment, see Cover, "Nomos and Narrative."

[29] Contra Thompson, *Patriarchal Narratives*, 255. Note Sarah's language in Gen. 16:2, "Look, the Lord has kept me from bearing. Consort with my maid; perhaps *I* shall have a son *through her*"; in "Some Cases," 193, Feigin sees in this verse the adoption of Ishmael by Sarah. See the next note, and on adoption, Chapter 3.

[30] Cf. the language in Gen. 17:23, 17:25, 21:11, 25:9, and 25:12. Abraham's naming of Ishmael (16:15) (rather than Hagar naming the child) may represent an act of legitimation (adoption by a family member). On the legitimation of Ishmael by Abraham, see Thompson, *Patriarchal Narratives*, 257; and Marcus, "Legal Dispute," 107. See also de Vaux, *Ancient Israel*, 1:53. For more on legitimation in the Bible, see Chapter 3.

[31] Either Sarah does not want Ishmael to succeed to the family leadership together with Isaac, or she does not want Ishmael to take exclusive possession of the leadership she believes is rightfully Isaac's.

[32] Marcus, "Legal Dispute," 107; cf. Sarna, *Genesis*, 146–147. See also Bird, "YRŠ," 215.

[33] On the fact that Ishmael would have inherited if he had not been cast out, see Marcus, "Legal Dispute," 107.

[34] See Yaron, *Gifts*, 4–5, 10; Hiers, "Transfer of Property," 148.

[35] For a discussion of whether Isaac and Ishmael are of the same rank or whether Isaac, by virtue of being born to the primary wife, automatically has a higher status than Ishmael, see Yaron, *Gifts*, 4; Falk, "Testate Succession," 72; van Seters, *Abraham in History*, 88; Brin, "Transfer of Hegemony," 49 n. 10; Frymer-Kensky, "Patriarchal Family Relationships," 213–214.

Once when Jacob was cooking a stew, Esau came in from the open, famished. And Esau said to Jacob, "Give me some of that red stuff to gulp down for I am famished." ... Jacob said, "First sell me your birthright." And Esau said, "I am at the point of death, so of what use is my birthright to me?" But Jacob said, "Swear to me first." So he swore to him and sold his birthright to Jacob. Jacob then gave Esau bread and lentil stew; he ate and drank, and he rose and went away. Thus did Esau spurn his birthright. (Gen. 25:29–34)

The background to these verses seems to be one in which, with great facility, the birthright is transferred from one brother to another. In a second episode (27:29), Jacob deceives his father in order to receive the firstborn's blessing intended for Esau. Westbrook suggests a legal interpretation: the first literary piece deals with the sale of Esau's extra inheritance portion whereas the second segment refers to the blessing that transfers the family leadership from father to son.[36] Whether we accept Westbrook's interpretation or not, it is clear that the Esau and Jacob traditions, too, like those about Ishmael and Isaac, showcase an inherent flexibility about the transfer of the firstborn's position and privilege.

The third storyline I consider here is no less informative than the previous two. It is Jacob himself, in the next generation, who takes the right and rank of the firstborn away from his firstborn son Reuben and transfers them to his children and grandchildren. Here, unlike in the other accounts, however, the rightful firstborn is punished, demoted as a consequence. Indeed, Reuben, the firstborn of Jacob from his wife Leah, is cursed by his father and stripped of his rights as firstborn (Gen. 49:3–4) for having lain with Jacob's concubine Bilhah (Gen. 35:22).[37] Westbrook argues that the punishment includes having his double portion and his status as family leader taken away.[38] The double portion is transferred to Joseph,[39] the favorite son from Jacob's preferred wife Rachel,[40] through Joseph's children Ephraim and Manasseh.[41] As implied by Gen. 48:5, Ephraim and Manasseh each receive the full portion of a son. The family leadership, however, is transferred to Judah, "You, O Judah, your brothers shall praise; ... Your father's sons shall bow low to you" (Gen. 49:8).[42]

---

[36] Westbrook, *Property and Family*, 137.

[37] Cf. 1 Chron. 5:1.

[38] Westbrook, *Property and Family*, 136.

[39] This may be the meaning of the phrase "one more portion than your brothers" (=*shkhem aḥad al aḥekha*) in Gen. 48:22. This understanding is preserved in the Targumim, Peshitta, and Vulgate; see also 1 Chron. 5:1; Jub. 45:14–15; and *Sifre to Deuteronomy*, par. 217 (250, Finkelstein ed.); Mendelsohn, "Preferential Status," 39 n. 9 (however, on Mendelsohn, see Brin, *Studies*, 238 n. 1); Yaron, *Gifts*, 9 n. 3; Brin, "Birthright," 1–4; Sarna, *Genesis*, 330 n. 10.

[40] On the language in Genesis, "Jacob 'loved Rachel more than Leah,' who was 'unloved' (Gen 29:30–31)" as reminiscent of the formulations in Deut. 21:15–17 (cited above in the body), see Levenson, *Death and Resurrection*, 55.

[41] See Josh. 14:4 and 17:14–18 where the tribes of Ephraim and Manasseh each receive a portion of the inheritance of the land when the tribes divide the Promised Land; and on this Westbrook, *Property and Family*, 136.

[42] Westbrook, *Property and Family*, 136.

Regardless of whether we fully accept Westbrook's interpretation or not, these three episodes express a fundamental flexibility concerning the transfer of a firstborn's portion and position to another.[43] And although it is clear that in each case the focus is a fight over the status of a father's firstborn son, Jon D. Levenson correctly reminds us, at least regarding Isaac and Joseph,[44] that each of these sons is a firstborn to his respective mother, suggesting that "Israelite primogeniture may at some time have involved matrilineal factors" as well.[45] Nevertheless, the practice presented in all three stories, reassignment of the firstborn to the *father*, is the one that is recognized throughout the ancient Near East, the cultural and literary landscape from which these narratives themselves claim provenance.[46]

The Ancient Near East

The privileged status of the firstborn and his receipt of an extra share of inheritance are traditions that are widespread in the ancient Near East,[47] as is the seemingly built-in flexibility to designate his replacement. Indeed, a major feature of a father's right to dispose of his property[48] is his ability to assign the firstborn's

---

[43] On two other biblical examples, 1 Chron. 26:10–11 and 2 Chron. 11:22, see Brin, *Studies*, 258–259.

[44] Levenson, *Death and Resurrection*, 56. On the rights of children from different mothers in ancient Near Eastern law, see Greengus, *Laws*, 72.

[45] On other matters of social rank by mother as related to the Genesis narratives and the ancient Near East, see Greengus, Laws, 77–79.

[46] The bibliography is vast, and the following is merely a sampling: Speiser, "New Kirkuk Documents," 48; Speiser, "Ethnic Movements," 44; Gordon, "Biblical Customs," 1–12; Paul, "The Patriarchate," 23–28. For a bibliography until its date of publication, see Thompson, *Patriarchal Narratives*, 280–285; see also Frymer-Kensky, "Patriarchal Family"; Westbrook, *Property and Family*,118–141.

[47] It may be that already in the Neo-Sumerian period the firstborn son received a larger portion of inheritance. A tablet involving the family of the *ugula* [=overseer] of the Inanna temple at Nippur deals with redistribution of inheritance and makes mention of the distinctions between the "eldest brother," *dumu šeš-gal* and the "younger brother," *dumu šeš-bàn-da*. On this translation, see Roth, "A Reassessment," 9 [= B. Lafont, "Les textes judiciaires," 49, no. 9]. See also text no. 12 in Falkenstein, *Die Neusumerischen Gerichtsurkunden*, 17–19, where one son receives a larger portion than his brothers. On this, see Bertrand and Lafont, "Neo-Sumerian Period (Ur III)," 207. The earliest clear designation of such in Mesopotamia, however, is only later (see the examples in the body of the text). See also some parallels listed in Greengus, *Laws*, 72–73.

[48] On the Neo-Sumerian period, see Roth, "Reassessment"; on the Old Babylonian period, see Laws of Lipit Ishtar 31 (Roth, *Law Collections*, 32) and Laws of Hammurabi 165 (Roth, *Law Collections*, 112); on the Old Assyrian period, see Veenhof, "Old Assyrian Period," 458; on the Middle Assyrian period, see Wilcke, "Assyrische Testamente," 198–199 and 201; on Nuzi, see Paradise, "Nuzi Inheritance Practices," 261–262; on the Neo-Babylonian period, see texts no. 34 and 36 in Wunsch, *Urkunden*, 112–115 and 120–121; on Emar, see text no. 186 in Arnaud, "Les hittites," 23; on Alalakh, see text no. 87 in Wiseman, *Alalakh Tablets*, no. 2, 53–54; on Ugarit, see Marquez Rowe, "Anatolia and the Levant," 729–730.

title,[49] status, and extra inheritance portion to a son other than the biological firstborn. According to evidence from the Old Babylonian period,[50] for example, a father can give the rights of the firstborn to another son or even an adoptee, as verified in a text from Mari:[51]

(If) Hillalum and Alitum should acquire (by adoption) many more sons, Iahatti-Il alone (is principal) heir, from the estate of Hillalum, his father, two (shares) he shall take. His younger brothers shall divide (the remainder of the inheritance), brother like brother (i. e., in equal shares).[52]

A Middle Babylonian period adoption/inheritance text from Hana declares that an adopted son is elected the eldest, entitling him to receive two inheritance shares, "Igmil-Dagan is the senior child and will enjoy two inheritance shares."[53] At Nuzi, a father removes a firstborn son from the position of primary heir and gives the double portion to another biological son, not yet born from a different wife:

Thus declares Zigi: If Šuwarhepa bears sons, then the eldest son of Šuwarhepa (shall be) as my eldest son. When he takes the (inheritance) portion, he shall take a double portion; and the remaining sons of Šuwarhepa shall take a single portion with the remaining sons of Zigi in their order of succession.[54]

At Alalakh a contract for a marriage settlement between Iri-halpa and his betrothed Naidu states:

If Naidu does not give birth to a son (then) the daughter of his brother Iwashshura (i. e., his niece) shall be given (to Iri-halpa as a wife); if ... (another wife) of Iri-halpa gives birth to a son first and after that Naidu gives birth to a son, the son of Naidu alone shall be the first-born.[55]

---

[49] Brin argues that whereas in the ancient Near East the rights of the firstborn and the title could be transferred, in ancient Israel only the rights could be transferred and not the title *bekhor* (Brin, *Studies*, 252, 259, 261–262; cf. Milgrom, "First-Born," 338).

[50] According to the Laws of Hammurabi (170), the firstborn selects his share of inheritance first. Westbrook says this refers to choosing an extra share of the property, not just the order in which he chooses (Westbrook, "Mesopotamia," 396); cf. the procedure found in the Middle Assyrian Laws where "the oldest son shall select and take a double share" (Roth, *Law Collections*, 176; see also 191); and see my comments below about the Athenian will of Pasion in n. 63. According to Mendelsohn, "Preferential Status," 40; and Davies, "Inheritance of Firstborn," 179–180, the firstborn choosing first does not refer to an extra share.

[51] There are two separate methods for computing this extra share. Tablets from Nippur, Ur, and Kutulla indicate that the firstborn receives an extra 10 percent of property, whereas tablets from Larsa, Mari, and Kutulla (again) record a double share of property; see Davies, "Inheritance of Firstborn."

[52] Mendelsohn, "Preferential Status," 38. For more on adoption, see Chapter 3.

[53] Podany, Beckman, and Colbow, "Adoption," 47.

[54] *Harvard Semitic Series* IX 24 cited in Paradise, "Nuzi Inheritance Practices," 260.

[55] Mendelsohn, "Preferential Status," 38. Wiseman translates as follows: "If Naidu has not borne an heir, the daughter of (his)? brother Iwaššura shall be given. If Irihalpa has earlier (sons

This text affirms a father's ability to disregard the law of primogeniture and to choose a firstborn. Legal texts from Ugarit also display a father transferring the extra share of the firstborn to another son or adoptee.[56] And, while it is unclear whether the firstborn has any special inheritance rights at Elephantine,[57] a father's right to allocate as he wishes may be inferred from the fact that the papyri include methods for bequeathing, even to people (presumably) outside of the regular order of succession.[58]

Ancient Near Eastern inheritance traditions provide a father with a right to reassign a firstborn's extra inheritance portion and accompanying rights and to grant a biological firstborn a single portion. If taken at face value, the demotion seemingly is adopted in biblical literature as well. Although in the case of the firstborn the dependence of the tannaim on antecedents from biblical and ancient Near Eastern sources cannot be definitively known, legal flexibility regarding a firstborn's extra inheritance is, seemingly, the local practice for centuries in the region and in all likelihood the tannaim were aware of it. Certainly the biblical narratives are familiar to them but despite this awareness, those tannaim who espouse flexibility regarding a firstborn's double portion do not use Scripture to advocate their position.[59] In the final analysis, I suggest that the existence of flexibility for allocating the firstborn's double portion in biblical and ancient Near Eastern texts may be one among several factors that lead to a flexible approach in tannaitic law. Two additional ingredients, of course, would be the family structure and landholding conditions in urbanized tannaitic Palestine (see the section entitled, "On the Textual and Archeological Evidence for the Presumed Family Structure and Landholding Patterns in the Bible and Tannaitic Literature" in the Introduction) and the absence of any formal status or supplementary inheritance allotment for the firstborn among the Greeks and Romans.

---

by another) and then Naidu has one Naidu will be the superior," implying that Naidu's son is designated the firstborn heir (Wiseman, *Alalakh Tablets*, 54–55, no. 92).

[56] Thureau-Dangin, "Trois contrats," 249; Rainey, "Family Relationships," 13; Vita, "Society of Ugarit," 481.

[57] Yaron, *Law of the Aramaic Papyri*, 67. However, see Botta, "Elephantine," 575, where the author contends that the fact that the whole Mibtahia archive ends up in the hands of Jedaniah suggests he is the firstborn and has special inheritance rights. See also the Ptolemaic text from Elephantine, in which an unmarried son who supports either of the parents receives a double portion [!]; text D3 in Porten, *Elephantine Papyri in English*, 412–413.

[58] See Chapter 3.

[59] And yet, e.g., mention is made in passing of Joseph's receipt of the double portion in *Sifre to Deuteronomy*, par. 217 (250, Finkelstein ed.) as proof that the phrase "double portion" in biblical texts means two parts and not two-thirds.

Ancient Greece and Rome

The laws of Greece and Rome give no primacy to the firstborn son, not by allocating to him a special status within the family or by granting him a greater portion of inheritance in the event of intestacy. Upon the death of the head of household, there is no framework whereby one immediate heir among several inherits or is appointed to the leadership of an entire household and his fellow heirs. Rather, the norm is the formation of separate households. In Athens, for example, where holding joint property after the death of the *kyrios* (head of household) is the exception,[60] equal division among sons is the practice if one dies intestate.[61] When the *kyrios* dies, the original *oikos* (household) is divided, and each son holds his own *oikos*, becoming its *kyrios*.[62] A father could confer a special advantage on a specific son, however, at times favoring the firstborn. So, for example, Demosthenes writes about Pasion enabling his older son, Apollodorus, to choose first from the significant inheritance he leaves, "[T]hey at once divided between them the bank and the shield-factory, and Apollodorus, having the choice, chose the shield factory in preference to the bank."[63] Pasicles, the second son, takes the bank.

Literature on Spartan inheritance practices,[64] most notably preserved in the writings of Plato, Polybios, and Plutarch, promotes a tradition that in Sparta a system of equal land shares among men obtains.[65] Lycurgus (8th–7th c. BCE) is

[60] MacDowell, *Law in Classical Athens*, 92.

[61] MacDowell, *Law in Classical Athens*, 92. Even in Seleucid Babylonia there is no evidence of the firstborn receiving an extra inheritance portion; see McEwan, "Inheritance in Seleucid Babylonia," 215. This may be due to the Hellenistic practice permeating Babylonian culture.

[62] MacDowell, "*Oikos*," 11. On this model as the ideal legal one in Athens, see Cox, *Household Interests*, 142.

[63] Demosthenes, *For Phormio*, 36.11 (329). The editor of the Loeb edition writes in footnote *b* that Apollodorus has the first choice by "right of seniority." Harrison (*Law of Athens*, 1:131 n. 4), however, argues that "[w]hen in a voluntary division of part of Pasion's estate Apollodoros has first choice between a factory and a bank we can hardly press this as a right secured by his being the elder." Harrison likely minimizes the "first choice" as being indicative of a privilege for the firstborn because Pasion allocates it in a will, and there is no evidence of such a practice in cases of intestacy. Note, however, that first choice is considered the firstborn's privilege in the Laws of Hammurabi (170; see n. 50). Accordingly, the parallel in Demosthenes should be investigated further among other legal and cultural parallels between Mesopotamia and ancient Greece, especially in light of the next two texts: "When he denies the will, ask him this, how it came that he received the lodging-house under the will *as being the elder*" (Demosthenes, *For Phormio*, 36.34 (347)) and "[b]esides, men of Athens, not one of you knows the number of the years, *for I shall say that I am the elder, and he will say that he is*, but you all understand the just way of reckoning," (Demosthenes, *1 Against Boeotos*, 39.29 (469)).

[64] See, generally, MacDowell, *Spartan Law*, 89–110.

[65] I cite the main texts. Plato's ambiguous formulation in *Laws*, 3.684D follows: "Their legislators, in their efforts to establish equality of property … so that they could divide up their land without dispute" (193); Polybius, *Histories*, 6.45.3 states: "The peculiar features of the Spartan state are said to be first the land laws by which no citizen may own more than another,

credited with establishing and implementing a system of equal landholdings for the citizenry of Sparta. The traditions conflict, however, and scholars dispute the ways in which such a system would have functioned and even if it ever existed.[66] Although privilege for primogeniture is not foreign to Sparta when appointing kings,[67] in the area of landholdings and inheritance it seems not to be standard.[68] Plutarch, in his biography of the third-century-BCE king Agis IV, states that "the number of families instituted by Lycurgus was still preserved in the transmission of estates and *father left to son* his inheritance."[69] Plutarch's statement assumes that even with the transfer of landholdings from one generation to the next, the original number of families and corresponding lots remains the same. Although according to Plutarch's single heir system each father could bequeath only to one son, the text does not articulate that the recipient is the firstborn son. In addition, the lack of mention of the firstborn in other texts discussing this system of land division and inheritance strongly suggests that the firstborn in Sparta does not have any privileged status with regard to inheritance.

Although the Law Code of Gortyn documents specific provisions for the division of the jointly owned estate,[70] the eldest son does not have a leadership role or receive an extra portion of inheritance. Sons, in general, do have a privilege, however. For some property they receive two portions each as opposed to daughters who receive one portion each. So states the Law Code of Gortyn without ambiguity, "And in case (the father) should die, ... all the rest of the property shall be fairly divided and the sons, no matter how many, shall each receive two parts, while the daughters, no matter how many, shall each receive one part" (Col. IV, 30–40).[71] The only clear evidence from Greek sources for the firstborn receiving

but all must possess an equal share of the public land" (373); and Plutarch, *Lycurgus*, 8.1.5–7: "A second, and a very bold political measure of Lycurgus, is his redistribution of the land ... he persuaded his fellow-citizens to make one parcel of all their territory and divide it up anew, and to live with one another on a basis of entire uniformity and equality" (227). Furthermore, he writes: "Offspring was not reared at the will of the father, but was taken and carried by him to a place called Lesche, where the elders of the tribes officially examined the infant, and if it was well-built and sturdy, they ordered the father to rear it, *and assigned it one of the nine thousand lots of land*" (255).

[66] For different ways of describing the Spartan system while acknowledging the testimony of all of the texts, see MacDowell, *Spartan Law*, 89–99. For a critique of previous scholarship and an erudite discussion of the possible fictitious nature of the Spartan institutions, see Hodkinson, "Land Tenure," 378–406 (although as per the postscript there, MacDowell's book had not yet been published when Hodkinson wrote his article); see also Hodkinson, *Property and Wealth*, 65–112.

[67] Herodotus, *Histories*, 6.52 (197–199).

[68] There is no mention of it in MacDowell, *Spartan Law*. However, see Asheri, "Sulla Legge di Epitadeo," 66, regarding privileges in the royal house deriving from the principle of primogeniture. For an informative critique of Asheri, see Hodkinson, "Land Tenure," 393 n. 70.

[69] Plutarch, *Agis*, 5.2 (13).

[70] Col. V, 28–34; see the discussion of this text in Westbrook, *Property and Family*, 139.

[71] Willetts, *Law Code of Gortyn*, 42 (for a discussion, see 65–66); and Schaps, "Women in Greek Inheritance Law," 55.

extra inheritance comes from the Greek papyri from Egypt of the Ptolemaic and Roman periods. Scholars attribute this to local Egyptian practice.[72] Although under provisions in the laws of writing a testament, anyone,[73] including the firstborn, could be instituted heir, the Roman law of intestacy does not grant the eldest son any privilege or extra inheritance portions.[74] Upon the death of the *paterfamilias*, the firstborn shares the inheritance equally with all of his brothers and sisters.[75] Even the one documented institution in Roman law, which deals with joint ownership of the estate of a *paterfamilias*[76] after his death, the early form of undivided inheritance in Roman law in which one might expect the firstborn to take on the role of administrator, is by definition a temporary arrangement and does not record the administration of the estate by a single heir. Gaius, in his *Institutes* (3:154a–154b),[77] discusses the Roman legal institution, *ercto non cito* (ownership undivided), already obsolete in his time, in which co-heirs hold the paternal estate in common.[78] This arrangement, unlike the parallel practice documented in biblical literature, enables each heir to act as owner over the whole property and does not include a single heir functioning as administrator.[79] In any case, *ercto non cito* is by definition a temporary and not preferred arrangement, division of the estate being the ultimate goal. Building on the words of Suzanne Dixon who, in her important study, *The Roman Family*, makes the essential point that, "[i]t does not follow from the fact that a Roman *paterfamilias*'s estate could be divided on his death among his wife, his children, and his son's children that all of these people necessarily inhabited the same house,"[80] it goes without saying that the household is not meant to be kept intact. In short, the structure of Greek and Roman households and their accompanying landholdings, like their tannaitic counterparts, are not consonant with the presumed framework of biblical literature's *bet av*.

---

[72] Seidl, "La Preminente Posizione," 192. On the Egyptian customs, see Mattha, "Rights and Duties of the Eldest Son," 113–118. Cf. Pestman, "Succession in Ancient Egypt," 80. See also Taubenschlag, *Law*, 139.

[73] See Chapter 3.

[74] Jolowicz and Nicholas, *Roman Law*, 125–126; Champlin, *Final Judgments*, 11.

[75] Jolowicz and Nicholas, *Roman Law*, 125–126. Nicholas, *Introduction to Roman Law*, 247. J. A. Crook refers to the fact that partibility is incompatible with the concept of the patriarchal joint family and primogeniture; see Crook, "Women in Roman Succession," 80 n. 6.

[76] On the role of the *paterfamilias* in the Roman household, see Saller, *Patriarchy, Property and Death*, 102–132.

[77] Gordon and Robinson, *Institutes of Gaius*, 168–169.

[78] Indeed, according to Saller, later jurists did not envisage the possibility of joint households, even headed by two brothers in *consortium* (*Patriarchy, Property and Death*, 82).

[79] For more on this legal institution, see Westbrook, *Property and Family*, 119.

[80] Dixon, *Roman Family*, 4.

Conclusions

Although the tannaitic laws of intestacy preserve the biblical mandate to grant the firstborn a double portion of inheritance – and some tannaitic sources even forbid adjusting this allocation – tannaitic law generally does not maintain the biblical concept of the *bekhor*'s leadership status within the family. Furthermore, the flexible approach to the apportionment of the firstborn's shares developed in *mBB* 8:5 is not the outcome of innovative scriptural interpretation. The legal flexibility, therefore, may be the result of the convergence of multiple factors: the adoption of gifting as a mechanism for transfer of property in the event of death, the absence of firstborn primacy in Greek and Roman legal writings, the pervasiveness of the nuclear family residing on privatized property in urban centers without a *bekhor* as family leader, and the long-standing local practice of flexibility in the region. However, that local practice of flexibility, reflected in some strata of the Bible and in some ancient Near Eastern sources, is distinct from the later development of tannaitic flexibility. In the earlier model, flexibility leads to the appointment of a "firstborn" because a family leader is required. In the later tannaitic approach, flexibility even leads to the possibility of no recognized "firstborn" at all.[81]

[81] See n. 5.

Chapter 3

Testate Succession in Tannaitic Law and in the Ancient World

Introduction

The discussion in Chapter 1 deals with the following primary elements that characterize tannaitic inheritance law as distinct from its biblical forerunner: partibility, gifting versus inheriting, transferring property to non-family members, and a newly recovered tannaitic opinion permitting testate succession among sons. Chapter 2 examines the implications of some of these factors for disposing of the firstborn's double portion. This chapter deals with an additional feature: testate succession to anyone in the agnatic line, that is, in the paternal line of descendancy (or ascendancy).[1] The promotion of this form of testate succession is attributed to the tanna Rabbi Yoḥanan ben Beroka.

In the ancient world testate succession, like gifting, circumvents the order of intestate succession. It accomplishes the transfer of property in case of death to other family members and, at times, even to strangers. More than just the mere passing on of possessions, however, testate succession also results in the appointment of an heir, a successor to the legal personality[2] of the decedent.[3] Heirs are appointed (often through an oral declaration) and, like their intestate counterparts, succeed universally to the estate of the deceased.[4] Accordingly, heirs

---

[1] Cf. Shilo and Elon, "Succession," 284.

[2] See Chapter 1. In some ancient societies a link also exists between succession to property and posthumous preservation of family sacra and ancestor worship (for a summary, see Driver and Miles, *Babylonian Laws*, 330 n. 4; and the literature cited in n. 65 below). However, this connection does not exist in tannaitic law as Urbach points out in "Inheritance Laws and After-Life," 135. For the implications of this absence, see my comments below in the body of the chapter.

[3] Not all of the legal traditions I discuss here describe succession to the legal personality of the deceased, i. e., universal succession, clearly or explicitly. I mention in the notes when there is lack of clarity, e. g., on the biblical tradition, see n. 27.

[4] In the ancient world, testate succession usually takes effect through an oral declaration. (At times written proof of the oral declaration is required; see, e. g., the citation from the Middle Assyrian laws below in the body of the chapter. In some places the written record eventually replaces the oral declaration). On the ancient Near East, see Westbrook, "Introduction," 58–59; on Greek written dispositions in general and on an oral disposition in particular, see Harrison, *Law of Athens*, 1:153; on Rome, see Buckland, *Text-book of Roman Law*, 284; Nicholas, *Introduction to Roman Law*, 256; and Watson, *Law of Succession*, 11.

inherit both rights and obligations and, unlike donees, "stand in the place" of the decedent, succeeding not only to currently held possessions (*muḥzakim*) but also to contingent assets (*re'uyim*).[5] With the advent of testate succession, therefore, the transfer of rights and obligations no longer relies on the force of the law of intestate succession alone. In the case of tannaitic law, testate succession empowers its adherents with a right previously reserved only for the function of divine law. Indeed, the presence of testate succession in tannaitic law – as another mechanism for dividing the estate – not only supports the thesis argued in Chapters 1 and 2 that tannaitic law promotes partibility, but it also represents the spirit of a context, one in which the selection of a successor – especially in light of the presumed Torah prohibition – is the greatest of freedoms.[6] Similar to gifting, testate succession may be the outcome of the social and economic contexts in which the tannaim find themselves, a place and time in which landholding patterns and family structure shifts to a reality not identifiable with that known from biblical texts. Moreover, the emergence of testate succession in tannaitic law may be an outcome of the contact between the sphere of Roman legal conceptualization and the world of tannaitic legal adaptation. For, as I suggest below, it is the Roman testament to the *sui heredes* – those in the direct line of succession and under the control of the head of household – that most closely resembles tannaitic testate succession among agnates.

Viable antecedents are not found in biblical law and literature, apocryphal narratives, ancient Near Eastern law, Greek law, or the Judean desert and Elephantine papyri. Biblical works exhibit a limited form of testate succession – if any at all – and apocryphal works together with the Elephantine papyri display too expansive a definition of who is eligible for appointment as a "family" heir (the eligible include relatives through marriage). Ancient Near Eastern and Athenian law require adoption into sonship to transfer inheritance *qua* inheritance, but adoption is a mechanism not evidenced in tannaitic law at all.[7] In Roman law,

---

[5] On the concept of "standing in the place of" and the right to contingent assets (*re'uyim*), see Chapter 1.

[6] The existence of a tannaitic approach promoting testate succession among agnates implies, along with its corollary testate succession among sons examined in Chapter 1, that mechanisms for the transfer of property exclusively for after death (i. e., without the accompanying transfer of any property during the lifetime of the donor/testator as well) are, at least according to some tannaim, permissible. Some scholars assume that Jewish law prefers practices whereby the transfer of some of the property, or some rights to it, is accomplished during the lifetime of the donor/testator (the remainder following after the death of the donor/testator). See Chapter 1 n. 61 and the Appendix n. 54.

[7] In fact, the Spanish scholar of Roman law Ursicino Álvarez Suárez concludes that the lack of influence of ancient systems of law on rabbinic law is exemplified by the fact that adoption, so prevalent in the ancient world, is not embraced by the rabbis, "[N]o es posible afirmar la existencia indudable de los influjos pretendidos, y más bien las características y autonomía del Derecho judío hablan en contra de ellos (por ejemplo, ausencia de la adopción)" (*Horizonte actual del derecho romano*, 191).

however, Rabbi Yoḥanan ben Beroka's proposition finds a reasonable counterpart. Testate succession in Rome does not require adoption, and among the *sui heredes* the appointment is universal, unilateral, and automatic (there is no right of refusal).

Although it cannot be definitively determined whether there was contact that led to the tannaitic legislation, certainly the proposal attributed to Rabbi Yoḥanan ben Beroka is appropriately formulated and conceptualized for the Roman context in the tannaitic Palestine in which it was conceived. Furthermore, even without the ability to show influence, comparing and contrasting the tannaitic and Roman approaches to testate succession undoubtedly results in a sharpened view of tannaitic innovation, an approach whose far-reaching implications are suppressed in post-mishnaic Talmudic literature and even in the works of some contemporary scholars.

Testate Succession in Tannaitic Law

Mishnah *Baba Batra* 8:5 (in MS Kaufmann 8:6) frames the tannaitic debate about testate succession by contrasting two approaches: the strict opinion of the anonymous tanna, forbidding all changes to the order of intestate succession, and the lenient view of Rabbi Yoḥanan ben Beroka, permitting changes among potential heirs, those in the agnatic line of succession. The anonymous tanna invokes biblical legislation (once again) as the source:[8]

V. האומר 'איש פלוני ירשני' במקום שיש בת, 'בתי תירשני' במקום שיש בן, לא אמר כלום, שהיתנה על הכתוב שבתורה.[9]	A man who says, "Such a man shall inherit from me," and he has a daughter; or "My daughter shall inherit from me," and he has a son, he has said nothing, for he has laid down a condition contrary to what is written in the Torah.

The source for the prohibition is the biblical order of intestate succession found in the book of Numbers,[10] paraphrased in *mBB* 8:2, "[t]his is the order of inheritance: ... the son precedes the daughter ... the daughter precedes the brothers (of the deceased)." By stating that one cannot bequeath an inheritance to a daughter in the presence of a son or to another relative (i. e., the brother of the deceased)

[8] See the discussion in Chapters 1 and 2 of paragraphs I–IV and VII of *mBB* 8:5.

[9] On the formulation *al hakatuv shebatorah*, see Chapter 1 n. 19.

[10] "If a man dies without leaving a son, you shall transfer his property to his daughter. If he has no daughter, you shall assign his property to his brothers. If he has no brothers, you shall assign his property to his father's brothers. If his father had no brothers, you shall assign his property to his nearest relative in his own clan, and he shall inherit it" (Num. 27:8–11).

in the presence of a daughter,[11] the anonymous tanna excludes the possibility for testate succession, even among family members.[12]

There is not total agreement regarding testacy, however. Our *mishnah* preserves a tradition in the name of Rabbi Yoḥanan ben Beroka, possibly opposing the dogma of the anonymous tanna.[13] This position permits making express changes to the biblical order of succession, such as appointing an heir from among family members in the agnatic line (*mi shehu ra'uy lo lirushah*):[14]

VI. רבי יוחנן בן ברוקא אומר: אם אמר על מי שהוא ראוי לו לירושה דבריו קיימין, ועל מי שאינו ראוי לו לירושה אין דבריו קיימין.	Rabbi Yoḥanan ben Beroka says: if he said this of one that was qualified to inherit from him, his words remain valid, but if of one that was not qualified to inherit from him, his words do not remain valid.

Read in light of par. V, Rabbi Yoḥanan ben Beroka expands the possibilities available for the allocation of assets.[15] He allows the appointment of an heir from among all those "qualified to inherit." The innovation enables the recitation of an oral declaration through which preference is given unilaterally to one among several heirs, promoting a *potential* heir to the status of *immediate* heir. Accordingly, the result is the appointment of a daughter instead[16] of a son or a brother instead of a daughter as heir (or anyone else in the agnatic line instead of the next heir in line).[17]

---

[11] The phrase *ish ploni* refers to the brother of the deceased (and not a stranger). Like the following clause, "'my daughter shall inherit from me,' and he has a son," our passage refers to circumventing the order of succession by appointing the next heir in line. In this case that would be the brother of the deceased. The classical Talmudic sources that discuss Rabbi Yoḥanan ben Beroka's opinion (see below in the body of the chapter) support my assumption.

[12] However, presumably the tanna permits gifting. On the anonymous opinion in *mBB* 8:5 and gifting, see Chapter 1.

[13] My interpretation below depends on the statement attributed to Rabbi Yoḥanan ben Beroka in par. VI being a response to par. V. For my reasoning, see the section below in the body of the chapter "Yaron on Rabbi Yoḥanan ben Beroka." The possibility remains, however, that the Rabbi Yoḥanan ben Beroka tradition in par. VI is a response to pars. I–II (see Chapter 1). And, although I reject this interpretation, it is perhaps how Yaron interprets it; see n. 123. Note that the *mishnah* in MS Leiden places the first clause of Rabbi Yoḥanan ben Beroka's statement immediately after par. I [!] and then the entire statement again in par. VI as here. The first occurrence may be attributable to scribal error, a matter which requires further investigation.

[14] On *ra'uy lo lirushah* as referring to the agnatic line specifically, see Schremer, *Male and Female*, 335; see also *Sifra*, *Behar*, Perek 6,8 (109a, Weiss ed.) and my discussion below, "Roman Law and Rabbi Yoḥanan ben Beroka."

[15] For other examples of an expansive approach preserved in tannaitic literature in the name of Rabbi Yoḥanan ben Beroka, see my article "*Rabbi Yoḥanan ben Beroka veshitato*" (in preparation).

[16] For another example of this use of the construction *bimkom she-*, see *mGit.* 5:2.

[17] Cf. Szubin, "Testamentary Succession in Jewish Law," 19 and 126 n. 46; and Falk, "Testate Succession," 77. Povarsky, in "*Shekhiv Me'ra* Will," 192, states that Rabbi Yoḥanan ben Beroka's ruling applies only when on one's deathbed (*shakhev mera*) probably because the declaration is oral. (On the oral implementation of a *mattenat shakhev mera,* see the Appendix.)

Later works of Talmudic literature significantly narrow the scope of Rabbi Yoḥanan ben Beroka's legal innovation. Perhaps the transmitters of those texts are troubled by the fact that a literal reading conflicts with the anonymous tanna's construction of Torah law.[18] Tosefta *Baba Batra* 7:18, for example, limits Rabbi Yoḥanan ben Beroka's position as follows:

רבי יוחנן בן ברוקה אומר: אם אמר על מי שראוי לו ליורשו דבריו קיימין, על מי שאינו ראוי לו ליורשו אין דבריו קיימין. כיצד? אמר על בת הבן בין הבנים ועל בן הבת בין הבנות דבריו קיימין, על הבת בין הבנים ועל האח בין הבנות לא אמר כלום.

Rabbi Yoḥanan Beroka says: "If he made the statement concerning someone who is qualified to inherit him, his statement is valid. [But if he said this] concerning someone who is not qualified to inherit him, his statement is not valid." How so? If he spoke concerning the daughter of the son among the other sons or concerning the son of the daughter among other daughters, his statement is valid. [If he made the statement concerning] *the daughter among the sons or the brother among the daughters, he has said nothing.*

With its qualified interpretation of the *mishnah*, the Tosefta rejects the historical meaning of the Rabbi Yoḥanan ben Beroka tradition.[19] It redefines the parameters of the concept, "qualified to inherit," requiring that the appointment of an heir can only be effective if: (a) the eventual beneficiary is in the biological line of an immediate heir, and (b) the competing heirs over whom the beneficiary is given precedence are of the same rank as the (original) immediate heir. Therefore, only "the daughter of the son among the other sons or ... the son of the daughter among the other daughters," is eligible. The Tosefta explicitly denies the original meaning of Rabbi Yoḥanan ben Beroka's statement by saying that even he forbids appointing a daughter heir in the presence of a son or a brother in the presence of a daughter (italicized in the citation above).

Two sources, one in the Palestinian Talmud (*pBB* 8:5, 16b [1254]) and the other in the Babylonian Talmud (*bBB* 130a), further limit the implications of Rabbi

---

However, I contend that Rabbi Yoḥanan ben Beroka's position does not refer to any form of gifting; see below, "Yaron on Rabbi Yoḥanan ben Beroka."

[18] In general, scholars view the interpretations found in these later works as representative of Rabbi Yoḥanan ben Beroka's historical position. For a reliance on the Tosefta's interpretation, see Zeitlin, "Testamentary Succession," 578–579. For the Talmud's interpretation, see Povarsky, "*Shekhiv Me'ra* Will," 192; and Rackman, "Jewish Philosophy of Property," 186. On Yaron's approach, see below "Yaron on Rabbi Yoḥanan ben Beroka."

[19] On the Tosefta as, generally, a commentary to the Mishnah (as in our example), see Goldberg, "Tosefta." In recent years, Shamma Friedman and Judith Hauptman have spearheaded two new approaches to the study of Mishnah and Tosefta parallels, focusing on the preservation in the Tosefta of material earlier than the Mishnah and the Mishnah as commentary on parts of the Tosefta. For a summary of these approaches and a bibliography, see Milgram, "Then and Now," 134–135.

Yoḥanan ben Beroka's assessment. As stated in these traditions, Rabbi Yoḥanan ben Beroka allows testate succession only among immediate heirs. Accordingly, only appointing a son heir among other sons and a daughter heir among other daughters is permissible, but not the appointment of other relatives.[20] Furthermore, like the tanna of the Tosefta tradition, in the following quotation from the Palestinian Talmud, Rabbi Yoḥanan explicitly denies that the literal rendering of Rabbi Yoḥanan ben Beroka's position in the *mishnah* is possible.[21]

Said Rabbi Yoḥanan: Rabbi Yoḥanan ben Beroka's statement applies only in a case in which the man spoke of one son among other sons or one daughter among other daughters. *He did not speak [however] of a daughter among [her own] brothers or a brother [of the deceased] among daughters.*	אמר רבי יוחנן: לא אמר רבי יוחנן בן ברוקה אלא על בן בין הבנים ועל בת בין הבנות. בת בין האחין אח בין הבנות לא.

According to Rabbi Yoḥanan, Rabbi Yoḥanan ben Beroka allows appointing an heir only from among several immediate heirs of the same rank. A *baraita* in *bBB* 130a, cited in the name of Rabbi Yoḥanan ben Beroka's son Rabbi Ishmael, preserves the same interpretation of Rabbi Yoḥanan ben Beroka's position, a rejection of the simple meaning of his words:[22]

Rabbi Yishmael the son of Rabbi Yoḥanan ben Beroka said: My father and the Sages did not disagree that in the case regarding a brother [of the deceased][24] instead of a daughter and in the case of a daughter instead of a son, he has said nothing. Regarding what did they disagree? [They disagreed] regarding the case of a son among sons and a daughter among daughters. Father says [the one appointed] inherits, and the sages say [the one appointed] does not inherit.	אמר רבי ישמעאל בנו של רבי יוחנן בן ברוקה: לא נחלק אבא וחכמים על אח[23] במקום בת ובת במקום בן שלא אמר כלום. ועל מה נחלקו? על בן בין הבנים ובת בין הבנות, שאבא אומר יירש וחכמים אומרים לא יירש.

[20] See Chapter 1 where I argue that a similar position is embedded and concealed within *mBB* 8:5.

[21] Compare the formulation in Hoffmann, *Midrash Tannaim*, 129, mentioned in Chapter 2 n. 4 and n. 15.

[22] The amoraim cited in *bBB* 130a also rule according to this interpretation of Rabbi Yoḥanan ben Beroka.

[23] As per MS Hamburg 165; the other textual witnesses examined read *aḥer* (see MS Escorial G-I-3, MS Munich 95, MS Paris [Bibliothèque nationale Suppl. Heb. 1337], MS Vatican 115, and the *editio princeps*, Pesaro 1511). Compare the text of *tBB* 7:18 cited above in the body of the text.

[24] See previous note.

Together, the three sources limit the force of Rabbi Yoḥanan ben Beroka's approach. They deny its original meaning and redefine the parameters of the category *ra'uy lo lirushah*. Although the authors of these sources narrow the scope of Rabbi Yoḥanan ben Beroka's pronouncement, they do not deny its fundamental assumption, namely, the right to appoint an heir (even if only among immediate heirs).

The liberalness inherent in Rabbi Yoḥanan ben Beroka's original opinion may be representative of the spirit of an age and a context in which the selection of a successor – especially in light of the assumed Torah prohibition – would have been valued as the greatest of freedoms. Below I engage in the search for parallels and antecedents to Rabbi Yoḥanan ben Beroka's notion of testate succession. As I demonstrate, testate succession among family members is quite common in the ancient world. In fact, in some of the legal traditions examined below, testate succession is only possible among family members, resulting in the use of adoption as a method to create the relationship required for the transfer of property, rights, and obligations to another. That is the case, indeed, for much of ancient Near Eastern and Athenian law (and perhaps even biblical law). After a discussion of testate succession among family members in multiple ancient legal traditions, below I suggest that the closest parallel to Rabbi Yoḥanan ben Beroka's conception is found in the testament to the *sui heredes* in Roman law. I begin with the biblical evidence.

Testate Succession in the Bible

Scholars debate whether any forms of testate succession are manifest in biblical literature.[25] Certainly biblical law allows some flexibility in the allocation of property among sons, a practice typically labeled by legal scholars as the right of distribution.[26] Namely, according to biblical law, a father may enjoy the right to distribute his property among his sons – choosing which fields to give to one or another son – as long as he does not deviate from the biblically commanded size of each son's share (however, on the firstborn, see Chapter 2).[27] Indeed, several

[25] See, e.g., the discussion in Maine, *Ancient Law*, 209; and the response in Herzog, *Main Institutions*, 296–298. See also the literature cited in Hiers, "Transfer of Property," 147 n. 106.

[26] See "Abbreviations, Terminology, and Transliteration."

[27] Although evidence for the concept of transferring property exists, explicit mention of universal succession is lacking. The most compelling data that may suggests that obligations are bequeathed along with rights according to biblical law is in Lev. 25:35–55, which states that members of the clan (*mishpaḥah*) are obligated to maintain or redeem the land of a fellow clansman or his dependents in debt. If members of the outer limits of an extended family have obligations regarding a fellow clansman's debt, is it not reasonable to assume that one's immediate heirs also have an obligation to repay debt after death according to the biblical construction of the law? See Chapter 1.

narrative and legal sections of the Bible and related literatures are best understood once we acknowledge that the texts assume such a right.[28] Of course, distribution and testate succession are not synonymous, and the search for testate succession in the Bible and related literatures, in fact, yields important results, even if only a few examples.

If we can read the patriarchal narratives in light of the biblical laws of succession in Numbers and Deuteronomy,[29] then perhaps the clearest depiction of possible testate succession in the Pentateuch – among family members and under very specific circumstances – is the narrative of Jacob's deathbed bequest (Genesis 48 and 49).[30] Jacob appoints Ephraim and Manasseh, his grandchildren from his favorite son Joseph[31] to (presumably) replace his firstborn son, Reuben. For, having lain with Jacob's concubine Bilhah (49:4),[32] Reuben is no longer worthy and is stripped of his rights as the firstborn.[33]

> Now, your two sons, who were born to you in the land of Egypt ... shall be mine; Ephraim and Manasseh shall be mine no less than Reuben and Simeon (48:5) ... Joseph took the two of them, Ephraim with his right hand – to Israel's left – and Manasseh with his left hand – to Israel's right – and brought them close to him. (48:13)

While some scholars maintain that in this episode Jacob legitimates[34] or adopts Ephraim and Manasseh,[35] others disagree.[36] In addition, it may be that, through Joseph, Jacob elevates Joseph's sons to the status of firstborn. Indeed, Gen. 48:5 implies that Ephraim and Manasseh are each to receive the full share of a son, possibly constituting the firstborn's two shares, which are transferred through

---

[28] See the discussion in Yaron, *Gifts*, 4–10. So, too, perhaps, the Parable of the Prodigal Son in Luke 15:11–32 may be understood. On the prodigal son, see also Chapter 1 n. 17. For a negative assessment of Yaron's understanding of *Sirach* and *Judith*, see Falk, "Testate Succession," 73; and for an unfavorable appraisal of Falk's interpretations, see Urbach, "Inheritance Laws and After-Life," 137 n. 46. See also my discussion below in the body of the chapter.

[29] Indeed, there is no reason to assume that the Genesis narratives must be representative of biblical laws found in other books of the Bible; see in the Introduction the section, "On the Relationship of Ancient Laws to Ancient Societies."

[30] On this episode and other deathbed bequests, see Malul, "Death-Bed Dispositions in the Hebrew Bible."

[31] On the possible reflection of the political reality of the biblical period in these verses, see Noth, *Das System der Zwölf Stämme Israels*; Brin, "Birthright of the Sons of Jacob," 4–8; and Westbrook, *Property and Family*, 136–137.

[32] Cf. 1 Chron. 5:1.

[33] See the discussion in Chapter 2.

[34] Some scholars distinguish between legitimation, adoption by a family member, and adoption by a stranger. See Marcus, "Legal Dispute," 105–114. Greengus notes what he calls "traces" of adoption only in later biblical texts such as 1 Chronicles, Proverbs, and Psalms; see Greengus, *Laws*, 79–80.

[35] Mendelsohn, "A Ugaritic Parallel," 180–183; Sarna, *Genesis*, 325–327. On the general interplay between adoption and inheritance in the ancient Near East, see also below in the body of the chapter.

[36] For the view that there is no evidence for adoption in biblical law or narrative, see Paul, "Leshonot imuts," 31–36; Frymer-Kensky, "Israel," 1015.

Joseph (see Chapter 2).[37] Our narrative, therefore, may contain two related, yet separate, acts of testate succession.[38] The first is an act of testate succession among sons, that is, Jacob's preference that Joseph rather than Reuben receive a double portion and the preference of Judah over Reuben for the family leadership.[39] The second is an example of testate succession among family members, that is, the elevation of Ephraim and Manasseh to the status of immediate heirs, a clear circumvention of the order of succession, preferring potential heirs (grandchildren) to an immediate heir (a son).[40]

The context of the narrative, the promotion of potential heirs as a result of the rightful heir's punishment, prevents us from arguing for the possibility of a biblical antecedent to Rabbi Yoḥanan ben Beroka's conception of testate succession. In fact, it may be that biblical law allows for testate succession among family members only under specific circumstances – such as a corollary to punishment – and, even then, only together with legitimation/adoption.[41] Both criteria, however, are absent from tannaitic law.[42]

An examination of texts in the book of Job, apocryphal works, and papyri at Elephantine demonstrates that the appointment of family members as heirs persists – even when not in the context of punishment or adoption. Furthermore, the pool of potential appointees expands. Daughters and wives, as well as other, non-consanguineous relatives, are appointed heirs.

Job, Judith, Tobit, and the Elephantine Papyri

In the book of Job a striking example of the expansion of heirs appears: daughters receive inheritance portions in the presence of sons! [43]Despite the fact that accord-

[37] The matter is complicated by the fact that Joseph is the firstborn to Jacob's second wife, Rachel; see Chapter 2.

[38] Cf. Greengus, *Laws*, 70.

[39] Westbrook, *Property and Family*, 136.

[40] Yaron's contention, therefore, that this narrative merely reflects distribution, is unfounded (*Gifts*, 8).

[41] On the theme of disinheritance as punishment in the ancient Near East, see Westbrook, "Introduction," 77.

[42] For a possible reference to punishment through disinheritance, see *mBB* 8:5, par. VII, "If a man assigned his goods to others and passed over his sons ... Rabban Simeon b. Gamliel says: Yet if his sons had not behaved aright, it should be accounted to his credit."

[43] For more on the topic of daughters inheriting in the presence of sons, see Chapter 4. On the episode in the book of Job, see Pope, *Job*, 353; Hiers, "Transfer of Property," 149; Yaron, *Gifts*, 5; Machinist, "Job's Daughters." Note that Urbach, in "Inheritance Laws and After-Life," 137 n. 46, which includes criticisms of Falk's review of Yaron ("Testate Succession," 73), states without elaboration that Job and Judith prove nothing (*einam mokhiḥim kelum*) regarding the antiquity of testate succession in "Hebrew custom" (as per Falk's terminology). It may be that Urbach, in translating Falk's term "testate succession" as *tzavaah*, thinks Falk is referring to some kind of written document (perhaps a *diathēkē*?) and therefore objects to the suggestion of

ing to Num. 27:8 inheritance passes to daughters only in the absence of sons,[44] Job gives his daughters "inheritance among their brothers" (42:15). Job giving inheritance to daughters in the presence of sons may represent a practice foreign to biblical law.[45] The other details of Job's inheritance division are unclear, a topic Richard Hiers considers in a recent essay.[46] For example, Hiers points to the difficulty involved in precisely labeling Job's act of disposition. The text mentions inheritance, usually realized at death, but also tells of Job living for 140 years *after* giving the inheritance.[47] Therefore, it is not possible to determine whether, strictly speaking, the disposition is an inheritance or a gift, or even whether the narrator attempts to base the storyline on any actual legal background at all.

Noteworthy are the bequests in the apocryphal books of Judith and Tobit.[48] According to the narrative, Judith's husband makes arrangements for the transfer of his estate to her upon his death (8:7)[49] despite the presence of relatives who would inherit under the laws of intestacy (16:24) and the absence of provision for the wife in the biblical laws of intestacy.[50] In Tob. 8:21 Raguel declares that upon his death, the remainder of his estate goes to his son-in-law Tobias,[51] the husband of his daughter Sarah. The reference to making a declaration may be legally significant and reveal something about the legal background of Tobit.[52] Perhaps without the pronouncement, the transfer of property would not be considered effective. For, it is by no means clear that otherwise the property goes to

---

its antiquity. However, it seems to me that Falk does not commit as to whether these texts refer to an oral or a written disposition. Rather, Falk's focus is on the antiquity of the practice of appointing an heir not in accordance with the biblical order of intestate succession. See also n. 50.

[44] See Chapter 4.

[45] For the view that this is an Israelite practice, however, see Hiers, "Transfer of Property," 149.

[46] Hiers, "Transfer of Property," 149.

[47] Hiers, "Transfer of Property," 149.

[48] On these bequests, see Hiers, "Transfer of Property," 130–134 and 150.

[49] See Grintz, *Sefer Yehudit*, 188–189.

[50] In his review of Yaron's *Gifts*, Falk writes that Sirach 33:19–24 may refer to testate succession and may, therefore, prove the antiquity of testate succession in "Hebrew custom" ("Testate Succession," 73). However, see the original remarks made by Yaron on Sirach (*Gifts*, 8) and the refutation of Falk by Urbach ("Inheritance Laws and After-Life," 137 n. 46) who emphasizes that the context in Sirach is negativity toward the concept of gifts in contemplation of death and similar practices and, therefore, Sirach cannot constitute evidence for the antiquity of embracing such practices. See also, Segal, *Sefer ben-Sira hashalem*, 214 (cited in Urbach) and the reference there to a negative view of gifting in contemplation of death in *bBM* 75b [incorrectly cited by Segal as 78b]. Also on Sirach, see Skehan, *The Wisdom of Ben Sira*, 405; Hiers, "Transfer of Property," 148–149. See also n. 43.

[51] Half of his property is transferred to Tobias at the end of the wedding feast. For a parallel from the Judean desert in which half of the property is given now and half after death, see Katzoff, "P. Yadin 19," 4.

[52] Hiers in "Transfer of Property," 130 n. 34 suggests the declaration is merely a confirmation of Tobias's right.

Tobias, despite the fact that he is Raguel's kinsman.[53] Indeed, at least according to the law in Numbers, Sarah is the rightful heir.[54] Therefore, the appointment of Tobias might be considered an act of testate succession.

The expansion of possible heir appointees discussed above is also evidenced in a more systematic way in the Elephantine papyri, and the relevant terminology descriptive of both gifting and inheriting benefits from a detailed study coauthored by Zvi Szubin and Bezalel Porten.[55] Indeed, the authors demonstrate that at Elephantine there may be testate succession. In the papyri the technical term *yhb*, "to give," describes the transfer of ownership from donor to donee through the mechanism of gifting, and the formula, *yhb brḥmn*, "to give in affection," together with the term *hntsl* "recover, reclaim, revoke," describes the transfer of ownership through testate succession and prevents reclamation of the transferred property.[56] In the following text, Anani engages in an act of testate succession when, in the presence of sons, he bequeaths to his daughter Jehoishma part of a house (adjoined to the one in which he lives):[57]

אנה ענני יהבת לך בתיא אלה ברחמה לא[58] אכהל אנה ענני אהנצל מ[נ]כי ולא אכהל אמר נפש אחרית אהנצל מנכי.	I, Anani, gave you these houses in love. I, Anani, shall not be able to reclaim (them) from you. And I shall not be able to say: "My soul desired (them). I shall reclaim (them) from you."[59]

[53] On the marriage of a daughter to kin for the purposes of inheriting, see Chapter 4.

[54] It may be reasonable to assume that Raguel's declaration has legal import whether Sarah is to inherit directly or whether she is to serve only as trustee of the inheritance for her sons. On the two options for understanding daughters' inheritance in Numbers, see Chapter 4. For the view that the actions in Tobit are simply a corollary to the laws in Numbers preventing daughters from inheriting directly (even in the absence of sons), see Hiers, "Transfer of Property," 129–130. Greengus in *Laws*, 74–75 suggests that the narrative in Tobit follows the prescriptions in Numbers that daughters marry relatives; Yaron, *Gifts*, 7, sees the action taken by Raguel as a possible adoption.

[55] Szubin and Porten, "Testamentary Succession at Elephantine"; the authors note on page 35 that the terms are neither constitutive nor operative but rather descriptive.

[56] The authors write: "The common denominator in all these cases is the promise not to reclaim the property through revocation. Such a right would not exist in *bona fide* gifts and sales, which are intrinsically irrevocable … Therefore, documents drawn up *brḥmn* should not be considered *bona fide* gifts but testamentary bequests akin to testaments and gifts in contemplation of death" (Szubin and Porten, "Testamentary Succession at Elephantine," 36). Note that the authors consider the documents using this formula comparable to testaments primarily because the property transferred cannot be reclaimed through revocation. On universal succession at Elephantine, see Chapter 1.

[57] As per the transcription in Kraeling, *Brooklyn Museum Aramaic Papyri*, 192. For smoother reading, I have removed the *sigla* included in the original edition.

[58] As correctly noted by Kraeling in *Brooklyn Museum Aramaic Papyri*, 196, the word *lo* was written above the line after the scribe forgot to include it. See, in Kraeling, the photograph of the original papyrus (#6) at the end of the book (unnumbered pages). In his translation, Porten (as in the next note) superimposes the word. I leave it as part of the text itself.

[59] TAD B3.7 (=Kraeling 6; see previous note). The English, as per Porten, *Elephantine Papy-*

As in this case of a father transferring inheritance to his daughter in the presence of sons, in all of the papyri where this specific formula is employed, the property is transferred to someone who, it is assumed, would likely not inherit under the regular laws of intestacy. In fact, the technical terminology for testate succession is employed in the papyri to bequeath to individuals within what seems to be a broadly defined familial relationship to the testator, at times even non-consanguineous. Property is not only transferred from father to daughter and mother to daughter, but also from husband to wife, brother to adopted sister, and father-in-law to son-in-law.[60]

In summary, in our *mishnah* Rabbi Yoḥanan ben Beroka limits testate succession to the appointment of agnates. And, whereas there is possible evidence for testate succession in various forms in the Bible, apocryphal literature, and Elephantine papyri, there is no clear antecedent among these to Rabbi Yoḥanan ben Beroka's conception. The context of the Genesis narrative seems to be castigation and, according to some, perhaps even adoption. The narrative in Job does not provide a clear context for determining the legal status of the property transferred. The broad spectrum of conceivable heir appointees evidenced in the books of Judith and Tobit, as well as in the Elephantine papyri, does not parallel the limited list of potential appointees encompassed in Rabbi Yoḥanan ben Beroka's category, *ra'uy lo lirushah*. Accordingly, the search for legal antecedents continues as we now turn to the laws of the ancient Near East and Greece.

Testate Succession in the Ancient Near East and in Ancient Greece

Testate succession exists throughout the ancient Near East and in Athens but is unlike the institution known from the legal traditions examined thus far.[61] Testate succession in the ancient Near East and in Athens requires adoption, an arrangement that is not bilateral in the sense that it requires an act of acquisition; however, it is still considered reciprocal in that it calls for the mutual consent of the parties[62] (in the case of minors, the parents' consent).[63] In the legal traditions

---

ri in English, 224–225. As already mentioned above in the body of the chapter, the term ברחמה may also be translated, "in affection."

[60] Szubin and Porten, "Testamentary Succession at Elephantine," 36.

[61] Yet it is absent from both Sparta and Gortyn (see below in the body of the chapter).

[62] In an earlier discussion of testate succession with adoption in Milgram, "Prolegomenon," 191, I did not make the distinction, made here, between bilateral and reciprocal sufficiently clear.

[63] Technical terminology in Old Babylonian contracts (as in BIN 2 75:2) indicates that the adoptee is adopted "with his consent"; see Westbrook, "Mesopotamia: Old Babylonian Period," 392. A Middle Babylonian period adoption/inheritance contract enables the adoptee's dissolution of the arrangement by reciting the formula, "You are not my father ... You are not my mother." See Podany, Beckman, and Colbow, "Adoption," 47. For the procedure in Athens, see Harrison, *Law of Athens*, 1:89–93.

of these societies, the beneficiary of an inheritance must be someone already entitled by the laws of intestate succession (usually members of the immediate family only). To circumvent this limitation, testate succession is vested under the institution of adoption. That is, adoption creates the relationship required for the act of inheritance to remain among family members, enabling the eventual transfer of property, rights, and obligations. Raymond Westbrook succinctly states the point when he writes that legitimate filiation is a conduit for the rights and duties of inheriting and that "[a]doption was therefore used as a mode of transferring [those] rights and duties."[64] The adoptee is not the only one to benefit, however. The adopting parents also gain, whether it is through the guarantee of care in their old age and attention to their burial arrangements, the safeguard that someone continues the family sacra,[65] or the assurance that the estate is managed adequately.

Adoption, however, is not found among the laws of the tannaim; and we should pause to consider the reasons for its rejection in light of the fact that testate succession with adoption is the most prevalent inheritance strategy throughout the region before the advent of the rabbinic movement. As we have seen up until now, the dominant voice among the tannaitic sources is the one that envisions as possible only testate succession among immediate heirs. Even Rabbi Yoḥanan ben Beroka, who champions a more expansive form of testate succession among heirs in the agnatic line, does not appropriate a practice that *creates* filiation. In that sense, the tanna remains faithful to a fundamental tenet of the biblical model: the land remains in family hands.

It may be that the absence of adoption in tannaitic inheritance law is related to the omission of ancestor worship from the rituals of the tannaim. As already pointed out by Ephraim Elimelech Urbach, whereas in the ancient Near East and Athens obligations pertaining to the maintenance of the family sacra, burial rites, and ancestor worship are thrust upon the heir (whether natural or adopted) after the demise of the parent, similar laws are entirely absent from tannaitic law.[66] I suggest that it stands to reason, therefore, that it was unnecessary to incorporate adoption into the tannaitic legal complex, a practice in principle linked to the testator's desire for the fulfillment of the posthumous rites that accompany the transfer of property.

---

[64] Westbrook, "Introduction," 51. Westbrook continues and states that adoption is also employed as a conduit for commercial transactions disguised as inheritance arrangements. However, the analysis of this role is beyond the scope of my discussion.

[65] See n. 2. For a short summary of the societies that link succession to property and ancestor worship, see Driver and Miles, *The Babylonian Laws*, 330 n. 4. See also, on the ancient Near East (with a focus on Babylonia), van der Toorn, *Family Religion*, 42–65; on Athens, Harrison, *Law of Athens*, 1:92, 123, 130, and the literature cited; on Rome, Scheid, "Sacrifices for Gods and Ancestors," 263–272.

[66] Urbach, "Inheritance Laws and After-Life," 135. See also the Preface to this book.

In contrast, inheritance and adoption are so intertwined in the ancient Near East that the Middle Assyrian Laws, for example, discuss adoption only in the context of inheritance:

> If a widow should enter a man's house and she is carrying her dead husband's surviving son with her (in her womb), he grows up in the house of the man who married her but no tablet of his adoption is written, he will not take inheritance from the estate of the one who raised him (A28).[67]

This text is about testate succession with adoption and although this form of testate succession may have existed as early as the Neo-Sumerian period,[68] the primary evidence is from the Old Babylonian period onward.[69] Indeed, adoption with inheritance rights is well documented in Old Babylonian,[70] Middle Babylonian,[71] Neo-Assyrian,[72] and Neo-Babylonian texts,[73] as well as in documents from Nuzi,[74] Ugarit,[75] Emar,[76] and Alalakh.[77] The arrangement enables a man to adopt a relative[78] (or at times a stranger)[79] to create a sonship/heirship between the parties. The adoption perforce affects the distribution of inheritance since it introduces someone new into the pool of heirs.

As in the ancient Near East, testate succession in Athens was not an independent legal act but, rather, required adoption. Legislation attributed to the

---

[67] Roth, *Law Collections*, 163.

[68] The wording in the following text, in which a slave is freed for heirship, may reflect such a practice: "His father Atu freed h[is?] slave … to (become his) heir." (Text #920 in Owen, *Neo-Sumerian Archival Texts*, 85; here as per the translation in Wilcke, "Care of the Elderly in Mesopotamia in the Third Millenium B. C.," 53). Note, however, that the language, "[h]is father" may actually indicate that the slave is the son of the owner by a slave woman. Although this example may indicate that the son of a master and his slave woman requires formal adoption in order to receive inheritance, it does not clearly establish that testate succession through adoption also is available for a complete stranger, nor that consent is required.

[69] See Stone and Owen, *Adoption in Old Babylonian Nippur*.

[70] See the previous note.

[71] See below in the body of the chapter.

[72] Radner, *Privatrechtsurkunden*, 140 and 142. In Neo-Assyrian documents the adoptees are always children, and the father or head of household gives away the child.

[73] In Neo-Babylonian texts adopted sons are not automatically entitled to a share of inheritance when other heirs are present. See Oelsner, Wells, and Wunsch, "Mesopotamia: Neo-Babylonian Period," 937 and 939; van Driel, "Care of the Elderly: The Neo-Babylonian Period," 161–197.

[74] Paradise, "Nuzi Inheritance Practices," 193–197, 233, 267, and 269–280.

[75] It seems that in Ugarit only adults are eligible. See Vita, "The Society of Ugarit," 479; Rowe, "Anatolia and the Levant: Ugarit," 727–728.

[76] See Beckman, "Family Values on the Middle Euphrates," 61–68 and 76–79; and, there, specifically on the formal declaration, "so-and-so is now my son."

[77] Text no. 16 in Wiseman, *Alalakh Tablets*. This is the only adoption document from Alalakh. For a discussion of its unique formulation "he took PN as his father," (as opposed to the reverse formula, which is what would have been expected), see Rowe, "Anatolia and the Levant: Alalakh," 711; and Yaron, "Varia on Adoption," 175–179.

[78] For two examples, see Mendelsohn, "A Ugaritic Parallel," 182 n. 11.

[79] Westbrook, "Introduction," 51.

sixth-century (BCE) legislator Solon[80] is credited with enabling a childless man[81] to perform such an adoption,[82] or *diathēkē* with *eispoiēsis*. Here, as in the ancient Near East, the arrangement designates a man or child the son of the testator. The adopted son universally succeeds his adoptive father and takes over the religious rites and management of the estate.[83] This arrangement is in stark contrast to the *diathēkē* without *eispoiēsis*, or *Legatentestament*, a disposition that transfers only a right or good (and does not require consent).[84]

Testate succession did not exist throughout ancient Greece, however. In Sparta and Gortyn, for example, there is no testate succession. Concerning Sparta, scholars look to two texts, one from Aristotle and the other from Plutarch, to shed light on what may have been groundbreaking legislation – the *Rhetra of Epitadeus* – which some assume enabled testate succession,[85] but more recent scholarship disputes. The two texts are discussed below.

Whereas Aristotle writes only, "but he [=the legislator] permitted those who wished to give it away and to bequeath it,"[86] Plutarch's testimony in *Life of Agis*, section 5, is more specific:

> But when a certain powerful man came to be *ephor*, who was headstrong and [of] a violent temper, Epitadeus by name, he had a quarrel with his son, and introduced a law permitting a man during his lifetime to give his estate and allotment to anyone he wished, or in his will and testament to leave it.[87]

Sima Avramović revisits the issue of testate succession in Sparta from philological and legal perspectives. As a result, he discounts Plutarch's (relatively late)[88] tes-

[80] As stated, e.g., in Demosthenes, *Against Leptines*, 20.102, "Solon made a law that every man could grant his property to whomever he pleased in default of legitimate offspring," (559–560), and affirmed, among others, by Isocrates, *Aeginiticus*, 19.49, "you should uphold the law which permits us to adopt children and to dispose wisely of our property, reflecting that for men who are childless this law takes the place of children," 327. See also Isaeus, *On the Estate of Menecles*, 2.13. For a list of sources attributing the law to Solon, see Asheri, "Laws of Inheritance," 7 n. 30.

[81] Because a man could not disinherit a son (MacDowell, *Law in Classical Athens*, 100); for the view that Athenians could, however, perform testamentary adoptions in the presence of sons, see Rubinstein, *Adoption*, 82–86.

[82] For a discussion of the distinct views on the development of this practice, see Rubinstein, *Adoption*, 82–86. See also the literature cited in Jackson, "Why the Name New *Testament*," 67 n. 155.

[83] Harrison, *Law of Athens*, 1:92, 123, and 130.

[84] For more on this type of disposition, see Chapter 1. Scholars dispute when the arrangements that did not require adoption came about. See Asheri, "Laws of Inheritance," 9–10; Ste. Croix, "Athenian Family Law," 390; Rubinstein, *Adoption*, 81.

[85] Although not connected directly to the concept of testate succession, adoption in Sparta, under the tutelage of the kings, was likely used by households with no male heirs; see Asheri, "Laws of Inheritance," 12.

[86] *Politics*, 1270A.15–34.

[87] "Plutarch's Lives," (13).

[88] It is composed about five hundred years after the *rhetra* and in a Roman context.

timony almost entirely and reinterprets and retranslates Aristotle's, establishing the *rhetra* not as a form of testament, at least not as it is known from classical Athens (requiring adoption; see above) or from Rome (with *institutio heredis*; see below) but rather as a form of gift.[89]

Avramović retranslates both of the texts above as follows: "He [the legislator] ... permitted those who wished, to make a gift or leave property" (Aristotle) and "Epitadeus ... proposed a *rhetra* that permitted free disposition over house and lot by gift *inter vivos* and by leaving them *mortis causa*" (Plutarch).[90] According to Avramović, the *rhetra* grants someone the freedom to dispose of his house and property lot by making a gift (during his lifetime) or leaving property (for after his death).[91] Similarly, in Gortyn, where there are no testaments, the father is given some control over the division of property,[92] as in Sparta, in terms of both gifting in his lifetime and for after his death but not for appointing an heir or adopting a universal successor.[93]

In summary, the form of testate succession known from the ancient Near East and Athens requires adoption. Accordingly, it is clear that this form of testate succession cannot be considered an antecedent to Rabbi Yoḥanan ben Beroka's disposition. As we see in the next section, Rabbi Yoḥanan ben Beroka's form of testate succession among family members most parallels the Roman testament to the *sui heredes*.

Roman Law and Rabbi Yoḥanan Ben Beroka

Roman law, like ancient Near Eastern and Athenian law, knows of the institution of adoption and, certainly, if a head of household adopts someone, the order of succession is affected.[94] However, in Roman law adoption is not *required* for testate succession. Testate succession is an act accomplished through an instrument known as the *testamentum*,[95] or testament, in the classical peri-

[89] On the distinction between inheriting and gifting, see Chapter 1.
[90] Avramović, "Rhetra," 182.
[91] Avramović, "Rhetra," 182.
[92] Willetts, *Law Code of Gortyn*, 20.
[93] Avramović, "Rhetra," 184. There, adoption seems to have been executed even in the presence of other male heirs (but in the absence of sons), potentially effecting changes to the regular order of succession; see Willetts, *Law Code of Gortyn*, 30 n. 10.
[94] Adoption in Rome, through which one leaves the *potestas* of one's father and enters that of another, has implications for succession, making the adopted son agnatically related to all of those in his adopted father's household and no longer related to those in his previous household. For a summary of the effects of adoption on succession, see Nicholas, *Introduction to Roman Law*, 77–80.
[95] In the body of the text I address the *testamentum per aes et libram*, or mancipatory testament, described in Gaius as existing in his day, although it is likely much older. On possible evidence for an earlier form of the *testamentum per aes et libram* in the XII Tablets that did not

od[96] executed through an oral ceremony.[97] The main function of the testament is *institutio heredis*, the appointment of the universal successor; as Gaius emphasizes, "the force of the will flows from the heir's appointment, which is its foundation and corner-stone" (*Institutes*, 2:229).[98] The appointment is effected by a specific formula *Titivs heres esto*, "Let Titius be heir" (2:117),[99] including the word *heres*, heir, taken from the vocabulary for intestate succession.[100] Like intestate succession, testamentary succession is unilateral, that is, it does not require an act of acquisition. Furthermore, the appointee can be anyone. There are procedural differences, however, dependent on the familial standing of the appointee. The appointment of a *suus heres* (plural, *sui heredes*),[101] in the legal sense a member of the *familia*[102] – that is, someone *in potestate*[103] such as a child or grandchild – is not only unilateral, but also universal and automatic (not re-

---

serve to institute an heir, see Watson, *Rome of XII Tables*, 59–61 and the discussion in Chapter 1. On the earlier forms of testaments, the *testamentum in comitiis calatis*, limited to two days per year, and the *testamentum in procinctu*, restricted to wartime, both obsolete by the end of the Republic, see the summaries in Buckland, *Text-book of Roman Law*, 288–289; and Nicholas, *Introduction to Roman Law*, 253; for a discussion of all three types, see Watson, *Law of Succession*, 8–21.

[96] However, by the time of the Republic, it was already customary to write the testament on wax tablets; see Tellegen-Couperus, *Testamentary Succession*, 20.

[97] On aspects of the ceremony, see Tellegen-Couperus, *Testamentary Succession*, 20. On the formula to institute the successor, see the text of Gaius (2:116–117) in Gordon and Robinson, *Institutes of Gaius*, 80–81; and 177–179. On the oral declaration *nuncupatio*, confirming the contents of the testament, see the text of Gaius (2:104) in Gordon and Robinson, *Institutes of Gaius*, 78 and 173. On the orality of the classical testament, see also Buckland, *Text-book of Roman Law*, 284; Nicholas, *Introduction to Roman Law*, 256; Watson, *Law of Succession*, 11; and Champlin, *Final Judgments*, 5. See also my discussion in Chapter 1.

[98] Gordon and Robinson, *Institutes of Gaius*, 239.

[99] Gordon and Robinson, *Institutes of Gaius*, 81 and 179.

[100] See, e. g., *Institutes* 3:1, "The Twelve Tables give the estate of an intestate first to his immediate *heirs*" (Gordon and Robinson, *Institutes of Gaius*, 268); "Intestatorum *hereditates* ex lege XII tabularum primum ad suos *heredes* pertinent" (Gordon and Robinson, *Institutes of Gaius*, 125); and the formulation in the earlier (and actual) XII Tablets V:4, "If he dies intestate, to whom there be no *suus heres* ..." "si intestato moritur, cui *suus heres* nec essit" (Crawford and Cloud, *Roman Statutes*, 641). On the modelling of testaments in the Greco-Roman papyri from Egypt after the classical Roman forms, see Taubenschlag, *Law*, 146.

[101] His wife in a *cum manu* marriage is included in this category and is considered like his daughter for the purpose of inheritance. See also Chapter 5.

[102] On the legal use of *familia*, see Ulpian, *Edict*, book 46 (D.50.16.195); and the discussion of this source in Saller, *Patriarchy, Property and Death*, 75–76. Ulpian (D.50.16.195) also discusses the (non-legal) social definition of the word *familia*, meaning all *agnati*; see Saller, *Patriarchy, Property and Death*, 76–77; and my discussion below in the body of the chapter as this pertains to Rabbi Yoḥanan ben Beroka.

[103] Someone *in potestate* is, to a certain degree, controlled by the head of household, the *paterfamilias*. For the clearest discussion of the historical development of this institution, see du Plessis, *Borkowski's Textbook*, 113–120.

quiring consent).[104] The appointment of a family member not considered a *suus heres* and the appointment of a stranger, though, requires consent.[105]

Elements of Rabbi Yoḥanan ben Beroka's disposition are parallel to the Roman testament to the *sui heredes*. In both, individuals already in the line of succession are appointed heirs and, in both, the dispositions are universal, unilateral, and automatic. The parallels are significant and appropriate because Rabbi Yoḥanan ben Beroka's position is formulated in the context of Roman Palestine.

One primary difference remains, however. For Rabbi Yoḥanan ben Beroka, the disposition applies to all those in the agnatic line of succession, a far more inclusive category than just those *legally* considered members of the Roman *familia* (the *sui heredes*). I emphasize here the *legal* usage of *familia* in Roman sources because a *non-legal* usage is also prevalent in common parlance and is relevant to this discussion. According to Ulpian,[106] *familia* also refers to "several people who descend by blood from the same original founder."[107] As Richard Saller points out regarding Ulpian's definition, "[t]hus all *agnati* were called *familia*, that is, the kin originating from the same house, and related by blood through males."[108] Indeed, the Roman *non-legal* meaning of *familia*, all those in the agnatic line, conceptually parallels the *legal* usage of *ra'uy lo lirushah* stated in the name of Rabbi Yoḥanan ben Beroka.[109]

The term also appears in *mSan* 3:4, and there, in the context of determining who is considered a family member for disqualification as a witness.[110] The *mishnah* states, "but the first *mishnah* [=*mishnah rishonah*] included his uncle and his first cousin and *all those qualified to inherit him*." Epstein notes that the language in "the first *mishnah*," an expression used in tannaitic literature to point to presumed early laws, "his uncle and his first cousin" (*dodo uven dodo*), is biblical.[111] In fact, *dodo uven dodo* is shorthand for *o dodo uven dodo yigalenu o misheer besaro* ***mimishpaḥto***, "or his uncle or his uncle's son shall redeem him, or **anyone of his clan** who is of his own flesh" (Lev. 25:49). Certainly for

---

[104] Nicholas, *Introduction to Roman law*, 238; du Plessis, *Borkowski's Textbook*, 227. See Gaius, *Lex Julia et Papia, book* 13: "In the case of the *sui heredes*, formal acceptance is not a requisite because they immediately fall to be heirs by operation of law" (D.38.16.14). For a discussion of intestacy, see Chapter 1.

[105] This is accomplished by a declaration (*cretio*) or an act that somehow signifies acceptance (*pro herede gestio*); for a discussion, see Watson, *Law of Succession*, 188–193.

[106] See note 102.

[107] D.50.16.195.

[108] Saller, *Patriarchy, Property and Death*, 76.

[109] Even though, strictly speaking, there are some differences in what constitutes the agnatic line in Roman and tannaitic law; see the examples given in Yaron, "Basics of Roman and Jewish Intestacy," 208. See also Hyamson, *Mosaicarum et Romanarum*, 133–149.

[110] The relatives listed in the *mishnah* are ineligible to testify for or against each other.

[111] Epstein, *Tannaim*, 21. In my interpretation of *mishnah rishonah*, I depart from Epstein's definition of the term, a matter I develop in a forthcoming study entitled "The Myth of the *Mishnah Rishonah*."

biblical Israel, the outermost limits of the agnatic line are in the *mishpaḥah*, male clan members,[112] who include even distantly related family, as these are explicitly listed as agnates.[113] But the evidence in these *mishnayot* demonstrates that the expression teaches not only about the patrilineal aspects of biblical inheritance practices.[114] It also instructs that the outer limits of the agnatic system – even for the tanna of the *mishnah rishonah* – are clan members. Accordingly, when the term, *ra'uy lo lirushah*, is repeated in the name of Rabbi Yoḥanan ben Beroka, the connotation of all agnates in the clan remains. Rabbi Yoḥanan ben Beroka draws, therefore, from the biblical model of the clan (=*mishpaḥah*) – a conglomerate of *batei avot* – for defining the limits of the agnatic relationship between testator and beneficiary,[115] a limit which, perhaps appropriately for the cultural and social contexts in which the source is produced, matches the social, non-legal, connotation of the word *familia* among Romans.

Yaron on Rabbi Yoḥanan Ben Beroka

Despite some of the parallels and the simple meaning of Rabbi Yoḥanan ben Beroka's position, Reuven Yaron argues against the idea that Rabbi Yoḥanan ben Beroka refers to a unilateral disposition, that is, testate succession. When discussing Rabbi Yoḥanan ben Beroka's opinion, he writes:

> It should be made clear that the controversy concerns merely the question of terminology. Though speaking of 'inheritance', R. Johanan b. Beroqa is not establishing a unilateral disposition by which preference is given to one among several heirs. Even where terms denoting an 'inheriting' are employed, acquisition by the beneficiary or on his behalf is just as essential as in cases of pure 'gift'.[116]

In his discussion, Yaron collapses the distinction between gifting and inheriting (in this case not referring to intestacy but rather to testate succession) so central to tannaitic inheritance law.[117] He denies the full import of Rabbi Yoḥanan ben Beroka's innovation, choosing to reduce the legal position to a mere mention of inheritance terminology, formulaically for testate succession, even when constituting gifting. According to Yaron, the transfer of property of which Rabbi Yoḥanan ben Beroka speaks is essentially bilateral, requiring a formal act of acquisition by (or on behalf of) the recipient, as usually required when gifting, even though terminology for testate succession, *yirasheni*, is employed in the

---

112 Milgrom, *Leviticus 23–27*, 2238.
113 Numbers 27:11.
114 Cf. Schremer, *Male and Female*, 335.
115 Rabbi Yoḥanan ben Beroka's category is an expansion of the order of intestate succession in *mBB* 8:2, which lists primarily those relatives that would make up the biblical *bet av*.
116 Yaron, *Gifts*, 38.
117 See Chapter 1.

mishnah.[118] Yaron's interpretation here accords with the general thesis of his entire book *Gifts in Contemplation of Death* that early Jewish law does not include any representations of what he terms Roman law's core innovation, unilateral dispositions in case of death, a view many scholars accept.[119]

It is likely that what prevents Yaron from accepting that Rabbi Yoḥanan ben Beroka refers to unilateral inheriting is the fact that the anonymous opinion of the *mishnah* unequivocally states that unilateral dispositions are contrary to (the *mishnah*'s construction of) biblical law.[120] Accordingly, Yaron interprets Rabbi Yoḥanan ben Beroka as referring to (a form of) gifting (and not to testate succession) so that the opinion of the tanna would not contradict biblical law! We have no reason to assume, however, that the Rabbi Yoḥanan ben Beroka tradition means anything other than testate succession, an essentially "unilateral disposition by which preference is given to one among several heirs," as dictated by the simple reading of the position in its context. Our *mishnah* (*BB* 8:5) deals generally with the ability to circumvent the biblical order of succession, and Rabbi Yoḥanan ben Beroka's opinion is placed in opposition to the anonymous position,[121] indicating disagreement (i. e., he cannot be referring to gifting). Rabbi Yoḥanan ben Beroka employs the word "inherit" (*y-r-sh*), a term that refers to a unilateral, universal, and automatic transfer of property in tannaitic Hebrew specifically,[122] and he mentions an oral declaration which, in our *mishnah*, refers to testate succession.[123] In truth, therefore, by effecting changes to the order of succession[124] –

[118] Compare Daube, "Johanan Ben Baroqa and Women's Rights," 55.

[119] See, most recently, Schwartz, *Were the Jews a Mediterranean Society?*, 127 n. 47.

[120] The *mishnah* states: "If a man said, 'Such a man shall inherit from me,' and he has a daughter; or 'My daughter shall inherit from me,' and he has a son, he has said nothing, for he has laid down a condition *contrary to what is written in the Torah*." An additional consideration for Yaron may be that the anonymous opinion states a position opposing Rabbi Yoḥanan ben Beroka's, and in amoraic literature the anonymous opinion in the *mishnah* is (often) considered authoritative. On the different manifestations of this concept in amoraic literature, see Brandes, "Beginnings of the Rules," 286–297.

[121] This is also one of the assumptions in *bBB* 130a. See also the comments in Halivni, *Baba Batra*, 245–247.

[122] See Chapter 1.

[123] This is why Yaron's proposition, perhaps based on the assumption that the Rabbi Yoḥanan ben Beroka tradition is composed in response to par. I–II of the *mishnah* (see Chapter 1, and n. 13 above), is equally unreasonable: "the majority view was that any change in the order of succession had to be effected by way of 'gift', and expressions denoting 'to give' had to be used. R. Johanan b. Beroqa distinguished: changes in favour of one who was entitled to a share in the inheritance were valid even if expressions denoting 'to inherit' were used" (*Gifts*, 125). I contend that if the Rabbi Yoḥanan ben Beroka tradition refers to gifting (at least within the contours of *mBB* 8:5), it would likely mention a written disposition and not an oral one. On the distinction see Chapter 1.

[124] Compare Falk's formulation in his critique of Yaron, "R. Yoḥanan ben Baroqa's opinion does not 'concern merely the question of terminology' (p. 38), but expressly validates changes of the rules of succession" ("Testate Succession," 77).

unilaterally[125] elevating members of the family circle from potential to immediate heirs – the Rabbi Yoḥanan ben Beroka tradition introduces testate succession, at least among agnates, into tannaitic law.[126]

Conclusions

Our survey of testate succession among family members in antiquity demonstrates that Rabbi Yoḥanan ben Beroka's proposition to circumvent the order of intestate succession is well rooted in ancient inheritance practices. While legal traditions throughout the ancient world exhibit forms of testate succession among family members, Rabbi Yoḥanan ben Beroka's specific proposal accords best with one particular approach – Roman law's testament to the *sui heredes*. Indeed, without the punishment that may appear in Genesis, the adoption – as in ancient Near Eastern and Athenian law – or bequeathing to members of a broadly defined family – as in the apocryphal literature and Elephantine papyri – Rabbi Yoḥanan ben Beroka's innovation cannot be considered parallel to the evidence in these legal traditions. Rabbi Yoḥanan ben Beroka's form of testate succession, as a unilateral, universal, and automatic disposition, therefore, remains conceptually closest – even if not identical – to the Roman testament to the *sui heredes*. While applying to a larger mix of relatives (all those in the agnatic line) than its Roman counterpart, Rabbi Yoḥanan ben Beroka's form of testate succession remains truly *inter familia*, at least in the social sense of the term *familia* as used among contemporary Romans.

125 Rivlin, in *Inheritance and Wills*, 152, also contends that the mechanism promoted by Rabbi Yoḥanan ben Beroka is unilateral.

126 And, therefore, it may be deduced – *a fortiori* – that Rabbi Yoḥanan ben Beroka's position allows testate succession among immediate heirs (the preferred interpretation and limitation of his words in the classical rabbinic literature; see above in the body of the text).

Chapter 4

Inheritance by Daughters in Tannaitic Law and in the Ancient World

Introduction

In the previous chapter, I discuss testate succession among agnates, the form of testate succession espoused in the name of the tanna Rabbi Yoḥanan ben Beroka in *mBB* 8:5. One of the two examples in that *mishnah* for bypassing the order of intestate succession is the appointment of a daughter as heir in the presence of a son. In this chapter I show that the tannaim enable transfers of property to a daughter not only with testate succession but through other means as well, both direct and indirect. According to the rules of intestate succession, for example, a daughter acquires an inheritance share, that is, ownership and the accompanying right to alienate the property, when there are no sons (*mBB* 8:2).[1] I call this direct inheritance by daughters. Receiving a dowry[2] or *parnasah*[3] from a father during his lifetime, or from his estate after his death, and also posthumously receiving maintenance, *mezonot,* from his assets until marriage are, what I call, indirect inheritance by a daughter from a father's estate. These property transfers, although from a father's assets, either are not always made after a father's death and/or do not always result in the property being fully owned by a daughter. That is, she does not always have the right to alienate the property (at least not while married; see below).[4] Therefore, I treat *parnasah* and *mezonot* as distinct from direct inheritance.

---

[1] In this case, the mechanism is identical to inheritance by sons (see Chapter 1).

[2] Historians argue that throughout the ancient Mediterranean region a father's gift of a dowry to his daughter represents the equivalent of her share in the inheritance; see, e. g., Saller, "Roman Dowry," 195–205; Cox, *Household Interests*, 116–120; and Schremer, *Male and Female*, 263–292. See also the bibliography of anthropological works cited in Schremer, *Male and Female,* 262 n. 5.

[3] On this term, see Schremer, *Male and Female*, 263 n. 10; and, before him, B. Cohen, *Jewish and Roman Law*, 353. The later Babylonian Aramaic term used for dowry, *nedunya*, is paralleled in the Akkadian *nudunum*, (see B. Cohen, *Jewish and Roman Law*, 350–351 and the bibliography in Schremer, *Male and Female*, 292 n. 115). On the use of the word *ketubbah* to mean dowry in some rabbinic sources, see M. Friedman, *Jewish Marriage*, 292 and 310–311. On Greek and Roman legal parallels, see B. Cohen, *Jewish and Roman Law*, 348–376, and Schremer, *Male and Female*, 263–285.

[4] The dowries include the provision in the father's estate to provide a dowry to a daughter when she marries (specifically, *nikhsei tson barzel*, which remains under the ownership of the

All of these tannaitic precepts stand in stark contrast to biblical literature's strict adherence to inheritance only among males in the agnatic line and, in the absence of sons, endogamy for inheritance purposes. A daughter is to marry a member of the family or tribe in order to serve as a conduit for the transfer of her father's property to eventual sons (the grandsons of the deceased).[5] That is, strictly speaking, the daughter does not own the property – she does not have a right to alienate the property. She holds the property only until such time as she transfers it to the rightful male heir(s) (her son or sons) of the original decedent. This, in theory, keeps the ancestral property among the male heirs of a (grand) father's family. Similar conventions are known from the ancient Near East and parts of ancient Greece (see below).

In the following pages, I discuss these traditions and, in addition, I argue that the application of source critical methods uncovers another tannaitic approach, one that endorses direct inheritance by a daughter even in the presence of a son![6] Direct inheritance is known in the region in urbanized societies, the earliest among them Sumer and, contemporaneous to tannaitic society, Rome. Among presumed representations of Jewish law, another form of inheritance by daughters in the presence of sons is present in the writings of Philo: an unmarried daughter secures a share equal to that of a brother from a father's assets because she has not yet received a dowry. Philo's testimony may, in fact, provide evidence for a middle stage in the conceptual continuum from the Bible's endogamy to the more inclusive tannaitic approaches for inheritance by daughters that I examine here.

The three principles developed and documented in tannaitic literature, namely, collection of an inheritance share, receipt of a dowry, and maintenance, are neither present in biblical literature nor the product of rabbinic scriptural interpretation. Following the approach of Jacob Milgrom, below I maintain that direct inheritance by daughters (actual ownership of the property and the right

---

husband for the duration of the marriage) and the maintenance of an unmarried daughter from the estate until she marries. On all these provisions, see below "Inheritance by Daughters in Tannaitic Law."

[5] For a discussion of the conflicting biblical sources, see below "Inheritance by Daughters in the Bible."

[6] A separate tradition, found in *tYad* 2:20 and paralleled in *Megillat Ta'anit* (24th of Av; Noam ed., 86), *pBB* 8:1, 16a (1252), and *bBB* 115b–116a (see also *bPes* 51a), records a dispute regarding inheritance by daughters in the absence of sons but in the presence of daughters of sons. According to rabbinic law when a man who is predeceased by his son, dies, the daughters of his son (in the absence of brothers), as next in the agnatic line, inherit directly from the decedent's estate while the deceased's daughters receive nothing. According to this tradition, the Sadducees argue that the daughters of the decedent should also inherit. On the legal conceptualization in these sources, see Yaron, "Sadducees and Pharisees"; on the relationship of the versions of the tradition to one another, see Noam, *Megillat Ta'anit*, 86 and 223. The recent contribution by Aharon Shemesh most convincingly and comprehensively resolves the textual and logical problems found in the traditions; see "*Mah gilah menashe ben ḥizkiyah batorah*?" 91–103.

to alienate it) – even in the absence of sons – is not documented in biblical literature. The predominant approach in the literature is endogamy for the purpose of inheriting (described above).[7] Regarding the dowry, as one scholar concisely puts it, "in biblical law, no laws regarding a dowry were formulated."[8] Finally, support for a non-married daughter from a deceased father's estate, while perhaps rightfully assumed, is not elucidated at all in biblical literature. Tannaitic literature, too, is silent about the scriptural underpinnings, if any, of these three institutions.[9] The presence of these principles in tannaitic law, therefore, should be seen as the product of a protracted process of adopting and adapting widespread ancient inheritance customs,[10] apparently appropriate to the social and economic conditions experienced by the rabbis (for more on this see below).[11]

Significant for comparison is the evidence for the social position of a daughter in the Roman society of the classical period. Judith Hallett, in her enlightening study *Fathers and Daughters in Roman Society*,[12] argues that the source material from ca. 220 BCE to ca. 130 CE that she analyzes shows what she calls, the "Roman cultural valuation of daughters."[13] She explains the degree to which the centrality of the daughter role remains a cultural constant during the classical

---

[7] This is even Milgrom's reading of Numbers 27, a chapter some scholars argue is evidence for a form of direct inheritance by a daughter in the absence of sons (see below, "Inheritance by Daughters in the Bible").

[8] Fleishman, "A Daughter's Demand," 355; cf. Greengus, *Laws*, 73. Scholars actually disagree about whether the dowry exists in biblical law at all; see, e.g., Wasserstein, "A Marriage Contract from the Province of Arabia Nova," 126, who argues that there is no legal institution of dowry in the Bible. This approach is also embraced, among others, by Schremer, *Male and Female*, 233 n. 19. Even for those who assume that the dowry is present in biblical law, the evidence for it is drawn primarily from comparison with ancient Near Eastern practices; e.g., Westbrook maintains the existence of the biblical dowry, or *shilukhim*; see Westbrook, *Property and Family*, 142–164; and, following his lead, Ben-Barak, *Inheritance by Daughters*, 6. For an independent discussion of dowries, see more recently Lemos, *Marriage Gifts and Social Change*, 50–59.

[9] Indeed, Rabbi Elazar ben Azariah does not resort to scriptural interpretation to provide proof for the maintenance of a daughter from a father's estate and, in an unusual move, he midrashically expounds the words of a *mishnah* (see below, "Inheritance by Daughters in Tannaitic Law").

[10] On the dowry in the Neo-Sumerian period, see Falkenstein, *Neusumerische Gerichtsurkunden*, 144–145 (no. 88) and 168–169 (no. 103). For the Old Babylonian period see n. 111; the Middle Babylonian period, see Podany, Beckman, and Colbow, "Adoption," 51; and see the discussion below in "Inheritance by Daughters in the Ancient World"; for Nuzi, see Grosz, "Dowry and Brideprice in Nuzi"; the Neo-Assyrian period, see Kwasman, *Neo-Assyrian Legal Documents*, no. 69; the Neo-Babylonian, see Wunsch, *Die Urkunden*, 113–114 (no. 137) and 173–174 (no. 209). On Emar, see the listing in Westbrook, "Emar and Vicinity," 679; on Ugarit, Marquez Rowe, "Ugarit," 730. See also the *Hittite Laws* 27 (in Roth, *Law Collections*, 220–221). On Athens, see MacDowell, *Law in Classical Athens*, 87–89; on Rome, see Saller, "Roman Dowry," 195–205.

[11] See also the Introduction.

[12] Hallett, *Fathers and Daughters*.

[13] Hallett, *Fathers and Daughters*, 97.

period, resulting in the daughter's continued prominent position in matters of inheritance despite legislation that attempts "to channel private wealth away from rich men's daughters and into the hands of males."[14] While still in her father's *potestas*, a daughter inherits from her father equally with her brother(s) in the event of intestacy;[15] however, the daughter's designation as heir to a large patrimony and her receipt of legacies come under attack when the *Lex Voconia* is issued in 169 BCE. Hallett explains that "any legacy left to a woman could not exceed what was left to the (male) heir or heirs."[16] Yet fathers seemingly find ways around the legislation, showing their deep affection for their daughters.[17] The time period examined by Hallett overlaps significantly with the dates for the data studied by Richard Saller (from ca. 200 BCE to ca. 235 CE) in his book *Patriarchy, Property and Death in the Roman Family*,[18] for which the source material is representative of an urbanized Rome made up primarily of nuclear families.[19] If Hallett's analysis is correct,[20] then perhaps, the "cultural valuation of daughters" – and its effect on inheritance practices – is a logical corollary to the presence of the nuclear family in an urbanized setting.[21] This would seem to be the case for ancient Rome and, as I suggest below, also for parts of the ancient Near East (see "Inheritance by Daughters in the Ancient Near East"). Tannaitic literature also originates in a social and economic context in which urbanization, privatization of land, and the nuclear family are predominant, and is roughly contemporary to the later material examined by both Hallett and Saller. Accordingly, I suggest that, while not conclusive, the innovations inclusive of daughters in tannaitic inheritance law may be the outcome not only of legal adaptation but also of accommodation. A major difference remains, however, between Roman and tannaitic conceptualization. Some Roman legislation seeks to frustrate the freedoms of daughters, only to have fathers restore the spirit of equal division that was original to Roman law. Their actions – not the legislation – are represen-

[14] Hallett, *Fathers and Daughters*, 96.

[15] Hallett, *Fathers and Daughters*, 90.

[16] Hallett, *Fathers and Daughters*, 93.

[17] See, e.g., the discussion of Cicero's second oration against Verres, in which the story of P. Annius Assellus appears. To ensure that his only daughter, indeed, inherits, he seemingly fails to register her at the census, exempting himself from the *Lex Voconia* (Hallett, *Fathers and Daughters*, 96).

[18] Saller, *Patriarchy, Property and Death.*

[19] See, e.g., Saller, *Patriarchy, Property and Death*, 4 and 82.

[20] For reservations concerning Hallett's argument, see Dixon, review of Hallett, *Fathers and Daughters in Roman Society*, 125–130.

[21] Indeed, Milgrom argues that the superior status of women, generally, and daughters, specifically, in ancient Mesopotamia's urbanized centers is evidenced by their full inheritance rights; see *Numbers*, 482 (see also "Inheritance by Daughters in the Ancient Near East" below). Schremer points to the parallel improvement of the status of the mother and wife in both Roman and rabbinic sources as a result of the predominance of the nuclear family; see *Male and Female*, 334–336. For more on both the possible effects of urbanization and the nucleation of the family on tannaitic law, see the Introduction.

tative of the "Roman cultural valuation of daughters." For the tannaim, however, it is the legislation itself that promotes the inclusion of daughters.

Although we cannot successfully argue that the Roman reality had any immediate implications for tannaitic law (or the society in which the tannaim lived), I raise the possibility that a parallel development to the Roman situation may be reflected in the tannaitic laws related to inheritance by daughters. That is, although it cannot be definitively demonstrated, the presence of developments inclusive of daughters in tannaitic law may be related to the social and economic contexts in which the tannaim themselves lived. Indeed, together, the three areas in which tannaitic law adds to its biblical antecedent – direct inheritance, dowry, and maintenance – may point to new ways of dealing with the concern for a daughter's welfare after she leaves her father's house or after he is no longer alive to care for her. And, perhaps, these three topics point to a newly perceived awareness of her exclusion from direct inheritance in the presence of sons, a situation that remained to be rectified.

The earlier biblical laws of endogamy related to inheritance prevent not only less-than-economically ideal land transfers between tribes and families. In theory, the laws also protect a daughter without a male provider (e.g., in the case of her father dying and the absence of a brother) by handing her marketable assets – landholdings – that would assist her in securing provision and protection through marriage. These young women are embraced by family members, men who theoretically might even have an interest in the woman's well-being beyond the acquisition of, and usufruct from, an uncle's estate. What the tannaim add – perhaps in light of the starkly different social and economic conditions in which they find themselves – is actual ownership of property and, due to this ownership, some amount of protection and position for a daughter.

In this way, tannaitic legislation even surpasses Roman regulation. For, according to tannaitic law, the married woman could own property of her own.[22] In early Roman law, however, a woman in a standard *cum manu* marriage does not own her own property;[23] even property she owns prior to the marriage passes to the ownership of her husband.[24] If we could argue that tannaitic law actually reflects a "cultural valuation" for daughters, different from the protection provided to daughters by biblical law, then this esteem is not only behind the three tannaitic innovations already outlined. It culminates in a tannaitic legal opinion,

---

[22] The property consists primarily of property she owns before the marriage or which is given to her upon marriage (see below). In biblical Israel, by contrast, women seemingly have no property rights while in many parts of ancient Mesopotamia, women do have rights in connection with both moveable and immoveable property; see Milgrom, *Numbers*, 482.

[23] And in a *sine manu* marriage, the property is owned by her father.

[24] Du Plessis, *Borkowski's Textbook*, 126. For a comparison of the legal traditions, see B. Cohen, *Jewish and Roman Law*, 179–278. On the paucity of source material from the ancient world indicating that land is given as property in dowries and the preference, instead, for movables; see Schremer, *Male and Female*, 272–276. See also Oudshoorn, *Relationship*, 296.

silenced in *mBB* 8:4 but uncovered by source critical tools, that promotes direct and equal inheritance by daughters *even in the presence of sons*! Certainly the prevalence of the nuclear family and privatized landholdings could bring with it a concern for the welfare of particular family members – especially daughters – as individuals in need of their own economic security through receipt of portions of the partible paternal estate. Furthermore, the onset of urbanization in tannaitic Palestine – as elsewhere in the ancient world – may have done its share, offering women opportunities for both social and economic advancement through the acquisition and ownership of property; and the effects of this upward social mobility may be reflected in tannaitic law. Accordingly, the inclusiveness of tannaitic law may be the result of the social and economic setting of tannaitic Palestine combined with the presence in the ancient Near East and Mediterranean of legal traditions allowing direct inheritance by daughters. The discussion of inheritance by daughters in tannaitic law in comparative context – with an emphasis on the newly revealed approach – continues below.

Inheritance by Daughters in Tannaitic Law

As mentioned previously, tannaitic law classifies inheritance by daughters into three categories: direct receipt of shares in the absence of sons, acceptance of a dowry from a father's estate, whether during his lifetime or posthumously, and maintenance from a father's property after his death until the daughter marries. I address these forms of inheritance for daughters in this section and also describe a fourth approach – the endorsement of direct inheritance by a daughter even in the presence of a son – embedded and camouflaged within *mBB* 8:4.

The direct receipt of an inheritance portion by a daughter in the absence of sons, rather than inheritance through endogamy, is assumed by the tannaitic legal collections. In fact, tannaitic *midrashim* declare explicitly that the institution of endogamy for the purpose of inheriting was only applicable in biblical times.[25] Actually, the whole institution of endogamy is transformed in post-biblical times, its radical recasting seemingly the outcome, at least in part, of social and economic changes. As Adiel Schremer demonstrates, though the practice of endogamy exists in the Second Temple and tannaitic periods, it is not linked to inheritance; and in post-biblical texts, it is presented exclusively as a way to ensure purity of lineage for marriage.[26] This thesis is supported by the exclusion

---

[25] *Sifra, Emor,* Parashah 4,3 (96a, Weiss ed.). See the insightful comments in *Perush Rabenu Hillel*, 58b. See also Targum Pseudo-Jonathan to Numbers 36:6; *pTa'anit* 4:11, 69c (738); *bBB* 120; see also Kahana, *Sifre to Numbers* 134 to lines 9–10 and 16–17 (60–61 [Hebrew character numbering], 1137, and 1139); my thanks to Menahem Kahana for providing me with a pre-publication copy of the relevant sections of his edition of *Sifre to Numbers*.

[26] *Male and Female*, 162–168 (first noted by A.S. Herschberg; see Schremer, *Male and Female*, 166 n. 29).

of a requirement in tannaitic law that daughters (without brothers) marry family members.[27]

By means of the dowry, a daughter receives an indirect inheritance in tannaitic law.[28] The dowry can be received from a father as a gift during his lifetime[29] or after his death from his estate.[30] The term "dowry" primarily means *nikhsei tson barzel* (iron sheep assets).[31] *Tson barzel* is property that the husband assumes ownership of and administers during a marriage. In the event of divorce or the husband's death, the wife receives the *tson barzel* property according to its original value.[32] *Nikhsei melug* (plucking assets),[33] on the other hand, are the private possessions of a wife brought into a marriage. Since these also can originate as a gift during the parents' lifetime (unrelated to the designated dowry), I treat them as indirect inheritance. *Melug* property remains under the ownership of the wife although the husband enjoys usufructuary rights to it and, at times, even manages it.[34] In the event of the husband's death (or divorce), she retains the property at its current value (i. e., after profit or loss since the time of marriage).[35]

The institutions of the dowry and maintenance for unmarried daughters from a father's estate after his death are intertwined in two rabbinic *takkanot* (sing., *takkanah*),[36] or enactments, legislated in *mKet* 4:10–11: *ketubbat benin*

---

27 See, e. g., *Sifre to Numbers* 134; and *mBB* 8:2–3.

28 Later Talmudic sources link the dowry to what would have been the daughter's inheritance share. On Talmudic traditions documenting whether a father is expected to grant his daughter a dowry in the amount equal to a son's inheritance portion, see M. Friedman, *Jewish Marriage*, 290 n. 5; and Schremer, *Male and Female* 265–267.

29 On the minimum dowry, see *mKet* 6:5.

30 For the dispute regarding the calculation of a dowry for one whose father has died, see *mKet* 6:6.

31 Possibly the dowry is called by this term because it figuratively denotes "iron security," (L. Epstein, *Jewish Marriage Contract*, 92 n. 12). I take that view to mean the dowry is ironclad security because it retains its original value even if the marriage ends many years later (see below in the body).

32 On all this, see *mYev* 7:1–2 and *tYev* 9:1–2. For a bibliography on these institutions, see M. Friedman, *Jewish Marriage*, 291 n. 8; and Schremer, *Male and Female*, 270–272, and 275.

33 "It describes property of which the husband plucks the fruit without carrying any responsibility for the safety of the principal" (L. Epstein, *Jewish Marriage Contract*, 92 n. 16).

34 On the ancient Near Eastern origins of the term *melug* property, see B. Levine, "Mulugu/ Melug," 271–285; and the critical comments by Kaufman, *Akkadian Influences on Aramaic*, 73 (as per M. Friedman, *Jewish Marriage*, 291 n. 8). See also the relevant discussions in Geller, "Ketubbah," 227–245.

35 Based on evidence from the Judean desert and Elephantine, however, Michael Satlow distinguishes between dowries and actual gifts of land given to daughters at or near the time of marriage. The latter would not be at all under the control of the husband. See Satlow, "Marriage Payments and Succession Strategies," 62–65; and Satlow, *Marriage*, 204–209. On a dowry being made up of movables and gifts of land, see Oudshoorn, *Relationship*, 296 (however see n. 24).

36 For a discussion of the father's obligation to support his daughters during his lifetime, see M. Friedman, *Jewish Marriage*, 356–358.

dikhrin[37] and *ketubbat benan nukban*.[38] *Ketubbat benin dikhrin* is a proviso that stipulates that the inheritance of a wife's dowry pass exclusively to *her* sons (see below).[39] The *ketubbat benan nukban* stipulation legislates the maintenance for daughters from a father's estate after his death.[40] These conditions are considered part of a wife's *ketubbah* (marriage document), even when not explicitly mentioned in it.[41] Another *mishnah*, *mKet* 4:6, states in the name of R. Elazar ben Azariah that "'the sons inherit and the daughters receive maintenance' – just like the sons inherit only after the father's death so too the daughters receive maintenance only after the father's death." Mordechai Friedman shows[42] that this (midrashic) exposition attributed to R. Elazar ben Azariah is actually a Hebrew paraphrase and interpretation[43] of the earlier Aramaic formulation[44] of the two aforementioned *takkanot*, found in *mKet* 4:10–11. Indeed, it is R. Elazar ben Azariah's statement that prescribes the exclusively posthumous application of the two *takkanot*.[45]

The concept behind the *ketubbat benin dikhrin* stipulation – paralleled elsewhere in the ancient world (see below) – has important implications for inheritance. Since a husband inherits his wife's assets,[46] fathers fear that the dowry they give their daughters eventually will fall into the hands of grandsons not their own. For, if a man has children both with a first and a subsequent wife,[47]

---

[37] In this context, meaning "the *ketubbah* (i.e., dowry money) of the male children." On *ketubbah* as also referring to dowry, see M. Friedman, *Jewish Marriage*, 310; and with reference specifically to the *ketubbat benin dikhrin*, see M. Friedman, *Jewish Marriage*, 383.

[38] In this context, meaning "provision for female children."

[39] See also *mKet* 10:2.

[40] On the textual history of this institution, see M. Friedman, *Jewish Marriage*, 356–360.

[41] As a *tenai beit din*, or provision of the court, binding even if not explicitly listed in the marriage document. For another provision of the court, see Chapter 5.

[42] Here I follow the convincing interpretation offered in M. Friedman, *Jewish Marriage*, 374–377. Friedman's position is against the interpretation offered by J. N Epstein (*Mavo*, 728) that Rabbi Elazar ben Azariah comments on *mKet* 13:3 (=*mBB* 9:1).

[43] M. Friedman, *Jewish Marriage*, 376.

[44] The *ketubbat benin dikhrin* clause reads, "Male children that you will have from me shall inherit your *ketubbah* in addition to the portion that they receive with their brothers" (*mKet* 4:10). The *ketubbat benan nukban* clause reads, "Female children that you will have from me shall reside in my house and receive maintenance from my goods until they marry husbands" (4:11). For more on *ketubbat benin dikhrin*, see Yaron, *Gifts*, 176–181; and Rivlin, *Inheritance and Wills*, 44–54; on *ketubbat benan nukban*, see Yaron, *Gifts*, 181; and Rivlin, *Inheritance and Wills*, 43–45.

[45] Since the *benan nukban* clause does not stipulate the death of the father in order for a daughter to receive maintenance, R. Elazar ben Azariah extrapolates from the *benin dikhrin* provision, in which it is implicit, that this is also the case for maintenance of daughters (see the formulations in the previous note). Read on its own, the *benan nukban* stipulation actually implies that a father has to support his daughters during his lifetime, but R. Elazar ben Azariah recognizes the legal claim only after the father's death; see M. Friedman, *Jewish Marriage*, 359.

[46] *mBB* 8:1.

[47] The same reasoning applies whether the wives are both married to the same man simultaneously (as in cases of polygamy) or successively.

then after his death, his second wife's children would take equal shares of the first wife's assets (along with the first wife's children). Strikingly, the rabbinic *ketubbat benin dikhrin* actually accomplishes the same goal as biblical endogamy for inheritance: it keeps the (grand)father's property strictly among those called his descendants.[48] A parallel to the tannaitic *ketubbat benin dikhrin* is known in the ancient Near East,[49] Athens,[50] and Elephantine.[51] A significant formulaic parallel to the tannaitic institution is found in an Edomite marriage contract from 176 BCE,[52] intimating that the rabbinic clause may originate in Aramaic common law.[53] According to classical Talmudic sources, the stipulation is implemented to encourage fathers to give larger dowries.[54] As mentioned, the *ketubbat benan nukban* stipulation ensures that daughters are provided for from a father's assets in his absence. The legal conditions of both the *ketubbat benan nukban* and *ketubbat benin dikhrin* seemingly also are attested in Judean desert marriage documents.[55] This fact may provide further evidence for living traditions from which the tannaim may draw when constructing their laws.[56]

Additional legislation regarding maintenance for daughters may exemplify the concern the rabbis have for their female offspring. Indeed, the fact that in the event of a father's death the welfare of daughters is paramount is clear from the mishnaic tradition, cited in the name of Admon, that if only a small estate is left behind, priority is given to the maintenance of unwed daughters: "if a man died and left sons and daughters and the property was great, the sons inherit and

[48] The difference that remains, however, is that in the Bible the name of the deceased grandfather is only considered to continue to exist as long as it is attached to ancestral land. This is implicit in the verse, "Let not our *father's name* be lost to his clan just because he had no son" (Numbers 27:4); see Milgrom, *Numbers*, 231. On this issue see, further, Westbrook, *Property and Family*, 29, 64, 75. For more on the issue see below, "Inheritance by Daughters in the Bible." No link between land and name seems to exist in tannaitic law.

[49] See, e.g., the Code of Hammurabi 167 (Roth, *Law Collections*, 113); see the listings in M. Friedman, *Jewish Marriage*, 380–381 nn. 5–6. Friedman emphasizes that the tannaitic institution, in all probability, is "an extension of the same Near Eastern tradition" (*Jewish Marriage*, 381).

[50] Harrison, *Law of Athens*, 1:57. On a possible parallel at Gortyn, see the discussion and notes in Schaps, *Economic Rights of Women*, 86.

[51] See M. Friedman, *Jewish Marriage*, 379–380 nn. 1–4.

[52] See Eshel and Kloner, "Aramaic Ostracon," 1–22 (esp., 13).The truncated text is found in Eshel and Kloner, "Aramaic Ostracon," 3; line 6 reads, בנין דכרין זי יהוון לי מנה] and line 7, ומראי ביתי וירתי מן].

[53] I thank Aaron Koller for bringing this to my attention.

[54] M. Friedman, *Jewish Marriage*, 290 n. 5; Schremer, *Male and Female*, 265–267.

[55] Cotton and Yardeni, *Aramaic, Hebrew and Greek Documentary Texts*, 270–273. However, the stipulations are omitted from Greek marriage documents found in the Judean desert (two of which mention Greek *nomos*). For a discussion, see Lapin, "Maintenance," 191–193.

[56] For more on the idea that the parallels likely indicate the tannaim draw from living traditions, see the Introduction and Chapter 5.

the daughters receive maintenance; but if the property was small, the daughters receive maintenance and the sons go a begging" (*mKet* 13:3=*mBB* 9:1).[57]

Even with all of the advances, which significantly circumvent the rigidity of the biblical intestate inheritance system and grant a daughter the right to property, scholars emphasize how the rabbis fall short of granting a daughter full rights of succession along with her brother(s), as do some of their urbanized neighbors and predecessors in the region.[58] In light of this, one other tannaitic tradition deserves particular attention, especially since a source critical analysis results in the unveiling of an approach promoting direct inheritance by daughters even in the presence of sons! Mishnah *Baba Batra* 8:4 states:

I.	אחד הבן ואחד הבת בנחלה	The son and the daughter are the same regarding inheritance
II.	אלא שהבן נוטל פי שנים בניכסי האב ואינו נוטל פי שנים בניכסי האם	except that [*ella she-*] the [firstborn] son takes a double portion of the father's property but does not take a double portion of the mother's property,
III.	והבנות ניזונות מנכסי האב ואינן ניזונות מנכסי האם.[59]	and the daughters receive maintenance from the father's property and do not receive maintenance from the mother's property.

Paragraph I of our *mishnah*, read in isolation, makes a striking statement, "the son and the daughter are the same regarding inheritance," that is, when the heirs include sons and daughters they inherit equally! And even though when read together with paragraphs II–III, the impression is that these are a qualification of paragraph I, a textual problem remains. The lack of agreement between the topic of paragraph I – the ability of a *son and a daughter* to inherit – and the subject matter of paragraphs II–III – rules governing the difference between allocations from the *father's estate versus the mother's estate*[60] – intimates that the

[57] See M. Friedman, *Jewish Marriage*, 376; and the discussion of this *mishnah* in Hauptman, *Rereading the Rabbis*, 179. See also below "Philo and the Tannaitic Traditions," where I discuss this *mishnah* in light of the writings of Philo.

[58] Consider, e. g., the comment by Milgrom, based on a private communication from Saul Lieberman, which is worth citing here in full: "That they [the rabbis] resisted both the practice of the outside world and the moral urgings of conscience can only mean that they were convinced that inheritance by agnates was an immutable postulate of the Torah" (Milgrom, *Numbers*, 484, and 519 n. 15).

[59] In MS Kaufmann, both occurrences of *nikhsei* in par. III are written without a *yod*, unlike in par. II.

[60] Hauptman's description of the discord between pars. I and II–III is informative: "Once it is established that sons and daughters are the same with respect to inheritance, one would expect the next clause, introduced by the expression *elah* (however), to indicate ways in which sons and daughters differ, i. e., sons and daughters are treated in the same way except for the following. But the *mishnah* goes on to list the ways in which inheriting a father's estate is different from inheriting a mother's estate, first for sons and then for daughters. The logical construction of

two sections, paragraph I, on the one hand, and paragraphs II–III, on the other, were originally two separate literary units. Two independent tannaitic sources are brought together here and linked by the phrase *ella she-*.

Already the Babylonian amoraim notice the dissonance between the issues addressed in paragraph I and paragraphs II–III, as well as the difficulty posed by the linking clause *ella she-* and its usage here.[61] In *bBB* 122b no less than four amoraic opinions are offered – by Rav Nachman bar Yitshak, Rav Papa, Rav Ashi, and Mar bar Rav Ashi – toward the goal of conceptually connecting the two parts of the *mishnah*. The *sugya* there concludes with the opinion of Mar bar Rav Ashi that, in truth, paragraph I should state, "the son and the daughter [when there are no sons] are the same regarding [inheriting] *a mother's assets and a father's assets* (=*shavin benikhsei ha'em uvenikhsei ha'av*)." By suggesting that the subject of paragraph I is the capacity of a son and a daughter (in the absence of sons) to inherit equally *from the assets of the mother and the assets of the father*, Mar bar Rav Ashi fills the gap to make paragraphs II–III, dealing with the rules for inheriting from each parent's estate, a qualification of paragraph I.

Although the amoraim propose solutions regarding the logical, there remain challenges regarding the *philo*logical. These are aptly addressed by J. N. Epstein who, building on the difficulty presented by the amoraim, suggests the two sources from which paragraph I, on the one hand, and paragraphs II–III, on the other, may originate, and how they are ultimately reworked and linked with the expression *ella she-*.[62] Epstein argues that paragraph I originally stated, "*eḥad haben ve'eḥad habat lenaḥalat ha'em*,"[63] "the son and the daughter are the same regarding inheritance *of the mother*['s estate]," a formulation conceptually parallel and linguistically very close to that presented by a chain of tannaim in *tBB* 7:10, "the son and the daughter are *equal regarding the assets of the mother* (=*eḥad haben ve'eḥad habat shavin benikhsei ha'em*).[64] Namely, the son does not precede the daughter when inheriting from the mother; rather, both the son and the daughter inherit equally from the mother, the son only preceding the daughter when inheriting from the father.

---

the *mishnah* is therefore faulty" (Hauptman, "Women and Inheritance in Rabbinic Texts," 231–232). And as concisely stated by my student Jordan Soffer what one would expect after *ella she-* is "distinctions between the son and the daughter, not (as the *mishnah* indeed goes on to do) a distinction between the father's property and the mother's property" (oral communication).

[61] Of the four examples given when explaining the use of *ella she-* in mishnaic Hebrew (*Suk* 4:9; *Ned* 9:10; *Sot* 3:5 and *BB* 8:4) in Azar, *Syntax of Mishnaic Hebrew*, 142, only *BB* 8:4 (our *mishnah*) seems to fit Azar's second definition: "and at times an element of rejecting a conclusion which could be arrived at from the preceding statement is felt (in its usage)" (translation mine). If so, then perhaps the original usage does not have this additional connotation. The secondary definition is the result of the combination of sources in this *mishnah*.

[62] Here J. N. Epstein follows Ginzberg, "Tamid," 41, regarding *ella she-* as a phrase which, at times, links two separate sources. See J. N. Epstein, *Mavo*, 660 n. 2.

[63] On the two versions, "*benaḥalah*" and "*lenaḥalah*," see J. N. Epstein, *Mavo*, 659.

[64] Compare this to Mar bar Rav Ashi's formulation in *bBB* 122b (cited above).

Epstein explains that our *mishnah*'s authors have this tradition but do not want to rule in accordance with the tannaim in the Tosefta who rule that, in fact, daughters inherit equally from the mother's assets. Rather, they want to rule like the anonymous opinion in *tBB* 7:10 that the son precedes the daughter *even* when inheriting from the mother. Accordingly, the *mishnah*'s authors remove the word *ha'em* and retain *benaḥalah*, yielding *eḥad haben ve'eḥad habat benaḥalah*, the contents of paragraph I. Epstein skillfully interprets this statement to mean that sons and daughters – in the absence of sons – are the same when inheriting from the father's or the mother's estate. Later, the abbreviated statement in paragraph I is joined to another tradition (pars. II–III) using the linking words *ella she-*. This tradition, made up of paragraphs II–III, is partially paralleled in *mBekh* 8:9.[65] According to Epstein, the disconnect between paragraph I and paragraphs II–III is evidence, therefore, of the editorial process that leads to the redaction of *mBB* 8:4. Certainly Epstein provides a meaningful model for reconstructing the process of the composition of *mBB* 8:4. His approach, however, is not without its difficulties and, although I follow Epstein's lead, below I propose an alternative reconstruction.

Epstein's contention that *ha'em* is removed from the phrase *lenaḥalat ha'em* in the original tradition to promote a son preceding a daughter even when inheriting from the mother's estate seems difficult. First, the presumed formulation *naḥalat ha'em* is not known in tannaitic literature, precluding the probability of the original tradition in paragraph I from stating this. The preferred expression is *nikhsei ha'em* (the formulation in *tBB* 7:10, the source Epstein cites as conceptually parallel to [the original] *mBB* 8:4 par. I).[66] Furthermore, the ensuing sentence, "the son and the daughter are the same regarding inheritance," does not, in and of itself, promote sons preceding daughters at all. Read on its own, it actually asserts that a son does *not* precede a daughter; rather, a son and a daughter inherit equally![67] A reconstruction of the redaction of *mBB* 8:4 that accounts for this meaning of paragraph I, therefore, is in order.

Indeed, because paragraph I reads perfectly well as an independent tradition and, in any case, does not match the exact language of *tBB* 7:10 (the tradition that Epstein presumes is conceptually associated with par. I in *mBB* 8:4), it seems reasonable to suggest that paragraph I – which read alone clearly states that a son and a daughter inherit equally – is, in and of itself, an independent tannaitic tradition. The formulation in paragraph I bears a resemblance, in fact, to the formulation of another talmudic tradition – of unknown provenance – preserved

[65] "The firstborn takes a double portion of his father's estate, but he does not take a double portion of his mother's estate" (*mBekh* 8:9).

[66] See also *mBB* 8:3 and pars. II and III of our *mishnah*, *BB* 8:4.

[67] On *eḥad … ve'eḥad* as equal, see also for example, *mKer* 2:4 and 2:6; cf. Hauptman, "Women and Inheritance," 231 and 233.

in the Palestinian Talmud, *BB* 8:1, 16a (1252), and there, in the mouths of "the sages of the gentiles!":

חכמי גוים אומרים בן ובת שוין כאחת.	The sages of the gentiles say, "son and daughter are equal [in matters of inheritance]."

Other Talmudic statements inclusive of direct inheritance by a daughter are also linked to non-Jews[68] and to non-rabbinic Jews.[69] What makes this tradition unique is that actual scriptural exegesis is put into the mouths of non-Jewish sages.[70] Whatever the origins of the comment,[71] the uniformity of its message with the contents of *mBB* 8:4 paragraph I, and the overlap between the words of the *ḥakhmei goyim*, *ben uvat shavin ke'eḥat*, and the formulation in paragraph I, *eḥad haben ve'eḥad habat benaḥalah*, is significant. A tradition promoting

[68] On *ḥakhmei umot ha'olam* in the Bavli, see Feintuch, "Daughters' Inheritance," 212 n. 25. A Babylonian Talmudic story in *bShab* 116b discusses tannaim – including Imma Shalom (Rabbi Eliezer's wife and Rabban Gamliel's sister) – and purports to quote a text from the Gospels [!] (not extant in Christian Bibles, however). Imma Shalom and Rabban Gamliel plan to ridicule and expose a judge, seemingly a sectarian, by bribing him. Imma Shalom gives him the bribe, a gold lamp, and when she requests a share of her father's estate, her brother R. Gamliel protests that this is illegal. The judge's response (according to Oxford Opp. Add. (fol. 23)) is: מן יומא דגליתון מן ארעכון איתנטילת אוריתא דמשה מנכון ואיתיהיבת לכון אוריתא דעון גיליון וכתי' ביה "ברא וברתא כחדא יירתון".

"Since the day that you were exiled from your land, the law of Moses was taken away from you, and the law of the Evangelicals (=Gospels) was given to you in which is written, 'a son and a daughter inherit equally'" (=*berah uveratah keḥadah yirtun*). The word "Evangelicals" appears in manuscripts (see MS Munich 95; MS Vatican 487.8; MS Klosterneuberg-Augustiner Chorherrenstift (129–130); MS British Library Or. 5558 A/14; JTS ENA 2069.6; and the Soncino printing [1489 or later]). The standard printed edition (Vilna), however, has "safra aḥariti" (= "another book"). The story ends with R. Gamliel bringing a more valuable bribe, a donkey, to the judge, causing him to forbid that the inheritance portion go to Imma Shalom (exposing the judge's corruption). On this story see Feintuch, "Daughters' Inheritance," 214–215 and n. 40 for a possible parallel in the *Syro-Roman Lawbook*.

[69] See my remarks about the dispute between the Sadducees and the rabbis regarding a daughter preceding a daughter of a son in the order of succession in n. 6. For an amoraic discussion (and without attribution to non-Jews) about a son and a daughter inheriting equally, see the discussion in *bBB* 110a–b.

[70] This fact leads Falk to conclude that the proponents of this approach are Jews influenced by non-Jews ("The Right of Inheritance of a Daughter and Widow," 12). Feintuch, "Daughters' Inheritance," assumes the non-Jews are advocates of Roman law (212) or actual Christian sages (214). Neither possibility is fully demonstrable.

[71] I claim that the origin of the tradition is unknown (cf. Feintuch, "Daughters' Inheritance," 214) because although it is in rabbinic Hebrew and preceded by what is clearly a *baraita* (*tani Rabi Yishmael*) – perhaps suggesting that this statement should be seen as a further tannaitic appendage to the *baraita* – the comment is followed by what is likely an explanation of Palestinian amoraic provenance: "דאינון דרשי. 'ובן אין לו'. הא אם יש לו שניהן שוין"; "for, they interpret [the verse], 'without leaving a son,' [to mean] indeed if he left a son, then the son and the daughter are equal [regarding inheritance]" (see also the continuation of the text). The logic proposed is to infer from Numbers 27:8, "[i]f a man dies *without leaving a son*, you shall transfer his property to his daughter," that when there are only daughters, the entire inheritance transfers to them; when there are sons and daughters, however, the inheritance is divided equally between both males and females!

the division of equal inheritance for daughters, even in the presence of sons, is extant in the tannaitic period and flourished afterward as well. In its former framing, it is camouflaged and, at least in its later laying out, is formulated as a non-rabbinic teaching.[72]

In the absence of anything that clearly can be defined as tannaitic interpretation of Scripture[73] – which can account for an equal approach to inheritance by a son and a daughter – I dedicate the rest of this chapter to charting the possible origins of this tannaitic tradition among the others concerning inheritance by daughters that I outline above. In the final analysis, I suggest that the tannaitic traditions may find their origin at the point of convergence between law and society. That is, the presence in tannaitic law of methods for distributing wealth from a father's estate to a daughter is the outcome of the rabbis adopting laws from their neighbors, which seemingly are appropriate to a nuclear family residing in an urban setting that the tannaim experience. But before addressing these matters in more detail, I take a short detour to describe the traditions about inheritance by daughters in the writings of Philo and their relationship to tannaitic precepts.

Philo and the Tannaitic Traditions

Significant for our study is the testimony of Philo of Alexandria who, in *The Special Laws*, describes two forms of inheritance by a daughter, the second of which entitles a non-dowered daughter to an equal share of an inheritance even in the presence of sons. Philo writes:

> Sons shall inherit their parents' property, but if there should be no sons, then the daughters would inherit ... But if virgins are left behind ..., no dowry having been set apart by the parents while they were still living, they shall receive a share equal to that of the males. (*The Special Laws* 2:124–125)[74]

Philo describes two separate matters pertaining to inheritance by a daughter. First, parallel to tannaitic law in the absence of sons, daughters inherit directly,

---

[72] See previous note. Implicit in my formulation is the possibility of a genetic link between the traditions in *mBB* 8:4 and the Palestinian Talmud (however, see Rosenthal and Lieberman, *Yerushalmi Nezikin*, 98, where the Escorial manuscript has *sheneihem shavin* and does not include *ke'eḥat*). My contention is *contra* Feintuch ("Daughters' Inheritance," 212, 214, 226) who sees no relationship between the traditions, per se, accepting Epstein's thesis regarding *mBB* 8:4, and presuming that the Palestinian Talmud's proposal is the product of real historical interaction between rabbinic Sages and either advocates of Roman law or Christians. See n. 70.

[73] Admittedly, the tradition I discuss above is presented as a biblical interpretation. However, the explanatory portion of the teaching may be of amoraic origin. Furthermore, the teaching in the Palestinian Talmud, by being attributed to non-Jews, is marginalized, i. e., excluded from the canon.

[74] *Works of Philo*, 580.

as he writes: "but if there should be no sons, then the daughters would inherit." Second, Philo explains that unmarried daughters ("virgins") inherit, even in the presence of sons, shares "equal to that of the males," in place of the dowries they did not receive before the death of their parents ("no dowry having been set apart by the parents while they were still living").

Samuel Belkin sees evidence for Alexandrian Jewry's extension of a tannaitic law for the protection of young women. As mentioned above, *mKet* 13:3 records a decision attributed to Admon that when an inherited estate is small, the assets are used for the benefit of the daughters' maintenance while the sons are sent begging.[75] Belkin writes: "the Alexandrian Jews went one step further and gave her a share in the inheritance if she was not provided for by her father."[76] To be sure, the tradition in *mKet* 6:6 affirming a daughter's receipt of a dowry from her father's estate after his passing is relevant to this discussion as well. Indeed, the *mishnah* assumes that, although not receiving a dowry equal in amount to her brother's inheritance, a daughter does benefit from a dowry in the event that her father dies before she is betrothed.

The degree to which Philo's statements can be taken as evidence of actual practice or simply as his interpretation of Scripture is unclear.[77] This is especially true regarding comments about family law because these often appear in his works linked to the biblical passages upon which he comments.[78] In a related context in *The Special Laws* (2:126), for example, Philo emphasizes that daughters should marry relatives to keep land allotments within the tribe, a remarkable pronouncement because by Philo's time, the tribal division of land shares is irrelevant. Here his comments must be considered, therefore, as explanatory or interpretive and not as descriptive of the context he experiences.

Returning to Philo's concept of granting a non-dowered daughter an equal inheritance share with a brother – these remarks could constitute a conceptual middle step from biblical endogamy to direct inheritance by a daughter (even in the presence of sons) in what may be broadly described as an evolutionary continuum of Jewish legal concepts. Below I continue the search for compelling parallels and antecedents to the tannaitic innovation. Certainly, there are no biblical sources that indicate that a daughter inherits equally with a son as is advocated in *mBB* 8:4, paragraph I (see the next section). Furthermore, as shown below, a daughter inheriting directly in the absence of a son is likely not evidenced in biblical literature despite the insistence of some biblicists to the contrary. In the final analysis, I demonstrate that the tradition embedded within *mBB* 8:4 is the culmination of a legal tendency in tannaitic sources toward enabling a daughter

[75] See my discussion above in the body of the chapter.

[76] Belkin, *Philo and the Oral Law*, 20.

[77] For a summary of scholarly approaches to the methodological problem, see Reinhartz, "Philo's *Exposition of the Law*," 9–13.

[78] Reinhartz, "Philo's *Exposition of the Law*," 7.

to partake of her father's fortune divorced from the notions prevalent in biblical literature and devoid of scriptural interpretation to buttress it. Such a trend is known in the ancient Near East and Mediterranean regions among other urbanized societies with privatized landholdings and nuclear family structures. Accordingly, I suggest that the social and economic contexts in which the rabbis live may contribute to their inclusive impulse. In the following section, I review the reigning biblical approach to inheritance by a daughter: endogamy.

Direct Inheritance by Daughters in the Bible

The primary Pentateuchal texts on inheritance by daughters appear in the book of Numbers in two separate accounts. The first, in chapter 27, tells the story of Zelophehad's daughters who approach Moses with a request to inherit because their father had no sons. They fear their father's name will be cut off (*yiggara*) because, without sons, there is no one to inherit the family/clan landholdings and, therefore, perpetuate the family name.[79] His daughters plead stating, "give us a holding among our father's kinsmen!"[80] This episode continues with Moses bringing the daughters' query to God who rules that the daughters' plea is reasonable, "you should give them a hereditary holding among their father's kinsmen; transfer (*veha'avarta*) their father's share to them."[81] The scene ends listing the order of intestate succession: "if a man dies without leaving a son, you shall transfer (*veha'avartem*) his property to his daughter."[82]

The second account, in chapter 36, is seemingly based on the first. The family heads of the tribe of Manasseh (Zelophehad's tribe) complain that if Zelophehad's daughters marry outside of their tribe, land will pass to their husbands' tribes, perforce diminishing the land portions of Israel allotted by God to Manasseh.[83] After consulting with God,[84] Moses declares that the daughters of Zelophehad must marry among the men of their father's tribe, thereby resolving the potential problem of the tribe of Manasseh losing landholdings to other tribes.

Bible scholars discuss the differences between chapter 27 and chapter 36 and their implications. Several argue that in chapter 27,[85] as a result of their plea, Zelo-

---

[79] On this see n. 48.

[80] Num. 27:4.

[81] Num. 27:6.

[82] Num. 27:8.

[83] Num. 36:1–4.

[84] See the language in Num. 36:5, "at the Lord's bidding" (=*al pi adonai*) even though the narrative does not state that Moses approaches God again, in accordance with Milgrom, *Numbers*, 297, in his commentary to the verse in question. However, see Westbrook, *Property and Family*, 164, who states that Moses acts "without recourse to divine ruling."

[85] B. Levine, *Numbers* 345 and 575; Ben-Barak, *Inheritance by Daughters*, 18; Greengus, *Laws*, 74; cf. Hauptman, *Rereading the Rabbis*, 192 n. 1; Westbrook, *Property and Family*,

phehad's daughters are entitled to direct inheritance[86] (since there are no sons) and to marry anyone they want, potentially transferring land to another family/clan or, even worse, to a different tribe. Despite the daughters' ownership of the land, the handing down of landholdings would still be through the paternal line (the line of the daughters' husbands).[87] So, once they marry, the land owned by the daughters transfers to their husbands. Zafrira Ben-Barak clearly states the problem in chapter 27, according to this view, and its resolution appears in chapter 36:

> Her marriage would be a threat to the patrimony, for both she and her property passed into the hands of her husband and his clan.[88] The daughter would become a means of transferring a patrimony from one family to another, and from one tribe to another, as was stated by the heads of the father's houses of the families... . The sons of the marriage, from the patriarchal standpoint, belonged to the husband's family, not the family of their maternal grandfather. This double danger was averted by the imposition of a severe restriction of the law of inheritance, obliging an inheriting daughter to marry only within her own tribe.[89]

According to Ben-Barak, therefore, whereas chapter 27, by empowering daughters to receive direct inheritance, enables the transfer of Zelophehad's estate to another family and/or to another tribe, chapter 36 limits the potentialities.

Milgrom, however, argues that the outcome of the plea of Zelophehad's daughters in chapter 27 is not that daughters receive direct inheritance. That is, that they actually own the property and have the right to alienate it (at least until the Jubilee year) and only upon marriage does the husband attain ownership. Milgrom argues that the daughters never own the land. The innovation in chapter 27 is that, in the absence of sons, inheritance transfers to the temporary stewardship of the daughters for the purpose of passing to their sons, the grandsons of the deceased, without detriment to the grandfather's legacy. These grandsons, despite their father's family affiliation, preserve Zelophehad's name.[90] That is, the daughters merely serve as trustees for their father's landholdings, not as heiresses with ownership, marrying whomever they wish without any eventual effect on

163–164. In addition, Westbrook tentatively suggests that the "thread of tradition" to which the resulting biblical ruling belongs (like the ruling in Lipit Ishtar, see below in the body of the text) is one that wants to avoid the unmarried daughter being deprived of her dowry because her father has died and there are no brothers (Westbrook, *Property and Family*, 163). He finds support for this position because in the restatement and emendation of the law in chapter 36 (discussed in the body of the chapter), the daughters are required to marry within the tribe; their land, and in Westbrook's opinion the equivalent of their dowry, being subsumed, like dowries were, into the assets of the husband. However, this reading does not acknowledge other elements about the family emphasized in chapter 27. See my summary of Milgrom's view below in the body of the chapter, where I make the case that his interpretation, and not Westbrook's, best incorporates all of the details of the biblical narrative.

[86] See the Introduction to this chapter where I define "direct inheritance."

[87] B. Levine, *Numbers*, 575.

[88] Ben-Barak's emphasis on "her property" presumes actual ownership of the property by a daughter and not just a trusteeship (see below).

[89] Ben-Barak, "Inheritance by Daughters," 26.

[90] Milgrom, *Numbers*, 231 and 482.

Zelophehad's family's landholdings.[91] Chapter 36 adds only, at least according to its current version (as per Milgrom; see below), that the concern is the transfer of property from one tribe to the next.

Milgrom cites two separate examples as proof that in biblical literature the grandfather's name continues regardless of whom the daughters marry. In 1 Chron. 2:34–35, Sheshan has no sons and gives his daughter Jarha to his Egyptian slave.[92] Their son Attai inherits the ancestral land. As Milgrom succinctly states it, "[t]hus the daughter acted as a vehicle for the transfer of her father's property to his grandchild."[93] The second example is recorded in Ezra 2:61 and Nehemiah 7:63. There, priests trace their lineage through the marriage of their father, whose name is not given, to one of Barzilai's daughters.[94] Milgrom sees a parallel between these two examples and the story of Zelophehad's daughters. He argues that the narrative of Zelophehad's daughters, as told in chapter 27, also ends with the daughters serving as trustees to their father's estate until such time that they will transfer the land, with his name attached to it, to their sons.[95]

In addition to being supported by further biblical examples, Milgrom's reading of chapter 27 is compelling because it accounts for all of the narrative and legal elements found in the chapter. First, Zelophehad's daughters' request is not to inherit land onto themselves but to acquire land for the purpose of preserving their father's name, a goal only accomplished by having the inheritance transferred to them and then passed on to grandsons (since males are required for the preservation of the estate's name). Second, Milgrom's interpretation accounts for the legal significance of the switch to the verb *a-v-r* (to pass or transfer) when referring to the daughters' receipt of inheritance as opposed to the verbs *n-t-n* and *n-ḥ-l*, which are used in the Bible when males inherit.[96] That is, in chapter 27 property transferred to the unqualified (=the daughters), and the use of this verb specifically, possibly carry a connotation regarding the daughters' eventual function of *passing* on the property to their sons (or husband).[97] Third,

---

[91] Milgrom, *Numbers*, 233.

[92] For more on daughters in the book of Chronicles, see Ben-Barak, *Inheritance by Daughters*, 81–83.

[93] Milgrom, *Numbers*, 231 and 232. See also Horovitz, *Siphre to Numbers*, 178.

[94] Milgrom, *Numbers*, 231. See also Ben-Barak, *Inheritance by Daughters*, 87.

[95] The model presented by Milgrom for transferring inheritance to grandsons through a daughter is attested to in the ancient Near East as well; see Ben-Barak, "Inheritance," 23–25 and 32. Milgrom, however, does not seem to make direct use of this example when presenting his findings in Numbers even though he cites Ben-Barak's article (Milgrom, *Numbers*, 518 n. 5). As if ancient Israel is unique in this practice of inheritance, he writes the following exclamatory sentence: "How then are we to explain the fact that the Bible gives women no inheritance rights except in the case where there are no sons? And in that situation, unmarried daughters inherit for the purpose of transferring the estate to his grandsons!" (Milgrom, *Numbers*, 482). Ben-Barak, on the other hand, while presenting this model for Sumer, Nuzi, and Ugarit (referenced above) does not see this as the practice in Numbers! (Ben-Barak, "Inheritance," 26).

[96] See Chapter 1.

[97] Milgrom, *Numbers*, 232. Cf. the opinion of Rabi (and its parallels) in *Sifre to Numbers* 134

only according to Milgrom's reading of chapter 27 is the strict agnatic principle of succession – assumed throughout the Bible – preserved because the eventual heirs, the grandsons, are males. For Milgrom, therefore, the legal distinction between chapter 27 and chapter 36 is not whether in the former daughters actually inherit while in the latter they do not. The distinction is in the framing of each narrative. The former, and historically earlier, story focuses on the family/clan, whereas the latter, and historically later, reworked composition, brings to the fore a new concern, the tribe.[98]

The absence in chapter 27 of any interest in the transfer of family land to another tribe is actually to be expected because the (tribal) census is structured according to family/clan groups, and the land is apportioned to these same clusters.[99] Chapter 36, in its current version, therefore, innovates, according to Milgrom, a new legal concern and represents an abrupt shift in the story line, or even a separate narrative, based on the tradition of chapter 27.[100] Milgrom even goes so far as to contend that originally chapter 36 possibly also referred to the family and not the tribe because the daughters marry their first cousins.[101]

In conclusion, there is no evidence from the narratives of Zelophehad's daughters that daughters actually ever receive direct inheritance according to biblical law – even in the absence of sons.[102] Accounts about other biblical daughters such as Rachel and Leah, the daughters of Laban (Genesis 29–31),[103] as well as

---

(Horovitz, *Siphre*, 178; Kahana, *Sifre to Numbers*, to lines 10–11, 60 and 1137–1138). B. Levine, on the other hand, does not appreciate the full import of the verb's legal ramifications, suggesting merely that, "[t]he implication is that something unusual is being prescribed, from a legal point of view" (*Numbers 21–36*, 347).

[98] Milgrom, *Numbers*, 512.

[99] Milgrom, *Numbers*, 512.

[100] Additionally, it may be that the preservation of the connection between the family name and the estate is independent of the larger social unit, the tribe. Namely, according to chapter 27, whereas the tribal affiliation of Zelophehad's landholdings may be transferred, the family name attached to the land parcels is not. The objection of the family heads in chapter 36, therefore, is that although transferring the landholdings to the daughters preserves Zelophehad's name and *bet av* through the daughters to the grandsons, such an arrangement can be detrimental to the tribe. If the daughters marry out of the tribe, the landholdings – while still perpetuating Zelophehad's name on his estate – will become landholdings of the tribes of the daughters' husbands.

[101] Milgrom suggests that originally chapter 36, like chapter 27, referred to the family/clan and not to the tribe and points to the Septuagint's use of the word "clan" (=*mishpaḥat*) two times (vv. 6 and 8) instead of tribe (=*matteh*) (Milgrom, *Numbers*, 512). Westbrook, however, states that the inheritance laws in chapter 27 reach only the level of the family due to the fact that in historical Israel this is the more likely allegiance, whereas tribal loyalty is based on fictional ancestry (*Property and the Family*, 22).

[102] On the possible significance of the retellings in Josh. 17:1–6 and I Chron. 7:14–19, see Ben-Barak, *Inheritance by Daughters*, 47–51.

[103] E. g., Ben-Barak addresses the story of Rachel and Leah, indicating that although the exact arrangements are not clear, it seems the daughters may inherit in the absence of sons (*Inheritance by Daughters*, 70–77). Milgrom, *Numbers*, 231, also suggests a similar interpretation, seemingly granting that perhaps this case is exceptional. However, as in Milgrom's reading of Numbers

Akhsah daughter of Caleb (Josh. 15:16–19; Judg. 1:12–15; and 1 Chron. 2:49),[104] and Job's daughters,[105] based on the evidence, remain inconclusive.[106]

In the final analysis, antecedents to the inheritance practices of the tannaim, including direct inheritance by daughters, whether in the presence or the absence of sons, are not to be found in the Bible. As is often the case, both biblical and tannaitic traditions are better understood in comparative relief. We continue, therefore, with a survey of ancient practices that enlighten regarding the background to biblical endogamy and that present the earliest origins and parallels to tannaitic traditions.

Inheritance by Daughters in the Ancient Near East

As illustrated in the story of Zelophehad's daughters, so, too, according to some ancient Near Eastern sources, in the absence of sons, the patrimony continues specifically through the line of the daughter because the grandsons of the deceased eventually inherit the estate. Perhaps the earliest example is at Sumer where King Urbaba of Lagash (third millennium BCE) continues the male line by adopting nephews and marrying them to his daughters.[107] However, daughters in these sources serve not only as catalysts for inheritance to their eventual sons. There is also evidence for the inclusion of daughters in the order of intestate succession, in the absence of sons, and other more inclusive practices enabling daughters to gain a part of their father's patrimony.

The earliest evidence for direct inheritance when no sons are present is from the end of the third millennium BCE (Sargonic period) in Mesopotamia in a reform attributed to Gudea of Lagash (Sumer), "[i]n the house that had no male heir, he installed its daughter as the heir" (Stat. B vii 44–46).[108] The Neo-Sumerian peri-

27, the impression is that Laban, Rachel and Leah's father, attempts to continue his household through his son-in-law Jacob.

[104] Ben-Barak contends that the narrative of Akhsah suggests daughters inherit in the absence of sons and, additionally, that they would lose their status upon the birth of a son, a practice paralleled at Nuzi (*Inheritance by Daughters*, 79–80).

[105] Ben-Barak emphasizes that the case of Job's daughters presents a new approach to inheritance by daughters in biblical literature (*Inheritance by Daughters*, 92). Westbrook, *Property and Family*, 147–148, however, takes the *naḥalah* given by Job to his daughters as referring to a dowry, most likely because it is given during Job's lifetime, a fact that leads Milgrom to the conclusion that this is a gift and not inheritance at all (Milgrom, *Numbers*, 483). See also, Greengus, *Laws*, 73.

[106] On related events in the book of *Tobit*, see my discussion in Chapter 3.

[107] Ben-Barak, *Inheritance by Daughters*, 114–115. See also the important example from Ur III of an adopted daughter (Ben-Barak, *Inheritance by Daughters*, 117). The example of the will tablet of Tarmiya from Nuzi is striking in that to preserve the household, the father stipulates that his daughters marry his sons from a different wife; see Ben-Barak, *Inheritance by Daughters*, 129–130.

[108] The translation is taken from Hallo, *The Context of Scripture*, 2:432. For a brief discussion of the source, see Ben-Barak, *Inheritance by Daughters*, 115–116; and Greengus, *Laws*, 76. For

od (Ur III) code of Lipit Ishtar allows this arrangement only for an unmarried daughter, "[i]f a man dies without male offspring, an unmarried daughter shall be his heir" (§b),[109] leading Westbrook to conclude that this legislation is instituted so as not to deprive a daughter of her dowry due to her father's death.[110] Documentation from the Old Babylonian period indicates that daughters inherit only through the institution of the dowry,[111] whereas Old Assyrian period evidence attests to sons and daughters inheriting equally.[112] An adoption/inheritance document from the Middle Babylonian period refers to "the inheritance share of Adda-nahda, which she took from the house of her father."[113] While the text's editors merely mention that the property in question is likely part of the dowry addressed earlier in the document,[114] Kathryn Slanski concludes that, "a daughter could receive a share of her paternal estate either as dowry or as inheritance."[115]

In the Middle Assyrian period, daughters at times inherited equally with sons and at times in accordance with special provisions.[116] The evidence from Nuzi on inheritance by daughters, as with other inheritance matters, provides perhaps the richest repository of primary material on our subject from the ancient Near East. Several models are evidenced in the Nuzi material and are systematically presented by Jonathan Paradise[117] and Ben-Barak,[118] including: a daughter inheriting jointly with her husband (an adopted son-in-law),[119] a daughter inheriting as sole heir in the absence of sons,[120] and even a daughter inheriting after being adopted as a son,[121] among others. Despite the aforementioned strategies and

---

a text from Nippur in which a father declares that the daughter is to receive a "portion in the inheritance," see Ben-Barak, *Inheritance by Daughters*, 113–114.

[109] The translation is from Roth, *Law Collections*, 26. See also Ben-Barak, *Inheritance by Daughters*,117–118; and Greengus, *Laws*, 76. If Claus Wilcke is correct, then the law is paralleled in the Code of Urnamma; see Wilcke, "Der Kodex Urnamma," 322.

[110] Westbrook, *Property and Family*, 163. The author reads this principle into the story of Zelophehad's daughters.

[111] Westbrook, "Mesopotamia: Old Babylonian Period," 397. Cf. Ben-Barak, "Inheritance," 23; and Ben-Barak, *Inheritance by Daughters*, 120. See, however, Westbrook, *Property and Family*, 158–159, where the author disagrees that the evidence is conclusive on the matter.

[112] Veenhof, "Old Assyrian Period," 458 and n. 140.

[113] Podany, Beckman, and Colbow, "Adoption," 48.

[114] Podany, Beckman, and Colbow, "Adoption," 51.

[115] Slanski, "Mesopotamia: Middle Babylonian Period," 507. For an example from Kassite Babylonia, see Ben-Barak, *Inheritance by Daughters*, 120–121.

[116] Lafont, "Mesopotamia: Middle Assyrian Period," 544. See, there, the reference to Wilcke, "Assyrische Testamente," 224–226.

[117] Paradise, "Daughter and Her Father's Property," 189–207; and Paradise, "Daughters as 'Sons' at Nuzi," 203–213.

[118] The scenarios are summarized most recently in Ben-Barak, *Inheritance by Daughters*, 123–152.

[119] On adoption, see Chapter 4.

[120] Ben-Barak, *Inheritance by Daughters*, 141–144. However, see the next note.

[121] See the critique by Westbrook of Ben-Barak's earlier conclusions regarding daughters inheriting only when granted male status (Ben-Barak, "The Legal Status of the Daughter as

scenarios, the fact remains that daughters are likely not included in the regular order of intestate succession[122] and that the documentation represents creative ways around that. That is to say, there is no automatic transfer of property to daughters even when there were no sons.

Similarly, at Emar, daughters inherit only by special order of the father (or mother), whether in the presence of sons or in their absence, and under other specific circumstances including adoption as a son.[123] An important document from Alalakh seemingly assumes that the daughter in question has a right to inherit with the son of the deceased[124] although specifics about the case remain unclear.[125] According to Ben-Barak, at least one document shows that at Ugarit a daughter can gain full possession of the patrimony as sole heir when there are no sons,[126] even though the assumption is that according to the laws of intestacy, daughters do not usually inherit. At least one Neo-Assyrian document attests to a father gifting a house to his daughter, but this should not be considered inheriting per se.[127] In fact, evidence suggests that daughters do not inherit according to intestacy laws.[128] The Neo-Babylonian evidence shows that generally daughters do not inherit according to the laws of intestacy.[129] However, one example of a daughter receiving an inheritance share from her father in addition to her dowry was published by Cornelia Wunsch.[130]

Although the ancient Near Eastern background for the tradition of endogamy for the purposes of inheritance in the Bible is clear, in light of the evidence another factor also comes to the fore. Unlike in biblical law, throughout the ancient Near East strategies inclusive of daughters, such as direct inheritance and dowries, existed. As already noted by Milgrom,[131] this inclusiveness likely was due to the fact that many societies in ancient Mesopotamia and the adjoining regions were centralized urban societies. Biblical law, however, holds steadfast to endogamy for inheritance because of the clan structure upon which biblical law is based, itself a possible reflection of the seminomadic society that is ancient Israel at the time of the earliest promulgation of its laws.[132] The fact that urban-

Heir," 96–97, in Westbrook, *Property and Family*, 160–161). For another critique of Ben-Barak regarding this matter, based on her analysis in Ben-Barak, "The Case of the Daughters of Zelophehad," 116–123, see Paradise, "Daughter and Her Father's Property," 191 n. 12.

[122] This seems to be the basic situation at Nuzi. See Ben-Barak, *Inheritance by Daughters*, 125.

[123] Ben-Barak, *Inheritance by Daughters*, 152–179.

[124] Wiseman, *Alalakh Tablets*, no. 2, 34–35 (no. 7).

[125] Ben-Barak, "Inheritance," 28–31.

[126] Ben-Barak, *Inheritance by Daughters*, 190–193.

[127] See text No. 69 in Kwasman, *Neo-Assyrian Legal Documents*, 79–80.

[128] Radner, "Neo-Assyrian Period," 900.

[129] Wunsch, "Women's Property and the Law of Inheritance," 2.

[130] Wunsch, *Die Urkunden*, 113–114 (no. 137) and 173–174 (no. 209).

[131] *Numbers*, 482.

[132] For more on this, see the Introduction.

ization may produce a more inclusive approach to inheritance by daughters is also evidenced in tannaitic law, which itself embraces strategies for both direct and indirect inheritance by daughters (see above). Below we continue with a survey of the evidence from additional ancient legal traditions.

The Elephantine and Judean Desert Papyri

Although there is no primary evidence regarding the status of a daughter in the line of intestate succession at Elephantine, scholars assume that daughters have some inheritance rights – probably in the absence of sons – because they are listed (along with sisters) as possible successors in documents related to property transfers.[133] One document, which deals with withdrawal from disputed land, lists those who are not allowed to file to reclaim the land after the withdrawal: "I shall not be able to institute against you suit or process – I, or son of mine or daughter of mine about that land (against) you."[134] Alejandro Botta[135] comments that the reference here to a daughter as claimant suggests that a daughter, at least when there are no sons, inherits. When discussing a different document from Elephantine, Bezalel Porten notes that often the order of people, as in our example, "adhered to a descending order of inheritance."[136] In the presence of sons, however, it is assumed that a daughter does not inherit directly but rather can receive (inheritance) gifts,[137] accounting for the high frequency of gifting to women at Elephantine.[138] Significantly, deeds of gift found in the Judean desert are issued exclusively to daughters (and wives). Based on the evidence, Hannah Cotton affirms that although not entirely conclusive, it may be that the gifting attests to fathers (and husbands) attempting to rectify the imbalance in the presumed laws of intestacy (never mentioned explicitly). That is, daughters do not inherit in the presence of sons.[139]

---

133 Yaron, *Law of the Aramaic Papyri*, 67–68.

134 B 24 (=TAD B2.2) in Porten, *Elephantine Papyri in English*, 161. For a transcription of the original Aramaic text and description, see Porten and Yardeni, *Textbook*, 20–21.

135 Botta, "Elephantine," 575.

136 Porten, *Elephantine Papyri in English*, 154 n. 22.

137 Botta, "Elephantine," 575.

138 Yaron, *Law of the Aramaic Papyri*, 68.

139 Initially Cotton concluded that, unlike biblical and rabbinic law, daughters did not inherit even in the presence of uncles; see Cotton, "Babatha's Property," 211–224; Cotton, "Deeds of Gift," 179–186. She later modified her view in Cotton, "The Law of Succession," 115–123.

Greece and Rome

As in several of the legal traditions treated above, the law in Athens also does not lack a way around the exclusion of daughters from the order of intestate succession. Here, as in the biblical model, the goal is to keep the estate intact despite the absence of male heirs; that is, to preserve the *oikos* of the deceased. These daughters (without brothers) are called *epikleroi* (sing., *epikleros*), and their role and function are aptly described by Douglas MacDowell: [140]

> If a man died leaving no legitimate son (or grandson or great-grandson), he might nevertheless leave a daughter (or granddaughter or great-granddaughter). In this case there was the prospect that she might eventually produce a son to inherit the property and continue the *oikos*... . The rule was then that the nearest surviving male relative of her deceased father was entitled to claim her in marriage.[141]

In Athens, therefore, as in biblical law and in sources from the ancient Near East, when a father dies without a son, a daughter marries a relative and serves as a conduit for the property, later to be inherited by her children, the grandchildren of the deceased. David Schaps explains that the eventual transfer of the *oikos* from grandfather to grandson is not necessarily automatic. It may be facilitated by the adoption of the grandson, albeit posthumously, as son of the grandfather:

> It appears to have been possible, though not required, for the husband of the *epikleros* to have one of her sons adopted posthumously as a son of her father... . Where the adoption did not take place, the *oikos* of the deceased became extinct, for its heirs – the children of the *epikleros* – belonged to their father's *oikos*, not their maternal grandfather's.[142]

Of utmost importance, therefore, is the preservation of the maternal grandfather's *oikos*, which can be accomplished by the *epikleros* being claimed by her closest next of kin on her father's side.[143]

At Gortyn, however, where these daughters are called *patroiokoi* (sing., *patroiokos*), there are some significant differences from the Athenian institution. For example, at Gortyn, unlike Athens, the daughter is the owner of the estate and not necessarily only a conduit for its transfer.[144] Indeed, even in the presence of sons, daughters at Gortyn directly inherit, for some parts of the estate,

---

[140] Lacey explains that the definition of *epikleros* is a woman who transmits a *kleros*, an estate of a deceased person or allotment of land, to her children. See Lacey, *The Family in Classical Greece*, 13. For a discussion of the *epikleros* in Athens, see Schaps, *Economic Rights of Women*, 25–42. For the Greek practice, as represented in the Greco-Roman papyri from Egypt, see Taubenschlag, *Law*, 140.

[141] MacDowell, *Law in Classical Athens*, 95.

[142] Schaps, *Economic Rights of Women*, 28.

[143] For the order of claimants, see Harrison, *Law of Athens*, 1:133.

[144] Schaps, *Economic Rights of Women*, 45. So, too, it seems in Sparta; see Schaps, *Economic Rights of Women*, 88.

half of what sons inherit.[145] The Law Code of Gortyn states, "And in case (the father) should die, ... all the rest of the property shall be fairly divided and the sons, no matter how many, shall each receive two parts, while the daughters, no matter how many, shall each receive one part" (Col. IV, 30–40).[146] Significantly for our immediate discussion, paternal relatives more distant than uncles and first cousins have no claim at Gortyn. This, perforce, prevents the estate of the grandfather from leaving his own father's extended family network.[147] Therefore, a greater concern for the preservation of property within the larger unit of the extended family is expressed in Gortyn than in Athens, where other male relatives have a claim as well. This concern is expressed through more limiting legislation regarding who can claim the heiress's hand (only uncles and first cousins). Accordingly, it remains unclear whether the eventual grandson at Gortyn is considered as belonging to the grandfather's *oikos*,[148] as in Athens, or not, even if it remains clear that a link to the great-grandfather's *oikos* continues due to the implementation of the laws.

The Gortynian model may be closer to the biblical one than the Athenian one.[149] The possible parallelism is not fleshed out by scholars and requires further investigation.[150] Following Milgrom's interpretation, as explained above, Numbers 27 and 36 (according to the hypothesized original version) are both based on the concept of preserving the land within the extended family/clan. The daughters of Zelophehad, as the Gortynian code would have it, actually marry their first cousins.[151]

Schaps argues that the institution in Gortyn is actually older than the practice in Athens;[152] and Michael Gagarin notes that even though the code's inscription is dated to 450 BCE, a considerable amount of its contents is likely earlier.[153] Elements of the older Greek practice,[154] therefore, may be parallel, in some respects, to the practice known from Numbers. Even though there is no evidence in Numbers that, as in Gortyn, the property is actually owned by daughters.

---

[145] However, upon receipt of her dowry, she forfeits her inheritance portion; see Schaps, *Economic Rights of Women*, 86.

[146] Willetts, *Law Code of Gortyn*, 42. For a discussion, see Willetts, *Law Code of Gortyn*, 65–66; and Schaps, "Women in Greek Inheritance Law," 55.

[147] Schaps, *Economic Rights of Women*, 44.

[148] Schaps, *Economic Rights of Women*, 44–45.

[149] Even so, Bible scholars usually stress the parallel with Athenian law. See, e.g., Milgrom, *Numbers*, 512.

[150] Westbrook notes the overlap between the Gortyn model and the biblical one; see *Property and the Family*, 164; and Westbrook and Wells, *Everyday Law in Biblical Israel*, 100–101.

[151] See Num. 36:10–12. See also regarding the daughters of Elazar in 1 Chron. 23:22 who also marry their first cousins (see Milgrom, *Numbers*, 512; and Japhet, *I & II Chronicles*, 417).

[152] Schaps, *Economic Rights of Women*, 45.

[153] Gagarin, *Early Greek Law*, 96.

[154] For a discussion of the evidence for the practice in Sparta, see Schaps, *Economic Rights of Women*, 43–44; and the innovative approach in Hodkinson, *Property and Wealth in Classical Sparta*, 94–104.

From its earliest documented beginnings, Roman law enables direct inheritance by daughters together with sons when a father dies intestate.[155] The provision of the XII Tablets states, "if he dies intestate, to whom there be no *suus heres*, the nearest agnate is to have the *familia* ? and goods?" (V:4).[156] As Alan Watson explains, "[a]ll *sui*, male or female, who were the children of the deceased, and his wife *in manu*, took equal shares."[157] And, as described earlier, although specific legislation attempts to uproot the original inclusiveness of the law, it ultimately fails.

Conclusions

By the advent of the tannaitic period, biblical endogamy for inheritance – whether it had ever really functioned in biblical Israel or not – does not exist. Without recourse to scriptural interpretation, tannaitic law adopts and adapts customs and practices for transferring property to daughters known in the region for millennia. Accordingly, the dowry, whether received from a father during his lifetime or from his estate after his death, the posthumous maintenance from the patrimony, and, in the event of intestacy and the absence of brothers, the direct acquisition of inheritance shares, are embraced by tannaitic law and may represent a (theoretical) response to the problem of the daughter's exclusion from the biblical order of intestate succession.

Another tannaitic approach, uncovered by the tools of source criticism and explicated in this chapter, even enables daughters to inherit equally with their brothers. I suggest that the conceptual move from biblical endogamy to direct inheritance rights (whether in the presence of sons or not) may be, in part, the result of the difference in the social and economic contexts as portrayed in biblical texts versus the social and economic conditions the rabbis experience. A middle stage along the legal continuum among presumed representations of Jewish law between biblical endogamy and inclusive tannaitic inheritance practices is also evident in the writings of Philo: unmarried daughters receive equal inheritance portions from their father's estate in place of the dowries they did not receive.

Certainly, the new ways of dealing with a daughter's welfare that dowry, maintenance, and direct inheritance represent are appropriate to the environment the tannaim experience, in which the nuclear family with privatized landholdings in an urban setting is prevalent. In light of the silence of tannaitic literature as to

[155] Indeed, women have equal rights with men when inheriting from fathers, brothers, or sisters. However, this is not the case when inheriting from others; see Crook, "Women in Roman Succession," 60.

[156] "Si intestato moritur, cui suus heres nec escit, adgnatus proximus familiam ?pecuniamque? habeto" (Crawford and Cloud, *Roman Statutes,* 641).

[157] Watson, *Law of Succession*, 176. See also Taubenschlag, *Law*, 139 and 142.

the scriptural underpinnings, if any, of the institutions described above, the presence of these precepts in tannaitic law perhaps can be considered the outcome of the interplay between the social and economic conditions known to the rabbis and their adoption, as well as adaption, of traditions regarding inheritance by daughters prevalent in the ancient Near East and Mediterranean.

Chapter 5

Inheritance by Wives in Tannaitic Law and in the Ancient World

Introduction

In the previous chapter, I argue that both the direct and indirect ways that the tannaim construct inheritance by a daughter enable a daughter, in theory, to gain a portion of her father's property. These constructions are indicative of the rabbis' concern for the financial well-being and independence of their daughters. This appreciation is appropriate, in fact, for the social and economic contexts in which the rabbis find themselves in tannaitic Palestine: an urbanized setting with private landholdings and predominantly nuclear families. These laws not only benefit daughters as daughters but also as future wives. The acquired assets offer extra protection in the event of a husband's death (or divorce).[1] For, as a father surely knows, his daughter – as wife – has no direct inheritance rights to the estate of her husband; she is not listed in the biblical or rabbinic orders of (intestate) succession.[2] Based on data from the ancient Near East, some scholars maintain that the wife's exclusion in biblical law makes sense since, presumably, the widow[3] would be cared for by her adult sons[4] or the firstborn.[5] This assumption may explain the deep concern of Scripture for the welfare of the childless widow;[6] she is left with no one to care for her.[7] Since explicit biblical evidence

[1] This chapter deals with inheritance by wives. On the husband's right to inherit his wife in tannaitic law, see Rivlin, *Inheritance and Wills*, 87–95; at Rome, see du Plessis, *Borkowski's Textbook*, 213–214; at Elephantine, Yaron, *Law of Aramaic Papyri*, 71. Regarding the absence of a right of the husband to inherit his wife's property in the ancient Near East, see Westbrook, "Introduction," 61.

[2] See Num. 27:8–11 and *mBB* 8:1.

[3] I use the word widow, in Hebrew *almanah*, to mean the wife of a deceased man and not in the technical biblical Hebrew sense. In biblical Hebrew, as in its Akkadian (*almattu*) and Sumerian (NU.MU.SU or NU.MA.SU) cognates, the word refers to a married woman who no longer has any means of financial support from any male member of her family, including her now deceased husband. See Roth, "Neo-Babylonian Widow," 2–3. For a rich discussion of the widow in the Bible and classical Jewish tradition, see Krauss, "Torat ha'almanah," 63–76.

[4] M. Friedman, *Jewish Marriage*, 427.

[5] In Deuteronomy, the firstborn son receives two shares of the inheritance, and some assume the second share is, in part, to provide for the mother (=widow) as in some places in the ancient Near East. See, e.g., Wells, "The Hated Wife," 132; and my comments in Chapter 2.

[6] See, e.g., Lev. 22:13.

[7] Cf. M. Friedman, *Jewish Marriage*, 427; and above n. 3.

about the widow's welfare is lacking, we must content ourselves with painting only an inadequate and partial picture, relying on the sparse and cryptic data available. Based on the existing information, it certainly seems that widows have no inheritance rights, direct or otherwise, in biblical law (see below).[8]

The tannaitic traditions, on the other hand, are rich and unambiguous. Although the tannaim do not add to the biblical law of intestate succession – enabling direct inheritance for a wife, as they do for a daughter – the rabbis do institute indirect ways for the wife of the decedent to profit from the patrimony.[9] For example, according to tannaitic law, in all likelihood a wife has a right to reclaim the contents of her dowry upon the death of her husband.[10] Furthermore, *mKet* 4:12 records a provision of the court, or *tenai beit din*,[11] establishing a widow's right to reside in her late husband's house and to be supported from his estate (until she remarries; see below).[12] In fact, this *mishnah* registers two approaches to a widow's rights, each attributed to a different geographic region. In Jerusalem and the Galilee, the widow chooses whether to accept support or collect her *ketubbah* debt;[13] in Judea the heirs choose.

In the absence of the scriptural underpinnings and rabbinic interpretive basis for such legal innovation, I argue that the tannaitic injunctions are the outcome of both the appropriation and alteration of practices the rabbis may have observed, as well as the integration of specific age-old traditions known in the region. For example, in many parts of the ancient Near East, Greece, and Rome, the widow's provision is connected to her original dowry; she reclaims what she brings with her into the marriage. In tannaitic law, in addition to recovering her dowry, the widow's support from her deceased husband's estate is, notably (and as mentioned), a statutory provision of the court. Her other option is to collect her *ketubbah* debt.[14]

---

[8] Cf. Frymer-Kensky, "Israel," 1019.

[9] Some tannaitic sources promote the use of gifts in contemplation of death to transfer property to wives. References to these gifts appear in the notes to this chapter, Chapter 1, and the Appendix. On gifts in contemplation of death in general, see Chapter 1.

[10] Cf. M. Friedman, *Jewish Marriage*, 292, and n. 9, there. The monetary portion of the dowry is increased by 50 percent. See *mKet* 6:3, and *tKet* 6:5; Yaron, *Gifts*, 178–179.

[11] That is, binding even if not explicitly stated. See the discussion below and, regarding other provisions of the court, Chapter 4.

[12] In rabbinic law regarding the husband's maintenance of his wife during his lifetime, see M. Friedman, *Jewish Marriage*, 167–178 (with a comparative discussion); Schremer, *Male and Female*, 329–333; Satlow, *Marriage*, 216–224; Lapin, "Maintenance," 184–198.

[13] Throughout this chapter I borrow the term, "*ketubbah* debt," used by Mordechai Friedman in *Jewish Marriage*, for the money pledged by the husband in the marriage document and collectable by the wife upon the dissolution of the marriage, whether by divorce or death of the husband (see M. Friedman, *Jewish Marriage*, 239–241). In the tannaitic texts the amounts collectable are standardized to 200 zuz for a virgin and 100 zuz for a widow or divorcee (see *mKet.* 5:1). The bibliography on the *ketubbah* debt is extensive. For partial listings, see Schremer, *Male and Female*, 233 nn. 19–21; and Lapin, "Maintenance," 187–188 n. 50. See also Satlow, *Marriage*, 213–216.

[14] An opinion appears in *mPe'ah* 3:7 that if a man leaves his wife any land whatsoever, she

Other parallels and antecedents to the tannaitic approaches include, for example, the notion that maintenance from the husband's estate and collection of the *ketubbah* debt are alternatives for the widow. This notion is paralleled in a fragmentary *ketubbah* from the Judean desert. The Judean practice, of which *mKet* 4:12 informs us, whereby the heirs choose when to cease support and grant the widow her *ketubbah* debt, is documented in Babatha's *ketubbah* (ca. 128 CE). Significantly, the right to reside in the deceased husband's home – prescribed by tannaitic law – is not recorded in Babatha's *ketubbah* at all. This right is seemingly granted by the Code of Hammurabi and, at least according to one scholar, also by texts from as early as the Neo-Sumerian period (Ur III). The right of a widow to reside in the her deceased husband's home is also made possible by strategies akin to gifts in contemplation of death in many parts of ancient Mesopotamia, Anatolia, and the Levant as well as at Elephantine, indicating that in all likelihood it is not an automatic right (on all this see below).

Certainly, the tannaitic proposals are representative of the high esteem the rabbis have for their wives and their desire to provide for them, even posthumously. In this regard, the concern and affection generally engendered by the structure of the nuclear family in its urbanized setting is reflected in tannaitic legislation on inheritance by wives as well.[15] If the law recorded in the Judean desert *ketubbot* represents typical practice in the Palestine of the tannaitic period, then in addition to adopting traditions they observe, the rabbis add the right of residence. Conceivably, they do so because of a sense of moral obligation to a widow, a matter made easier, perhaps, by the precedents in the region for providing a widow with the right to occupy her husband's home (see above). In the following pages I discuss in detail the tannaitic approaches for supporting a widow in light of the parallels and antecedents in the ancient world.

Inheritance by Wives in Tannaitic Law

Mishnah *Ketubbot* 4:12 discusses two alternative plans of action for the widow in the event of her husband's death. The first option is a provision of the court: a widow is to be supported from her husband's estate (*mezonot*),[16] and she is

forfeits her *ketubbah* debt. Gulak impressively shows the influence of the Roman *edictum de alteruto* on tannaitic law; see Gulak, "Peah 3:7," 121–126; and on this further, Hayes, "Abrogation," 671–672; Rivlin, *Inheritance and Wills*, 73 n. 37; Lieberman, *Tosefta: Zera'im*, 45; *Tosefta ki-fshuṭah: Zera'im* 1:141–143. See also in the continuation of *mPe'ah* 3:7; and my comments in the Appendix.

[15] The evolving position of the wife within the nuclear family in ancient Rome, for example, is well documented. Schremer points to the parallel improvement of the status of the wife (and mother) in rabbinic sources on marriage; see *Male and Female*, 334–336. On the possible effects of family structure on inheritance by daughters, see Chapter 4.

[16] The same term is used for maintenance of daughters; see Chapter 4.

to reside in his residence. Like other court stipulations, according to tannaitic law this is binding even if not explicitly stated in the marriage document.[17] The second possibility is payment of the *ketubbah* debt, an amount determined by the status of the wife at the time of marriage.[18] The text of *mKet* 4:12 (in MS Kaufmann 4:11–4:12) follows:

I.	"ואת תהוויין יתבה בביתי ומתזנה מן נכסיי כל ימי מגר ארמלותייך בביתי"[19] חייב, שהוא תניי בית דין. כך היו אנשי ירושלם כותבין.	[If he had not written for her], "You shall dwell in my house and receive maintenance from my goods so long as you remain a widow in my house," he is still liable [thereto], since this is a provision of the court. And so the people of Jerusalem used to write.
II.	ואנשי הגליל היו כותבין כאנשי ירושלם.	And the people of Galilee used to write as the people of Jerusalem.
III.	וביהודה היו כותבין "עד שירצו היורשים ליתן לה כתובתה". לפיכך, [20]ואם רצו היורשים נותנין לה כתובתה ופוטרים אותה.	And in Judea they used to write, "until such time as the heirs want to give her the *ketubbah*." Therefore, if the heirs wanted, they could give her the *ketubbah* and let her go.

This *mishnah* states that the wife is maintained from the estate of her deceased husband all the days of her widowhood in her husband's house, implying that remarriage or relocation[21] results in cessation of support and issuance of the *ketubbah* debt.[22] Furthermore, the *mishnah* preserves two different formulae for the *ketubbah*'s court provision, each representing a distinct approach attributed to regional practice.[23] Implicit in paragraphs I–II is that in Jerusalem and the Galilee, the widow has the choice whether to be supported or accept the *ketubbah* debt.[24] According to paragraph III, in Judea the heirs are given the choice.[25]

Significantly, the tannaitic idea that collection of maintenance and the right to residence or payment of the *ketubbah* debt are two independent approaches to the widow's benefits is paralleled in a fragmentary *ketubbah* from the Judean

[17] See Chapter 4.

[18] See n. 13.

[19] Compare the formulation in *tKet* 11:5.

[20] The letter *vav* may have been erased in the original manuscript.

[21] See also *mKet* 12:3 and *tKet* 12:3.

[22] See M. Friedman, *Jewish Marriage*, 429 and n. 9.

[23] On the fact that in our *mishnah* the Jerusalem/Galilee formula is in Aramaic and the Judean in Hebrew, see the discussion in M. Friedman, *Jewish Marriage*, 434–435.

[24] On the two mishnaic traditions in general, see the important discussion in M. Friedman, *Jewish Marriage*, 428–429 and 433–435. On the fact that the mishnaic statement that the widow is supported from the estate implies the *ketubbah* money is not disbursed (postponing such disbursal until remarriage), see M. Friedman, *Jewish Marriage*, 429–432.

[25] See also *mKet* 12:3 regarding the establishment of a home for the widow in accordance with her honor and the statement in *tKet* 12:3 that the widow may not be forcibly removed from her husband's house due to her husband's honor.

desert. This is stated explicitly, ארמלו די לא מן כת[בתיך.]; support is during "widowhood, exclusive of [your] *ket*[*ubbah*] (money)."[26] That is, as implied in the *mishnah* above, maintenance ends with remarriage.[27] This legal distinction is not the only one evidenced in the Judean desert. As already noted by Yigael Yadin,[28] the formulation in Babatha's *ketubbah* conforms to the practice mentioned in the *mishnah* as Judean (par. III).[29] Babatha's *ketubbah* states:[30]

ואם אנה אהך לבית עלמי קדמך תהוין יתבא ומתזנן מן ביתי מן נכסי עד זמן די יצבון ירתי למנתן לך כסף כתבתך.[31]	And if I should go to my eternal home before you, you will reside (in your widowhood) and (continue to) be provided for until the time that my heirs will agree to give you the silver of your *ketubba*.[32]

The presence of the two parallels to mishnaic law found in the Judean desert documents suggests that when drafting their inheritance laws, the tannaim may draw, partially, from the living traditions they observe and experience.[33]

Differences between the law preserved in the Judean desert *ketubbot* and rabbinic law remain, however. In addition to the return of the dowry (see above), our *mishnah* implies that financial support is provided to the widow as long as she resides in her husband's house. Our *mishnah* states, *yatva beveiti*, that she will reside in her husband's home (literally, "in my house") during her widowhood (i.e., until remarriage) in addition to being financially maintained. This residence requirement is absent from Babatha's *ketubbah*. Babatha's *ketubbah*

---

[26] The Hebrew and the translation both as per M. Friedman, *Jewish Marriage*, 429. Friedman prefers the reconstruction of the text suggested by Birnbaum, *Bar Menasheh Marriage Deed*, 19, and not as per the original publication of the text in *Discoveries in the Judaean Desert* 2, no. 20, 110.

[27] M. Friedman, *Jewish Marriage*, 429.

[28] Yadin, "Expedition D," 245.

[29] Babatha's *ketubbah* is the subject of considerable scholarly discussion that I do not review here. See, e.g., the text's original publication in Yadin, "Expedition D," 244–246; Yadin, Greenfield, and Yardeni, "Babatha's *Ketubba*," 75–101; M. Friedman, "*Babatha's Ketubba*," 55–76.

[30] P. Yadin 10, lines 15–16; see next note. For smoother reading, I have removed the *sigla* included in the original edition.

[31] As per the reconstruction in Yadin, *Documents*, 126.

[32] This is based on the translation in Yadin, *Documents*, 127 with some minor editorial additions on my part. See also the discussion of P. Yadin 5 in Oudshoorn, *Relationship*, 220, where in addition to the *ketubbah* debt a further debt owed by the husband to the wife is mentioned. Oudshoorn argues there that the mention of the debt indicates the wife did not inherit from the husband.

[33] The argument that the parallels between the Judean desert *ketubbot* and tannaitic sources are indicative of the influence of rabbinic legislation on common Jewish practice is difficult to sustain in the absence of meaningful extra-textual data on the rabbinic movement in general and further overlapping evidence. Furthermore, there are still differences between tannaitic law and the traditions attested to in the *ketubbot*. According to tannaitic law, a widow has the right to live in her husband's house (see below in the body of the chapter). See also the Judean desert (and earlier) parallels for *ketubbat benin dikhrin* and *ketubbat benan nukban* mentioned in Chapter 4 and my comments on methodology in the Introduction.

merely states, *yatva*,[34] indicating that she is supported during her widowhood.[35] Namely, according to the law recorded there, the widow has no right to reside in her late husband's home.[36]

Mention of a widow living in the house of her deceased husband also appears in the Elephantine papyri. There the context is a childless widow's rights. The text of Cowley 15 (17–19) states:[37]

מחר או יום א[חר]ן ימות אסחור ובר דכר ונקבה לא איתי לה מן מפ[ט]חיה אנתתה מפטחיה הי שליטה בביתה זי אסחור ונכסוהי וקנינה וכל זי איתי לה על אנפי ארעא.[38]	Tomorrow or (the) n[ex]t day, should Eshor die not having a child, male or female, by Mipta[h]iah his wife, it is Miptahiah (who) has right to the house of Eshor and [hi]s goods and his property and all that he has on the face of the whole earth.[39]

In this text, the deceased husband's house is mentioned since the childless widow receives the rights, or control (see below), to the house upon her husband's death. As Reuven Yaron correctly reminds his readers, the text does not describe inheritance by the widow in accordance with the laws of intestacy. Rather, it outlines a contractual arrangement between husband and wife (in the event he predeceases her). In that sense, the agreement is akin to a gift in contemplation of death (see Chapter 1) and not a provision of the court (in the event of intestacy), as discussed in our *mishnah*.[40] Furthermore, the contract deals specifically with the case of a childless widow, that is, a woman who does not have children to support her after her husband's death. Note the use of the word *shalita*, here rendered as "right," also "control," and not a form of the root *y-r-t* (inherit). The latter is employed at Elephantine exclusively in connection with the widower's rights to his deceased wife's property (and not her rights to his assets).[41] Alejandro Botta proposes that *sh-l-t* transfers possession whereas *y-r-t* passes on ownership[42] and points to possible Ptolemaic parallels for the

[34] Other Judean desert marriage documents (in Greek; two mention "*nomos*") omit the specific requirement for maintenance of the wife during widowhood found in our *mishnah* and paralleled in Babatha's *ketubbah*. Rather they link the maintenance to the original dowry (see below in the body of the chapter on the Greek practice regarding maintenance during widowhood and the dowry). For a discussion of these Greek documents and a bibliography, see Lapin, "Maintenance," 191–193.

[35] On *y-sh-v/y-t-v* as meaning a widow who remains unmarried, see M. Friedman, *Jewish Marriage*, 428 n. 6.

[36] M. Friedman, "Babatha's Ketubba," 73–74.

[37] Also found as text B28 in Porten, *Elephantine Papyri in English*, 181.

[38] As per Porten and Yardeni, *Textbook*, 30.

[39] As per Porten and Yardeni, *Textbook*, 33.

[40] Yaron, *Law of Aramaic Papyri*, 71.

[41] Yaron, *Law of Aramaic Papyri*, 71; see also Chapter 1.

[42] Possession includes the right to enjoyment and use but not the right to alienation, the transfer of property to another party. Ownership, however, also includes the right to alienate by sale, gift, or otherwise.

distinction.[43] The house in this context, the object under the control and in the possession of the widow, therefore, is also where the widow likely resided. This also seems to be the case according to the (partial) parallel in Hammurabi 171,[44] except that there the right is automatic:[45]

> [T]he first-ranking wife shall take her dowry and the marriage settlement, which her husband awarded to her in writing, and she shall continue to reside in her husband's dwelling; as long as she is alive, she shall enjoy use of it, but she may not sell it.[46]

According to the Code of Hammurabi, therefore, a widow has the right to possession of her deceased husband's home. However, she has no power of alienation, that is, she does not have ownership of the home.

In light of the data available, it seems that in appropriating elements of the provisions for a widow that the rabbis may observe among second- and third-century Judeans, the rabbis also may supplement the provisions with the right to reside in the deceased husband's home because of a sense of moral obligation to a widow. This could be the expected outcome for the social and economic context in which the rabbis live and function. Adding such a benefit is made easier, perhaps, due to the precedents evidenced in earlier traditions in the region, even if not exhibited in the biblical canon, to which we now turn.

Inheritance by Wives in the Bible

Not only is a widow's right to reside in her husband's home absent from the Bible, biblical literature is almost completely silent regarding the plight of the widow. As previously mentioned, based on data from the ancient Near Eastern context in which the Bible is authored and various hints in biblical literature, some scholars think the biblical assumption is that a widow is supported by her firstborn son or all of her sons collectively.[47] A clearer picture is unattainable, however.

An examination of the few biblical texts about widows clarifies very little. The conclusion remains that in all likelihood a widow does not inherit directly or even indirectly according to biblical law, an expected situation, perhaps, in

---

[43] Botta, "Legal Function," 199–200. For more on the distinction between possession and ownership in Ptolemaic law, see Taubenschlag, *Law*, 173–174. See also in Porten, *Elephantine Papyri in English*, 181 n. 36, the reference to an early Greek will from Elephantine in which surviving spouses take control of property but do not inherit it.

[44] In the following case, the widow is not childless.

[45] For a possible right to residence in the earlier, Neo-Sumerian period, see below in the body of the chapter.

[46] As per Roth, *Law Collections*, 114; see also Code of Hammurabi 172 (in Roth, *Law Collections*, 115) and there regarding the widow's departure from the house upon remarriage.

[47] See note 5 and cf. Frymer-Kensky, "Israel," 1019.

a literary complex in which land is connected inalienably through the male family line.[48] As correctly pointed out by Raymond Westbrook, the few and obscure biblical references to women possibly owning land mention women with sons.[49] This may indicate that according to biblical law women do not actually own land but are, at most, trustees for their sons' inheritance.[50] It also affirms that, in fact, wives do not inherit directly (at least not according to the laws of intestacy).[51]

A look at the book of Ruth, a situation in which the widow Naomi's sons die, complicates the picture. There the impression is that Naomi possesses and controls the sale of her late husband Elimelech's landholdings despite the fact that there are no longer sons for whom to serve as trustee (4:3).[52] Scholars wrestle with the legal question of whether Naomi acquires the land as a type of inheritance from her husband or not.[53] In the case of this narrative specifically, perhaps because Naomi's sons die, she functions as trustee of the property for kin, the redeemer Boaz, who eventually acquires the land.[54] The possibility of polemics in Ruth,[55] however, impairs our ability to penetrate in what way – if any – the book is representative of historical law or local custom. In the final analysis, therefore, based on the evidence available, it is unlikely that according to biblical law either direct or indirect inheritance is available to wives.[56]

---

[48] See Chapters 1 and 4.

[49] Westbrook, *Property and Family*, 65 and n. 2 there. For a discussion on biblical women who may own moveable property, see Rivlin, *Inheritance and Wills*, 69–70; Hiers, "Property Transfer," 130–134.

[50] See my discussion in Chapter 4.

[51] Cf. Westbrook, *Property and Family*, 65. For a possible case of testate succession in the later book of Judith, see Chapter 3.

[52] The sons Maḥlon and Chilion died previously.

[53] See Beattie, "Ruth," 253–255 for a summary of medieval and modern opinions. Beattie argues that, in fact, the book of Ruth is evidence that in biblical Israel, wives inherit directly (Beattie, "Ruth," 256; for a similar view see also Hiers, "Transfer of Property," 133). Sasson (*Ruth*, 108–120 and 139–140), argues against the idea that Naomi inherits any land. For the view that the book of Ruth cannot easily be used to reconstruct the legal history of ancient Israel, see Zakovitch, *Ruth*, 20–21 and 104–105. Falk, "Inheritance of a Daughter and Widow," 14, makes the important observation that if the land had been inherited by Naomi, then she would have owned it; and its redemption would have fallen on her family and not her late husband's family.

[54] Cf. Beattie, "Ruth," 255, discussing one of the suggestions by Neufeld. For a more recent treatment of the possibilities for inheritance by widows as expressed in the book of Ruth, see Jackson, "Ruth," 100–104.

[55] For a summary of opinions, see Hubbard, *Ruth*, 35–39.

[56] In her summary of Israelite law, Frymer-Kensky discusses an ostracon from ancient Israel, a petition by a childless widow pleading for a plot of land that is, perhaps, owned by her husband. The details of the case, and whether the text deals with inheritance at all, are disputed by scholars. See Frymer-Kensky, "Israel," 1019; see also the comments in Jackson, "Ruth," 103–104.

Inheritance by Wives in the Ancient Near East, Greece, and Rome

The assumption of scholars that the biblical widow does not inherit but, rather, serves as trustee of her husband's estate and is supported by her offspring reflects but one ancient Near Eastern approach. Other models exist in the ancient Near East as well, with some parallels even among Greek and Roman practices. The provision during widowhood, for example, is usually linked to the dowry originally brought into the marriage. That is, rights to the dowry, under the husband's control and ownership for the duration of the marriage, are given to the widow after her husband's death. In addition, where relevant, the husband's marital gift to his bride, issued at the time of marriage, is also passed on to the widow upon his death. The evidence points, at times, to widows managing their deceased husband's estates on behalf of minor children and adult children supporting their widowed mother (see below). However, the right to reside in the marital home after her husband's death, a provision of the court in tannaitic law, is not assumed throughout the ancient world although, as mentioned, important ancient Near Eastern exceptions did exist. We turn now to the evidence.

In the Early Dynastic and pre-Sargonic periods in Mesopotamia, upon the death of the husband, the wife takes control of the management of the estate for the benefit of the sons.[57] According to Sophie Lafont and Westbrook, in the Neo-Sumerian period the widow gains control of her original dowry, as well as control of the administration of the husband's estate, acting on behalf of her minor children.[58] David Owen,[59] building on the research of Edmond Sollberger,[60] argues for the elevated status of the widow in the Ur III period. He contends that texts imply the widow has the right to reside in the deceased husband's home until she remarries.[61] As already discussed above,[62] according to the Old Babylonian Code of Hammurabi 171, the widow has the right to reside in her dead husband's home. Furthermore, upon her husband's death, her dowry is returned to her along with any other marital settlement her husband gives her.[63] Old Assyrian period tablets from Kültepe list the widow as first [!] in the order

[57] Wilcke, "Neue Rechtsurkunden," 48–50. This includes obligations; see, e.g., Wilcke, "Neue Rechtsurkunden," 47. See also Chapter 1.

[58] Lafont and Westbrook, "Neo-Sumerian Period," 208. The authors also cite a bequest of the estate to the wife in Falkenstein, "Neusumerische Gerichtsurkunden," text no. 7, 10–12.

[59] Owen, "Widow's Rights," 174.

[60] Sollberger, "Legal Documents," 441. See also on this text, Wilcke, "Care of Elderly," 48.

[61] Owen, "Widow's Rights," 175. Furthermore, Owen argues, a widow's inheritance rights precede that of her son(s).

[62] See my discussion above.

[63] For more on the widow's residence, see also the Code of Hammurabi 172 (Roth, *Law Collections*, 114–115); note that if her husband does not make a marriage settlement, then she inherits a portion equal to one heir. Gulak, "Peah 3:7," 125, sees a parallel to this in *bBB* 122b. However, see the critique in Rivlin, *Inheritance and Wills*, 73 n. 40.

of heirs receiving shares.[64] The Middle Assyrian Laws (A 46)[65] report that the wife does not inherit directly[66] but is supported by her sons;[67] she is also given her original marital gift for the purpose of maintenance.[68] In the Neo-Babylonian period in Mesopotamia, although wives have no direct inheritance rights, they are at times gifted property[69] and maintained by their sons.[70] Martha Roth asserts that the explicit provision made by a husband for the residence of his widowed wife in his home likely indicates that, "there was no recognized legal right of a Neo-Babylonian widow to remain in her husband's home."[71] At Nuzi, the wife of the decedent is, at times, appointed the guardian of the family estate, which would later be divided among the heirs, providing her with adequate support during her lifetime as well.[72] In Ugarit widows do not inherit, only acquiring property by gift;[73] so, too, at Emar.[74] Furthermore, the husband at Emar could grant his wife the right to reside in his home after his death,[75] indicating that the right probably is not hers otherwise.

In Athens the widow does not inherit directly but has two claims against the estate of her husband or his heirs. The first entitlement is the collection of her entire dowry (*dikē proikos*), and the second is maintenance from the dowry (*dikē sitou*).[76] The significant difference between the tannaitic institution of maintenance and the Athenian one is that, in Athens, maintenance for a widow comes from the capital value of the dowry itself at an interest rate of 18 percent and not

[64] Veenhof, "Old Assyrian Period," 458. See also the discussion of the arrangements for the widow to stay in the deceased husband's house (460). See also Veenhof, "Care of Elderly," 139–142.

[65] Roth, *Law Collections*, 171–172.

[66] See, however, the discussion of a text in which the husband designates his wife sole heir to property, which after her death will pass to her son (Lafont, "Middle Assyrian Period," 545).

[67] See also the conditions regarding whether she resides in her husband's house or the house of one of her sons, and compare these to the discussion above regarding the *mishnah*, Babatha's *ketubbah*, and the law of the Elephantine papyri.

[68] Lafont, "Middle Assyrian Period," 541. On leaving the husband's estate to remarry, see Lafont, "Middle Assyrian Period," 537.

[69] Oelsner, Wells and Wunsch, "Neo-Babylonian Period," 938–939. On all aspects of the widow's rights and her husband's provisions for after death, see Roth, "Neo-Babylonian Widow," 1–26.

[70] Wunsch, "Women and Property," 2. On a widow without sons, see Roth, "Neo-Babylonian Widow," 6.

[71] Roth, "Neo-Babylonian Widow," 25–26.

[72] Zaccagnini, "Nuzi," 601–602. At Emar a marital gift, at times including land, is given with the intention of future use during widowhood; see Westbrook, "Emar," 680. At Ugarit, the impression is that the wife acquires inheritance rights only by "express grant" (Márquez Rowe, "Ugarit," 730–731). Regarding similar gifts to wives in the Neo-Assyrian period in Mesopotamia, see also Radner, *Privatrechtsurkunden*, 163 and 164.

[73] See Rowe, "Ugarit," 730–731.

[74] Westbrook, "Emar," 681 and 684.

[75] Westbrook, "Emar," 681 and 684.

[76] Harrison, *Law of Athens*, 1:57–60. See also n. 34 regarding the Judean desert marriage documents in Greek and the practice of maintenance from the dowry recorded in them.

from the husband's estate (as in tannaitic law).[77] That is, there seems to be no statutory provision for a widow's maintenance from her husband's assets.[78] Only a pregnant woman or one with young children has the right to remain in her deceased husband's home; if her children are adults, they provide for the widow's maintenance (independent of the dowry).[79] At Gortyn the dowry belongs to a woman even during her marriage, and it automatically follows her in the event of her husband's death. The same is assumed for Sparta.[80] In Roman law, a wife in a marriage *cum manu*[81] is counted among the *sui heredes* and accordingly regarded as a daughter, inheriting equally with the offspring of the deceased.[82] She could also recover her dowry from her husband's heirs,[83] often for the purpose of her own maintenance,[84] or be bequeathed its contents in the husband's testament.[85] So, too, in the absence of an automatic right to reside in her husband's house, at times the husband uses the testament to ensure the widow's access to the property.[86]

Conclusions

In tannaitic law the widow not only recovers her dowry upon her husband's death, but her maintenance and the right to reside in her deceased husband's home are guaranteed by a statutory provision of the court. Alternatively, she can be paid her *ketubbah* debt. In the absence of biblical precedents and rabbinic scriptural interpretations that serve as background for these legal innovations, I argue that the tannaitic regulations are the result of a combination of integrating local customs the rabbis might observe, as well as maintaining ancient traditions known in the region. The addition, in particular, of the widow's right to residence stands out among the practices known from the contemporaneous Judean desert *ketubbot,* which do not provide the widow with such a privilege. So, too, many

[77] Harrison, *Law of Athens*, 1:57.

[78] Cf. Lacey, *Family in Classical Athens*, 216.

[79] Schaps, *Economic Rights of Women*, 81. However, as pointed out by Schaps, *Economic Rights of Women*, 145 n. 69, residing in the home is not the universal choice; taking the dowry instead is also evidenced.

[80] Schaps, *Economic Rights of Women*, 88.

[81] By the time of the later republic, however, marriages are usually *sine manu,* and the wife loses her privilege. Husbands make up for this in testaments. For a summary of the scholarship on the issue, see Champlin, *Final Judgments*, 120–124.

[82] Du Plessis, *Borkowski's Textbook*, 210; Nicholas, *Introduction to Roman Law*, 238. For a sociological discussion, see Dixon, *Roman Family*, 42–43. For examples in the Babylonian Talmud of a wife inheriting with sons, see *bBB* 122b, 128b, 133a; with daughters, see, *bBB* 122b. For a limitation on these practices, see *bBB* 131b.

[83] Du Plessis, *Borkowski's Textbook*, 133.

[84] Gardner, *Women*, 107.

[85] Champlin, *Final Judgments*, 122–123.

[86] Champlin, *Final Judgments*, 123.

ancient Near Eastern traditions in addition to Greek, Roman, and Elephantine sources do not automatically give the widow a right to live in her husband's home although the benefit can be granted through a gift in contemplation of death. Notably, the Code of Hammurabi (and perhaps also Neo-Sumerian traditions) is an exception because it provides a widow with the right to reside in her husband's home.

The tannaitic laws are, undoubtedly, representative of the rabbis wish to adequately provide for their wives even after death. This concern is appropriate for the social and economic contexts in which the rabbis find themselves as heads of nuclear households in the urbanized centers of Roman Palestine. The social and economic contexts, therefore, may provide the necessary conditions for the appropriation and expansion of existing laws.

Conclusions

How Jewish is Jewish Inheritance Law?

If we are willing to entertain the question of "how Jewish is Jewish inheritance law?"[1] and if we assume that grounding in the Hebrew Bible and in its interpretation are primary criteria, based on the analysis in this book in all likelihood we would conclude with "not so Jewish." For, as I demonstrate throughout this work, tannaitic inheritance law is often unrelated to the Hebrew Bible or its interpretation. If tannaitic inheritance law can, at all, be considered "Jewish," it is primarily in spirit and not because of the origins of its concepts and its technical terminology. The identity of tannaitic inheritance law arises from its ability to innovatively breathe fresh legal life into a variety of inheritance laws that pervade the ancient Near East and the Mediterranean region. The end result is a magnificent collection of laws that – even in all of their variety – generally fosters freedom for allocation of assets to its potential adherents and new opportunities, especially for its would-be female followers. Below I reiterate the major tannaitic innovations I allude to above and indicate in parentheses the chapters where the reader can find the discussions leading to my conclusions.

Many concepts in tannaitic law are simply part and parcel of the way inheritance is envisioned in the ancient Near East and the Mediterranean region, cross-culturally, from time immemorial. These include the conceptual distinction between gifting in contemplation of death and inheriting (Chapter 1); the appointment of heirs through testate succession (Chapter 3); and the existence of dowry and maintenance for daughters (Chapter 4) and for wives (Chapter 5). Frequently, though, the laws and terms are likely the product of the adoption and adaptation of existing terminology, conceptions, and practices external to the biblical canon, and, readily identifiable in other ancient legal collections. The Greek word *diathēkē* (Chapter 1 and the Appendix) and the terms *mattanah* and *yerushah* – corresponding to their Roman legal equivalents of *donatio* and *hereditas* (Chapter 1) – enter tannaitic legal discourse. Rabbi Yoḥanan ben Beroka's testate succession among agnates parallels the Roman *testamentum* for the *sui heredis* (Chapter 3). I base my conclusions on the broad comparative legal study I engage in here and on my insistence on introducing into the discussion traditions from thousands of years of ancient law as well as from fields not usually associated by scholars.

[1] Compare, Jackson, "How Jewish is Jewish Family Law?," 201–229.

I also show that the laws and traditions embraced by the rabbis – generally more inclusive than their biblical antecedent laws – oftentimes correspond to the social and economic contexts the rabbis know and experience: the nuclear family with privatized landholdings in an urban setting, a far cry from the presumed biblical order of the extended family on its jointly owned estate in rural surroundings. Although I do not argue for direct causation, that is, that the social and economic conditions of Roman Palestine cause the rabbis to adopt existing laws, I make my observations about the possible relationships between the laws and the contexts because I choose to cultivate the methodologically most sophisticated argument for the combined conditions (social, economic, and legal) that could culminate in the production of tannaitic inheritance laws. Thus, I explain the appropriateness of certain rabbinic innovations to the social and economic contexts of Roman Palestine, including the presence of multiple forms for transferring assets (Chapters 1, 3, and the Appendix), the existence of dispositions of property even to non-relatives (Chapters 1), the diminished status of the firstborn son (Chapter 2), the inclusion of daughters in the order of succession (Chapter 4), and automatic asset allocation for the protection of widows (Chapter 5).

The prominence of a philological-historical analysis of tannaitic sources throughout this study proves to be invaluable in gaining a deeper appreciation of the variegated make-up of the tannaitic laws of inheritance. We are not dealing with a cohesive system of inheritance law. Rather, we are witness to competing and conflicting traditions that are, at times, interwoven with one another, waiting to be discovered and mined for the richness they add to the complex web of tannaitic inheritance traditions.

It is my hope that based on the methodological advances of this study, future projects on diverse areas of tannaitic law will tackle other variations of my question, "How Jewish is Jewish inheritance law?" all of which, like my question, ultimately lead to the question of questions "How Jewish is Jewish law?"

Appendix

Gifts in Contemplation of Death in Tannaitic Law and Ancient Parallels

Introduction

Tannaitic law recognizes four different gifts. Three of these (the exception is the *mattenat shakhev mera*; see below) are effected by an act of acquisition. One is the simple gift or *mattanah*. It takes immediate effect, requires an act of acquisition by or on behalf of the donee,[1] and is irrevocable.[2]

The other three gifts are specifically gifts in contemplation of death. That is, they take full effect only after the death of the donor.[3] For clarity and convenience, although dealing with tannaitic gifts, I refer to two of the three gifts in contemplation of death by their commonly known amoraic names.[4]

The *mattenat bari* (literally, gift of one in good health)[5] is a gift with retention of usufruct.[6] The *mattenat shakhev mera* (literally, the gift of one lying ill)[7] is a deathbed gift or bequest effected orally. The fourth type of gift is the *diathēkē*,[8] Greek for a written disposition in case of death.[9] I discuss the terms and conditions of each gift with reference to parallels in other ancient legal traditions in the sections below.[10]

---

[1] On acts of acquisition in tannaitic law, see Chapter 1.

[2] For more on gifting, see Chapter 1. On the irrevocability of each gift, see the corresponding section for each gift below.

[3] See "Abbreviations, Terminology, and Transliteration" and Chapter 1.

[4] Although the terms *mattenat bari* and *mattenat shakhev mera* do not occur in tannaitic literature, the conceptual distinction between a disposition by one who is critically ill vs. one who is healthy may exist; see *mBB* 9:6 and below in the body. Rabinowitz, "Neo-Babylonian Legal Documents and Jewish Law," 165 n. 115 argues for the great antiquity of distinguishing between gifting by the healthy and the ill.

[5] The following are examples of occurrences in amoraic literature: *pPe'ah* 3:7, 17d; *pBB* 8:8, 16c; *bKet* 55b; *bGit* 59a; *bBB* 135b.

[6] In my use of Roman legal terminology here, i. e., usufruct, I follow Daube, "Inheritance in Two Lukan Pericopes," 326–334; see also Jackson, "Prodigal Son," 118.

[7] For occurrences in amoraic literature, see n. 28.

[8] MS Kaufman reads, דְּיֵיאתְּקֵי, and MS Parma, דיאתיקי. I use the transliteration of the Greek in the body of the text even when referring to the tannaitic institution.

[9] On the use of other Greek terminology, i. e., דיאתימון, for gifting in contemplation of death that is not dealt with here, see Gulak, *Das Urkundenwesen*, 133 (=Gulak, *Legal Documents*, 160, and the bibliography the editor lists in n. 22). See also Sperber, *Greek*, 163–164; Sperber, *Dictionary*, 81–82 and the bibliography cited.

[10] The bibliography below is meant to be representative; it is not exhaustive.

The Tannaitic Mattenat Bari

Reuven Yaron aptly describes the *mattenat bari*:

> [In this gift] ownership is immediately transferred to the donee; use and management are retained by the donor. The donee has immediate power of alienation, though with effect from the donor's death only. Any subsequent dispositions of the donor are of effect only for his lifetime. At his death full control passes to the donee or his alienee.[11]

That is, if during the father's lifetime the son sells any land the father gifted to him previously, the sale only takes effect after the father's death. If the father sells any part of the land he gifted prior, it is considered to be sold (and the buyer benefits from the produce) only until the father dies. Then it reverts back to the donee (i. e., the son).[12] The arrangement is seemingly irrevocable from the initial time of gifting even though full ownership is not acquired by the donee until after the donor's death.[13]

Below I cite *mBB* 8:7,[14] dealing with *mattenat bari*, and divide it into two parts. Following the translation of the citation, I discuss the form of the source and then the content. Mishnah *Baba Batra* 8:7 (in MS Kaufmann 8:9) states:

I.	הכותב נכסיו לבניו צריך שיכתוב 'מהיום לאחר מותי',[15] דברי רבי יהודה. ורבי יוסה אומר אינו צריך.	If a man assigns his goods to his sons in writing, he must write, "From today (and) after my death." These are the words of R. Judah. And R. Jose says: He need not do so.
II.	הכותב נכסיו לבנו לאחר מותו האב אינו יכול למכור מפני שהן כתובים לבן, והבן אינו יכול למכור מפני שהן ברשות האב. מכר האב, מכורין עד שימות. מכר הבן, אין ללוקיח בהן כלום עד שימות האב. האב תולש ומאכיל לכל מי שירצה. ומה שהיניח תלוש הרי הוא שליורשים.	If a man assigns his goods to his son in writing for after his [the father's] death, the father cannot sell them since they are assigned to his son, and the son cannot sell them since they are in the father's possession. If the father sold them, they are sold [only] until he dies; if the son sold them, the buyer has no claim on them until the father dies. The father may pluck up [the crop of a field that he has so assigned] and give to whom he wants; and if he left anything already plucked up, it belongs to [all] his heirs.

[11] Yaron, *Gifts*, 49.

[12] On this arrangement possibly applying to the older son in the New Testament narrative of the prodigal son, see Jackson, "Prodigal Son," 118.

[13] Cf. Edrei, "Mattanah," 5–6. On the irrevocability of the amoraic *mattenat bari*, see Yaron, *Gifts*, 50–53.

[14] In MS Kaufmann, MS Parma, MS Lowe, and MS Leiden, 8:9. See also the parallel in *tKet* 8:5, discussed below.

[15] So, too, MS Lowe. MS Parma reads, *mehayom uleaḥar moti*. MS Leiden, the Mishnah in Bavli manuscripts (MS Paris [Bibliothèque nationale Suppl. Heb. 1337], MS Vatican 115, MS

Paragraph I presents a tannaitic dispute regarding the necessity for a formula when effecting a *mattenat bari* while par. II describes the terms and conditions of the gift. Although in par. I R. Judah requires a formula for the *mattenat bari* (as opposed to R. Jose who does not), the *mishnah* is silent about why R. Judah requires the formula. Tosefta *Ketubbot* 8:5 (seemingly working off of a *mishnah* very similar, if not identical, to ours)[16] cryptically adds the reasoning behind R. Judah's position: the date on a deed only proves the "date it was written."

Saul Lieberman interprets the Tosefta to mean that R. Judah requires the formula, "from today (and) after my death," so that it is clear the gift is being made also for during the donor's lifetime and not for after his death only.[17] A gift solely for after death cannot be gifted since after death the donor no longer owns the property.[18] Furthermore, Lieberman explains that R. Judah requires the date on the deed to indicate that only the possessions owned as of that date, and not those acquired by the donor afterward,[19] are gifted to the donee.[20]

Joseph Rivlin adds that the formula "from today (and) after my death" indicates immediate cession of the possession, but not its usufruct, which is only ceded upon death.[21] That is, each separate clause in the formula "from today" and "until death" refers to a different part of the arrangement inherent in the *mattenat bari* and implied in par. II of the *mishnah*.[22] "From today" refers to the ownership of the principal, gifted at the time of the issuance of the deed, and "until death" addresses the usufruct, passed on only after the donor's demise.[23]

Hamburg 165 and MS Munich 95) and printed editions of Mishnah have the formula as *mehayom uleaḥar mita*.

16 Cf. Lieberman, *Tosefta ki-fshuṭah: Nashim*, 319.

17 Yaron, *Gifts*, 114, contends that the inclusion of *mehayom* in the rabbinic formula is to clarify what is ambiguous in the original Greek formula, whether ownership passes immediately or only on the donor's death. For more details, see below, "The Formula of the Tannaitic *Mattenat Bari* and Gifting Formulae at Elephantine."

18 This assumption seems to be what is behind the reasoning in some sources, and Lieberman invokes it when apparently appropriate. See, e. g., Lieberman, *Tosefta ki-fshuṭah: Neziqin*, 427. The tannaitic basis for this assumption requires further consideration. See also my comments in Chapter 1 n. 61; Chapter 3 n. 6; below n. 54.

19 See also Gulak, *Das Urkundenwesen*, 133 (=Gulak, *Legal Documents*, 161); Edrei, "Mattanah," 7.

20 Lieberman, *Tosefta: Nashim*, 85; and Lieberman, *Tosefta ki-fshuṭah: Nashim*, 319.

21 Rivlin, *Inheritance and Wills*, 163; and, as per the medieval rabbinic literature cited by Rivlin at n. 18, he states emphatically, "this is the only [possible] interpretation of this formula." For an English summary, see Rivlin, "Gift and Inheritance Law," 176–177. See also the citations to Lieberman in the previous note; and Edrei, "Mattanah," 6.

22 Rivlin, *Inheritance and Wills*, 163 n. 18, argues that there is no connection between tannaitic and Elephantine gifting formulae primarily because the formulae examined from Elephantine are employed for immediate gifts and not gifts comparable to the *mattenat bari*. See my discussion in the section below entitled, "The Formula of the Tannaitic *Mattenat Bari* and Gifting Formulae at Elephantine."

23 Aryeh Edrei argues for an entirely different approach to the matters addressed here by Lieberman and Rivlin primarily because he chooses to find a conceptual background to the tannaitic dispute that does not incorporate the Tosefta tradition; see Edrei, "Mattanah," 1–23.

Another Tosefta text also dealing with gifting, *tBB* 8:10, is interpreted in two different ways in the Palestinian and Babylonian Talmuds, the latter linking the Tosefta text to our *mishnah* regarding the *mattenat bari* (*mBB* 8:7, cited above). The text of the Tosefta follows:

ח:י	8:10
הכותב ... מתנה אין יכול לחזור בו ... אי זו היא מתנה מן היום יינתנו נכסיו לפלני.	He who writes a (deed of) gift may not retract ... which is a (deed of) gift? Any in which it is written: "from today his possessions will be given to so-and-so."

When discussing this source, the Palestinian Talmud states that the possessions will be given to so-and-so "from now, and let it be written in it [the deed of gift] 'from today' [=*mehayom*]." [24] According to this source, the word *mehayom* in the Tosefta indicates that the transfer of possession with full rights takes immediate effect, categorizing this as a simple gift, an interpretation considered by some as the historical meaning of the Tosefta text.[25] Based on the greater context in both the Tosefta and the Palestinian *sugya*, however, Lieberman argues that both texts refer to a deathbed bequest, or *mattenat shakhev mera*,[26] a point to which we return later in the section entitled "Yaron on the Tannaitic *Diathēkē*" in our discussion of the *mattenat shakhev mera* as compared to the *diathēkē*.

With the formula of the *mattenat bari* in place in *mBB* 8:7, the Babylonian Talmud seeks to root this gift and its formula in the Babylonian version of the Tosefta tradition above (*tBB* 8:10) as well. Indeed, the Babylonian Talmud at *bBM* 19a and *bBB* 135b preserves the text of *tBB* 8:10, appending to it the formula known from *mBB* 8:7: "a gift, any in which it is written: *from today and after death* (=*mehayom uleaḥar mita*)."[27] The original Tosefta version, as cited above, does not allude to the formula of the *mattenat bari*; it only states that the gift is effective "from today." The transmitters of this Tosefta tradition in the Babylonian Talmud seem to view the phrase "from today" in the *baraita* as an abbreviation of the entire phrase "from today and after death," known to them from *mBB* 8:7. Accordingly, they register this formula as part of the *baraita* itself.

The Tannaitic Mattenat Shakhev Mera

Unlike the *mattenat bari* whose terms are explained in tannaitic literature, what comes to be called the *mattenat shakhev mera* by the amoraim[28] is not ade-

---

[24] See *pPe'ah* 3:7, 17d (94).

[25] Yaron, *Gifts*, 27; see also the discussion in Rivlin, *Inheritance and Wills*, 162–163.

[26] Lieberman, *Tosefta ki-fshuṭah: Neziqin*, 428.

[27] This is the formula according to MS Vatican 115.

[28] For occurrences in amoraic literature, see *pKet* 9:1, 33a; *pBB* 8:8, 16c; *bKet* 55b; *bGit* 9a, 59a, 66a; *bBB* 135b, 137a.

quately described in tannaitic sources. Tannaitic traditions mention only that the donor is "lying ill" (*shakhev mera*). Accordingly, it may be that the *mattenat shakhev mera*, like the classical Roman *donatio mortis causa* (see below), can be made only due to fear of death from a certain danger such as illness.[29] In the absence of further specifications in tannaitic literature, it is left to the amoraim to creatively infer from other details in the tannaitic traditions the terms and conditions of the *mattenat shakhev mera*.

Two major features distinguish the amoraic *mattenat shakhev mera* from other gifts. According to the Talmud, out of consideration for the mental strain on an ill person if one's dying wishes might not be accomplished, the amoraim rule that the donor can gift, even all possessions, without the transfer depending on a formal act of acquisition.[30] Furthermore, the amoraic *mattenat shakhev mera* is revocable upon the recovery of the donor[31] (and seemingly at a later time in the amoraic period even at pleasure).[32] Although there is no explicit statement in tannaitic traditions that the *mattenat shakhev mera* is revocable upon recovery,[33] scholars assume it is revocable because of later Talmudic interpretation, the possible parallel to the Roman *donatio mortis causa*[34] and, at least according to one scholar, the lack of necessity for tannaitic traditions to be explicit about revocation.[35]

The fact that already some tannaim do not require an act of acquisition for the *mattenat shakhev mera* is alluded to in *mBB* 9:7 (in MS Kaufmann 9:9):[36]

המחליק[35] נכסיו על פיו רבי אליעזר אומר אחד בריא אחד מסוכן, נכסים שיש להן אחריות ניקנים בכסף ובשטר ובחזקה, ושאין להן אחריות אינן ניקנים אלא במשיכה.	If a man apportions his goods by word of mouth, R. Eliezer says: whether he was in health or at the point of death, property for which there is security can be acquired only

[29] In addition, the classical Roman *donatio mortis causa* could be effected in fear of death due to dangerous travel but not merely in abstract contemplation of mortality; see Nicholas, *Introduction to Roman Law*, 266.

[30] See *bBB* 147b; the rabbis treat the words of a *shakhev mera* "as if written and delivered" (=*kikhetuvim u-mesurin*); see *bBB* 151a, 175a; *bGit* 13a, 15a.

[31] See *bBB* 151a.

[32] So states Yaron, "The *mattenath šekhiv mera*ʿ revocable at will, even prior to recovery, is a creation of the Amoraim" (Yaron, *Gifts*, 64). On the effect of the donor's recovery in amoraic law, see Yaron, *Gifts*, 81–84. For more on the amoraic *mattenat shakhev mera*, see Rivlin, *Inheritance and Wills*, 142–150.

[33] In fact, one possible reading of *tBB* 8:10 implies that the tannaitic *mattenat shakhev mera* is irrevocable [!] (see below "The Tannaitic *Diathēkē*").

[34] See Yaron, *Gifts*, 1; Yaron, "Acts of Last Will," 36. See also Taubenschlag, *Law*, 154.

[35] Yaron states, "[A] stipulation of revocation on recovery would have been unnecessary as being implied by it. Under Tannaitic law, if the donor survived the illness, the gift became by that fact either void or revocable" (Yaron, *Gifts*, 64). See also Rivlin, *Inheritance and Wills*, 146.

[36] As per, MS Kaufmann, *hamaḥalik*. MS Parma, MS Lowe, MS Leiden and the Mishnah in Bavli manuscripts (MS Paris [Bibliothèque nationale Suppl. Heb. 1337], MS Vatican 115, MS Hamburg 165 and MS Munich 95) read *hameḥalek*, as expected.

by money or by deed or by usucaption; that for which there is no security can be acquired only by the act of drawing into possessions.

R. Eliezer's emphasis on "whether he was in health or at the point of death" reads almost like a response to a contention that distinguishes between the mechanisms for transfer of property by the critically ill versus the healthy. The parallel in *tBB* 10:12 gives a context for R. Eliezer's position:

A person in danger [of death] who divided his property by word of mouth whether this was on a weekday or on the Sabbath, the statements made by the decedent are to be carried out. But in the case of a healthy person, [they are carried out] only if [the donee] will make acquisition through money, a deed, or usucaption. R. Eliezer says, "property for which there is security is acquired through money, a deed, or usucaption; and that for which there is no security is acquired only through being drawn [into the possession of the one who acquired it].	המסכין שחלק נכסיו על פיו בין בחול בין בשבת דברי המת יעשו. אבל בריא, עד שיקנה בכסף ובשטר ובחזקה. רבי אליעזר אומר נכסים שיש להן אחריות נקנין בכסף ובשטר ובחזקה ושאין להן אחריות אין נקנין אלא במשיכה.

The implication of the anonymous tannaitic opinion indeed supports a legal distinction (later adopted by the amoraim): while the healthy are subjected to the use of mechanisms for the transfer of property, the critically ill need not be burdened (for the amoraic understanding, see above). According to the tradition in R. Eliezer's name, however, the distinction is not applicable.

Another set of parallel tannaitic sources – *mPe'ah* 3:7 and *mBB* 9:6[37] – discusses the *mattenat shakhev mera*. These sources are interpreted by the amoraim as teaching about the revocability of the gift. However, the case can be made for the tannaitic sources originally teaching about something else: the prohibition against disinheriting one's immediate heirs (i.e., sons). Below I cite both *mishnayot*, briefly discuss the Palestinian Talmud's *sugya,* and then elaborate on the interpretation of the tannaitic sources I prefer:

Pe'ah 3:7	פאה ג:ז
If one that lay dying assigned his goods in writing and kept back any property whatsoever, his gift is valid; but if he had kept back no property whatsoever, his gift is not valid.	הכותב נכסיו שכיב מרע שייר קרקע כל שהוא מתנתו קיימת, לא שייר קרקע כל שהוא אין מתנתו קיימת.

[37] In MS Kaufmann 3:8 and 9:8, respectively.

בבא בתרא ט:ו	*BB* 9:6
שכיב מרע שכתב[38] נכסיו לאחרים שייר קרקע כל שהוא, מתנתו קיימת. לא שייר קרקע כל שהוא אין מתנתו קיימת.	If one that lay dying assigned his goods in writing to others and kept back any property whatsoever, his gift is valid; but if he had kept back no property whatsoever, his gift is not valid.

The Palestinian Talmud, *Pe'ah* 3:7, 17d (94), infers from the negative statement "his gift is *not* valid" that if a dying man gifts all of his property, his gift is not valid as a *simple* gift but would be valid as a *deathbed* gift. Because his declaration is made with dying in mind, if he recovers from his illness the gift is considered void, and the donor recuperates it.[39] On the other hand if the dying man retains some property, "his gift is valid" as a *simple* gift and would not be valid as a *deathbed* gift. If he recovers from his illness, he will not recuperate what he gifts.

However, this may not be the simplest reading of the tannaitic texts, as correctly noted by Rivlin.[40] I add that one would expect that because the subject is one who is critically ill, the phrase "his gift is not valid" and the parallel clause "his gift is valid" refer specifically to the type of gift effected (or not effected) because of the illness – what the amoraim call the *mattenat shakhev mera*,[41] and not the *simple* gift. Read this way, the tannaitic traditions state that retaining some property validates the gift – the *mattenat shakhev mera* – while not retaining any property invalidates it.[42] Accordingly, if the gift is not valid because the donor gifts his (entire) estate to non-heirs [=*aḥerim*], the *mishnah* may actually be referring to a prohibition of disinheritance.[43] To circumvent the potential prohibition, when disposing of assets the donor must retain some property for the heirs – even if just a minimal amount – thereby validating the *mattenat shakhev mera*.

Ancient Parallels to the Mattenat Bari and Mattenat Shakhev Mera

Although strictly speaking neither the *mattenat bari* nor the *mattenat shakhev mera* are evidenced in biblical literature, scholars point to possible deathbed

---

[38] So too MS Parma, MS Lowe, and MS Hamburg 165 (Bavli). MS Leiden, the Mishnah in the following Bavli manuscripts – MS Paris [Bibliothèque nationale Suppl. Heb. 1337], MS Vatican 115, and MS Munich 95 – and printed editions read, *kol nekhasav* (= all of his goods).

[39] See also *bBB* 151a; cf. Yaron, *Gifts*, 61 and 64.

[40] Rivlin, "Inheritance, Wills and Legacies," 170.

[41] While there seems to be no specific tannaitic name for the gift under discussion, the way in which the gift of the lying ill functions is implied by the tannaitic sources; see my discussion above.

[42] See previous note. This may, in fact, also be Yaron's interpretation. See Yaron, *Gifts*, 67–68, 85. See also Rivlin's important comments at 171 n. 20 regarding the opinion of Falk.

[43] For support for such an interpretation in medieval Jewish works, see Rivlin, "Inheritance, Wills and Legacies," 169–70.

dispositions and their terminology in the Hebrew Bible[44] – most notably the patriarch Isaac's disposition in Genesis 27:1–4 – and possible parallels from Nuzi.[45] Possible parallels to the tannaitic *mattenat bari* and *mattenat shakhev mera* (and even the amoraic *mattenat shakhev mera*) are attested to in documents from the Neo-Babylonian period.[46] A gift with retention of usufruct is recorded,[47] and Cornelia Wunsch published another document that contains the essential characteristics of both forms of gifting. It is a disposition of the businessman Itti-Marduk-balātu, from the Egibi family, in which before going on a (potentially dangerous?) long journey, he bequeaths all of his property to his wife while retaining for himself the usufruct for life.[48]

Another Neo-Babylonian document, from the period between the reigns of Xerxes and Alexander, recently examined by Matthew W. Stolper, is a conceptually closer parallel to the amoraic *mattenat shakhev mera* (and the Roman *donatio mortis causa*). It begins with an unambiguous statement regarding the donor's expectation that he will not survive his illness:[49] "Mannu-kâ-Attar, servant of Šum-iddin, who [contracted?] an illness in Babylon, did not believe that he would recover."[50] The donor retains ownership for his lifetime, and the terms of the document are revoked should Mannu-kâ-Attar recover from his illness.[51] So, too, documents possibly akin to the amoraic *mattenat shakhev mera*/*donatio mortis causa* exist among the Elephantine papyri. Although these documents do not necessarily deal with critically ill donors, they do employ terminology relating to their revocability. Zvi Szubin and Bezalel Porten discuss the Elephantine gifts in light of the *mattenat shakhev mera* and the *donatio mortis causa*, as well as Roman testaments.[52]

---

[44] Also on this topic, see Chapter 3.

[45] See C. Gordon, "Biblical Customs and the Nuzu Tablets," 8; Speiser, "I Know Not the Day of My Death," 252–256. The relationship of these biblical parallels to ancient Near Eastern institutions is strongly disputed by Thompson, *Historicity*, 285–293; however, see the most recent and eloquent defense of the relationship between the ancient Near Eastern and biblical deathbed bequests in Malul, "Death-Bed Dispositions in the Hebrew Bible." See also Gulak, *Das Urkundenwesen*, 125–126 (=Gulak, *Legal Documents*, 154–155), and Gulak, *Yesodei hamishpat haivri*, 3:142, who argues for the biblical origins of deathbed bequests (cf. Rivlin, *Inheritance and Wills*, 135) and the refutation in Yaron, *Gifts*, 8.

[46] Gulak, *Das Urkundenwesen*, 133 (=Gulak, *Legal Documents*, 161) already points to an Old Babylonian parallel to the *mattenat bari*.

[47] See Oelsner, Wells, and Wunsch, "Mesopotamia: Neo-Babylonian Period," 937, where such texts are described briefly.

[48] Wunsch, *Urkunden*, 214–215 (Text No. 260). See also Wunsch, "Women's Property," 6.

[49] Cf. VAS 5:21 in which a man's donation of a prebend begins, "For some time I have been ill," cited in Stolper, "Mannu-kâ-Attar," 471.

[50] The text is BM 16562+16806 as transcribed and translated in Stolper, "Mannu-kâ-Attar," 470.

[51] Stolper, "Mannu-kâ-Attar," 473.

[52] Szubin and Porten, "Testamentary Succession at Elephantine," 36. See also my discussion in Chapter 3.

Yaron points to Greek and Roman parallels to the *mattenat bari* and the *mattenat shakhev mera*.[53] The former, he states, is a result of the importation of the Greco-Egyptian *meta tēn teleutēn* gift[54] and is parallel to the Roman *donatio deducto usufructu*,[55] while the latter roughly corresponds to the classical Roman *donatio mortis causa*.[56] It may be that the *mattenat shakhev mera*, like the classical Roman *donatio mortis causa*, can only be made due to fear of death from certain danger such as illness (or travel, and, not merely in abstract contempla-

[53] Yaron, *Gifts*, 1, 46–60. On Katzoff's argument for the modeling of the *mattenat bari* (and *diathēkē*) on analogous Greek institutions only before the middle of the first century CE, see Katzoff, "P. Yadin 19," 1–8; and on Katzoff's argument, Rivlin, *Inheritance and Wills*, 143 n. 65; and Jackson, "Why the Name New Testament," 71 n. 193.

[54] Yaron, *Gifts*, 47. Yaron was preceded by Gulak, *Das Urkundenwesen*, 133 (=Gulak, *Legal Documents*, 161) in pointing to the parallel concept and partial formulaic overlap of the tannaitic *mattenat bari* and the Greco-Egyptian gift. However, see my discussion below, "The Formula of the Tannaitic *Mattenat Bari* and Gifting Formulae at Elephantine." For a possible objection to the Greco-Egyptian parallel, see Falk, "Testate Succession," 75; and Rivlin, *Inheritance and Wills*, 143 n. 65; and see n. 75, below. Rivlin contends that in tannaitic times, the *mattenat bari* arises in response to the problem of donors wanting a gift to transfer after death (despite a prohibition of stipulating so) and of donors not wanting to irrevocably transfer possessions immediately, thereby losing the rights to the use of the property during their lifetimes. (For a similar suggestion, see Edrei, "Mattanah," 5–7.) Rivlin sees the presence of the *mattenat bari* in tannaitic law as the final stage in a process beginning with the assimilation of the Greek *diathēkē* for use both by the ill and the healthy, followed by a shift to the use of the *diathēkē* only by the ill and then the creation of the *mattenat bari* arrangement for use only by the healthy (see Rivlin, *Inheritance and Wills*, 138–150, 162–165; Rivlin, "Gift and Inheritance Law," 172–179). Rivlin's reconstruction of the historical process is rooted in his assumption that two legal positions, "a deed has no validity after death" and "there is no transfer of title after death" are adopted during the tannaitic period. These two positions are explicitly recorded only in the Babylonian Talmud and in the name of the amora Shemuel (although Rivlin argues that the argument for tannaitic origins may find support in the prohibitions regarding declarations of divorce for after death in *mGit* 7:3; see Rivlin, *Inheritance and Wills*, 141 n. 57; specifically on possible tannaitic support for the amoraic view [at least according to R. David Pardo], see Lieberman, *Tosefta ki-fshuṭah: Neziqin*, 427). The contention, therefore, must be reexamined. See Chapter 1 n. 61 and Chapter 3 n. 6. See also my comments on Lieberman's approach in n. 18. On the usage of the term *diathēkē* even for *meta tēn teleutēn* gifts, see Jackson, "Why the Name New Testament," 64.

[55] Yaron, *Gifts*, 59–60. Boaz Cohen argues that, in general, the concept of usufruct in Jewish law is borrowed from Roman law (although he does not deal with the *mattenat bari*); see B. Cohen, *Jewish and Roman Law*, 557–577. We now know of legal arrangements involving usufruct from other ancient legal contexts as well (even if not gifts in contemplation of death with retention of usufruct). On Elephantine, see Szubin and Porten, "A Life Estate of Usufruct," 29–45; on the ancient Near East, see Magdalene and Wunsch, *Manumission, Emancipation, and Oblation*, 76. See also my discussion above on the work of Wunsch and Stolper.

[56] Yaron, *Gifts*, 1; Yaron, "Acts of Last Will," 36. For one possible case of a Greek disposition dependent on the donor not recovering, see Yaron, *Gifts*, 64. On *donatio mortis causa* in general, see Buckland, *Text-Book of Roman Law*, 257–259; di Paola, *Donatio Mortis Causa*; and Borkowski, *Deathbed Gifts*. On Egyptian *donatio mortis causa* with *meta tēn teleutēn* terminology, see the references to Taubenschlag's work and that of other scholars in Jackson, "Why the Name New Testament," 64 n. 117.

tion of mortality; see above).[57] In addition, the *donatio mortis causa* is revocable[58] and requires an act of acquisition.[59] In the absence of explicit evidence for the revocability of the tannaitic *mattenat shakhev mera,* it may be that it remains distinct from the classical Roman *donatio mortis causa*, a matter requiring further reflection.[60] As previously mentioned, its amoraic counterpart is revocable. Finally, only Rabbi Eliezer's opinion in *mBB* 9:7, requiring an act of acquisition for the execution of a *mattenat shakhev mera*, parallels the same requirement for the classical Roman *donatio mortis causa.*

Not only conceptual parallels but also terminological overlap exists between tannaitic gifts and those known in other ancient legal traditions (even if not always from a context of gifts in contemplation of death). Indeed, in Neo-Babylonian deeds of gift, the donor's retention of the right to the income or usufruct of donated property is indicated by the verb *akālu*, "to consume,"[61] whose verbal equivalent, the Hebrew root *a-kh-l*, is used to designate the same arrangement in varying scenarios involving rights to usufruct in tannaitic law[62] and in the papyri from the Judean desert.[63] On a possible relationship between Elephantine gifting formulae and the formula of the tannaitic *mattenat bari*, see below "The Formula of the Tannaitic *Mattenat Bari* and Gifting Formulae at Elephantine."

A Mattenat Bari From the Judean Desert?

Although not recorded in tannaitic literature, at least one other gift in contemplation of death (in addition to the *mattenat bari*, *mattenat shakhev mera*, and *diathēkē*) survives from Palestine in the tannaitic period. A deed of gift from the "Cave of Letters," P. Yadin 7,[64] written in Aramaic and dated July 13, 120 CE is, in the strictest sense of the term, a gift in contemplation death, as correctly

[57] Nicholas, *Introduction to Roman Law*, 266. Only in later Roman law can the *donatio mortis causa* be made in general contemplation of mortality; see Nicholas's comments there, and Yaron, "Some Remarks on *Donatio Mortis Causa*," 493–512; Yaron, "Donatio Sola Cogitatione Mortalitatis," 369–375.

[58] Nicholas, *Introduction to Roman Law*, 266.

[59] See Talamanca, *Istituzioni di Diritto romano*, 778. On delivery specifically, see Borkowski, *Deathbed Gifts*, 5–7.

[60] See n. 56.

[61] See Stolper, "Mannu-kâ-Attar," 469.

[62] See *mKet* 4:4 and 6:1; and also *mBB* 8:7 (cited above) where the father can "feed" others from the usufruct. For more on *a-kh-l* and its parallels, see Rabinowitz, "Neo-Babylonian Legal Documents and Jewish Law," 158–159.

[63] Yadin, *Documents*, 98.

[64] A second papyrus, P. Yadin 19, written in Greek and dated 128 CE, possibly displays yet another gift in contemplation of death unattested in tannaitic law, in which one half of the gift is gifted immediately and the other half after the death of the donor (on the parallel in Tobit, see Katzoff, "P. Yadin 19," 4; and Chapter 3). On this deed, see Cotton, "Deeds of Gift and the Law of Succession," 180–181; Rivlin, "Gift and Inheritance Law," 166–167.

pointed out by Hannah Cotton.[65] For, the transfer of the gift is dependent on and effected by the death of the donor.[66] In the deed, Shimon son of Menaḥem[67] grants his wife, Miriam, daughter of Yosef son of Menashe, an irrevocable gift (*mattenat olam*) of all of his property and any property that he might acquire during his lifetime, on the condition that the transfer of ownership only take place after his death. Part of the (lengthy) text follows:

אנה שמעון בר מנחם די עמר במחוזא לכי אנתי מרים אנתתי ברת יוסף בר מנשה ית כל מה די איתי לי במחוזא ... ושאר כל מנדעם די איתי לי די לא וציף עם כל די אקנא ויהוא לי מן כען יהבת לכי מתנת עלם ... יהבת לכי אנתי מרים אנתתי מתנת עלם על אסרה די אהוא אכל ומחסן ופרע פרעון מלכהון ועמר ומעמר בדרתא ובתיא כל יומי חיי וכדי אהך לבית עלמי תהוין רשיה ושליטה באתרי מתנתא דא או במה די [א]שבוק מנהון וד[י לא אשתרהן] ולא אתזבן לפרנוס נפשי מן באתר דנה ובבל נכסין ודמי נכסין ומאני בי וכל מנדעם זעיר וסגיא די יהוא לי מן כען [ועד עלם] די וציף בשטר מתנתא דנה.[68]

I, Shim'on, son of Menaḥem, who resides in Maḥoza', to you; you, Miryam, my wife, daughter of Yoseph, son of Menasheh, all that I possess in Maḥoza; ... and whatever else I (may) possess that is not described, together with all that I may acquire and (that) will become my possession from this time (forth) – I have given to you as a gift forever ... I have given to you; you, Miryam, my wife, as a gift forever, on the binding agreement that I may enjoy the usufruct, and retain possession, and remit payment of their property taxes; and reside and install (others) as residents, in the courtyards and houses, all the days of my life. And when I go to my eternal home, you shall become the rightful possessor of the sites of this gift, or of what [I shall] leave of them behind, (and) whi[ch will not have been pledged (as security)], and (which) will not have been sold for my own subsistence subsequent to this (time). And (similarly), over all properties, and income of property, and household utensils, and anything (whatsoever), small or large, that I will possess from this time forth [and forever], that is described in this document of gift ...[69]

Unlike the *mattenat shakhev mera*, P. Yadin 7 is not written by a critically ill donor. Unlike the *mattenat bari*, sale by the donor in P. Yadin 7 is not only in effect for his lifetime. Rather, in P. Yadin 7 the donor retains the right to sell possessions from the principal for his own sustenance and, upon his death, the

[65] Cotton, "Archive of Salome Komaise," 183. Cf. Cotton, "Deeds of Gift and the Law of Succession," 179.

[66] See the definition I provide in "Abbreviations, Terminology, and Transliteration" and Chapter 1 n. 1.

[67] He is the father of the famed Babatha from the same archive.

[68] Yadin, *Documents*, 80–82. Some of the *sigla* in the original edition were removed for easier reading.

[69] Yadin, *Documents*, 81–83.

donee receives only what is left of the principal, if anything ("And when I go to my eternal home, you shall become the rightful possessor of the sites of this gift ... and [which] will not have been sold for my own subsistence subsequent to this [time]"). Furthermore, the terms of the gift allow the donor to cede ownership even of property that has yet to be acquired ("together with all that I may acquire and [that] will become my possession from this time [forth]").

Despite the fundamental differences between the gift in the papyrus and the *mattenat bari* and based on the fact that the donor retains the usufruct for his lifetime, Yaron[70] and, following him, Rivlin,[71] consider P. Yadin 7 a (form of) *mattenat bari.*[72] However, in light of the fact that in P. Yadin 7 the donor can sell part of the principal and only gift the remaining property and that the donor gifts property he will own in the future, the parallel to the *mattenat bari* is difficult to sustain. It is likely, therefore, that the gift in P. Yadin 7 either represents an institution independent of the *mattenat bari* or a special arrangement unattested in tannaitic law.[73]

The Formula of the Tannaitic Mattenat Bari and Gifting Formulae at Elephantine

Despite Rivlin's hesitation to examine the formula of the tannaitic *mattenat bari* in light of Elephantine formulae,[74] an attempt to learn from the overlap may prove productive. Maximally, the exercise can result in the discovery of a possible genetic link between the later tannaitic formulae and antecedents at Elephantine. Minimally, a review of the possible meanings of Elephantine formulae can yield a sharper interpretation of the formula of the *mattenat bari.*

Here I look at two different gifting formulae known from the Elephantine papyri (with reference to Judean desert formulae when relevant), each of which contains two clauses. The first is *min yoma zenah ve'ad olam*, "from this day and forever." The second is *beḥayay uvemoti*, "in my life and in my death." Each one of the two clauses in R. Judah's formula for the *mattenat bari*, *mehayom leaḥar moti*, is parallel to one half of each of the formulae known from Elephantine (underlined above): *mehayom* = *min yoma zenah* and *leaḥar moti*= *uvemoti.*

The commonalities may be instructive even if at Elephantine the formulae are not employed specifically for gifts in contemplation of death with retention of usufruct (i. e., *mattenat bari* type arrangements). If the parallels are, indeed, in

[70] Yaron, "Acts of Last Will," 45.

[71] Rivlin, "Gift and Inheritance Law," 165–166.

[72] Indeed, Rivlin alludes to a possible link between the formula of the *mattenat bari* and that of P. Yadin 7. See Rivlin, "Gift and Inheritance Law," 166.

[73] For more on inheritance by wives in the Judean desert, see Chapter 5.

[74] See n. 22.

any way indicative of a relationship between the earlier and later formulae, then perhaps the tannaim rework and adapt the older general gifting formulae to the gift in contemplation of death that they know and embrace, seemingly modeled after the Greco-Egyptian *meta tēn teleutēn*.[75]

In the Elephantine papyri the first part of the formula (underlined), *min yoma zenah ve'ad olam*, "from this day and forever," indicates that a contract is entered into immediately.[76] That is, its irrevocability is effected as of now.[77] The second part of the formula, *ve'ad olam* (="and forever"), instructs that the transaction established by the deed, such as being taken in marriage or receiving a gift, is not, a priori, limited by time.[78] In the context of gifting, it may affirm that the gift's said irrevocability is forever. Significantly, a similar formula appears in documents from the Judean desert papyri, *min ke'an yahavat lekhi mattenat olam*, – "from this time (forth) I have given to you as a gift forever" – indicating that the gift takes effect from this time or from now (=*min ke'an*) and is "a gift forever, a perpetual gift," a *mattenat olam*.[79] As stated, I highlight the overlap between the first clause in the Elephantine formula, *min yoma zenah*, and the first clause in the tannaitic formula, *mehayom*. If at Elephantine this clause indicates the immediacy of the effect of the contract, then perhaps *mehayom* in our *mishnah* similarly instructs.[80]

---

[75] On other possible ancient parallels, see the section above entitled "Ancient Parallels to the *Mattenat Bari* and *Mattenat Shakhev Mera*." Falk, "Testate Succession," 75, actually casts doubt on the parallel between the Greco-Egyptian gift and the tannaitic *mattenat bari*, at least on the terminological level, since Yaron, preceded by Gulak, argues that the tannaitic *mattenat bari* includes only a translation of the key words *meta tēn teleutēn* – *le'aḥar mita* preceded by the word *mehayom* – "from today," and not a fuller parallel formula; on Yaron and Gulak's position, see n. 54. Falk, himself, prefers the suggestion that the tannaitic formula is an adaptation of either Elephantine (or biblical) terminology (Falk, "Testate Succession," 75), a matter I develop here.

[76] Szubin and Porten, "Testamentary Succession at Elephantine," 39.

[77] On aspects of irrevocability at Elephantine and in Neo-Babylonian documents, see Rabinowitz, "Neo-Babylonian Legal Documents and Jewish Law," 159–160; and in relation to Roman law, Rabinowitz, "Neo-Babylonian Legal Documents and Jewish Law," 162–163.

[78] Yaron, "Aramaic Marriage Contracts," 31–32. Yaron emphasizes how the use of our formula in marriage contracts is unique to the Jewish context at Elephantine; the parallel formula in other legal traditions is not employed for marriage. For a demotic parallel, see Porten, *Elephantine Papyri in English*, 166 n. 31.

[79] Yadin, *Documents*, 81 and 92. For part of a text in which this phrase appears, P. Yadin 7, see above "A *Mattenat Bari* from the Judean Desert?" Compare also the term used in Neo-Babylonian documents, *ana ūmu ṣâtu*, "in perpetuity," to indicate that the donee's ownership after the donor's death is not limited; and on this, Stolper, "Testament of Mannu-kâ-Attar," 469 and 473.

[80] As noted earlier, Lieberman's position is that the function of *mehayom* is to clarify that the gift is not just for after death (for him a forbidden arrangement) but for during life as well. Rivlin sees in *mehayom* an indication of the immediate cession of the principal. Yaron, assuming the Greek origin of the formula of the *mattenat bari*, thinks *mehayom* in the rabbinic formula is added to clarify (what was ambiguous in the original Greek formula) whether ownership passes immediately or only after the death of the donor. See n. 54 and n. 75.

A second formula at Elephantine *beḥayay uvemoti*, "in my life and after my death" also appears in the context of gifting. Scholars debate what the actual force of the formula is. Yochanan Muffs argues that the formula[81] indicates the gift is transferred and final from the moment of the donation and is not affected (or effected) by the donor's death.[82] That is, the gift is given from now ("in my life[time]") and forever ("after my death"). Daniel Boyarin disagrees and suggests that in fact the formula may mean the gift is final from the moment of the donation ("in my life[time]") but only takes effect after the donor's death ("after my death").[83] If we follow Boyarin's lead and read *uvemoti* (underlined above) as technical terminology for when the gift takes full effect, then perhaps we can assign a similar function to the phrase *leaḥar moti*, "after my death" in the *mattenat bari*.[84]

In light of the formulaic antecedents used at Elephantine, the origins and the meaning of the formula advocated by R. Judah for the *mattenat bari* can be reexamined. As shown, each part of the double-tiered formula effecting the *mattenat bari*, *mehayom leaḥar moti*, is parallel to one part of each of the two formulae known for gifting from Elephantine. Although not conclusive, R. Judah's formula may be a tannaitic reworking or adaptation. If so, we can affirm that the *mattenat bari* is final – that is, irrevocable – from today (*mehayom*), the point from which it transfers the principal. It takes full effect, transferring also the usufruct, after the death (*leaḥar moti*) of the donor. Furthermore, if the above is correct, then the idea that the *mattenat bari* is parallel to the Greco-Egyptian *meta tēn teleutēn* is primarily conceptual. That is, although the tannaitic institution may have been modeled after the Greco-Egyptian antecedent, its formula may be based on Elephantine formulaic antecedents.[85]

Yaron on the Tannaitic Diathēkē

We now turn to an analysis of the term *diathēkē*, Greek for a written disposition in case of death, and its usage in tannaitic literature. Yaron correctly points out

[81] The Talmud in *bBB* 153a actually discusses the use of a similar phrase *beḥayyim uvemavet* in deeds of gift, and it presents a debate between Rav and Shemuel, first generation Babylonian amoraim, who argue about whether the terminology designates a gift, a *mattenat bari*, taking effect while the donor is still alive (Shemuel), or a *mattenat shakhev mera*, taking effect after the death of the donor (Rav). See Yaron, *Gifts*, 76 and 120–121; Muffs, *Studies*, 36 n. 1; Boyarin, review of *Studies*, 59; Rabinowitz, *Jewish Law*, 202 n. 42; and Epstein, "Notizen," 364.

[82] Muffs, *Studies*, 36 n. 1. See also Yaron, *Gifts*, 121; Yaron, *Aramaic Papyri*, 78; Szubin and Porten, "Testamentary Succession at Elephantine," 39; and Porten, *Elephantine Papyri in English*, 164 n. 12. See also the observation in Jackson, "Prodigal Son," 117 n. 18.

[83] Boyarin, review of *Studies*, 59.

[84] This interpretation of *leaḥar moti* is in keeping with the scholarly suggestions offered above in "The Tannaitic *Mattenat Bari*" but points to the possible origins from Elephantine.

[85] Contra Yaron, see n. 54, n. 75, and n. 80.

that the *diathēkē* always appears in tannaitic literature in the context of dispositions in contemplation of death.[86] Significantly, he discovers that the formula used in the original Greek *diathēkē*, "be it (given) to me to be in good health and to live," is paralleled in the rabbinic formula, *tehe li liḥyot la'amod*, as attested in one textual witness of Talmudic literature, MS Vatican 133 to *pPe'ah* 3:7, 17d (94),[87] definitively demonstrating the adoption of the original Greek formula (and not just the name *diathēkē*) by the rabbis.[88] In addition, Yaron emphasizes the bilateralness of the *diathēkē* in tannaitic law – requiring an act of acquisition by or in favor of the donee[89] – as opposed to the unilateral Greek *diathēkē* without *eispoiēsis* (*Legatentestament*) and the Roman *testamentum*,[90] correctly coming to the conclusion that the tannaitic *diathēkē* is a gift. The tannaitic sources he examines on this issue do, in fact, seem to reflect the bilateralness to which he refers.[91] I suggest that when the term *diathēkē* assimilates into tannaitic law, the bilateralness of the original *diathēkē* with *eispoiêsis* (adoption) – both the adopter's and adoptee's consent[92] – transforms into a requirement for an act of acquisition (in the absence of adoption in tannaitic law, the bilateralness is expressed through procedures known for gifting).

Lastly, Yaron subjects the tannaitic sources on *diathēkē* to careful analysis, attempting to show a unified conception in tannaitic law that: (1) the *diathēkē* is reserved for use by the critically ill whereas the *mattanah* is used by the healthy;[93] (2) the *diathēkē* in tannaitic times is originally revocable upon recovery, only later in amoraic times does it become freely revocable;[94] and (3) the *diathēkē* later evolves into the *mattenat shakhev mera*.[95] Although some of the sources Yaron analyzes do in fact support these conclusions, a close look at a cluster of three

---

[86] Yaron, *Gifts*, 19.

[87] Yaron, *Gifts*, 23–26. For the text of Vatican 133, see Schäfer and Becker, *Synopse zum Talmud Yerushalmi*, 318. See Gulak, *Das Urkundenwesen*, 126 (=Gulak, *Legal Documents*, 155) who preceded Yaron in noticing that one part of the formula in the original Greek *diathēkē* parallels the tannaitic formula (see also the next note).

[88] The formula that Yaron discovers is not in textual witnesses of the Tosefta; see Lieberman, *Tosefta ki-fshuṭah: Neziqin*, 427, where all (the text is cited below in the body) preserve *lihyot* and not *liḥyot*. Despite this, Lieberman agrees with Yaron (see Lieberman, *Tosefta ki-fshuṭah: Nashim*, 18, in the Introduction; Lieberman, *Tosefta ki-fshuṭah: Neziqin*, 427). See also Rivlin, *Inheritance and Wills*, 139–140, and esp. n. 49. In light of the above, Urbach's claim ("Inheritance and After-life," 134 n. 21) that Yaron may have been incorrect does not stand. Although, the degree to which the different spellings may reflect different pronunciations requires consideration.

[89] Yaron, *Gifts*, 32–34. However, Rivlin does not consider there to be an act of acquisition in these examples; rather, he sees an act demonstrating final intent to bequeath possessions; see Rivlin, *Inheritance and Wills*, 142; and Rivlin, "Gift and Inheritance Law," 173.

[90] See Chapter 3.

[91] See *mBB* 8:6; *tBB* 8:9 and 8:11; and on these, see Yaron, *Gifts*, 65.

[92] On the Greek institution, see Chapter 3.

[93] Yaron, *Gifts*, 23, 48, 50.

[94] Yaron, *Gifts*, 61, 64, 71.

[95] Yaron, *Gifts*, 48.

traditions found in the eighth chapter of Tosefta *Baba Batra* may yield different findings. For, under the assumption that the sources on *diathēkē* speak in one conceptual voice, Yaron overlooks or reinterprets the fundamental differences between the sources. Indeed, he attempts to treat all of the sources on *diathēkē* as representing the same exact institution, a thesis for which we suggest several challenges below. In the reanalysis what emerges is the identification of a series of conflicting sources on the definition of the term *diathēkē* in tannaitic law.[96] Below is a review and critique of Yaron's position regarding the history of the *diathēkē* with references in the notes to the work of other scholars.

Three *baraitot* in *tBB* 8:9–8:11 discuss different aspects of the gift and the *diathēkē*,[97] the texts of which follow:

ח:ט בריא שכתב דייתיקי, שכיב מרע שכתב נכסיו מתנה אף על פי שזיכה לאחר מתנה לא עשה כלום.	8:9 A healthy person who wrote a *diathēkē*, a dying person who wrote his property as a gift, even though he gave possession of the gift to another, he has done nothing.
ח:י הכותב דייתיקי יכול לחזור בו מתנה אין יכול לחזור בו. אי זו היא דיותיקי 'דא תהא לי לעמוד ולהיות אם מתי יינתנו נכסיי לפלני' אי זו היא מתנה 'היום יינתנו נכסיו לפלני'.	8:10 He who writes a *diathēkē* may revoke it. He who writes a (deed of) gift may not. Which is a *diathēkē*? "This is to stand and to be to me, that if I die, my possessions will be given to so-and-so." Which is a (deed of) gift? Any in which it is written "from today my possessions will be given to so-and-so."
ח:יא הכותב דיותיקי עד שלא זכה ... יכול לחזור בו משזכה ... אין יכול לחזור בו.	8:11 He who writes a *diathēkē*, before he gives possession ... he can revoke; once he has given possession ... he cannot revoke.

Tosefta *Baba Batra* 8:9 states that if a healthy person writes a *diathēkē* and a dying person writes a deed of gift, neither is valid, intimating as Yaron points out, that the *diathēkē* is reserved exclusively for use by the critically ill, and the *mattanah* is reserved for the healthy.[98] This text is central to Yaron's thesis that not only is each deed of gift – *diathēkē* and *mattanah* – reserved for a person in a specific state of health, but also that eventually the term *diathēkē* falls out of use. Its later name *mattenat shakhev mera*[99] is based on the exclusive identification of the document with the donor's state of health.[100]

96 Gulak, *Das Urkundenwesen*, 125 (=Gulak, *Legal Documents*, 154), notices that the sources are in conflict.

97 Lieberman, *Tosefta ki-fshuṭah: Neziqin*, 157–158.

98 Yaron, *Gifts*, 23, 48, 50.

99 Cf. Gulak, *Das Urkundenwesen*, 125 (=Gulak, *Legal Documents*, 154).

100 Yaron, *Gifts*, 48.

Although this source may imply different documents for persons of differing degrees of health, we need go no farther than the next paragraph in the Tosefta (8:10) to see that all tannaitic sources are not in agreement. Tosefta *Baba Batra* 8:10 explains that whereas a *diathēkē* may be revoked, a *mattanah* may not; and 8:10 also gives the formula for each method of transfer. Yaron understands the formula for the *diathēkē*, "This is to stand and to be to me, that if I die, my possessions will be given to so-and-so,"[101] as describing the donor's current state of health. If the donor dies from his illness, the possessions are distributed; if he recovers, they are not.[102] It is possible, however, that the formula in the tannaitic *diathēkē* is just a formula, as in Greek and Greco-Egyptian sources,[103] and is not a written description of the donor's current state of health. Yaron appears to insist that the formula in *tBB* 8:10 refers to the donor's state of health because *tBB* 8:9 implies that a valid *diathēkē* may only be written by someone who is critically ill.[104] However, based on our reading of *tBB* 8:10 indicating that the formula is not descriptive of the donor's state of health, the *diathēkē* may even be executed by the healthy [!],[105] a potential contradiction to *tBB* 8:9.

When interpreting the next part of *tBB* 8:10, Yaron considers the word "gift" to refer to "a simple gift, to take immediate effect, and in no way dependent on the death of the donor."[106] For Yaron the gift here must be a simple gift since the text states that it is irrevocable and because it is juxtaposed with the *diathēkē*, which Yaron insists is solely for the critically ill. He excludes the possibility of the gift being a *mattenat shakhev mera* because he contends that the *diathēkē* and the *mattenat shakhev mera* are the same institution (preventing their mention together here) and that even the tannaitic *mattenat shakhev mera* is revocable. However, as mentioned earlier, there is no explicit tannaitic evidence for the revocability of the *mattenat shakhev mera* and, as Lieberman points out, since

---

101 On the formula, see above in the body and nn. 87–88.

102 Yaron, *Gifts*, 25.

103 Yaron in *Gifts*, 25, states himself that in Greek and Greco-Egyptian sources the formula does not reflect the state of health of the donor. See also the next note.

104 Note Yaron's formulation: "The transplantation of the Greek formula into Jewish law involved a subtle change in its meaning. In the Greek and Greco-Egyptian wills the formula does not reflect the state of health of the testator; it merely expresses his wish for a long life and good health. In Jewish law the use of the *deyathiqi* is restricted; it is the disposition in contemplation of death of a sick man" (Yaron, *Gifts*, 25).

105 So, too, Rivlin, *Inheritance and Wills*, 141 (and esp. nn. 55–56), regarding the *diathēkē* when it originally enters the sphere of tannaitic legal discourse (compare his comments in Rivlin, "Gift and Inheritance Law," 173) in the later tannaitic period to become exclusively for the lying ill. Rivlin, however, seems to misinterpret Yaron's approach by including him in a list of scholars (Rivlin, *Inheritance and Wills*, 141 n. 55), including Gulak and Falk, who contend that the tannaitic *diathēkē* is also for the healthy. Yaron, *Gifts*, 23, only states that there are sources that are not explicit about the *diathēkē* being exclusively for the lying ill.

106 Yaron, *Gifts*, 27. This is also the interpretation accepted by Rivlin, "Gift and Inheritance Law," 173. See *pPe'ah* 3:7, 17d (94) and my discussion of this interpretation above in the body of the text.

the greater context of Tosefta chapter 8 is dispositions in case of death, *mattanah* in 8:10 may in fact mean *mattenat shakhev mera*.[107] The *mattanah* in *tBB* 8:10, therefore, may actually refer to a document for the critically ill, again a potential contradiction to *tBB* 8:9. Accordingly, 8:10 may compare two types of dispositions in case of death: one (even) for the healthy and revocable (*diathēkē*) and the other for the critically ill and irrevocable (*mattanah*), the opposite of the rulings in 8:9! These interpretive suggestions impact Yaron's conclusion that the *diathēkē* and the *mattenat shakhev mera* are essentially the same institution (the former eventually being called the latter name in the amoraic period). In light of these findings, it may be that according to *tBB* 8:10 these two types of dispositions in case of death exist side by side, albeit each one legally distinct from the other.

Tosefta *Baba Batra* 8:10 is also relevant for the question of the revocability of the *diathēkē* because it states clearly that the *diathēkē* is revocable whereas the *mattanah* is not. The following Tosefta paragraph, 8:11, preserves an alternate tradition: the *diathēkē* is in fact *not* revocable, at least not after delivery. The possible contradiction between 8:10 and 8:11 does not go unnoticed by Yaron and clearly pushes him to reinterpret 8:11, stating, "[t]his cannot be a complete ban on revocation, or else the distinction between *deyathiqi* and *mattana*, in 8:10, would be meaningless."[108] He prefers, therefore, to reinterpret 8:11 in a way that does not contradict 8:10 deducing, "[t]he only possible solution is to conclude that, if the donor died without having recovered, the *deyathiqi*, once delivered, was irrevocable."[109] Namely, Yaron interprets *tBB* 8:11 to mean that a *diathēkē* generally may be revoked but is irrevocable after delivery (to the second or third party) until the ill donor recovers, at which time the *diathēkē* is once again revocable. Note, however, that *tBB* 8:11 makes no mention of the recovery of an ill donor and merely states that a *diathēkē* is not revocable once delivered.

To summarize Yaron's method, under the assumption that all three Tosefta paragraphs complement one another and cannot contradict, he reinterprets the paragraphs in light of one another. Taking *tBB* 8:9 as a rule that only the ill may issue a *diathēkē*, he processes both 8:10 and 8:11 as if the *diathēkē* in these paragraphs refers to a gift from an ill donor as well. Accordingly, the revocability or irrevocability of the *diathēkē* in 8:11 must be dependent on the donor's recovery.[110] However, 8:10 may refer to the formula of the *diathēkē* and not to

---

[107] Lieberman, *Tosefta ki-fshuṭah: Neziqin*, 428. So, too, Katzoff, "P. Yadin 19," 6. Katzoff, "An Interpretation," 564. See my discussion of Lieberman's interpretation above.

[108] Yaron, *Gifts*, 66.

[109] Yaron, *Gifts*, 66.

[110] See also Yaron's forced interpretation of *mBB* 8:6 in Yaron, *Gifts*, 65–66, where he states that the words *devarav kayamin* in that *mishnah* refer to the irrevocability of the *diathēkē* until recovery. In truth, the interpretation that the *diathēkē* is valid, rejected there by Yaron but accepted by H. Albeck, *Mishnah: Nezikin*, 146, is, to my mind, preferable.

the state of the donor's health, as in the original Greek sources, and 8:11 may indicate that the *diathēkē* is irrevocable under certain circumstances (i. e., after delivery) and freely revocable under others (i. e., before delivery and not dependent on recovery). In fact, another *baraita* preserved in *pBB* 8:6, 16b (1255)[111] cites the opinion of Rabbi Shimon ben Gamliel who supports the contention that a *diathēkē* is freely revocable:

תני רבן שמעון בן גמליאל אומר דייתיקי מבטלת דייתיקי.	It was taught: Rabbi Shimon ben Gamliel says: a (new) *diathēkē* revokes a (former) *diathēkē*.[112]

This *baraita*, together with *tBB* 8:11, shows that the concept of free revocability of the *diathēkē* is known in tannaitic sources (and is not the innovation of the amoraim).[113]

In summary, viewing the paragraphs in the eighth chapter of Tosefta as a cluster of independent traditions on the *diathēkē* yields more precise conclusions about the historical meaning of the Tosefta *baraitot*, ones that do not accord with Yaron's harmonized reading. That is, the term *diathēkē* in tannaitic sources is not employed consistently. It may be that upon the assimilation of the term into tannaitic legal discourse, conflicting traditions regarding the *diathēkē* developed.[114] Three of these conflicting traditions are taught together in *tBB*, chapter

[111] Cf. *bBB* 135b and 152b. See Yaron's discussion of this source in Yaron, *Gifts*, 71, where he minimizes the significance of the opinion of Rabbi Shimon ben Gamliel preserved here, insisting that free revocability is achieved only by the amoraim.

[112] Gulak, *Das Urkundenwesen*, 130 (=Gulak, *Legal Documents*, 158), says the principle of a later *diathēkē* revoking an earlier one is taken from Roman law. For more on this principle, see Yaron, *Gifts*, 71; Rivlin, *Inheritance and Wills*, 142; and Jackson, "Why the Name New Testament," 72.

[113] Contra Yaron, *Gifts*, 61, 64, 71. A late Palestinian amoraic tradition preserved in *pPe'ah* 3:7, 17d (94) states that the *diathēkē* is not only for the ill and the *mattana* is not only for the healthy, and both are freely revocable without qualification: "רבי יוסי בי רבי בון ... בריא שכתב דייתיקי ושכיב מרע שכתב מתנה חוזר בו," "Rabbi Yose be Rabbi Bun ... a healthy person who wrote a *diathēkē* and a *shakhev mera* who wrote a deed of gift may revoke."

[114] Keenly aware of the difficulties confronting a scholar's attempt to make sense of the *diathēkē* traditions, Bernard Jackson lists the pertinent challenges along with related obstacles for the study of tannaitic gifts in contemplation of death, in general, worth citing here in full: "[t]he methodological difficulties involved in ascertaining the inter-relationships between some of these different forms include: (1) the lack of terminological precision and consistency, particularly as regards the term *diathēkē* and its associated verbal forms, which could refer to both gifts in contemplation of death or wills, even though the latter appears to have been the more typical; (2) the fact that the Greek *meta tēn teleutēn* is found in papyrological practice documents rather than formal statements of law, while the converse largely applies to the Rabbinic *mattenat bari*; (3) while the Rabbinic *diatiki* is mentioned in the Mishnah and related documents, its legal characteristics are not systematically set out, so that it remains debatable whether the loan word is simply an earlier name for the rabbinic *shekhiv mera*, or the genuine adoption of a foreign institution, perhaps by adaptation of a rabbinic form" (Jackson, "Why the Name New Testament," 72–73).

eight. Finally, in light of the above, the tannaitic *diathēkē* should be viewed as an independent deed of gift, unrelated to the *mattenat bari* and *mattenat shakhev mera.*[115]

[115] On the methodological question of how to classify the tannaitic *diathēkē* among other tannaitic forms of gifting in contemplation of death, see Jackson, "Why the Name New Testament," 71–72.

Bibliography

Abramson, Shraga. "Acquisition." *Encyclopaedia Judaica.* 1st ed. 2:216–221. Jerusalem: Keter; New York: Macmillan, 1971–72.

Albeck, Hanokh. *Mavo lamishnah*. Jerusalem: Mosad Bialik, 1959.

–. *Shishah Sidre Mishnah*. Jerusalem: Mosad Bialik; Tel-Aviv: Devir, 1952–59.

Albeck, Shalom. *Principles of Talmudic Private Law*. [In Hebrew.] Ramat Gan: Bar Ilan University Press, 1994.

Alon, Gedalia. "Beneihem shel Chachamim." *Tarbiz* 20 (1949): 84–95.

Álvarez Suárez, Ursicino. *Horizonte actual del Derecho Romano*. Madrid: Consejo Superior de Investigaciones Científicas, 1944.

Appelbaum, Alan. "Rabbi's Successors: The Later Jewish Patriarchs of the Third Century." *Journal of Jewish Studies* 40 (2012): 3–11.

Applebaum, Shimon. "The Settlement Pattern of Western Samaria from Hellenistic to Byzantine Times: A Historical Commentary." In Shimon Dar and Shimon Applebaum, *Landscape and Pattern: An Archaeological Survey of Samaria: 800 B. C. E.–636 C. E.*, 255–269. Oxford: B. A. R. International Series, 1986.

Aristotle. *Politics*. Translated by Harold P. Cooke. Loeb Classical Library. London: William Heinemann; Cambridge, MA: Harvard University Press, 1932.

Arnaud, Daniel. "Les hittites sur le moyen-Euphrate: Protecteurs et indigènes." In *Hethitica VIII: Acta Anatolica E. Laroche Oblata*, 9–27. Paris: Louvain, 1987.

Asheri, David. "Laws of Inheritance, Distribution of Land and Political Constitutions." *Historia* 12:1 (1963): 1–21.

–. "Sulla Legge di Epitadeo." *Athenaeum* 39 (1961): 45–68.

Avramović, Sima. "Differences of Substance and the Legal Nature of the Roman Testament and the So-Called Legacy by Testament of the Old Greek Law." [In Serbian Cyrillic.] *Anali PFB* 1 (1987): 9–18.

–. "The Rhetra of Epithadeus and Testament in Spartan Law." *Symposion 2001* (2005): 175–186.

Azar, Moshe. *The Syntax of Mishnaic Hebrew*. [In Hebrew.] Jerusalem: The Academy of Hebrew Language; Haifa: University of Haifa, 1995.

Babylonian Inscriptions (in the Collection of J. B.) Nies, edited by Clarence Elwood Keiser. New Haven: Yale University Press; London: Humphrey; Milford: Oxford University Press, 1918.

Baer, Isaac F. "The Historical Foundations of the Halakhah." [In Hebrew.] *Zion* 27 (1962): 117–155.

Bar-Asher, Moshe. "Mishnaic Hebrew: An Introductory Survey," In *Literature of the Sages*, edited by Shmuel Safrai, Zeev Safrai, Joshua Schwartz, and Peter J. Tomson, 567–596. Amsterdam: Royan Van Gorcum; Minneapolis: Fortress, 2006.

Barkay, Gabriel. "Burial Caves and Burial Practices in Judah in the Iron Age." In *Graves and Burial Practices in Israel in the Ancient Period*, edited by Itamar Singer, 96–164. [In Hebrew.] Jerusalem: Yad Izhak Ben-Zvi and Israel Exploration Society, 1994.

–. "The Iron Age II–III." In *The Archaeology of Ancient Israel*, edited by Ben-Tor Amnon. Translated by R. Greenberg, 302–373. New Haven, CT: Yale University Press; Israel: Open University of Israel, 1992.

Barmash, Pamela. *Homicide in the Biblical World*. Cambridge: Cambridge University Press, 2005.

Beattie, D. R. G., "The Book of Ruth as Evidence for Israelite Legal Practice." *Vetus Testamentum* 24 (1974): 251–262.

Beckman, Gary. "Family Values on the Middle Euphrates in the Thirteenth Century B. C. E." In *Emar: The History, Religion, and Culture of a Syrian Town in the Late Bronze Age*, edited by Mark W. Chavalas, 57–79. Bethesda, MD: CDL, 1996.

Belkin, Samuel. *Philo and the Oral Law*. Cambridge, MA: Harvard University Press, 1940.

Ben-Barak, Zafrira. "The Case of the Daughters of Zelophehad in Connection with a New Document from Nuzi." In *Shnaton: An Annual for Biblical and Near Eastern Studies III*, edited by Moshe Weinfeld, 116–123. Jerusalem: Magnes, 1978.

–. "Inheritance by Daughters in the Ancient Near East." *Journal of Semitic Studies* 25:1 (1980): 22–33.

–. *Inheritance by Daughters in Israel and the Ancient Near East*. Jaffa, Israel: Archaeological Center, 2006.

–. "The Legal Status of the Daughter as Heir in Nuzi and Emar." In *Society and Economy in the Eastern Mediterranean (c. 1500 BC–1000 BC)*, edited by M. Heltzer and E. Lipinski, 87–98. Leuven: Peeters, 1988.

Bendor, Shunya. *The Social Structure of Ancient Israel: The Institution of the Family (Beit Ab) from the Settlement to the End of the Monarchy*. Jerusalem: Simor, 1996.

Benoit, P., J. T. Milik, and R. de Vaux. *Les grottes de Murabba'at (Discoveries in the Judaean Desert II*. 2 vols. Oxford: Clarendon, 1961.

Berkowitz, Beth. *Execution and Invention: Death Penalty Discourse in Early Rabbinic and Christian Cultures*. Oxford: Oxford University Press, 2006.

Bird, Phyllis. "YRŠ and the Deuteronomic Theology of the Conquest." PhD diss., Harvard University, 1971.

Birnbaum, Salomo A. *The Bar Menashe Marriage Deed: Its Relations with Other Jewish Marriage Deeds*. Istanbul: Nederland Historisch-Archaeologisch Instituut in het Nabije Oosten, 1962.

Bokser, Baruch. "Jacob N. Epstein on the Formation of the Mishnah." In *The Modern Study of the Mishnah*, edited by Jacob Neusner, 37–55. Leiden: Brill, 1973.

–. "Jacob N. Epstein's *Introduction to the Text of the Mishnah*." In *The Modern Study of the Mishnah*, edited by Jacob Neusner, 13–36. Leiden: Brill, 1973.

Boling, Robert G. *Judges*. Garden City, NY: Doubleday, 1975.

Borkowski, Andrew. *Deathbed Gifts: The Law of Donatio Mortis Causa*. Shrewsbury, UK: Blackstone, 1999.

Botta, Alejandro. *The Aramaic and Egyptian Legal Traditions at Elephantine: An Egyptological Approach*. London: T&T Clark, 2009.

–. "Elephantine, Elephantine Papyri." In *The Eerdman's Dictionary of Early Judaism*, edited by John J. Collins and Daniel C. Harlow, 574–577. Grand Rapids, MI: Eerdmans, 2010.

–. "The Legal Function and Egyptian Background of the שליט Clause: A Reevaluation." *Maarav* 13:2 (2006): 193–209.

–. "A Reevaluation of the Use of זבן and יהב in Elephantine." *Antiguo Oriente* 6 (2008): 95–104.

Boyarin, Daniel. Review of *Studies in the Aramaic Legal Papyri from Elephantine*, by Yochanan Muffs. *Journal of the Ancient Near Eastern Society* 3 (1970–71): 57–62.

Brandes, Yehuda. "The Beginnings of the Rules of Halachic Adjudication." PhD diss., Hebrew University of Jerusalem, 2002.

Brin, Gershon. "The Birthright of the Sons of Jacob." [In Hebrew.] *Tarbiz* 48:1–2 (1979):1–8.

–. "The First-Born in Israel in the Biblical Period." [In Hebrew.] PhD diss., Tel Aviv University, 1971.

–. *Studies in Biblical Law: From the Hebrew Bible to the Dead Sea Scrolls.* Sheffield, UK: Sheffield Academic, 1994.

–. "The Transfer of Hegemony and the Problem of the Title Bekor." [In Hebrew.] In *Ha-Zevi Yisrael: Sefer le-Zekher Braude*, edited by Gershon Brin and Jacob Licht, 47–55. Tel Aviv: Mifalim Universitaim, 1976.

–. "Two Problems in the Laws of Inheritance during the Biblical Period – A Comparative Study." [In Hebrew.] *Diné Israel* 6 (1975): 231–249.

Büchler, Adolph. *The Adolph Büchler Memorial Volume: Studies in Jewish History.* London: Oxford University Press, 1956.

Buckland, William Warwick. *A Text-Book of Roman Law from Augustus to Justinian.* Cambridge: Cambridge University Press, 1966.

Burkert, Walter. *Babylon, Memphis, Persepolis: Eastern Contexts of Greek Culture.* Cambridge, MA: Harvard University Press, 2004.

Carmichael, Calum, ed. *Collected Works of David Daube.* Berkeley: Robbins Collection, 2000.

Champlin, Edward. *Final Judgments: Duty and Emotion in Roman Wills 200 B.C–A. D. 250.* Berkely and Los Angeles: University of California Press, 1991.

Charlesworth, James H., ed. *The Old Testament Pseudepigrapha.* Garden City, NY: Doubleday, 1983.

Chavel, Simeon. "Biblical Law." In *The Literature of the Hebrew Bible – Introductions and Studies*, edited by Ziporah Talshir, 227–272. [In Hebrew.] Jerusalem: Yad Ben-Zvi, 2014.

Childe, Vere Gordon. "The Urban Revolution." *Town Planning Review* 21:1 (April 1950): 3–17.

Cohen, Boaz. *Jewish and Roman Law.* New York: Jewish Theological Seminary of America, 1966.

Cohen, David. "Introduction." In *The Cambridge Companion to Ancient Greek Law*, edited by Michael Gagarin and David Cohen, 1–26. Cambridge: Cambridge University Press, 2005.

–. "Problems, Methods, and Models in the Study of Greek Law." *Zeitschrift der Savigny-Stiftung für Rechtsgeschichte* 106 (1989): 81–105.

Cohen, Shaye J.D. "The Judaean Legal Tradition and the 'Halakhah' of the Mishnah." In *Cambridge Companion to Talmud and Rabbinic Literature*, edited by Charlotte Fonrobert and Martin Jaffee, 121–143. Cambridge: Cambridge University Press, 2007.

Cohn, Naftali. *The Memory of the Temple and the Making of the Rabbis.* Philadelphia: University of Pennsylvania Press, 2012.

Collins, John J., and Gregory E. Sterling, eds. *Hellenism in the Land of Israel.* Southbend, IN: University of Notre Dame Press, 2001.

Cotton, Hannah. "The Archive of Salome Komaise Daughter of Levi: Another Archive from the 'Cave of Letters.'" *Zeitschrift für Papyrologie und Epigraphik* 105 (1995): 171–208.

–. "Babatha's Property and the Law of Succession in the Babatha Archive." *Zeitschrift für Papyrologie und Epigraphik* 104 (1994): 211–224.

–. "Deeds of Gift and the Law of Succession in the Documents from the Judaean Desert." *Archiv für Papyrusforschung* 3 (1997): 179–186.

–. "The Law of Succession in the Documents from the Judaean Desert Again." *Scripta Classica Israelica* 17 (1998): 115–123.

–. "Marriage Contracts from the Judaean Desert." *Materia Giudaica Bolletino dell' Associazione Italiana per lo Studio del Giudaismo* 6 (2006): 2–6.

–. "The Rabbis and the Documents." *Jews in a Graeco-Roman World*, edited by Martin Goodman, 167–179. Oxford: Clarendon, 1998.

–. "Women and Law in the Documents from the Judaean Desert." *Studia Hellenistica* 37 (2002):123–147.

Cotton, Hannah and Ada Yardeni, *Aramaic, Hebrew and Greek Documentary Texts from Nahal Hever and Other Sites.* Discoveries in the Judaean desert XXVII. Oxford: Clarendon, 1997.

Cover, Robert M., "The Supreme Court, 1982 Term – Foreword: Nomos and Narrative," *Harvard Law Review* 97:4 (1983): 4–68.

Cox, Cheryl Anne. *Household Interests: Property, Marriage Strategies, and Family Dynamics in Ancient Athens.* Princeton: Princeton University Press, 1998.

Crawford, M., and J. Cloud, eds. *Roman Statutes.* Bulletin of the Institute of Classical Studies. Supplement, 641. London: Institute of Classical Studies, School of Advanced Study, University of London, 1996.

Crook, John A. "Women in Roman Succession." In *The Family in Ancient Rome: New Perspectives*, edited by Beryl Rawson, 58–82. Ithaca, NY: Cornell University Press, 1986.

Danzig, Nachman. "Hitpatḥut hamunaḥ baraita veteruts hatalmud baraita delo shmia leih." *Sinai* 85 (1979): 217–224.

–. "Lehitpatḥut hamunaḥ baraita." *Sinai* 89 (1981): 240–247.

Dar, Shimon. "Agriculture and Agricultural Produce in Eretz-Israel in the Roman-Byzantine Period." [In Hebrew.] In *Man and Land in Eretz-Israel in Antiquity*, edited by A. Kasher, A. Oppenheimer, and U. Rappaport, 142–169. Jerusalem: Yad Izhak ben Zvi, 1986.

Dar, Shimon, and Shimon Applebaum. *Landscape and Pattern: An Archaeological Survey of Samaria: 800 B. C. E.–636 C. E.* Oxford: B. A. R. International Series, 1986.

Daube, David. "Consortium in Roman and Hebrew Law." *The Juridical Review* 42 (1950): 71–91.

–. "Inheritance in Two Lukan Pericopes," *Zeitschrift der Savigny-Stiftung für Rechtsgeschichte*, Rom. Abt. 72 (1955): 326–334.

–. "Joḥanan Ben Baroqa and Women's Rights." In *Jewish Tradition in the Diaspora: Studies in Memory of Professor Walter J. Fischel*, edited by Mishael Maswali Caspi, 55–65. Berkeley: Judah L. Magnes Memorial Museum, 1981.

–. "Mancipatio of *rec nec mancipi.*" In *Festschrift für Erwin Seidl zum 70 Geburtstag*, edited by H. Hübner, E. Klingmüller, and A. Wacke, 35–38. Cologne: Hanstein, 1975.

Davies, Eryl. "The Inheritance of the Firstborn in Israel and the Ancient Near East." *Journal of Semitic Studies* 38 (1993): 175–191.
–. "The Meaning of Pî Šenayim in Deuteronomy XXI:17." *Vetus Testamentum* 36 (1986): 341–347.
de Colquhoun, Patrick Mac Chombaich. *A Summary of the Roman Civil Law: Illustrated by Commentaries on and Parallels from the Mosaic, Canon, Mohammedan, English and Foreign Law*. London: V. and R. Stevens and Sons, 1849–1860.
de Ste. Croix, Geoffrey E.M. "Athenian Family Law." Review of *The Law of Athens*, by A.R.W. Harrison. *Classical Review* (New Series) 20:3 (December 1970): 387–390.
de Vaux, Roland. *Ancient Israel: Its Life and Institutions*. New York: McGraw Hill, 1965.
Demosthenes. *I: Olynthiacs, Philippics, Minor Public Speeches, Speech Against Leptines I–XVIII, XX*. Translated by J.H. Vince. Loeb Classical Library. London: William Heinemann; Cambridge, MA: Harvard University Press, 1930.
Demosthenes. *IV: Private Orations XXVII–XL*. Translated by A.T. Murray. Loeb Classical Library. London: William Heinemann; Cambridge, MA: Harvard University Press, 1984.
di Paola, Santi. *Donatio mortis causa: Corso di diritto romano*. Napoli: Eugenio Jovene, 1969.
Diamond, Eliezer, "Rabbinics in the New *Encyclopaedia Judaica*." *Judaica Librarianship* 16/17 (2011): 173–195.
Dixon, Suzanne. Review of *Fathers and Daughters in Roman Society*, by Judith P. Hallett. *The American Journal of Philology* 107:1 (Spring 1986): 125–130.
–. *The Roman Family*. Baltimore: Johns Hopkins University Press, 1992.
Driver, Godfrey Rolles, and John Charles Miles. *The Babylonian Laws*. Oxford: Clarendon, 1952.
du Plessis, Paul. *Borkowski's Textbook on Roman Law*. 4th ed. New York: Oxford University Press, 2010.
Edrei, Aryeh. "'To Fulfill the Wishes of the Deceased': On the Validity of Wills in Rabbinic Literature." [In Hebrew.] *Hebrew Union College Annual* 69 (1998): 105–141.
–. "Halakhic Responsibility of the Deceased: A Further Study of the Concept of Inheritance in Talmudic Thought." *Israel Law Review* 33:4 (1999): 821–854.
–. "Matanah 'mehayom uleaḥar mita' bamishnah uvatalmud." *Shenaton Hamishpat Haivri* 20 (1997): 1–23.
–. "Mitsvah al hayetomim lifro'a ḥov avihem." In *Studies in Jewish Law*, edited by Aharon Arendt and Sinai Deutsch. Ramat Gan: Bar Ilan, 1999.
–. "Shi'abud nekhasim: Mah bein nikhsei halakoaḥ lenikhsei hayoresh." *Mishpatim* 25 (1995): 291–332.
Eisser, G., and J. Lewy, eds. *Die altassyrischen Rechtsurkunden vom Kültepe*. Leipzig: J.C. Hinrichs, 1930–1935.
Elman, Yaakov. "Authoritative Oral Tradition in Neo-Assyrian Scribal Circles." *Journal of the Ancient Near Eastern Society* 7 (1975): 19–32.
–. "Babylonian Echoes in a Late Rabbinic Legend." *JANES* 4 (1972): 12–19.
Epstein, Jacob Naḥum. "Hamada hatalmudi utserakhav." In *Studies in Talmudic Literature and Semitic Languages* 2:1, 1–18. Jerusalem: Magnes, 1988.
–. *Mavo lenusaḥ hamishna*. Jerusalem: Magnes, 1948.
–. *Mevoot lesifrut hatannaim*. Jerusalem: Magnes; Tel Aviv: Devir, 1957.
–. "Notizen zu den jüdisch-aramäischen Papyri von Assuan." *Jahrbuch der jüdisch-literarischen Gesellschaft* 6 (1909): 359–373.

Epstein, Louis. *The Jewish Marriage Contract*. New York: Jewish Theological Seminary of America, 1927.

Eshel, Esther, and Amos Kloner. "An Aramaic Ostracon of an Edomite Marriage Contract from Maresha, Dated 176 B.C.E." *Israel Exploration Journal* 46:1/2 (1996): 1–22.

Fabry, Heinz-Josef. "Nātan." In vol. 10 of *Theological Dictionary of the Old Testament*, edited by G.J. Botterweck and H. Ringgren, 90–108. Grand Rapids, MI: Eerdmans, 1974.

Falk, Zeev. *Introduction to Jewish Law of the Second Commonwealth*. Leiden: E.J. Brill, 1978.

–. "The Right of Inheritance of a Daughter and Widow in Bible and Talmud." [In Hebrew.] *Tarbiz* 23, no. 1 (October 1951): 9–15.

–. "Testate Succession in Jewish Law." Review of *Gifts in Contemplation of Death in Jewish and Roman Law*, by Reuven Yaron. *Journal for Jewish Studies* 12:1–2 (1961): 67–77.

Falkenstein, Adam. *Die Neusumerischen Gerichtsurkunden*. Munich: Bayerischen Akademie der Wissenschaften, 1956.

Faust, Avraham. *The Archaeology of Israelite Society in Iron Age II*. Eisenbrauns: Winona Lake, IN, 2012.

Faust, Avraham, and Shlomo Bunimovitz. "The Judahite Rock-Cut Tomb: Family Response at a Time of Change." *Israel Exploration Journal* 58 (2008): 150–170.

Feigin, Samuel. "Some Cases of Adoption in Israel." *Journal of Biblical Literature* 50:3 (1931): 186–200.

Feintuch, Yonatan. "Daughters' Inheritance: Halakha, Law and Literature (In the Footsteps of the Story of R. Yehudah Nesi'ah)." *Shenaton Ha-Mishpat Ha-Ivri* 28 (2015): 203–227.

Fiensy, David A. *The Social History of Palestine in the Herodian Period: The Land Is Mine*. Lewiston, NY: Edwin Mellen, 1991.

Finkelstein, J.J. "The Ox That Gored." *Transactions of the American Philosophical Society* Vol. 71, No. 2 (1981): 1–89

Finkelstein, Louis. *Sifre to Deuteronomy*. [In Hebrew.] New York and Jerusalem: Jewish Theological Seminary of America, 1993.

Fleishman, Joseph. "A Daughter's Demand and a Father's Compliance: The Legal Background to Achsah's Claim and Caleb's Agreement: Joshua 15, 16–19; Judges 1, 12–15." *Zeitschrift für die Alttestamentliche Wissenschaft* 118:3 (September 2006): 354–373.

Flusser, David. *Judaism of the Second Temple Period: The Jewish Sages and their Literature*. Translated by Azzan Yadin. Grand Rapids, MI: Eerdmans, 2009.

Freydank, Helmut. "*bitqī batāqu* 'Abschneidungen abschneiden'?" *Altorientalische Forschungen* 24 (1997): 105–114.

Friedman, Mordechai A. *Jewish Marriage in Palestine: A Cairo Genizah Study*. Tel-Aviv: Tel-Aviv University, 1980.

Friedman, Shamma. "The Case of the Woman with Two Husbands in Talmudic and Ancient Near Eastern Law." *Israel Law Review* 15:4 (1980): 530–558.

–. "Mi haya Ben-Drosai?" *Sidra* 14 (1998): 77–91.

–. "The 'Plotting Witness' and Beyond: A Continuum in Ancient Near Eastern, Biblical, and Talmudic Law." In *Birkat Shalom Studies in the Bible, Ancient Near Eastern Literature, and Postbiblical Judaism: Presented to Shalom M. Paul on the Occasion of His Seventieth Birthday*, edited by Chaim Cohen et al., 801–829. Winona Lake, IN: Eisenbrauns, 2008.

Frymer-Kensky, Tikva. "Israel." In *A History of Ancient Near Eastern Law*, edited by Raymond Westbrook, 2:975–1046. Leiden: Brill, 2003.
–. "Patriarchal Family Relationships and Near Eastern Law." *The Biblical Archeologist* (Fall 1981): 209–214.
Furstenberg, Yair. "Eating in a State of Purity in the Tannaitic Period: Tractate Toharot and Its Historical and Cultural Contexts." [In Hebrew.] PhD diss., Hebrew University of Jerusalem, 2010.
Gafni, Chanan. "The Emergence of Critical Scholarship on Rabbinic Literature in the Nineteenth Century: Social and Ideological Contexts." PhD diss., Harvard University, 2005.
Gafni, Isaiah. "*Maamadah shel eretz yisrael batodaah hayehudit beikvot mered bar kokhva.*" In *The Bar-Kokhva Revolt: A New Approach*, edited by Aaron Oppenheimer and Uriel Rappaport, 224–232. Jerusalem: Yad Izhak ben Zvi, 1984.
Gagarin, Michael. *Early Greek Law*. Berkeley and Los Angeles: University of California Press, 1986.
–. "Inscribing Laws in Greece and the Near East." *Symposion 2003* (2006): 9–20.
–. "Unity of Greek Law." In *The Cambridge Companion to Ancient Greek Law*, edited by Michael Gagarin and David Cohen, 29–40. Cambridge: Cambridge University Press, 2005.
–. *Writing Greek Law*. Cambridge: Cambridge University Press, 2008.
Gardner, Jane F. "The Recovery of Dowry in Roman Law." *Classical Quarterly* (New Series) 35 (1985): 449–453.
–. *Women in Roman Law and Society*. Bloomington: University of Indiana Press, 1986.
Gelb, Ignace J. "Household and Family in Early Mesopotamia." In *State and Temple Economy in the Ancient Near East*, edited by Edward Lipinski, 1–98. Leuven: Orientaliste, 1979.
Gelb, Ignace J., P. Steinkeller, and R.M. Whiting. *Earliest Land Tenure Systems in the Ancient Near East: Ancient Kudurrus*. Chicago: Oriental Institute, 1991.
Geller, Markham, "The Influence of Ancient Mesopotamia on Hellenistic Judaism." In *Civilizations of the Ancient Near East*, edited by Jack Sasson, 43–54. New York: Charles Scribner's Sons, 2002.
–. "New Sources for the Origins of the Rabbinic *Ketubah*." *Hebrew Union College Annual* 49 (1978): 227–245.
Gil, Moshe. "The Decline of the Agrarian Economy in Palestine under Roman Rule." *Journal of the Economic and Social History of the Orient* 49:3 (2006): 285–328.
Ginzberg, Louis. "Tamid, The Oldest Treatise of The Mishnah." *Journal of Jewish Lore and Philosophy* 1 (1919): 33–44.
Goldberg, Abraham. *Commentary to the Mishna Tractate Eruvin*. Jerusalem: Magnes, 1986.
Goldin, Judah. "The Youngest Son or Where Does Genesis 38 Belong?" *Journal of Biblical Literature* 96 (1977): 27–44.
Gordon, Cyrus. "Biblical Customs and the Nuzu Tablets," *Biblical Archeologist* (February 1940): 1–12.
Greenberg, Moshe. "The Terms *Nafal* and *Hipil* in the Context of Inheritance." In *Ki Baruch Hu: Ancient Near Eastern, Biblical, and Judaic Studies in Honor of Baruch A. Levine*, edited by Robert Chazan, William W. Hallo, and Lawrence H. Schiffman, 251–259. Winona Lake, IN: Eisenbrauns, 1999.

Greenfield, Jonas C. "*Našû-nadānu* and Its Congeners." In *'Al Kanfei Yonah: Collected Studies of Jonas C. Greenfield on Semitic Philology*, edited by Shalom M. Paul, Michael E. Stone, and Avital Pinnick, 720–724. Jerusalem: Magnes, 2001.

Greengus, Samuel. "Filling Gaps: Laws Found in Babylonia and in the Mishna but Absent in the Hebrew Bible." *Maarav* 7 (1991): 149–171.

–. *Laws in the Bible and Early Rabbinic Collections: The Legacy of the Ancient Near East.* Eugene, OR: Cascade, 2011.

–. "The Old Babylonian Marriage Contract." *Journal of the American Oriental Society* 89:3 (1969): 505–532.

–. "Some Issues Relating to the Comparability of Laws and the Coherence of the Legal Tradition." In *Theory and Method in Biblical and Cuneiform Law: Revision, Interpolation and Development*, edited by Bernard Levinson, 60–87. Sheffield, UK: Sheffield Academic, 1994.

Grintz, Yehoshua. *The Book of Judith: A Reconstruction of the Original Hebrew Text with Introduction, Commentary, Appendices and Indices.* [In Hebrew.] Jerusalem: Bialik, 1957.

–. *Chapters in the History of Second Temple Times.* [In Hebrew.] Jerusalem: Makor, 1969.

Grosz, Katarzyna, "Dowry and Brideprice in Nuzi." In *Studies on the Civilization and Culture of Nuzi and the Hurrians*, edited by M. A. Morrison and D. I. Owen. Winona Lake, IN: Eisenbrauns, 1981, 1:161–182.

Guijarro, Santiago. "The Family in First-Century Galilee." In *Constructing Early Christian Families*, edited by Halvor Moxnes, 42–65. London and New York: Routledge, 1997.

Gulak, Asher. *Legal Documents in the Talmud In Light of Greek Papyri and Greek and Roman Law.* [In Hebrew.] Edited and supplemented by Ranon Katzoff. Jerusalem: Magnes; Hebrew University, 1994.

–. *Das Urkundenwesen im Talmud.* Jerusalem: Rubin Mass, 1935.

–. *Yesodei hamishpat haivri: Seder dinei hamamonot beyisrael al pi mekorot hatalmud vehaposkim.* Warsaw: Universal, 1913.

Hachlili, Rachel, and Ann Killebrew. *Jericho: The Jewish Cemetery of the Second Temple Period.* Jerusalem: Israel Antiquities Authority, 1999.

–. "Jewish Funerary Customs during the Second Temple Period in the Light of the Excavations at the Jericho Necropolis." *Palestine Exploration Quarterly* 115 (1983): 109–139.

Halivni, David. *Sources and Traditions: Baba Batra.* [In Hebrew.] Jerusalem: Magnes, 2007.

Hallett, Judith P. *Fathers and Daughters in Roman Society: Women and the Elite Family.* Princeton: Princeton University Press, 1984.

Hallo, William W., ed. *The Context of Scripture: Monumental Inscriptions from the Biblical World.* Leiden: Brill, 2000.

Halpern, Baruch. "Jerusalem and the Lineages in the Seventh Century BCE: Kinship and the Rise of Individual Moral Liability." In *Law and Ideology in Monarchic Israel*, edited by Baruch Halpern and Deborah W. Hobson, 11–107. Sheffield, UK: JSOT Press, 1991.

Harrison, Alick R. W. *The Law of Athens.* 2nd ed. Indianapolis and Cambridge: Hackett, 1998.

Hauptman, Judith. *Rereading the Rabbis: A Woman's Voice.* Boulder, CO: Westview, 1998.

–. "Women and Inheritance in Rabbinic Texts: Identifying Elements of a Critical Feminist Impulse." In *Introducing Tosefta: Textual, Intratextual, and Intertextual Studies*, edited by Harry Fox and Tirzah Meacham, 221–240. Hoboken, NJ: KTAV, 1999.

Hayes, Christine. "The Abrogation of Torah Law: Rabbinic Taqqanah and Praetorian Edict." In *The Talmud Yerushalmi and the Graeco-Roman World*, edited by Peter Schäfer, 643–674. Tübingen: Mohr Siebeck, 2002.

–. *Between the Babylonian and Palestinian Talmuds: Accounting for Halakhic Difference in Selected Sugyot from Tractate Avodah Zarah*. Oxford: Oxford University Press, 1997.

Herodotus. Translated by A. D. Godley. Loeb Classical Library. London: William Heinemann; Cambridge, MA: Harvard University, 1921.

Herzog, Isaac. *The Main Institutions of Jewish Law*. London and New York: Soncino, 1936.

Hiers, Richard. "Transfer of Property by Inheritance and Bequest in Biblical Law and Tradition." *Journal of Law and Religion* 10:1 (1993): 121–155.

Hillel bar R. Elyakim (me'eretz yavan). *Sifra devei Rav hu sefer torat kohanim*, edited by Shakhne Koliditski. Jerusalem: Sifriyah Toranit, 1991.

Hirschfeld, Yizhar. *The Palestinian Dwelling in the Roman-Byzantine Period*. Jerusalem: Franciscan Printing and Israel Exploration Society, 1995.

Hodkinson, Stephen. "Land Tenure and Inheritance in Classical Sparta." *The Classical Quarterly* 36:2 (New Series) (1986): 378–406.

–. *Property and Wealth in Classical Sparta*. London: Duckworth and Classical Press of Wales; Oakville, CT: David Brown, 2000.

Hoffmann, David Tsvi. *Midrash tannaim al sefer devarim*. Berlin: Ts. H. Iṭtsḳoysḳi, 1908–1909.

Holtz, Shalom. "'To Go and Marry Any Man That You Please': A Study of the Formulaic Antecedents of the Rabbinic Writ of Divorce." *Journal of Near Eastern Studies* 60:4 (October 2001): 241–258.

Honoré, A. M. *Gaius*. Oxford: Clarendon, 1962.

Horovitz, H., ed. *Siphre d'be rab fasciculus primus: Siphre ad numeros adjecto siphre zutta*. Jerusalem: Wahrman, 1966.

Hubbard, Robert L. *The Book of Ruth*. Grand Rapids, MI: Eerdman's, 1988.

Hudson, Michael. "Acknowledgments Page." In *Privatization in the Ancient Near East and Classical World*, edited by Michael Hudson and Baruch A. Levine, unnumbered. Cambridge, MA: Peabody Museum of Archaeology & Ethnology, 1996.

–. "The Dynamics of Privatization: From the Bronze Age to the Present." In *Privatization in the Ancient Near East and Classical World*, edited by Michael Hudson and Baruch A. Levine, 33–72. Cambridge, MA: Peabody Museum of Archaeology & Ethnology, 1996.

–. "New Economic Archaeology of Urbanization." In *Privatization in the Ancient Near East and Classical World*, edited by Michael Hudson and Baruch A. Levine, 9–15. Cambridge, MA: Peabody Museum of Archaeology & Ethnology, 1996.

Hyamson, Moses. *Mosaicarum et Romanarum Legum Collatio*. London: Oxford University Press, 1913.

The Institutes of Gaius. Translated and with an introduction by W. M. Gordon and O. F. Robinson. Texts in Roman Law. Ithaca, NY: Cornell University Press, 1988.

Isaeus. *On the Estate of Menecles*. Translated by Edward Seymour Forster. Loeb Classical Library. London: William Heinemann; Cambridge: Harvard University Press, 1962.

Isocrates. Translated by Laura Van Hook. Loeb Classical Library. London: William Heinemann; Cambridge, MA: Harvard University Press, 1968.

Jackson, Bernard S. "Evolution and Foreign Influence in Ancient Law." *American Journal of Comparative Law* 16 (1968): 372–390.

–. "History, Dogmatics and Halakhah." In *Jewish Law in Legal History and the Modern World*, edited by Bernard S. Jackson, 1–26. Leiden: Brill, 1980.

–. "How Jewish is Jewish Family Law?" *Journal of Jewish Studies* 55:2 (2004): 201–229.

–. "The Jewish Background to the Prodigal Son: An Unresolved Problem." In *Essays on Halakha in the New Testament*, edited by Bernard Jackson, 111–150. Leiden: Brill, 2008.

–. "On the Problem of Roman Influence on the Halakah and Normative Self-Definition in Judaism." In *Jewish and Christian Self-Definition*, edited by E. P. Sanders, 157–203. Philadelphia: Fortress, 1981.

–. "Ruth, the Pentateuch and the Nature of Biblical Law: In Conversation with Jean Louis Ska." In *The Post-Priestly Pentateuch. New Perspectives on Its Redactional Development and Theological Profiles* (Ska Festschrift), edited by Konrad Schmid and Federico Giuntoli, 75–111. Tübingen: Mohr Siebeck, 2015.

–. "Why the Name New *Testament*?" *Melilah: Manchester Journal of Jewish Studies* 9 (2012): 50–100.

Japhet, Sarah. *I & II Chronicles: A Commentary*. Louisville, KY: Westminster/John Knox, 1993.

Jolowicz, Herbert F., and Barry Nicholas. *Historical Introduction to the Study of Roman Law*. 3rd ed. Cambridge: Cambridge University Press, 2008.

Kahana, Menahem I. *Sifre to Numbers: An Annotated Edition*. [in Hebrew.] Jerusalem: Magnes, 2011.

–. *Sifre Zuta on Deuteronomy: Citations from a New Tannaitic Midrash*. [in Hebrew.] Jerusalem: Magnes, 2002.

Katzoff, Ranon. "Children of Intermarriage: Roman and Jewish Conceptions." In *Rabbinic Law in Its Roman and Near Eastern Context*, edited by Catherine Hezser, 277–286. Texts and Studies in Ancient Judaism. Tübingen: Mohr-Siebeck, 2003.

–. "An Interpretation of P. Yadin 19: A Jewish Gift after Death." In *Proceedings of the 20th International Congress of Papyrologists*, edited by A. Bülow-Jacobson, 562–565. Copenhagen, 1994.

–. "P. Yadin 19: A Gift after Death from the Judean Desert." In *Proceedings of the Tenth World Congress of Jewish Studies, Jerusalem 1989*, Division C, Volume 1, 1–8. Jerusalem, 1990.

–. "*P. Yadin 21* and Rabbinic Law on Widows' Rights." *Jewish Quarterly Review* 97:4 (Fall 2007): 545–575.

Kaufman, Stephen A. *The Akkadian Influences on Aramaic*. Chicago: University of Chicago Press, 1974.

Kelley, Donald R. "Gaius Noster: Substructures of Western Social Thought." *The American Historical Review* 84:3 (June 1979): 619–648.

Kohler, J., and A. Ungnad. *Assyrische Rechtsurkunden*. Leipzig: von Eduard Pfeiffer, 1913.

Koschaker, Paul. "Drei Rechtsurkunden aus Arrapha." *Zeitschrift für Assyriologie und vorderasiatische Archäologie* 48 (1944): 161–221.

Kraeling, Emil G. *The Brooklyn Museum Aramaic Papyri: New Documents of the Fifth Century B. C. from the Jewish Colony at Elephantine*. London: Oxford University Press, 1953.

Kraus, F. R. "Erbrechtliche Terminologie im alten Mesopotamien." In *Essays on Oriental Laws of Succession*, edited by J. Brugman, et. al., 18–57. Leiden, 1969.

Krauss, Samuel. "Torat haalmanah beyisrael." *HeAtid* 6 (1926): 63–76.

Kristensen, Karen Rørby. "Inheritance, Property, and Management: Gortynian Family Law Revisited." *Symposion 2005* (2007): 89–104.

Kwasman, Theodore. *Neo-Assyrian Legal Documents in the Kouyunjik Collection of the British Museum*. Rome: Editrice Pontificio Istituto Biblico, 1988.

Lacey, W. K. *The Family in Classical Greece*. Ithaca, NY: Cornell University Press, 1968.

Lafont, Bertrand. "Les textes judiciaires sumeriens." In *Rendre la justice en Mesopotamie: Archives judiciaires du Proche-Orient ancien*, edited by F. Joannès, 35–68. Saint-Denis: Presses Universitaires Vincennes, 2000.

Lafont, Bertrand, and Raymond Westbrook. "Neo-Sumerian Period (Ur III)." In *A History of Ancient Near Eastern Law*, edited by Raymond Westbrook, 1:183–226. Leiden: Brill, 2003.

Lafont, Sophie. "Mesopotamia: Middle Assyrian Period." In *A History of Ancient Near Eastern Law*, edited by Raymond Westbrook, 1:486–520. Leiden: Brill, 2003.

Lanni, Adriaan. "Relevance in Athenian Courts." In *The Cambridge Companion to Ancient Greek Law*, edited by Michael Gagarin and David Cohen, 112–128. Cambridge: Cambridge University Press, 2005.

Lapin, Hayim. "The Construction of Households in the Mishnah." In *The Mishnah in Contemporary Perspective*, edited by Alan J. Avery-Peck and Jacob Neusner, 55–80. Leiden: Brill, 2006.

–. *Early Rabbinic Civil Law and the Social History of Roman Galilee: A Study of Mishnah Tractate Baba' Meṣi'a'*. Atlanta: Scholars, 1995.

–. "Maintenance of Wives and Children in Early Rabbinic and Documentary Texts from Roman Palestine." In *Rabbinic Law in Its Roman and Near Eastern Contexts*, edited by Catherine Hezser, 177–189. Tübingen: Mohr Siebeck, 2003.

–. *Rabbis as Romans: The Rabbinic Movement in Palestine 100–400 C. E.* Oxford: Oxford University Press, 2012.

Leibner, Uzi. *Settlement and History in Hellenistic, Roman, and Byzantine Galilee*. Tübingen: Mohr Siebeck, 2009.

Lemos, T. M. *Marriage Gifts and Social Change in Ancient Palestine*. Cambridge: Cambridge University Press, 2010.

Levenson, Jon D. *The Death and Resurrection of the Beloved Son: The Transformation of Child Sacrifice in Judaism and Christianity*. New Haven, CT: Yale University Press, 1993.

Levine, Baruch A. "Farewell to the Ancient Near East: Evaluating Biblical References to Ownership of Land in Comparative Perspective." In *Privatization in the Ancient Near East and Classical World*, edited by Michael Hudson and Baruch A. Levine, 223–252. Cambridge, MA: Peabody Museum of Archaeology & Ethnology, 1996.

–. "Mulugu/Melug: The Origins of a Talmudic Legal Institution." *Journal of the American Oriental Society* 88 (1968): 271–285.

–. *Numbers: 21–36*. New York: Doubleday, 2000.

Levine, Lee I. *The Rabbinic Class of Roman Palestine in Late Antiquity*. Jerusalem: Yad Izhak ben-Zvi; New York: Jewish Theological Seminary of America, 1989.

Lévy, Edmond. *La codification des lois dans l'antiquité: Actes du colloque de Strasbourg: 27–29 novembre 1997*. Paris: Boccard, 2000.

Lieberman, Saul. *Greek in Jewish Palestine*. New York: Jewish Theological Seminary, 1942.

–. *Hellenism in Jewish Palestine*. New York: Jewish Theological Seminary, 1950.

–. *Tosefta ki-fshuṭah: Nashim*. 3rd ed. Jerusalem and New York: Jewish Theological Seminary, 2007.

–. *Tosefta ki-fshuṭah: Neziqin*. New York: Jewish Theological Seminary, 1988.

–. *Tosefta ki-fshuṭah: Zera'im*. 3rd ed. Jerusalem and New York: Jewish Theological Seminary, 2001.

–. *Tosefta: Nashim*. 3rd ed. Jerusalem and New York: Jewish Theological Seminary of America, 2007.

–. *Tosefta: Neziqin*. New York: Jewish Theological Seminary of America, 1988.

–. *Tosefta: Zera'im*. 3rd ed. Jerusalem and New York: Jewish Theological Seminary of America, 2001.

Lipinski, Edward. "Naḥal." In *Theological Dictionary of the Old Testament*, edited by G. Johannes Botterweck, Helmer Ringgren, and Heinz-Josef Fabry, 9:319–335. Grand Rapids, MI: Eerdmans, 1998.

Livy (Titus Livius). *Ab Urbe Condita Libri* (*History of Rome*). Paderborn, GE: Ferdinand Schöningh, 1889.

Lohfink, Norbert. Yaraš. In *Theological Dictionary of the Old Testament*, edited by G. Johannes Botterweck, Helmer Ringgren, and Heinz-Josef Fabry, 6:370–376. Grand Rapids, MI: Eerdmans, 1990.

MacDowell, Douglas M. *The Law in Classical Athens*. Ithaca, NY: Cornell University Press, 1978.

–. "The *Oikos* in Athenian Law." *The Classical Quarterly* (New Series) 39:1 (1989): 10–21.

–. *Spartan Law*. Edinburgh: Scottish Academic, 1986.

Machinist, Peter. "Job's Daughters and Their Inheritance in the Testament of Job and Its Biblical Congeners." In *The Echoes of Many Texts: Reflections on Jewish and Christian Traditions: Essays in Honor of Lou H. Silberman*, edited by William G. Dever and J. Edward Wright, 67–80. Atlanta: Scholars, 1997.

Maeir, Aren M. "The Rephaim in Iron Age Philistia: Evidence of a Multi-Generational Family?" In "*Vom Leben umfangen*": *Ägypten, das Alte Testament und das Gespräch der Religionen, Gedenkschrift für Manfred Görg*, edited by Stefan Jakob Wimmer and Georg Gafus, 289–297. Münster, GE: Ugarit-Verlag, 2014.

Magdalene, F. R., and C. Wunsch. *Manumission, Emancipation, and Oblation: On Changing Personal Status in Neo-Babylonian Times*. Dresden: Islet, 2014.

Maine, Henry James Sumner. *Ancient Law: Its Connection with the Early History of Society and Its Relation to Modern Ideas*. New York: H. Holt, 1888.

Malul, Meir. "'Āqēb' "Heel" and 'āqab' "To Supplant" and the Concept of Succession in the Jacob-Esau Narratives." *Vetus Testamentum* 46:2 (April 1996): 190–212.

–. *The Comparative Method in Ancient Near Eastern and Biblical Legal Studies*. Kevelaer, GE: Butzon and Bercker; Neukirchen-Vluyn, GE: Neukirchener, 1990.

–. "Death-Bed Dispositions in the Hebrew Bible." In *A Common Cultural Heritage: Studies on Mesopotamia and the Biblical World in Honor of Barry L. Eichler*, edited by Grant Frame, Erle Leichty, Jeffrey Tigay, Karen Sonik, and Steve Tinney, 35–63. Bethesda, MD: CDL, 2011.

–. *Studies in Mesopotamian Legal Symbolism*. Kavelaer, GE: Butzon and Bercker, 1988.

Marcus, David. "The Legal Dispute between Jephthah and the Elders." *Hebrew Annual Review* 12 (1990): 105–114.

Martin, Roland. *L'Urbanisme dans la Gréce antique.* 2nd ed. Paris: A. & J. Picard, 1974.
Mattha, Girgis. "Rights and Duties of the Eldest Son According to the Native Egyptian Laws of Succession of the Third Century B. C." *Bulletin of the Faculty of Arts, University of Cairo* 12 (1950): 113–118.
McEwan, G. J. P. "Inheritance in Seleucid Babylonia." *Bulletin of the School for Oriental and African Studies* 47 (1984): 211–227.
Melamed, Ezra Zion. *Pirkei mavo lesifrut hatalmud* [An Introduction to Talmudic Literature]. Jerusalem, 1973.
Mendelsohn, Isaac. "On the Preferential Status of the Eldest Son." *Bulletin of the American Schools of Oriental Research* 156 (1959): 38–40.
–. "A Ugaritic Parallel to the Adoption of Ephraim and Manasseh." *Israel Exploration Journal* 9:3 (1959): 180–183.
Meyers, Eric. "Roman-Period Houses from the Galilee: Domestic Architecture and Gendered Spaces." In *Symbiosis, Symbolism, and the Power of the Past*, edited by William G. Dever and Seymour Gitin, 487–499. Winona Lake, IN: Eisenbrauns, 2003.
Milgram, Jonathan. Review of *Essays on Halakhah in the New Testament*, by Bernard Jackson. *Catholic Biblical Quarterly* 73:2 (April 2011): 431–433.
–. "Mishnah Baba Batra 8:5: The Transformation of the Firstborn Son from Family Leader to Family Member." In *Talmuda de-Eretz Israel: Archaeology and the Rabbis in Late Antique Palestine*, edited by Steven Fine and Aaron Koller, 19–28. Boston and Berlin: De Gruyter, 2014.
–. "Prolegomenon to a New Study of Rabbinic Inheritance Law on the Fiftieth Anniversary of Yaron's *Gifts In Contemplation of Death.*" *Jewish Law Association Studies* 23 (2012): 181–192.
–. "Then and Now: A Summary of Developments in the Field of Talmudic Literature through Contributions to the First and Second Editions of the *Encyclopaedia Judaica.*" *Currents in Biblical Research* 11:1 (October 2012): 126–140.
Milgrom, Jacob. "First-Born." In *Interpreter's Bible Dictionary Supplement*, 336–338. New York: Abingdon, 1976.
–. *Numbers: The Traditional Hebrew Text with the New JPS Translation.* The JPS Torah Commentary. Philadelphia: Jewish Publication Society, 1990.
Mirsky, Aharon, ed. *Midrash Tanaim li-vereshit*, Jerusalem: Mossad Harav Kook, 2000.
Modrzejewski, Joseph Mélèze. "Jewish Law and Hellenistic Legal Practice in the Light of Greek Papyri from Egypt." In *An Introduction to the History and Sources of Jewish Law*, edited by N. S. Hecht, et al., 75–99. Oxford: Oxford University Press, 1996.
Moscovitz, Leib. "Legal Fictions in Rabbinic Law and Roman Law: Some Comparative Observations." In *Rabbinic Law in Its Roman and Near Eastern Context*, edited by Catherine Hezser, 105–132. *Texts and Studies in Ancient Judaism.* Tübingen: Mohr-Siebeck, 2003.
Muffs, Yochanan. *Love and Joy: Law, Language, and Religion in Ancient Israel.* New York: Jewish Theological Seminary of America, 1992.
–. *Studies in the Aramaic Legal Papyri from Elephantine.* Leiden: E. J. Brill, 1969.
Neusner, Jacob. *Judaism: The Evidence of the Mishnah.* 2nd ed. Atlanta: Scholars, 1988.
–, ed. *The Modern Study of the Mishnah.* Leiden: Brill, 1973.
Nicholas, Barry. *An Introduction to Roman Law.* Clarendon Law Series. Oxford: Clarendon; New York: Oxford University Press, 1996. First published 1962.
Nickelsburg, G. W. E. "Stories of Biblical and Early Post-Biblical Times." In *Jewish Writings of the Second Temple Period: Apocrypha, Pseudepigrapha, Qumran Sectarian*

Writings, Philo, Josephus, edited by Michael E. Stone, 33–88. Assen: Van Gorcum; Philadelphia: Fortress, 1984.

Noam, Vered. *Megillat Ta`anit: Versions, Interpretation, History.* [in Hebrew.] Jerusalem: Yad Ben-Zvi, 2003.

–. "Between Qumran and Rabbinic Midrash: Common Exegesis and Implied Polemics." [In Hebrew.] *Meghillot* 7 (2009): 71–98.

–. *From Qumran to the Rabbinic Revolution.* [In Hebrew.] Jerusalem: Ben Zvi, 2010.

Noth, Martin. *Das System der Zwölf Stämme Israels.* Darmstadt, GE: Wissenschaftliche Buchgesellschaft, 1966.

Novick, Tzvi. "The 'Borer' Court: New Interpretations of mSan 3." *Zutot* 5:1 (2008): 1–8.

Oelsner, Joachim, Bruce Wells, and Cornelia Wunsch. "Mesopotamia: Neo-Babylonian Period." In *A History of Ancient Near Eastern Law*, edited by Raymond Westbrook, 2:911–974. Leiden: Brill, 2003.

Oudshoorn, Jacobine. *The Relationship between Roman and Local Law in the Babatha and Salome Komaise Archives: General Analysis and Three Case Studies on Law of Succession, Guardianship and Marriage.* Leiden: Brill, 2007.

Owen, David I. *Neo-Sumerian Archival Texts Primarily from Nippur in the University Museum, the Oriental Institute, and the Iraq Museum (NATN).* Winona Lake, IN: Eisenbrauns, 1982.

–. "Widow's Rights in Ur III Sumer." *Zeitschrift für Assyriologie und vorderasiatische Archäologie* 70:2 (1981): 170–184.

Paradise, Jonathan. "A Daughter and Her Father's Property at Nuzi." *Journal of Cuneiform Studies* 32, no. 4 (October 1980): 189–207.

–. "Daughters as 'Sons' at Nuzi." In *Studies on the Civilization and Culture of Nuzi and the Hurrians*, edited by D. I. Owen and M. A. Morrison, 203–213. Winona Lake, IN: Eisenbrauns, 1987.

–. "Marriage Contracts of Free Persons at Nuzi." *Journal of Cuneiform Studies* 39:1 (1987): 3–7.

–. "Nuzi Inheritance Practices." PhD diss., University of Pennsylvania, 1972.

Paul, Shalom. "Leshonot imuts." *Eretz Israel* 14 (1978): 31–36.

–. "The Patriarchate in the Light of the Nuzi Documents." *Diné Israel* 2 (1970): 23–28.

Pestman, P. W. "The Law of Succession in Ancient Egypt." In *Essays on Oriental Laws of Succession*, edited by J. Brugman, M. David, F. R. Kraus, P. W. Pestman, and M. H. van der Valk, 58–77. Leiden: E. J. Brill, 1969.

Pfeiffer, Robert H. *Excavations at Nuzi II: The Archives of Shilwateshub, Son of the King.* Harvard Semitic Studies IX. Cambridge: Harvard University Press, 1932.

Philo of Alexandria. *The Works of Philo: Complete and Unabridged.* Translated by C. D. Yonge. Peabody, MA: Hendrickson, 1993.

Piatelli, Daniella, and Bernard S. Jackson. "Jewish Law during the Second Temple Period." In *An Introduction to the History and Sources of Jewish Law*, edited by N. S. Hecht, et al., 19–56. Oxford: Oxford University Press, 1996.

Plato. *Laws.* Translated by R. G. Bury. Loeb Classical Library. London: William Heinemann; Cambridge, MA: Harvard University Press, 1967.

Plutarch. "Plutarch's Lives." Translated by Bernadotte Perrin. London: William Heinemann; Cambridge, MA: Harvard University, 1914.

Podany, Amanda, Gary M. Beckman, and Gudrun Colbow. "An Adoption and Inheritance Contract from the Reign of Iggid-Lim." *Journal of Cuneiform Studies* 43–45 (1991): 39–51.

Polybius. *The Histories of Polybius.* Translated by W.R. Paton. Loeb Classical Library. London: William Heinemann; Cambridge, MA: Harvard University Press, 1979.

Pope, Marvin. *Job.* Anchor Bible Commentary. Garden City, NY: Doubleday, 1965.

Porten, Bezalel. *Archives from Elephantine: The Life of an Ancient Jewish Military Colony.* Berkeley and Los Angeles: University of California Press, 1968.

–. *The Elephantine Papyri in English: Three Millennia of Cross-Cultural Continuity and Change.* Leiden: Brill, 1996.

Porten, Bezalel, and Ada Yardeni, eds. *Textbook of Aramaic Documents from Ancient Egypt.* Vol. 2: *Contracts.* Winona Lake, IN: Eisenbrauns, 1989.

Povarsky, Haim. "The *Shekhiv Me'ra* Will: Composition and Scope." [In Hebrew.] *Diné Israel* 7 (1976): 191–203.

Rabinowitz, J.J. *Jewish Law: Its Influence on the Development of Legal Institutions.* Bloch: New York, 1956.

–. "Neo-Babylonian Legal Documents and Jewish Law." *Journal of Juristic Papyrology* 12 (1961): 131–175.

Rackman, Emmanuel. "A Jewish Philosophy of Property: Rabbinic Insights on Intestate Succession." *Jewish Quarterly Review* 67, nos. 2–3 (October 1976–January 1977): 65–89.

Radner, Karen. "Mesopotamia: Neo-Assyrian Period." In *A History of Ancient Near Eastern Law*, edited by Raymond Westbrook, 2:883–910. Leiden: Brill, 2003.

–. *Die neuassyrischen Privatrechtsurkunden als quelle für Mensch und Umwelt.* SAAS. Helsinki: Neo-Assyrian Text Corpus Project, 1997.

Rainey, Anson F. "Family Relationships in Ugarit," *Orientalia* 34 (1965): 10–22.

Reinhartz, Adele. "Philo's *Exposition of the Law* and Social History: Methodological Considerations." In *SBL Annual Meeting 1993 Seminar Papers*, edited by Eugene H. Lowering Jr., 9–13. Atlanta: Scholars, 1993.

Rivlin, Joseph. "Gift and Inheritance Law in the Judaean Desert." In *Law in the Documents of the Judaean Desert*, edited by Ranon Katzoff, 165–183. Leiden: Brill, 2005.

–. *Inheritance and Wills in Jewish Law.* Ramat Gan: Bar Ilan University, 1999.

–. "Inheritance, Wills and Legacies." *Diné Israel* 13–14 (1988): 167–192.

Roaf, Michael. *Cultural Atlas of Mesopotamia and the Ancient Near East.* Oxfordshire, UK: Andromeda Oxford, 1996.

Rofé, Alexander. *Deuteronomy: Issues and Interpretations.* London: T&T Clark, 2001.

Rosenfeld, Ben Zion, and Haim Perlmutter, "Landowners in Roman Palestine 100–300 C.E.: A Distinct Social Group." *Journal of Ancient Judaism* (2011): 2:327–352.

Rosenthal, Eliezer Shimshon. "Leferushah shel mishnat Ta'anit 1:1–2." In *Yad Reem.* Jerusalem, 1975, 261–270.

–. "Hamoreh," *PAAJR* 31 (1963): 1–71.

Rosenthal, Eliezer Shimshon, and Saul Lieberman, *Yerushalmi Nezikin.* [In Hebrew.] Jerusalem: *Ha'akademia hale'umit hayisra'elit lemada'im*, 1983.

Rosen-Zvi, Ishay. *Mishnaic Sotah Ritual: Temple, Gender, and Midrash.* Leiden: Brill, 2012.

Roth, Martha. *Babylonian Marriage Agreements, 7th–3rd Centuries B.C.* Kevelaer, GE: Butzon and Bercker, 1989.

–. *Law Collections from Mesopotamia and Asia Minor.* Atlanta: Scholars, 1995.

–. "The Neo-Babylonian Widow." *Journal of Cuneiform Studies* 43–45, (1991–1993): 1–26.

–. "A Reassessment of RA 71 (1977) 125ff." *Archiv für Orientforschung* 31 (1984), 9–14.

Rowe, Ignacio Marquez. "Anatolia and the Levant: Alalakh." In *A History of Ancient Near Eastern Law*, edited by Raymond Westbrook, 1:693–718. Leiden: Brill, 2003.

–. "Anatolia and the Levant: Ugarit." In *A History of Ancient Near Eastern Law*, edited by Raymond Westbrook, 1:719–736. Leiden: Brill, 2003.

Rubin, Nissan. *The End of Life: Rites of Burial and Mourning in the Talmud and Midrash.* [In Hebrew.] Tel Aviv: Hakibbutz Hameuchad, 1997.

–. "For Whom Does One Mourn? A Sociological Analysis of Talmudic Sources." [In Hebrew.] *Bar Ilan* 10 (1972): 111–122.

Rubinstein, Lene. *Adoption in IV. Century Athens.* Copenhagen: Museum Tusculanum, 1993.

Sabato, Mordechai. "Elu hen hakerovin: Iyun meḥudash bireshimot hakerovim hapesulim le'edut." *Diné Israel* 29 (2013): 71–123.

Safrai, Shmuel. "Home and Family." In *The Jewish People in the First Century*, edited by S. Safrai, et al. Philadelphia: Fortress, 1976.

Safrai, Zeev. "Family Structure during the Period of the Mishna and the Talmud." [In Hebrew.] *Milet* 1 (1983): 129–156.

–. *Hanose, Baalut al hakarka bitekufat hamishnah vehatalmud: Tahalikhim umaavakim.* Hamakhon leḥeker shimushei karka: haḥug lemediniut karkait, 1998.

Saller, Richard P. *Patriarchy, Property and Death in the Roman Family.* Cambridge: Cambridge University Press, 1994.

–. "Roman Dowry and the Devolution of Property in the Principate," *Classical Quarterly* 34, no. 1 (1984): 195–205.

Saller, Richard P., and David I. Kertzer, "Historical and Anthropological Perspectives on Italian Family Life." In *The Family in Italy*, edited by Richard P. Saller and David I. Kertzer, 1–22. New Haven, CT: Yale University Press, 1991.

Sarna, Nahum M. *Genesis: The Traditional Hebrew Text with New JPS Translation.* JPS Torah Commentary. Philadelphia: Jewish Publication Society, 1989.

Sasson, Jack. *Ruth: A New Translation with Philological Commentary and a Formalist-Folklorist Interpretation.* Baltimore: Johns Hopkins University Press, 1979.

Satlow, Michael. "Beyond Influence: Toward a New Historiographic Paradigm." In *Jewish Literatures and Cultures: Context and Intertext*, edited by Anita Norich and Yaron Z. Eliav, 37–53. Providence, R. I.: Brown University Press, 2008.

–. *Jewish Marriage in Antiquity.* Princeton, NJ: Princeton University Press, 2001.

–. "Marriage Payments and Succession Strategies in the Documents from the Judaean Desert." In *Law in the Documents of the Judaean Desert*, edited by Ranon Katzoff and David Schaps, 51–65. Supplements to *Journal for the Study of Judaism* 96. Leiden: Brill, 2005.

Schäfer, Peter, and Hans-Jürgen Becker, eds. *Synopse zum Talmud Yerushalmi.* Vol. 1, 1–2: Ordnung Zeraʿim: Berakhot und Peʾa. Tübingen: Mohr-Siebeck, 1991.

Schaps, David M. *Economic Rights of Women in Ancient Greece.* Edinburgh: Edinburgh University Press, 1979.

–. "Women in Greek Inheritance Law." *Classical Quarterly* New Series 25, no. 1 (May 1975): 53–57.

Scheid, John. "Sacrifices for Gods and Ancestors." In *A Companion to Roman Religion*, edited by Jörg Rüpke, 263–272. Malden, MA: Blackwell, 2007.

Schiffman, Lawrence. *The Halakhah at Qumran.* Leiden: Brill, 1975.

–. *Law, Custom, and Messianism in the Dead Sea Scrolls.* [In Hebrew.] Jerusalem: Israel Historical Society and Shazar, 1993.

–. *Sectarian Law in the Dead Sea Scrolls: Courts, Testimony, and the Penal Code*. Chico, CA: Scholars, 1983.
Schloen, J. David. *The House of the Father as Fact and Symbol: Patrimonialism in Ugarit and the Ancient Near East*, Winona Lake, IN: Eisenbrauns, 2001.
Schremer, Adiel. *Male and Female He Created Them*. [In Hebrew.] Jerusalem: Zalman Shazar Center, 2003.
Schwartz, Seth. *Imperialism and Jewish Society, 200 B. C.E to 640 C. E.* Princeton, NJ: Princeton University Press, 2001.
–. "The Political Geography of Rabbinic Texts." In *The Cambridge Companion to Talmud and Rabbinic Literature*, edited by Charlotte Fonrobert and Martin Jaffee, 75–96. Cambridge: Cambridge University Press, 2007.
–. "Political, Social and Economic Life in the Land of Israel, 66–c. 235." In *The Cambridge History of Judaism*, edited by Steven Katz, 4:23–52. Cambridge: Cambridge University Press, 2006.
–. *Were the Jews a Mediterranean Society?* Princeton, NJ: Princeton University Press, 2010.
Segal, Moses Hirsch. *Sefer ben-Sira hashalem*. Jerusalem: Bialik, 1958.
Seidl, Erwin. "La preminente posizione successoria del figlio maggiore nel diritto dei papiri." *Rendiconti dell'Istituto Lombardo: Classe di Lettere* 99 (1965): 185–192.
Shemesh, Aharon, "Mah gilah menashe ben hizkiyah batorah? Al seridei halakhah tzedukit-kitatit besifrut hazal." *Megillot* 2 (2004): 91–103.
Shilo, Shmuel, and Menachem Elon. "Succession." In *Encyclopaedia Judaica*. 2nd ed. Edited by Michael Berenbaum and Fred Skolnik, 19:284–290. Detroit: Macmillan Reference USA, 2007.
Skehan, Patrick W., and Alexander A. De Lella, eds. *The Wisdom of Ben Sira*. Anchor Bible. New York: Doubleday, 1987.
Slanski, Kathryn. "Mesopotamia: Middle Babylonian Period." In *A History of Ancient Near Eastern Law*, edited by Raymond Westbrook, 1:485–520. Leiden: Brill, 2003.
Smith, Michael E. "Centenary Paper: V. Gordon Childe and the Urban Revolution: A Historical Perspective on a Revolution in Urban Studies." Town Planning Review 80, no. 1 (2009): 3–29.
Smith, Morton. Review of *Jewish and Roman Law: A Comparative Study* by Boaz Cohen. *Journal of Biblical Literature* 86:2 (June 1967): 238–241.
Snijders, L. A. "Genesis XV: The Covenant with Abraham." *Oudtestamentische Studien* 12 (1958): 261–279.
Sollberger, Edmond. "Some Legal Documents of the Third Dynasty of Ur." In *Kramer Anniversary Volume: Cuneiform Studies in Honor of Samuel Noah Kramer*, edited by Barry Eichler, 435–450. Kevelaer, GE: Butzon and Bercker, 1976.
Soloveitchik, Haym. "Can Halakhic Texts Talk History?" *AJS Review* 3 (1978): 153–196.
–. "Halakhah, Hermeneutics and Martyrdom in Medieval Ashkenaz (Part 1 of 2)." *Jewish Quarterly Review*, 94:1 (Winter 2004): 77–108.
Speiser, E. A., "Akaddian Documents from *Ras Shamra.*" *Journal of the American Oriental Society* 75:3 (1955): 160–165.
–. "Ethnic Movements in the Near East in the Second Millennium." *The Annual of the American Schools of Oriental Research* 13 (1933): 13–54.
–. "I Know Not the Day of My Death." *Journal of Biblical Literature* 74 (1955): 252–256.
–. "New Kirkuk Documents Relating to Family Laws." *The Annual of the American Schools of Oriental Research* 10 (1928): 1–73.

Sperber, Daniel. *A Dictionary of Greek and Latin Legal Terms in Rabbinic Literature.* Ramat Gan: Bar Ilan University, 1984.
–. *Greek in Talmudic Palestine*. Ramat Gan: Bar Ilan University, 2012.
–. *The City in Roman Palestine*. Oxford: Oxford University Press, 1998.
Stager, Lawrence E. "The Archaeology of the Family in Ancient Israel." *Bulletin of the Schools of Oriental Research* 260 (1985): 1–35.
Stein, Peter. "Lex Falcidia." *Athenaeum* 65 (1987):454–457.
Stolper, Matthew W. "The Testament of Mannu-kâ-Attar." In *Veenhof Anniversary Volume: Studies Presented to Klaas R. Veenhof on the Occasion of His Sixty-Fifth Birthday*, edited by W.H. van Soldt, 467–473. Leiden: Nederlands Instituut voor het Nabije Oosten, 2001.
Stone, Elizabeth C. "The Development of Cities in Ancient Mesopotamia." In *Civilizations of the Ancient Near East*, edited by Jack M. Sasson, 235–248. Peabody, MA: Hendrickson, 2000.
Stone, Elizabeth C., and David I. Owen. *Adoption in Old Babylonian Nippur and the Archive of Mannum-mešu-liṣṣur.* Winona Lake, IN: Eisenbrauns, 1991.
Surenhuys, Willem. *Mischna: sive totius Hebraeorum juris, rituum, antiquitatum, ac legum oralium systema.* Amstelaedami: Excudunt Gerard & Jacobus Borstius, 1698–1703.
Sussmann, Yaakov. "Torah shebe'al peh peshutah kemashma'ah," *Meḥkerei Talmud* 3:1 (2005): 209–384.
Szubin, H.Z. "Testamentary Succession in Jewish Law." PhD diss., Dropsie College, 1965.
Szubin, H.Z., and Bezalel Porten. "A Life Estate of Usufruct: A New Interpretation of Kraeling 6." *Bulletin of the American Schools of Oriental Research* 269 (February 1988): 29–45.
–. "Testamentary Succession at Elephantine." *Bulletin of the American Schools of Oriental Research* 252 (Autumn 1983): 35–46.
Talamanca, Mario. *Istituzioni di Diritto romano*. Milano: Dott. A. Giuffré Editore, 1990.
Taubenschlag, Rafal. *The Law of Greco-Roman Egypt in the Light of the Papyri, 332 B.C.–640 A.D.* New York: Herald Square, 1944.
Tellegen-Couperus, O.E. *Testamentary Succession in the Constitutions of Diocletian*. Zutphen, NL: Uitgeverij Terra, 1982.
Thompson, T.L. *The Historicity of the Patriarchal Narratives: The Quest for the Historical Abraham.* Berlin: W. de Gruyter, 1974.
Thureau-Dangin, F. "Trois contrats de Ras Shamra." *Syria* 18 (1937): 245–255.
Tigay, Jeffrey. *Deuteronomy: The JPS Torah Commentary.* Philadelphia: Jewish Publication Society, 1996.
Todd, Stephen. "Law and Oratory at Athens." In *Cambridge Companion to Ancient Greek Law*, edited by Michael Gagarin and David Cohen, 97–111. Cambridge: Cambridge University Press, 2005.
Tropper, Amram. "Children and Childhood in Light of the Demographics of the Jewish Family in Late Antiquity." *Journal for the Study of Judaism* 37, no. 3 (2006): 299–343.
–. "The Economics of Jewish Childhood in Late Antiquity." *HUCA* 76 (2005): 189–233.
Tsevat, Matitiahu. "Chalaq II." In *Theological Dictionary of the Old Testament*, edited by G. Johannes Botterweck, Helmer Ringgren, and Heinz-Josef Fabry, 4:447–451. Grand Rapids, MI: Eerdmans, 1980.
Urbach, Ephraim Elimelech. "Inheritance Laws and After-Life." In *Fourth World Congress, Union of Jewish Studies.* Vol. 1:133–141. Jerusalem, 1967.

Van der Toorn, Karel. *Family Religion in Babylonia, Syria and Israel.* Leiden: E.J. Brill, 1996.

Van Driel, G. "Care of the Elderly: The Neo-Babylonian Period." In *The Care of the Elderly in the Ancient Near East*, edited by S.P. Vleeming and Marten Stol, 161–197. Leiden: Brill, 1998.

Van Seters, John. *Abraham in History and Tradition.* New Haven, CT: Yale University Press, 1974.

Veenhof, Klaas R. "Mesopotamia: Old Assyrian Period." In *A History of Ancient Near Eastern Law*, edited by Raymond Westbrook, 1:431–484. Leiden: Brill, 2003.

Vita, Juan-Pablo. "The Society of Ugarit." In *Handbook of Ugaritic Studies*, edited by Wilfred G.E. Watson and Nicolas Wyatt, 455–498. Leiden: Brill, 1999.

Vorderasiatische Schriftdenkmäler der Königlichen Museen zu Berlin. Herausgegeben von der Vorderasiatischen Abteilung [ed. Friedrich Delitzsch]. Leipzig: J.C. Hinrichs, 1907–1917.

Wald, Steven "Baraita, Baraitot." In *Encylcopaedia Judaica.* 2nd ed., edited by Fred Skolnik and Michael Berenbaum, 3:124–128. Detroit: Macmillan Reference USA, 2007.

Wasserstein, Avraham. "A Marriage Contract from the Province of Arabia Nova: Notes on Papyrus Yadin 18." *Jewish Quarterly Review* 80, nos. 1–2 (October 1989): 93–130.

Watson. Alan. *The Law of Succession in the Later Roman Republic.* Oxford: Clarendon, 1971.

–. *Legal Transplants: An Approach to Comparative Law.* Charlottesville: University Press of Virginia, 1974.

–. "From Legal Transplants to Legal Formants." *The American Journal of Comparative Law* 43 (1995): 469–476.

–. *Rome of the XII Tables: Persons and Property.* Princeton, NJ: Princeton University Press, 1975.

–. *Society and Legal Change.* 2nd ed. Philadelphia: Temple University Press, 2001.

Watson, Alan, ed. *The Digest of Justinian.* Text by T. Mommsen with the aid of P. Kreuger. Philadelphia: University of Pennsylvania Press, 1985.

Weiss, Avraham. "Laḥeker hasifruti shel hamishnah." *HUCA* 16 (1941): 1–33.

Weiss, Isaac Hirsch, ed. *Sifra devei rav hu sefer torat kohanim.* Vienna: Yaakov Hakohen Schlossberg, 1862.

Weissberg, Dvora E. *Levirate Marriage and the Family in Ancient Judaism.* Waltham, MA: Brandeis University Press, 2009.

Wells, Bruce. "The Hated Wife in Deuteronomic Law." *Vetus Testamentum* 60 (2010): 131–146.

Wells, Bruce, and F. Rachel Magdalene, eds. *Law from the Tigris to the Tiber: The Writings of Raymond Westbrook.* Winona Lake, IN: Eisenbrauns, 2009.

Westbrook, Raymond. "Emar and Vicinity." In *A History of Ancient Near Eastern Law*, edited by Raymond Westbrook, 1:657–692. Leiden: Brill, 2003.

–. "Introduction." In *A History of Ancient Near Eastern Law*, edited by Raymond Westbrook, 1:1–92. Leiden: Brill, 2003.

–. "Mesopotamia: Old Babylonian Period." In *A History of Ancient Near Eastern Law*, edited by Raymond Westbrook, 1:361–430. Leiden: Brill, 2003.

–. *Property and the Family in Biblical Law.* Journal for the Study of the Old Testament Supplement Series. Sheffield, UK: Journal for the Study of the Old Testament Press, 1991.

Westbrook, Raymond, and Bruce Wells. *Everyday Law in Biblical Israel: An Introduction*. Louisville, KY: Westminster John Knox, 2009.

Whitley, James. "Cretan Law and Cretan Literacy." *American Journal of Archaeology* 101:4 (1997): 635–661.

Wilcke, Claus. "Assyrische Testamente." *Zeitschrift für Assyriologie* 66 (1976): 198–233.

–. "Care of the Elderly in Mesopotamia in the Third Millennium B.C." In *The Care of the Elderly in the Ancient Near East*, edited by S.P. Vleeming and Marten Stol, 23–58. Leiden: Brill, 1998.

–. *Early Ancient Near Eastern Law, A History of Its Beginnings, The Early Dynastic and Sargonic Periods*. Munich: Verlag der bayerischen Akademie der Wissenschaften, 2003.

–. "Der Kodex Urnamma (CU): Versuch einer Rekonstruktion." In *Riches Hidden in Secret Places: Ancient Near Eastern Studies in Memory of Thorkild Jacobsen*, 291–333. Winona Lake, IN: Eisenbrauns, 2002.

–. "Neue Rechtsurkunden aus der Altsumerischen Zeit." *Zeitschrift für Assyriologie* 86 (1996): 47–67.

Willetts, R.F. *The Law Code of Gortyn*. Translation and a commentary. Kadmos Supplement. Berlin: De Gruyter, 1967.

Wiseman, D.J. *The Alalakh Tablets*. Occasional Publications of the British Institute of Archaeology at Ankara, no. 2. London: British Institute of Archaeology at Ankara, 1953.

Witt, John Fabian. "Contingency, Immanence, and Inevitability in the Law of Accidents." *Journal of Tort Law* 1, no. 2 (2007): 1–41.

Wood, Gordon S. *The Radicalism of the American Revolution*. New York: A.A. Knopf, 1992.

Woolf, Jeffrey. "Methodological Reflections on the Study of Halakhah." *EAJS Newsletter* 11 (October 2001): 9–14.

Wunsch, Cornelia. *Das Egibi-Archiv*. Groningen, NL: Styx Publications, 2000.

–. "Und die Richter berieten . . : Streitfälle in Babylon aus der Zeit Neriglissars und Nabonids." *Archiv für Orientforschung* 44–45 (1997–1998): 59–100.

–. *Die Urkunden des babylonischen Geschäftsmannes Iddin-Marduk*. Groningen, NL: Styx, 1993.

–. *Urkunden zum Ehe-, Vermögens- und Erbrecht aus verschiedenen neubabylonischen Archiven*. Dresden: Islet, 2003.

–. "Women's Property and the Law of Inheritance in the Neo-Babylonian Period." In *Women and Property in Ancient Near Eastern and Mediterranean Societies*. Washington, DC: Center of Hellenic Studies: Harvard University, 2003. http://chs.harvard.edu.

Yadin, Yigal. "Expedition D – The Cave of the Letters." *Israel Exploration Journal* 12:1 (1962): 227–257.

Yadin, Yigal, Jonas C. Greenfield, and Ada Yardeni. "Babatha's *Ketubba*." *Israel Exploration Journal* 44 (1994): 75–101.

Yadin, Yigal, Jonas C. Greenfield, Ada Yardeni, and Baruch A. Levine, eds. *The Documents from the Bar Kokhba Period in the Cave of Letters: Hebrew, Aramaic and Nabatean-Aramaic Papyri*. Jerusalem: Israel Exploration Society; Institute of Archeology, Hebrew University; Shrine of the Book, Israel Museum, 2002.

Yaron, Reuven. "Acts of Last Will in Jewish Law." *Recueils de la Société Jean Bodin pour l'Histoire Comparative des Institutions* 59 (1992): 29–45.

–. "Aramaic Marriage Contracts from Elephantine." *Journal of Semitic Studies* 3, no. 1 (January 1958): 1–39.

–. "Basics of Roman and Jewish Intestacy." In *Critical Studies in Ancient Law, Comparative Law and Legal History*, edited by John W. Cairns and Olivia F. Robinson, 201–210. Oxford: Hart, 2001.

–. "Donatio Sola Cogitatione Mortalitatis." *Revue internationale des droits de l'antique* 13 (1966): 369–375.

–. *Gifts in Contemplation of Death in Jewish and Roman Law*. Oxford: Clarendon, 1960.

–. *Introduction to the Law of the Aramaic Papyri*. Oxford: Oxford University Press, 1961.

–. "Sadducees and Pharisees: Two Controversies." *Israel Law Review* 33, no. 4 (1999): 743–755.

–. "Some Remarks on *Donatio Mortis Causa*." *Revue internationale des droits de l'antique* 3 (1956): 493–512.

–. "Varia on Adoption." *Journal of Juristic Papyrology* 15 (1965): 175–179.

Zaccagnini, Carlo. "Nuzi." In *A History of Ancient Near Eastern Law*, edited by Raymond Westbrook, 2:565–618. Leiden: Brill, 2003.

Zacovitch, Yair. *Ruth: Introduction and Commentary.* Vol. 1 of Mikra leyisra'el: A Bible Commentary for Israel, edited by Moshe Greenberg and Shmuel Ahituv. Tel Aviv: Am Oved; Jerusalem: Magnes, 1990.

Zeitlin, Solomon. "Testamentary Succession: A Study in Tannaitic Jurisprudence." *Jewish Quarterly Review* 57 (1967): 574–581.

Index of Foreign Terms

Index of Contemporary Authors

Index of Sources

Hebrew Bible

Second Temple Literature

New Testament

Ancient Translations

Ancient Near Eastern Sources

Greek Sources

Roman Sources

Mishnah (*m*)

Tosefta (*t*)

Halakhic Midrash

Palestinian Talmud (*p*)

Babylonian Talmud (Bavli)

Talmudic Commentaries

Judean Desert Papyri

Elephantine Papyri

Index of Subjects

Postscript to the Paperback Edition

The republication of *From Mesopotamia to the Mishnah* provides me with the unique opportunity to reflect on some aspects of my methodology more explicitly, to append new material and, primarily in the footnotes, to address some of the more substantive observations about my book made in recent reviews. Since I view the identification of the correspondence between tannaitic inheritance terminology and conceptualization and their Roman counterparts as one of the most significant contributions of my book, I direct my remarks in this postscript to that relationship.[1] I begin, in the first section below, with an overview of some of the methodological aims of *From Mesopotamia to the Mishnah*. Then, I enter into a discussion of the use of parallels in the study of tannaitic inheritance law. Following, in each of the three subsequent sections, I summarize the findings of three of the book's chapters and then discuss additional evidence. In the final section, as in the concluding chapter of the book, I briefly address the question,

---

[1] In "Rabbis and Romanization," 218–245, Ishay Rosen-Zvi argues that by offering a complete alternative to Roman law, the publication of the Mishnah is evidence of a sophisticated and antagonistic rabbinic movement that rejected Romanization on multiple levels (compare similar remarks in Rosen-Zvi, "Is the Mishnah a Roman Composition?," 506). Even if Rosen-Zvi is correct regarding the broad implications of the Mishnah's publication (a matter which still requires further consideration), that would not preclude the possibility of the tannaim integrating elements of Roman legal thinking—in the case of inheritance law, terminology and conceptualization—into their sphere of legal inquiry. In "Is the Mishnah a Roman Composition?," Rosen-Zvi writes that he entertains the question, "why is the Mishnah so deeply different from everything else around it?" (490). However, what the author really addresses in the article is, why are the rabbis—the creators of the Mishnah—so deeply different from everyone else around them? And, to what degree does the publication of the Mishnah provide us with an answer? In the article's final paragraph he writes: "To conclude: scholars are hard pressed to find parallels between the Mishnah and Roman law … I have offered a more general context to this somewhat unsuccessful scholarly endeavor, suggesting to treat it as part of the question of Romanization at large. Seeing the Mishnah as an alternative to Rome does not contradict all sorts of undeliberate influences, but it does significantly reduce the openness to Roman legal models, whether in the context of specific laws or in the composition at large" (508). What Rosen-Zvi concludes, therefore, is that in light of the seemingly global rejection of Romanization evidenced by the publication of the Mishnah, we should not be surprised when we take a micro approach and find few (and undeliberate) overlapping laws among the Romans and the tannaim. I would like to add a warning: we should not prevent ourselves from seeing specific parallels, and even noting their potentially deliberate inclusion, because of our assumption that the rabbis rejected Romanization in a global sense. As noted by Rosen-Zvi in both articles, the rabbis did adopt elements of the Roman world around them. I merely point out the possibility here that regarding inheritance law the overlap may be telling in the opposite direction of Rosen-Zvi's approach. If, in fact, the rabbis ever hoped to create a collection of living laws that they would eventually be able to legislate, what better construction to create than one which deliberately conformed to some of the legal presumptions of Roman law? (For more on this see below, "So, how Jewish is Jewish is Inheritance Law?" and my earlier comments in Milgram, *From Mesopotamia to the Mishnah, 33*).

"So, how Jewish is Jewish inheritance law?" and I note the possible significance of the tannaitic construction of inheritance laws for the study of rabbinic self-perception of leadership.

Tannaitic Inheritance Law in Comparative Context: Goals, Methods and Parallels

On the most basic level, the goal of the legal comparatist is to find possible parallels between legal traditions and then to mine them for the potential significance of their similarities and differences.[2] Supported by a philological and source critical analysis that revealed multiple strands of tannaitic traditions about inheritance, in *From Mesopotamia to the Mishnah* I located parallels in ancient near eastern and Mediterranean legal traditions dating from before and during the tannaitic period, in order to highlight the similarities and differences between the laws. I suggested the significance of specific similarities, at times pointing to the possible sources of tannaitic traditions in foreign legal compilations from the ancient world.[3] In light of the lack of overlap with biblical modes of inheritance procedure and the absence of the expected—interpretation of Scripture to buttress rabbinic innovation—I argued that the likely source of much of rabbinic inheritance practice can be found in other legal traditions. Moreover, I provided an additional explanation for the dramatic differences between biblical and tannaitic inheritance laws, ascribing some of the developments, perhaps, to the social and economic contexts in which the rabbis found themselves.[4]

---

[2] See the statement in Watson, *Legal Transplants*, 9. For a useful methodological presentation, see Danneman, "Comparative Law: Study of Similarities or Differences?," 384–419.

[3] In his review essay, "Inheritance Laws in their Greco-Roman Context: Review of Milgram," Yair Furstenberg deals in detail with several of the issues I tackled in *From Mesopotamia to the Mishnah*. I address a number of Furstenberg's comments in the forthcoming footnotes. I should note from the outset that in his essay Furstenberg prefers to compare and contrast the finally redacted Mishnah with other ancient legal traditions. The main goal of my book, however, was the opposite: mining the finally redacted Mishnah for its multiple tannaitic voices and sources and then comparing these to potentially parallel legal material in several ancient legal traditions (See, especially, Furstenberg, "Inheritance Laws in their Greco-Roman Context: Review of Milgram, 255–258). Certainly, this difference in approach, among other differences, has resulted in a fruitful scholarly debate on fundamental methodological issues (see below in the footnotes and also Milgram, "Min hamizrach hakadum vead lamishnah," (forthcoming)).

[4] Regarding this final point, I attempted to be very cautious, from a methodological perspective, not to label the social and economic situation as a cause for the institution of certain laws, while at the same time accounting for the role that specific social and economic conditions may have had on the production of laws; see Milgram, *From Mesopotamia to the Mishnah*, 146 (and in the Preface). I fear the subtlety in my contention may have been misunderstood by several of my reviewers; see n. 8. See also, below, "So, How Jewish is Jewish Inheritance Law?," for an expansion of these ideas. Note, also, that in Hezser, "Review of *From Mesopotamia to the Mishnah*," 1176, the author attempts to discredit the assertion, appearing throughout my book, that the tannaim likely resided in urban centers. This notion is not of my creation. I relied on

Certainly, every scholar of comparative law—whether ancient, medieval or modern—must contend with the possibility that the overlap between traditions, terms, and concepts is merely incidental. Indeed, the conundrum of the comparatist has always been, and inevitably will always remain: when is a parallel a parallel? More specifically, does the partial overlap between a rule, term, or procedure in two legal traditions from the same general geographic region and/or time period constitute a parallel?[5] Some scholars argue that to demonstrate that an element from one legal tradition enters another, it must transfer *in toto*.[6] Such a requirement not only denies the scholar the ability to engage in rich and creative work, but also prevents the researcher from observing and charting the potentially nuanced and complex process of adoption and adaptation (whether conscious or not) of terms, formulae and concepts that occurs between legal traditions.[7] With

---

the scholarship of several historians and archeologists (see Milgram, *From Mesopotamia to the Mishnah*, 31 nn. 182–186). Indeed, it seems that by the beginning of the third century, the time by which the Mishnah as a literary work would have been crystallized, most rabbis did live in cities. In fact, Hezser herself argues for the presence of rabbis in cities in the first, second and third centuries; see Hezser, *Social Structure*, 157–165. Furthermore, while I agree with Hezser's contention that the urbanization of Palestine was a gradual process, we should not assume that the social and economic developments, no matter how protracted, could not have had an impact on the burgeoning laws of the tannaim at every stage of their extended development.

[5] In his, now classic, *Legal Transplants*, Alan Watson engaged in what can be called a 'rules based' inquiry. Watson observed individual rules or laws that traversed cultural, historical and linguistic boundaries, charting the, at times, partial parallels between legal systems. He pointed to the overlap and the significance of the changes that took place during the process of transplantation. In *From Mesopotamia to the Mishnah*, I embraced aspects of Watson's approach (see Milgram, *From Mesopotamia to the Mishnah*, 11–17).

[6] In "The Impossibility of 'Legal Transplants,'" (and several other publications) Pierre Legrand took issue with Watson's vision, pointing out that law is not just about rules in isolation. He argued that rules cannot be devoid of context, which provides them with meaning. Accordingly, Legrand disputed the existence of a legal transplant unless, when transplanted, the individual rule was accompanied by its original meaning and context upon being transferred. He went further: since this cannot really happen, legal transplants, therefore, cannot exist. Legrand's formulation is worth citing here in full: "If one agrees that, in significant ways, a rule receives its meaning from without and if one accepts that such investment of meaning by an interpretive community effectively partakes in the ruleness of the rule, indeed the *nucleus* of ruleness, it must follow that there could only occur a meaningful 'legal transplant' when both the propositional statement as such *and* its invested meaning—which jointly constitute *the rule*—are transported from one culture to another. Given that the meaning invested into the rule is itself culture-specific, it is difficult to conceive, however, how this could ever happen" (Legrand, "The Impossibility of Legal Transplants," 116–117); and, furthermore, "No rule in the borrowing jurisdiction can have any significance as regards the rule in the jurisdiction from which it is borrowed. This is because, as it crosses boundaries, the original rule necessarily undergoes a change that affects it *qua* rule," ibid., 120; italics in both of the quotes are in the original; see also Legrand, "Against a European Civil Code," 44.

[7] The result of such processes are what Watson calls "legal transplants." In a rebuttal of Legrand entitled, "Legal Transplants and European Private Law," Watson affirmed that when arguing for the existence of legal transplants he always suggested that only individual rules,

regards to the tannaitic situation, if we were to argue that a partial parallel is, in fact, not a parallel at all, we could potentially miss noticing something significant about the partial and fragmented assimilation, integration, and absorption of legal terms and traditions into the legal matrix of the tannaim.[8] One example from the world of inheritance procedure will illustrate this point: the well-known tannaitic institution of the דייתיקי.[9]

Scholars agree that the word דייתיקי in tannaitic sources finds its origins in the Greek word *diathēkē* of similar meaning, that is, a written disposition in case of death. And, as demonstrated by Reuven Yaron, the formula of the tannaitic institution, "be it (given) to me to be in good health and to live," matches the Greek, the former being a translation of the latter.[10] Despite the definitive correspondence between the two instruments, there remain significant differences between the original Greek *diathēkē* and its tannaitic counterpart. The tannaitic form does not require adoption, as does the original Greek, and it requires an act of acquisition that is not present in the Greek.[11] Furthermore, the tannaitic *diathēkē* is not presented consistently in tannaitic literature. A case in point is the cluster of three

---

concepts and institutions were transplanted and not entire legal systems; or as he put it, not "the spirit of a legal system." For, how could an entire legal context actually transfer? Based on the abundant evidence for the transfer of individual rules—whether linguistic, historical or otherwise—Watson, too, contended that context produces meaning, but it is a meaning that can change as a rule travels from one legal sphere to another: "a rule once transplanted is different in its new home." His insistence on pointing out overlap between individual rules and legal structures, while acknowledging the transformation undergone by transplantation, has been the hallmark of his work.

[8] To be sure, Yair Furstenberg's requirements for demonstrating a relationship between Roman and tannaitic laws do not mirror those of Legrand. In his own work, Furstenberg has argued for the adaptation of Roman legal classification by the tannaim (see most recently Furstenberg, "The Rabbis and the Roman Citizenship Model" and Furstenberg, "Inheritance Laws in their Greco-Roman Context: Review of Milgram," 255–258). However, it seems that Furstenberg requires a more complete integration of Roman elements into the tannaitic legal sphere before he is willing to grant that a relationship between traditions exists; hence, his objection to my analysis, where I have argued for pointed and partial terminological and conceptual overlap, while accounting for transformation, as evidence of possible connections. Furthermore, I have introduced the social and economic contexts of Roman Palestine into the equation, another methodological matter to which Furstenberg objects (and has, perhaps, even misunderstood); see Furstenberg, ibid., 250 and n. 4 above. For a favorable view of my inclusion of the social and economic contexts, see Vicent, "Reseña de Milgram, *From Mesopotamia to the Mishnah*," 769.

[9] For a detailed discussion on this instrument for disposing of assets, see Milgram, *From Mesopotamia to the Mishnah*, 160–166.

[10] For more on this, see Milgram, *From Mesopotamia to the Mishnah*, 165–166.

[11] See Milgram, *From Mesopotamia to the Mishnah*, 161, where I suggested the possibility that when the Greek institution was assimilated into tannaitic law the bilateralness of the original (=adoption) was transformed into the bilateralness of requiring an act of acquisition in the latter. On the later *diathēkē* without adoption see the literature cited in Milgram, *From Mesopotamia to the Mishnah*, 62 n. 143 and 97 n. 84.

conflicting traditions that appears in the eighth chapter of Tosefta Baba Batra.[12] Together, the inconsistent presentation of the tannaitic *diathēkē* and the incomplete entry of the Greek institution, I would argue, attest to the fluid and, at times, only partial importation of traditions into the legal sphere of the tannaim. Based on the incomplete and conflicting reception(s) of the original Greek *diathēkē* in tannaitic law, would anyone argue that a foreign institution was not assimilated into tannaitic legal discourse? I do not think so. Certainly, the terminological and formulaic overlap are determinative. The partial, incomplete and even contradictory entry of traditions about the *diathēkē*, therefore, should not pose problems for our understanding of the reception of foreign elements into the legal discourse of the rabbis. Actually, it appropriately problematizes the assumptions of some about the reception of law, legal borrowing, and legal transplants—assumptions which may not be in sync with the regnant approach to comparative law[13]—and helps us arrive at a more nuanced and sophisticated evaluation of the tannaitic situation. The example of the *diathēkē* may attest to what we should expect: partial, broken, and inconsistent overlap.[14]

In *From Mesopotamia to the Mishnah*, I dealt with several examples of partial parallels, arguing that, at times, one can identify in tannaitic inheritance law some of the elements of inheritance traditions and terminology found in other ancient legal collections. I specifically highlighted the similarities between tannaitic and Roman legal terminology (Chapter 1) and conceptualization (Chapter 3) that I encountered. Furthermore, I explored the possibility of comparable social and economic contexts—such as the Roman condition and the tannaitic—to result in similar laws (Chapter 4). In short, I argued that varying degrees of parallel—even when partial—are meaningful. This is especially true when the overlap is between tannaitic law and Roman law, specifically, and to the exclusion of all of the other ancient legal traditions from the same general region.

In the following sections, I deal with the three cases from the three aforementioned chapters, and I explore, further, their relationship to Roman law and life. In the first section, "On the Distinction between Gifting and Inheriting," relating to Chapter 1, I deal with the terminology used by the tannaim for distinguishing between gifting and inheriting, which I argue was likely borrowed from Roman law, and I offer Hebrew terms the tannaim may have rejected. In this example I see the linguistic parallels as determinative. In the second part, "On Testate Succession," I address testate succession for

[12] For my analysis of this literary cluster of three conflicting Tosefta traditions, see Milgram, *From Mesopotamia to the Mishnah*, 160–166.

[13] See Graziadei, "Comparative Law as the Study of Transplants and Receptions," 442–474.

[14] Despite the incomplete reception of the *diathēkē* in tannaitic law, Furstenberg proclaims the *diathēkē* to represent the "*she'ila gemura,*" the "complete borrowing" [!], of a foreign institution; see Furstenberg, "Inheritance Laws in their Greco-Roman Context: Review of Milgram," 254.

family members in both Roman and tannaitic law, a matter I discussed in Chapter 3, and I explore further the complex of contexts—both legal and social—that led to the integration of such an approach into tannaitic law. In the third segment, "On Inheritance by Daughters," I take up, once again, equal inheritance by daughters considering social and economic parallels from the ancient world, an issue investigated in Chapter 4. Here, I offer additional evidence for my position and consider the post-tannaitic history of the literary and legal approach that I identified.

On the Distinction between Gifting and Inheriting

In Chapter 1, "Gifting and Inheriting in Tannaitic Law and in the Ancient World," I suggested that the legal terms employed in tannaitic inheritance law, *mattanah* and *yerushah*, are Hebrew renditions of the Roman legal terms (in Latin) *donatio* and *hereditas*, respectively.[15] This was not to say that the Hebrew words etymologically originated from the Latin. The words *mattanah* and *yerushah* certainly existed in the classical Hebrew lexicon before the tannaim may have encountered the terms employed in Roman inheritance law. Rather, I argued that it cannot be maintained that the tannaitic usage of *mattanah* versus *yerushah*—that is, including the legal differences inherent in the two terms—originated in biblical Hebrew usage, or any other Hebrew or Aramaic usage known to us from antiquity.[16] The two words are, at times, even synonymous [!] in biblical texts.[17] Furthermore, had the tannaim based the terms to distinguish between gifting and inheriting on words from the classical Hebrew lexicon, that is, without terminology external to that word-stock impinging on the range of the words' meanings, perhaps we would have expected the appearance of *naḥalah* (for inheriting) opposite *nedavah* or *terumah* (for gifting). The word *naḥalah* refers with regularity to inheritance of land;[18] and, although both *nedavah* and *terumah* are used within the realm of the cultic in biblical religion (like *mattanah*),[19] either word could have served as an appropriate term for gifting. Indeed,

---

[15] Brown, "From Mesopotamia to the Mishnah, by Jonathan S. Milgram," 1, incorrectly asserts that *mattanah* and *donatio*, and, *yerushah* and *hereditas*, were "already established as parallel terms" before my study. While it is true that, as I mention in *From Mesopotamia to the Mishnah*, 64 n. 164, Surenhuys used *hæreditatem* for *yerushah* and *dona* for *mattanah* in his translation of *mBB* 8:5 into Latin, I have not located any scholarly treatment of these terms as parallel prior to my work. Perhaps the most well-known attempts to identify translations of Roman legal terms in tannaitic literature are Gans, "Grundzüge," 419–471 and Krochmal, *More Nebochei ha-seman*, 156–157 (unnumbered footnote), neither of whom address our terms. For a critique of Krochmal, see Herzog, *Main Institutions*, 77–81.

[16] See Milgram, *From Mesopotamia to the Mishnah*, 52–55 and 60–65.

[17] Milgram, *From Mesopotamia to the Mishnah*, 54–55.

[18] See Lipinski, "Naḥal," 326.

[19] See Farby, "nāṯan," 102–107.

while *nedavah* refers primarily to a "freewill offering" given outside of the regular sacrificial system,[20] it carries with it the basic meaning of a free and voluntary gift.[21] Similarly, the dominant definition of the word *terumah* (though its etymological origins are in dispute[22]) is "gift."[23]

In light of the evidence, the choice of the tannaim to employ the terms *mattanah* and *yerushah* for inheritance procedures seems to occur due to the presence of the Roman legal terms *donatio* and *hereditas*.[24] Admittedly, this terminological overlap is not accompanied, for example, by all of the other formal elements of inheritance procedure present in Roman law, such as the ceremony for transfer of ownership in the presence of witnesses.[25] That is, there is no complete copying of inheritance and gifting practices and procedures from the Roman legal sphere to the tannaitic. Even so, an additional element overlaps for gifting: both Roman and tannaitic law (and to the exception of other ancient legal systems) require an act of acquisition on the part of the donee.[26]

These partial parallels should not be considered merely coincidental. Rather, they should be expected. The parallels evidenced are especially significant because of the terminological overlap—the possible linguistic link strengthening the potential relationship between the legal traditions. The case to which we now turn our attention, testate succession, is representative of conceptual overlap alone.

---

[20] Conrad, "Ndb," 221.

[21] Conrad, "Ndb," 220.

[22] See Muffs, *Studies*, 128–137; Milgrom, *Leviticus 1–16*, 475; and the discussion in Anderson, *Sacrifices*, 137–144.

[23] Milgrom, *Leviticus 1–16*, 473.

[24] *Contra* Ranon Katzoff who, in his review of Daniel Sperber's *A Dictionary of Greek and Latin Legal Terms in Rabbinic Literature*, writes: "Even more striking is the state of affairs of Latin legal terms. As has been noted above a surprisingly large number of the terms collected in the volume under review are Latin. Yet not a single one seems to have entered the rabbis' active legal vocabulary. In other words, whatever familiarity the rabbis had with Roman law was not translated into institutions consciously adopted from Roman law along with their terminology (Katzoff, "Review of Sperber," 204). Compare his remarks in Katzoff, "Children of Intermarriage," 286.

[25] See Furstenberg's critique of my suggestion about the relationship between the Roman and tannaitic terminology. He contends that the existence of the relationship cannot be maintained if more commonalities between the institution from which tannaitic law is borrowing (and that are unique to it) and tannaitic law are not observed; see Furstenberg, "Inheritance Laws in their Greco-Roman Context: Review of Milgram," 251. However, he in no way accounts for the peculiar, innovative and otherwise unprecedented usage of the terms *mattanah* and *yerushah* among the tannaim.

[26] Milgram, *From Mesopotamia to the Mishnah*, 42–43.

On Testate Succession

In Chapter 3, "Testate Succession in Tannaitic Law and in the Ancient World," I suggested that tannaitic law knew of at least one form of testate succession that was promoted in the name of the tanna, Rabbi Yoḥanan ben Beroka. And this is so, despite the seemingly prevalent approach in the Mishnah prohibiting testate succession. Testate succession was forbidden because, according to the construction of inheritance procedures of some tannaim, it violated biblical law.[27] Even so, Rabbi Yoḥanan ben Beroka permitted adjustments to the biblical order of succession, even the appointment of a daughter as heir in the presence of a son and the brother as heir in the presence of a daughter![28]

In that chapter, I argued that the tannaitic form was possibly parallel to one type of testate succession known from antiquity: Roman law's testament to the *sui heredes* (all those *in potestate*, under the control of the head of household, or *paterfamilias*, and legally members of the *familia*; these included children, grandchildren, and, in a *cum manu* marriage, the wife). Indeed, considering the meaningful overlap between this type of Roman testament and Rabbi Yoḥanan ben Beroka's conception—according to both a potential heir (someone *ra'uy lo lirusha* in the tanna's terminology) is appointed to a universal, unilateral, and automatic succession—I suggested the appropriateness of the tanna's position in the context of Roman Palestine.[29]

From a methodological perspective, differences are no less significant than similarities, and the primary distinction between Rabbi Yoḥanan ben Beroka's position and Roman law's institution is how broadly, from among family members, one may appoint an heir. Rabbi Yoḥanan ben Beroka proposes the possibility of appointing anyone in the agnatic line of succession, a broader category than those legally considered members of the Roman *familia* (as in the testament to the *sui heredes*; see above). Yet, the range of potential heirs eligible according to the tanna's view does correspond to the group considered members of the Roman *familia* in the non-legal usage of the term *familia* found in some Roman sources.[30] That is, the line of family members included in this latter usage coincides with those family members who are a part of Rabbi Yoḥanan ben Beroka's category, *ra'uy lo lirushah*.

Certainly, when observing tannaitic legal innovation, consultation of possible biblical antecedents is essential. As I noted in Chapter 3, Rabbi Yoḥanan ben Beroka's classification, *ra'uy lo lirushah*, also corresponds to the biblical category of the clan, or *mishpaḥah*, the term used in biblical

---

[27] On this, see Milgram, *From Mesopotamia to the Mishnah*, 85–86.

[28] *From Mesopotamia to the Mishnah*, 86–87.

[29] Significantly, no analogous types of appointments of heirs are present in any of the other legal traditions examined; see Milgram, *From Mesopotamia to the Mishnah*, 89–98.

[30] See Milgram, *From Mesopotamia to the Mishnah*, 100.

texts for defining the limits of the agnatic line.[31] That is, according to the tanna, one can appoint anyone from among the members of the biblically defined *mishpaḥah* to be heir. Rabbi Yoḥanan ben Beroka, therefore, seems to draw on the biblical model which, at the same time, is appropriate for the cultural and social contexts of the Roman non-legal usage of the category *familia*.[32] In light of the fact that we observe in Rabbi Yoḥanan ben Beroka's teaching overlap with two ancient traditions, we should pause to consider the implications of arguing that his position primarily subsumes the assumptions of only one. To say that Rabbi Yoḥanan ben Beroka's approach is primarily grounded in biblical conceptualization[33] would be to negate the innovation inherent in his rejection of the limits of the biblical order of succession: as noted before, he allows appointing a daughter instead of a son and a brother instead of a daughter.[34] So too, attributing his innovation to the impact of Roman conceptualization alone would be to ignore two essential ingredients found in this comparative study: (a) that in addition to the possible Roman parallel, a biblical antecedent exists and (b) that Rabbi Yoḥanan ben Beroka's vision only corresponds to one type of Roman testament (to the members of the *familia*) and does not include the most radical innovation of Roman testate succession, found in other Roman testamentary instruments,—the right to designate anyone (even outside of the *familia*) as universal heir.[35]

This example provides us with an important model of the methodological challenges involved in comparative work. The question that remains is, therefore, can we provide a more nuanced view of the role of legal similarities when they may be paralleled in multiple traditions and when they are not coupled with a total transfer of legal procedures and presumptions? I would argue that, appropriately, Rabbi Yoḥanan ben Beroka's approach, whatever the unrecoverable background of its historical development actually is,

---

[31] Milgram, *From Mesopotamia to the Mishnah*, 100–101. On the term, *ra'uy lo lirushah*, compare the recent remarks in Sabato, *Sanhedrin*, vol. 2, 501 and 505–506. I should add here a note on the interpretive move accomplished when the term, *ra'uy lo lirushah*, is taken from its original location in *mSan* 3:4 and placed in the mouth of Rabbi Yoḥanan ben Beroka. In its original location the term refers to agnates, all those in the order of (intestate) succession in the event of death *intestate* (likely the only kind of inheritance known in the Bible; see Milgram, *From Mesopotamia to the Mishnah*, 89–94). However, Rabbi Yoḥanan ben Beroka's usage, in a move turning the original usage on its head, refers specifically to this list as including those who can be appointed heirs, that is, through *testate* succession, even at the expense of the original biblical order.

[32] See Furstenberg, "Inheritance Laws in their Greco-Roman Context: Review of Milgram," 253–254, who states that I argued for the specific influence of Roman law on tannaitic law at the expense of noticing the biblical overlap.

[33] As per Furstenberg, "Inheritance Laws in their Greco-Roman Context: Review of Milgram," 254.

[34] Also see above in the body of the Postscript and my discussion in Milgram, *From Mesopotamia to the Mishnah*, 86.

[35] On this, see Milgram, *From Mesopotamia to the Mishnah*, 99.

represents, yet again, that parallels between tannaitic law and other legal traditions will only be partial. What is so important about this observation is that the incomplete adoption of traditions in this example applies equally to the use of the biblical heritage as it does to the integration of other legal traditions (here, possibly the Roman). As I concluded in my chapter, Rabbi Yoḥanan ben Beroka's innovation remains, therefore, among the finest examples of a tannaitic opinion which is the product of *all* of its legal and social contexts.

On Inheritance by Daughters

In Chapter 4, "Inheritance by Daughters in Tannaitic Law and in the Ancient World," I argued that a source critical analysis of *mBB* 8:4 uncovers a previously concealed tradition promoting equal inheritance from the father's estate for both sons and daughters![36] Mishnah Baba Batra 8:4 states:

I. אחד הבן ואחד הבת בנחלה
II. אלא שהבן נוטל פי שנים בניכסי האב ואינו נוטל פי שנים בניכסי האם
III. והבנות ניזונות מנכסי האב ואינן ניזונות מנכסי האם.[37]

I. The son and the daughter are the same regarding inheritance

II. except that [*ellah she-*] the [firstborn] son takes a double portion of the father's property but does not take a double portion of the mother's property

III. and the daughters receive maintenance from the father's property and do not receive maintenance from the mother's property.

I pointed to the lack of agreement between the topic of paragraph I (the ability of a *son and a daughter* to inherit) and the subject matter of paragraphs II–III (the rules governing the difference between allocations from the *father's estate* versus the *mother's estate*). I argued that the discord intimates that the two sections, paragraph I, on the one hand, and paragraphs II–III, on the other, were originally two separate literary units.[38] The two

---

[36] Milgram, *From Mesopotamia to the Mishnah*, 114–118; Hezser has misunderstood me to mean that the direct inheritance of which I speak is only from the mother's estate: "Against M., I read the initial statement (>>The son and the daughter are the same regarding inheritance<<) as referring to both of them inheriting from the father's property only and not from the mother's" (Hezser, "Review of *From Mesopotamia to the Mishnah*," 1177).

[37] In MS Kaufmann, both occurrences of *nikhsei* in par. III are written without a *yod*, unlike in par. II.

[38] The incongruity was already noticed by the amoraim; see Milgram, *From Mesopotamia to the Mishnah*, 115. For two additional formulations of the problem, see Milgram, *From Mesopotamia to the Mishnah*, 114 n. 60.

independent tannaitic sources were brought together here and linked by the phrase *ellah she-*.[39]

In further support of my argument, I submit here that the word *naḥalah* in *mBB* 8:4 par. I marks the end of a self-contained literary unit (*kovets*), a collection of *mishnayot* beginning with *mBB* 8:1 that specifically uses the word *naḥalah* throughout and concludes here. The *mishnayot* after *mBB* 8:4 par. I—that is, *mBB* 8:4 par. II and beyond (at least until the end of this chapter of Mishnah) linked to the previous literary unit by the phrase *ellah she-*, are part of a separate collection that is appended here. That collection consistently employs the words *nekhasim* (or variations of it) and *yerushah*, but not *naḥalah*. The word *naḥalah* in par. I, therefore, was in this location in the Mishnah from its earliest form[40] and should be defined as it is in the rest of the *mishnayot* that precede it in chapter 8 (that is, that are part of the same collection). Accordingly, the ensuing sentence in *mBB* 8:4 par. I, "the son and the daughter are the same regarding inheritance," asserts that a son and a daughter inherit equally from their mutual father's estate![41]

Certainly, embracing my interpretation of *mBB* 8:4 par. I (as well as others in my book) requires accepting a number of methodological assumptions that are present throughout my work (these are discussed, at length, in the "Introduction"). Firstly, individual *mishnayot* are, at times, made up of more than one source. Secondly, the separation of the component parts of a mishnah may result in the (re)discovery of a camouflaged approach. Finally, the uncovered source can be put into dialogue with legal positions from other ancient legal traditions in order to teach us about the possible origins of tannaitic laws.[42] The example of inheritance by daughters in *mBB* 8:4 is particularly significant since I argue that the camouflaged position, in this case silenced by the process of redaction,[43] contained a singular approach

---

[39] Here I build on the observations of J.N. Epstein; see Milgram, *From Mesopotamia to the Mishnah*, 115–116.

[40] And should not be seen as a source not originally included in Mishnah *Baba Batra* chapter 8, imported from elsewhere (such as *tBB* 7:10), and truncated at the word *naḥalah*, as suggested by Epstein, *Mavo*, 659–660. For more on Epstein's view and my own reconstruction of the evidence, see Milgram, *From Mesopotamia to the Mishnah*, 115–116.

[41] Furstenberg, "Inheritance Laws in their Greco-Roman Context: Review of Milgram," 255, uses the presence of the word *naḥalah* in par. I to argue that the word *naḥalah* is used in the entire earlier collection due to the general concern in the *mishnayot* with explicating the biblical background of *naḥalah*. Namely, the word *naḥalah* is used because of its presence in biblical texts on the topic. While Furstenberg is correct that the word *naḥalah* is used because of its presence in biblical texts, he ignores how the meaning of the word *naḥalah* is applied in the context of all of these *mishnayot*, and, as a result, in 8:4 par. I. See related comments in Milgram, *From Mesopotamia to the Mishnah*, 116.

[42] See note 3.

[43] While, unquestionably, one could posit that the effects of the process of redaction should be mined for their ideological and interpretive significance, I simply did not observe any pattern that would lead me to any definitive conclusions, *per se*. Here I specifically respond

to inheritance by daughters, otherwise unattested in what may verifiably be considered the literature of the tannaim. Indeed, the outcome of applying source critical methods to mishnaic texts is that, at times, the approach revealed may be an otherwise unattested opinion in the corpus of tannaitic texts. This certainly should not preclude the interpretation's viability, however. Furthermore, while the source I identify in *mBB* 8:4 par. I and my interpretation of it are seemingly not present in other tannaitic collections, I pointed to a possible tannaitic parallel tradition preserved in amoraic literature. The Palestinian Talmud, *pBB* 8:1, 16a,[44] states: "The Sages of the Gentiles say: a son and daughter are equal in inheritance" (חכמי גוים אומרים בן ובת שוין כאחת.). In the Palestinian Talmud's *sugya*, following the statement by the Gentile Sages, their interpretive strategy is explained. According to this approach, one can infer from Numbers 27:8—"[if] a man dies without leaving a son, you shall transfer his property to his daughter"—that when there is no son the inheritance transfers to the daughter; but, when there are sons and daughters, the inheritance is divided equally among them![45] As I illustrated in Chapter 4, the statement of the Gentile Sages may not only

---

to the thoughtful remarks by Matthew Hass in his review, where he states, "there was perhaps more opportunity to discuss the activity of the Mishnah(s) redactors and later interpreters of tannaitic traditions" (Hass, "Review of Mesopotamia to the Mishnah"). There, in addition to the example of inheritance by daughters in which, as mentioned, the process of redaction affects the meaning of a tradition, Hass cites two more examples from my book. The first relates to my philological-historical study of *mBB* 8:5 (see *From Mesopotamia to the Mishnah*, 48–52) where I argue that glosses made during the process of redaction alter the meaning of a tannaitic opinion from being one that advocates for testate succession among sons to an approach only permitting gifting among sons. The second example deals with the opinion of Rabbi Yoḥanan ben Beroka which, I argue, refers to testate succession among family members (that is, appointing a daughter heir in the presence of a son, etc.; see *From Mesopotamia to the Mishnah*, 85–89 and the section in the body of the Postscript entitled, "On Testate Succession") and is reinterpreted in later talmudic sources, including the Tosefta, Palestinian Talmud and Babylonian Talmud, in a way that narrows the scope of Rabbi Yoḥanan ben Beroka's innovation (limiting the area of tannaitic controversy; see *From Mesopotamia to the Mishnah*, 87–89). At this time, I can only suggest that in all three of the cases the changes in meaning, whether as a result of redactional reframing or later interpretation of a tannaitic source, seem to concur with the anonymous views presented in a number of other tannaitic traditions: testate succession of any kind is forbidden and daughters do not inherit in the presence of sons. My observations are likely in line with the general tendencies already observed by scholars of previous generations. On the view that the anonymous opinion is promoted and/or developed by the Mishnah's redactors see, for example, Epstein, *Tannaim*, 192–193; on the readiness of the Babylonian Talmud to limit the scope of tannaitic controversies, see, for instance, Goldberg, "Babylonian Talmud," 328.

[44] In his effort to dispute my interpretation of this source, Furstenberg's contention ("Inheritance Laws in their Greco-Roman Context: Review of Milgram," 255) that no other rabbinic tradition so blatantly contradicts Torah law regarding inheritance by daughters is surprising; for, yet a third and fourth example of this inclusive approach appear in the Babylonian Talmud, see below in the body of the text.

[45] See Milgram, *From Mesopotamia to the Mishnah*, 117 and n. 71 there.

be conceptually parallel, but even linguistically parallel,[46] to the tannaitic position uncovered in *mBB* 8:4, a matter which may have some significance for the textual history of this specific approach. I also document other cases in Talmudic literature in which claims for inheritance by daughters are put in the mouths of non-Jews and non-rabbinic Jews,[47] although, to the best of my knowledge, no other attributions to the "Sages of the Gentiles" occur.[48] One tradition at *bShab* 116b, about tannaim, purports to cite a text from the Gospels (not actually extant in Christian Bibles), that is possibly a translation into Aramaic of the tradition under discussion here, "a son and a daughter inherit equally" (=*berah uveratha keḥadah yirtun*), potentially providing yet another link in the literary history of this legal tradition.[49] Following, I present an additional tradition promoting equal inheritance by sons and daughters, preserved in the Babylonian Talmud (*BB* 110b) in the name of

---

[46] See Milgram, *From Mesopotamia to the Mishnah*, 117 where I discuss the linguistic overlap between *ben uvat* *shavin* *ke'ehat* in the Palestinian Talmud text and *ehad haben ve'ehad habat benaḥalah* in *mBB* 8:4 par. I.

[47] See Milgram, *From Mesopotamia to the Mishnah*, 117 nn. 68–69.

[48] Immediately preceding the statement by the Sages of the Gentiles the text, seemingly in the name of Rabbi Ishmael, states, "*ibur hadin hu shehabat yoreshet.*" The term *ibur hadin* here should be translated as "a distortion of the law" (see the use of the same phrase in Midrash Deuteronomy Rabbah, *Vaetḥanan* p. 49 in Lieberman ed. and the comments in Lieberman, "Review of Finkelstein," 329 n. 1; see also the related phrase, *ibru alav et hadin*, in *mMiddot* 2:2 according to the MS Kaufmann and on the term, in general, Bar-Asher Siegal, "*Iber*," 56–59); that is, the entire sentence in *pBB* should be translated, "it is a distortion of the law that a daughter inherit." However, Tal Ilan, in her article, "The Daughters of Zelophehad," 184, argues that the tannaitic school of Rabbi Ishmael advocates for direct inheritance by daughters (see also Ilan, *Silencing the Queen*, 144–145). She seemingly takes the word *ibur* to be a paraphrase of the word "*veha'avartem*" (both words have the same root) in the biblical verse, "if a man dies without leaving a son, you shall transfer (*veha'avartem*) his property to his daughter" (Num. 27:8). Accordingly, she mistranslates the text of *pBB* as, "With 'pass' the law is that a daughter inherits" [!] (for a similar critique of Ilan, see Hidary, "Hellenism and Hermeneutics," 181 n. 97). In truth, on the hermeneutic level, the choice of the phrase ***ibur hadin*** is intentional since it has the same root as ***veha'avartem***. The implication is that that the biblical verse already alludes to the fact that daughters do not actually inherit. On the complex transmission history of another text that Ilan cites in support of her thesis, *Sifre to Numbers*, 134 (p. 450 lines 22–24 in Kahana ed.), see Kahana, *Sifre to Numbers*, 1140–1141 and my comments in Milgram, "*Min hamizrach hakadum vead lamishnah*" (forthcoming). Here, too, it is unlikely that the tannaitic text supports Ilan's contention.

[49] See the previous note. Feintuch ("Daughters' Inheritance," 215 n. 40) suggests the possibility that the tradition appearing in Aramaic in *bShab* 116b, *berah uveratha keḥadah yirtun*, may find its source in the Syro-Roman Law Book which states: "If a man dies and does not write a testament and he shall leave his children behind, male and female, they inherit equally" (Vööbus, *Syro-Roman Law Book*, 2). Because of the formulaic overlap with both *mBB* 8:4 par. I and the tradition of the Sages of the Gentiles in *pBB* 8:1, 16a, I suggest that the Aramaic formulation in *bShab* 116b may be related to the earlier talmudic traditions, and not necessarily to the Syro-Roman law. However, the matter requires further consideration.

Rav Papa, attesting to the persistence of an inclusive approach to inheritance by daughters in the literature of the Sages.

The discussion in the Babylonian talmudic *sugya* addresses the question, what is the source for sons preceding daughters in inheritance? The text of Bavli *BB* 110a–110b continues:

מנלן? דכתיב, "איש כי ימות" וגו' טעמא דאין לו בן. הא יש לו בן, בן קודם ...	From where is this derived? It is written, "If a man dies, [and has no son, then you shall cause his inheritance to pass unto his daughter] (Num. 27:8). [From this we infer that] the reason is he has no son; if he has a son, a son takes precedence ...
אמר ליה רב פפא ... הכי קא אמינא איכא בן ובת לא האי לירות כוליה ולא האי לירות כוליה, אלא כי הדדי לירתו ...	R. Papa said to him [=Abaye]: This is what I [meant to] say, [it can be inferred from the verse that] if there is a son and daughter, neither this one nor the other one should inherit the entire [estate]. Both should inherit equally*...

* Compare the phrase, ליפלוג כי הדדי, "let them divide equally" (*bBekh* 18a; MS Florence and MS Vatican 120). For more on this see Sokoloff, *Dictionary of Jewish Babylonian Aramaic*, 362.

Rav Papa suggests to Abaye that one can infer from the verse, "if a man dies without leaving a son, you shall transfer (*veha'avartem*) his property to his daughter," that if a man dies without leaving a son, the daughter inherits; but if the son and daughter are both present they both inherit equally. This interpretation parallels the reasoning given in the Palestinian Talmud in the name of the "Sages of the Gentiles" (although the formulation is different),[50] and its bottom line is consistent with the concealed approach in *mBB* 8:4 par. I as well.

The trajectory of the idea that sons and daughters inherit equally can be traced in tannaitic and amoraic literature, therefore. The rabbinic innovation is significant; for as I demonstrated in Chapter 4, the view is absent from biblical literature.[51] In summary, an original and inclusive tannaitic view concealed by the process of redaction (*mBB* 8:4 par. I) was transformed into a stance marginalized and placed in the mouths of those not within

[50] See Halivni, *Baba Batra*, 196 n. 3, who suggests Rav Pappa is somehow responding to the position of the Sages of the Gentiles in the Palestinian Talmud. See also Hidary, "Hellenism and Hermeneutics," 181–182 n. 97.

[51] See Milgram, *From Mesopotamia to the Mishnah*, 120–124.

the rabbinic tradition (*pBB* 8:1, 16a),[52] and, later, in an unexpected move, the position was presented as an amoraic assertion (*bBB* 110b).

What likely spawned the inclusive approach in its earliest stage among some tannaim was a combination of factors including legal, social, and economic. The presence of comparable legal traditions in both the ancient Near East and Mediterranean may have contributed to some rabbis embracing a more inclusive approach.[53] Moreover, the case of direct inheritance by daughters in tannaitic literature, more than representing any definitively traceable genetic link between individual legal traditions, may enable a morphological analysis: the inclusion of daughters in inheritance may be expected in an urbanized setting where the ownership of private land among nuclear families is prevalent.[54]

So, How Jewish is Jewish Inheritance Law?

The final chapter of my book is entitled, "Conclusions: How Jewish is Jewish Inheritance Law?" There I used the question, "How Jewish is Jewish Inheritance Law?", as a metaphor for a matter I address on almost every page of *From Mesopotamia to the Mishnah*, "How biblical is tannaitic inheritance law?"[55] Certainly, the main thrust of my book is that tannaitic inheritance law is, for the most part, not biblical at all. I attempt to label the "identity" of tannaitic inheritance laws, therefore, based on recurring trends and tropes within the body of the tannaitic traditions that I identify. In the final analysis, the identity of tannaitic inheritance law—whether we call it "Jewish" or anything else—comes from the creative impulse of the rabbis to successfully integrate a variety of conflicting laws about inheritance procedure, most of the laws, seemingly, with a common thrust and unified ethos: to grant the adherents of tannaitic law the right to allocate assets more freely. The result is in stark opposition to the centralized and rigid biblical model, whereby the collective family heritage is to be maintained. By embracing new approaches and creating innovative opportunities, especially for wives[56] and daughters, the tannaim teach that a legacy ultimately belongs to the individual.

[52] On the rabbis placing what they perceive as problematic views in the mouths of the marginalized, see most recently Hayes, *What's Divine about Divine Law?*, 262.

[53] Furstenberg, "Inheritance Laws in their Greco-Roman Context: Review of Milgram," 249 and 254, states that I conclude some tannaim embraced the inclusive approach specifically due to Roman influence. My actual suggestion was more nuanced, as in the final statement above in the body of the text.

[54] On the general approach of the tannaim towards the inclusion of daughters within the realm of inheritance, see Milgram, *From Mesopotamia to the Mishnah*, 105–110.

[55] For an unsympathetic response to my use of this motif, see Cohen, "Review of Milgram, *From Mesopotamia to the Mishnah*," 448-449. For a thoughtful reaction to my question see Schwartz, "Review of Milgram, *From Mesopotamia to the Mishnah*," 189.

[56] See Milgram, *From Mesopotamia to the Mishnah*, 133–144.

In light of the observations above, the comprehensive reframing of the purpose and objective of inheritance laws by the tannaim should be mined for its greater significance within the world of the rabbis. In *From Mesopotamia to the Mishnah* I wrote:

> By ensuring that their inheritance laws correspond to the social and economic contexts of Roman Palestine, perhaps the rabbis prepare laws that would be appropriate in the event they are to legislate. Or, put differently, it may be that the construction of these inheritance laws is an expression of the rabbis' desire to legislate a livable law for their time or for a time when their laws would be accepted.[57]

At the time of that writing, I limited my suggestion to the applicability of the laws I identified in relation to the social and economic contexts of Roman Palestine. This approach can be broadened. The overlap with the general inheritance practices known from the ancient Near East and Mediterranean, coupled with the individual parallels to Roman law and conceptualization to which I point, add, not insignificantly, to the portrait that can be painted of rabbinic engagement with the world outside of their inner circles and to a possible directed purpose in their legal construction. If any intentionality can be conjectured—admittedly not a self-evident proposition and stated here merely as a suggestion—then the creation of a law that was in accordance with the social conditions that would-be followers experienced was not the only hope of some tannaim. The vision was also to fashion a law that was not allergic to "foreign" elements and that would have been readily recognizable in the legal and social contexts of Roman Palestine. Here I refer specifically to (a) the terminological and legal distinction between gifting and inheriting and (b) testate succession to family members, both of great pragmatic significance for the accomplishment of the ultimate goals of flexibility and independence in the disposition of assets. The rabbis ultimate desire may have also been to legislate, therefore, a law consonant with the legal idiom of their time and place.[58]

---

[57] Milgram, *From Mesopotamia to the Mishnah*, 33.

[58] These suggestions may have implications for the larger question of the desire of the tannaim to be the leaders of the Jewry of their time. The general tendency in scholarship has been to assume that the rabbis did not have interest in said leadership; see, for example, Cohen, "Place of the Rabbi," 157–173 and Schwartz, *Imperialism*, 113, among others.

Bibliography to the Postscript

* Books cited in the Postscript that were previously cited in the main body of the book are not listed again here. The original Bibliography should be consulted.

Anderson, Gary. *Sacrifices and Offerings in Ancient Israel: Studies in their Social and Political Importance*. Atlanta: Scholars Press, 1987.

Bar-Asher Siegal, Michal. "*Iber, Ibur hadin ufarashat haibur: iyunim leshoniyim.*" *Leshonenu* 78:1/2 (2016): 43–59.

Brown, William. Review of *From Mesopotamia to the Mishnah*, by Jonathan S. Milgram. *The Biblical Review*, thebiblicalreview.wordpress.com/2016/09/18/from-mesopotamian-to-the-mishnah-by-jonathan-s-milgram/.

Cohen, Shaye J.D. "The Place of the Rabbi in Jewish Society of the Second Century." In *The Galilee in Late Antiquity*, edited by Lee Levine, 157–173. New York: Jewish Theological Seminary of America, 1992.

–. Review of *From Mesopotamia to the Mishnah*, by Jonathan S. Milgram. *AJS Review* 42:2 (November 2018), 447-449.

Conrad, J. Ndb. In *Theological Dictionary of the Old Testament*, edited by G. Johannes Botterweck and Helmer Ringgren, 9: 219–226. Grand Rapids, MI: Eerdmans, 1998.

Danneman, Gerhard. "Comparative Law: Study of Similarities or Differences?" In *The Oxford Handbook of Comparative Law*, edited by Mathias Reimann and Reinhard Zimmerman, 384–419. Oxford: Oxford University Press, 2008.

Furstenberg, Yair. "Inheritance Laws in their Greco-Roman Context." Review Essay on *From Mesopotamia to the Mishnah*, by Jonathan S. Milgram. [In Hebrew.] *Shenaton Hamishpat Haivri* 29 (2016–2018): 245–248.

–. "The Rabbis and the Roman Citizenship Model: The Case of the Samaritans." In *Citizenship(s) and Self-Definition(s) in the Roman Empire: Roman, Greek, Jewish and Christian Perspectives*, edited by K. Berthelot and J. Price. Leuven: Peeters, forthcoming.

Gans, Eduard. "Grundzüge des mosaisch-talmudischen Erbrechts." In *Zeitschrift für die Wissenschaft des Judenthums* 1:3, edited by Leopold Zunz, 419–471. Berlin: Verein für Kultur und Wisseschaft der Juden, 1823.

Goldberg, Abraham. "The Babylonian Talmud." In *The Literature of the Sages: First Part*, edited by Shmuel Safrai, 323–366. Philadelphia: Fortress Press, 1987.

Graziadei, Michele. "Comparative Law as the Study of Transplants and Receptions." In *The Oxford Handbook of Comparative Law*, edited by Mathias Reimann and Reinhard Zimmerman, 442–474. Oxford: Oxford University Press, 2008.

Hass, Matthew. Review of *From Mesopotamia to the Mishnah*, by Jonathan S. Milgram. *Jewish Law Association Studies* 28, forthcoming.

Hayes, Christine. *What's Divine about Divine Law? Early Perspectives*. Princeton: Princeton University Press, 2015.

Hezser, Catherine. Review of *From Mesopotamia to the Mishnah*, by Jonathan S. Milgram. *Theologische Literaturzeitung* 142 (2017): 1175–1177.

–. *The Social Structure of the Rabbinic Movement in Roman Palestine*. Tübingen: Mohr Siebeck, 1997.

Hidary, Richard. "Hellenism and Hermeneutics: Did the Qumranites and Sadducees use *qal va-ḥomer* Arguments?" In *Hā-'îsh Mōshe: Studies in Scriptural Interpretation in the Dead Sea Scrolls and Related Literature in Honor of Moshe J. Bernstein*, edited by Binyomin Y. Goldstein, et. al., 155–189. Leiden and Boston: Brill, 2018.

Ilan, Tal. "The Daughters of Zelophehad and Women's Inheritance: the Biblical Injuction and its Outcome." In *From Exodus to Deuteronomy: A Feminist Companion to the Bible* (2nd series), edited by Athalya Brenner, 176–186. Sheffield: Sheffield Academic Press, 2000.

–. *Silencing the Queen: The Literary Histories of Shelamzion and Other Jewish Women*. Tübingen: Mohr Siebeck, 2006.

Jacobs, Sandra. Review of *From Mesopotamia to the Mishnah*, by Jonathan S. Milgram. *Journal for the Study of the Old Testament* 41:5 (2017): 16.

Katzoff, Ranon, "Sperber's Dictionary of Greek and Latin Terms In Rabbinic Literature—A Review Essay." *Journal for the Study of Judaism in the Persian, Hellenistic and Roman Period* 20:2 (1989): 195–206.

Krochmal, Nachman. *More Neboche ha-seman*, edited by Leopold Zunz. Lemberg: M. Wolf, 1863.

Legrand, Pierre. "Against a European Civil Code." *Modern Law Review* 60:1 (January 1997): 44–63.

Lieberman, Saul. "The Impossibility of Legal Transplants." *Maastricht Journal of European and Comparative Law* 4:2 (1997): 111–124.

–. *Midrash Debarim Rabbah*, 2nd edition (with additional notes and corrections). Jerusalem: Shalem Books, 1992.

–. Review of *Sifre on Deuteronomy*, by Louis Finkelstein. [In Hebrew.] *Kiryat Sefer* 14 (1937–1938): 323–336.

Milgram, Jonathan. *From Mesopotamia to the Mishnah: Tannaitic Inheritance Law in its Legal and Social Contexts*. Tübingen: Mohr Siebeck, 2016.

–. "*Min hamizraḥ hakadum vead lamishnah: Hilkhot hayerushah shel hatanaim beheksheran hamishpati vehaḥevrati*" (forthcoming).

Milgrom, Jacob. *Leviticus 1–16: A New Translation with Introduction and Commentary*. New York and London: Doubleday, 1991.

Rosen-Zvi, Ishay. "Is the Mishnah a Roman Composition?" In *The Faces of Torah: Studies in the Texts and Contexts of Ancient Judaism in Honor of Steven Fraade*, edited by Michal Bar-Asher Siegal, et. al., 487–508. Bristol: Vandenhoeck and Ruprecht, 2017.

–. "Rabbis and Romanization: A Review Essay." In *Jewish Cultural Encounters in the Ancient Mediterranean and Near Eastern World*, edited by Mladen Popović et. al., 218–245. Leiden and Boston: Brill, 2017.

Sabato, Mordechai. *Talmud Bavli Sanhedrin Chapter 3: Critical Edition and Commentary*. [In Hebrew.] Jerusalem: Bialik Institute, 2018.

Schwartz, Joshua. Review of *From Mesopotamia to the Mishnah*, by Jonathan S. Milgram. *Religious Studies Review* 43:2 (June 2017): 189.

Sokoloff, Michael. *Dictionary of Jewish Babylonian Aramaic of the Talmudic and Geonic Periods*. Ramat Gan and Baltimore: Bar Ilan University Press and Johns Hopkins University Press, 2002.

Syro-Roman Law Book: The Syriac Text of the Recently Discovered Manuscripts accompanied by a Facsimile Edition and Furnished with an Introduction and Translation, edited by Arthur Vööbus. Stockholm: ETSE, 1983.

Vicent, Rafael. Reseña de *From Mesopotamia to the Mishnah*, por Jonathan S. Milgram. *Salesianum* 79 (2017) 4:768–769.

Watson, Alan. "Legal Transplants and European Private Law." *Electronic Journal of Comparative Law* 4:4 (December 2000), http://www.ejcl.org/ejcl/44/44-2.html.

CPSIA information can be obtained
at www.ICGtesting.com
Printed in the USA
BVHW042157030519
547363BV00003B/9/P

9 781644 690277